POLYANDRY IN INDIA

POLYANDRY IN INDIA

(Demographic, Economic, Social, Religious and Psychological Concomitants of Plural Marriages in Women)

Edited with an Introduction by
MANIS KUMAR RAHA

Associate in Editing
PALASH CHANDRA COOMAR

GIAN PUBLISHING HOUSE
DELHI - 7

GIAN PUBLISHING HOUSE
29/6 Shakti Nagar, Delhi-110007

ISBN 9788121201056

Views, if any, expres sed in the articles of this book are of the authors. The editors are not responsible for the same.

PRINTED IN INDIA

Published by Gian Publishing House, Delhi (India) and
Printed at Mohan Printing Corporation
(Composing at Godwall Printers), Delhi.

To

My brother, Amitava and
sisters, Mira, Maya, Chaya, Sabita and Hashi
who did so much for me.

PREFACE

Polyandry is in existence in India since *Vedic* ages, even earlier. A good number of people inhabiting from the Himalayas to the southern tip of India have been practising polyandry since time immemorial. Polyandrous system of some of these societies has been studied by individual scholars, no doubt, but no systematic study of polyandry in India has since been done till 1963 when H.R.H. Prince Peter undertook very detailed study on polyandry among some contemporary polyandrous societies and published his monumental volume, *A Study of Polyandry*. Later on Dr. S. D. Singh undertook detailed study on this institution as prevalent in ancient India and published his very interesting book, *Polyandry in Ancient India* (1978). These are their own studies, and no doubt very helpful for the scholars.

My idea of compiling a book having articles on polyandry as prevalent in different societies in India, cropped up in me when I started my research project, *A Study of Polyandry in the Himalayas*, which is the outcome of my interest and long standing experience among the polyandrous societies in the Himalayas, which I studied for years. I thought that for the students of Anthropology, Sociology, and allied disciplines of under-graduate and post-graduate classes, some compilation work on the studies of polyandry as prevalent in different societies in India, would be of great help. It is also a long standing demand from the scholars of anthropology, sociology and other disciplines for such a book. This compilation of works would enlighten them about structure and function of this plural marriage system as practised by different societies in India, of past and present, and also about varied reasons for its origin and development and also causes of decline. In order to adjust with the particular environmental and cultural situations a particular society/ethnic group adopts certain cultural traits; and polyandry is the product of some such unique scholar in different cases. No one factor is responsible everywhere as no one situation is prevalent everywhere.

Again for the influence of different forces, the same trait/ institution may decline, as polyandry is declining everywhere. This book, we firmly believe, will also help our scholar in understanding such geo-cultural situations which compelled various human societies to bear the unique system of marriage between one or more women and more than one man, and also the reasons for its decay. This book we believe, will meet the long felt need of the students and scholars of Anthropology, Sociology and other allied disciplines for a book on polyandry in India.

Editors

ACKNOWLEDGEMENTS

We express our deep sense of gratitude to Dr. A.K. Danda, Director, Anthropological Survey of India for his constant encouragement for such a book. Prof. P.K. Bhowmick of the Department of Anthropology, Calcutta University, and Dr. A.K. Das, Director, Cultural Research Institute, Govt. of West Bengal were our constant source of encouragement. We are also grateful to them. We are really thankful to the authorities of the following journals who have so kindly permitted us to reprint in this book some important articles on polyandry and allied issues which were earlier published in these journals.

1. Ethnology
2. Journal of the Royal Anthropological Institute of Great Britain and Ireland
3. Man in India
4. Sociological Bulletin
5. Journal of Indian Anthropological Society
6. Bulletin of the Anthropological Survey of India
7. American Anthropologist
8. American Ethnologist.

We are also thankful to the authors of these articles for their kind co-operation. They have also permitted us to incorporate these articles in our book. We are also identically thankful to our other contributors without whose kind co-operation this programme would not have been successful.

We are indebted to all our colleagues who constantly encouraged us and helped us in different ways in finalising this book. But we simply cannot resist mentioning Shri Ramashis Bhattachariya, Shri Nilmoni Das, Smt. Anima Pal, Miss Geeta, Shri Anand Minj and Shri Pitambaru, and particularly Shri Sudip De and Smt. Vimla who extended their hand of co-operation ungrudgingly and helped us by typing the entire manuscripts. Our gratefulness are due to Shri Swapan Das who also assisted us in different ways.

We express our gratitude to our publisher, Gian Publishing House, Delhi, whose interest, skill and experience made this book published so early.

Finally, we are thankful to the people of all polyandrous societies in India without whose active co-operation it would not have been possible to prepare this book.

Editors

CONTRIBUTORS

1.	Prof. John. H. Crook D. Sc.	Deptt. of Psychology University of Bristol, Bristol U.K.
2.	Shri T.K. Ghosh	Assistant Keeper Anthropological Survey of India, Dehra Dun
3.	Dr. M.K. Raha	Deputy Director Anthropological Survey of India, Port Blair
4.	Shri P.C. Coomar	Senior Technical Assistant Anthropological Survey of India, Port Blair
5.	Dr. Ramesh Chandra	Anthropologist Anthropological Survey of India, Udaipur
6.	Prof. Gerald D. Berreman	Professor of Anthropology California University California, USA
7.	Prof. Melvyn. C. Goldstein	Professor and Chairman Deptt. of Anthropology Case Western Reserve Univ. Ohio, U.S.A.
8.	Dr. V.K. Sishaudia	Lecturer Deptt. of Sociology, DAV College, Dehra Dun.
9.	Dr. (Mrs.) K.P. Singh	Reader Deptt. of Sociology Punjab University, Chandigarh.

10.	Prof. E. Kathleen Gough	Formerly in the Deptt. of Anthropology, University of Oregon
11.	Prof. A. Aiyappan	Former Professor, Utkal University and Curator Madras Museum, Madras.
12.	Dr. K. Raman Unni	Formerly in the School of Planning and Architecture, New Delhi
13.	Prof. David G. Mandelbaum	Deptt. of Anthropology California University, California
14.	Dr. I. Verghese	Senior Personnal Manager Hindustan Photo Films Mfg. Co. Ltd. Ootacamund
15.	Dr. B.K. Das Gupta	Superintending Anthropologist Anthropological Survey of India, Nagpur.
16.	Dr. N. Sarkar	Deputy Director, Deptt. of Research, Arunachal Pradesh
17.	Shri Sumit Ghosal	Senior Technical Assistant Anthropological Survey of India, Calcutta.
18.	Dr. K. Pakrasi	Professor and Head Anthropometry and Human Genetics Unit Indian Statistical Institute, Calcutta
19.	Dr. B.B. Goswami	Joint Director Anthropological Survey of India, Calcutta
20.	Dr. G.S. Bhatt	Former Head, Deptt. of Sociology, DAV College, Dehra Dun.
21.	Dr. (Miss) S.D. Jain	Head, Deptt. of Sociology M.K.P. College, Dehra Dun
22.	Dr. S.B. Nandi	Deputy Director Anthropological Survey of India, Mysore.

CONTENTS

PART ONE

INTRODUCTION

INTRODUCTION

The institution of polyandry cannot be considered as the 'rare cultural oddity' nor an 'ethnographic fossil of a bygone stage in the evolution of the family' (Sangrec & Lavin, 1980 : 1), as it is still in existence in India and some neighbouring countries like Tibet and Sri Lanka, and also in many other countries of the world as custom and social norm among many communities.

Polyandry, no doubt, as Berreman has rightly pointed out, 'has long been a popular subject for speculation and occasionally, for research by anthropologists' (1962 : 60). This institution has definitely fascinated and challenged anthropologists from early evolutionists to contemporary structural-functionalists (Berreman, 1975 : 127). It surely has intrigued anthropologists who have come forward to study it' (Goldstein, 1978 : 325).

The word polyandry has been derived from the Greek word 'polyandria' meaning thereby a woman having many husbands (*polys* = many ; *aner*, *andres* = man). *Notes and Queries on Anthropology* defines it as a custom 'by which a woman is permitted to have more than one husband at the same time' (1971 : 71). Besides, a number of scholars have tried to define this type of marriage system in human society while working among different polyandrous communities (Berreman, 1962 ; 60; Kapadia, 1984 : 52 ; Goldstein, 1976 : 223 ; Radcliffe-Brown, 1950 : 5 ; Fischer, 1956 : 92 ; Leach, 1955 : 199 ; Gough, 1959: 32 ; Prince Peter, 1955 : 179-181 ; 1956 : 46 ; 1957 : 35 ; 1963 : 21).

II

Aristotle felt that 'the union of man and woman has no name' (Politics, 1, 3, 2, ef Needham, 1971 : 6). But many anthropologists and others have searched for a suitable definition to the word 'marriage' and experimented by their own views and definitions.

The definition of marriage as given in the *Notes and Queries on Anthropology* (6th Edition, Reprinted 1971) that *marriage is a union between a man and a woman such that children born to the woman are the recognized legitimate offsprings of both partners* (1971 : 110) has raised much controversy. Many anthropologists could not agree with this definition and are of opinion that this definition is not adequate and that this cannot define all types of marriage as prevalent in different parts of the world.

> 'If this definition was to be accepted a union of a man with several women, or of a woman and several men, or of a woman and another woman, can not be called marriage' (Sarana, 1969 : 159).

In this regard, as Sarana puts it that 'the attempt made in the *Notes and Queries on Anthropology* to define marriage universally has failed' (*op. cit.* : 160-161). Leach also feels that 'all universal definitions of marriage are vain.' The reason he stated in favour of his assertion is that 'the institutions commonly described as marriage do not all have the same legal and social concomitants' (1961 : 105, 108).

It is true that the above definition does not satisfy all types of marriage prevalent all over the world. For example, the above definition can not clarify polyandry in which, 'a woman is permitted to have more than one husband at the same time' as defined by *Notes and Queries on Anthropology* (1971 : 71). No doubt the definition that 'marriage is a relationship established between a woman and one or more other persons....' put forward by Gough (1959 : 32), satisfies the polyandrous marriage though of course, it does not define a polygynous marriage or woman to woman marriage and ghost marriage among the Nuer as described by Evans-Pritchand (1960 : 108, 109). It also does not define polygynandrous marriage in which 'all men of each generation who are brothers marry together with... more than one wife.' (Majumdar, 1963 : 72). It is 'a combination of paternal polyandry and polygyny' (*ibid*) or it is 'multiple, husband *and* wife' (Berreman, 1980 : 377). We may thus tune with the words of Leach that 'all universal definitions of marriage are vain' as marriage 'is... a bundle of rights' (1961 : 105) until we get an actual and just definition of marriage.

Polyandry has also been defined by different scholars. But unlike the definition of marriage, the definitions of polyandry by different scholars have been set almost in one tune. Definition of the *Notes and Queries on Anthropology* (6th Edition, Reprint) has already been stated. Besides this definition some others have also defined polyandry. To McLannan polyandry is the marriage of one woman to more than one man. He also feels that 'wifedom begins with polyandry which is a contract' (1896 : 50-51). But Spencer accepted polyandry 'as one of the kinds of marital relations emerging from the primitive unregulated state...' (1921 : 656-657). Briffault considered polyandry as a relics of group marriage (1927 : 1 : 628-629). According to Prince Peter, 'polyandry is the marriage of one woman to more than one man' (1955 : 21). Brereman has defined it as a 'form of marriage in which a woman has more than one husband at a time.' (1962 : 60). Goldstein thinks that 'polyandry is a form of marriage where two or more males share a bride....' (1976 : 223). Kapadia's definition is that 'polyandry is a form of union in which a woman has more than one husband at a time, or in which brothers share a wife or wives in common' (1984 : 52). Levine and Sangree assert that,

> 'The term 'polyandry' can be used in reference to any situation in which a woman is married to two or more men simultaneously'

and,

> 'It does not apply to circumstances in which women are

> permitted or encouraged to engage in extra-marital liaisons of the sort which may be termed cicibeism, a form of polykoity' (1980 : 388).

The definition of polyandry as given in the *Notes and Queries on Anthropology* and also by other scholars is apparently simple. But unfortunately like the definition of marriage as given in the *Notes and Queries on Anthropology* (6th Edition, *Reprinted*), the above definitions of polyandry do not fit with *polyandry* as prevalent in different human societies all over the world. There are two basic difficulties in this definition. Firstly in case of polyandrous marriage whether all 'husbands' may be treated as actually the husbands. That means if all the 'husbands' are actually married to the girl. And secondly whether the children born of the 'union' actually get the identity of their paternity. In case of the 'marriage' of the 'individuals' (may or may not be brothers) with a girl to become her 'husband,' it is seen that the so called social husbands in many polyandrous societies may not have actually married the girl or performed any marriage ritual at all. Or in certain societies marriage ceremony in case of adelphic polyandry, may take place with one of the 'brother-husbands,' preferably the eldest, brother. The other brother-husbands have sexual access to their 'common-wife.' But question is whether 'the access to the wife for sexual congress' by the so called 'husbands' (or brothers) who have not actually married the girl through ritual, or their 'union' with the girl obeys the very definition of marriage? Or whether these so called 'husbands,' may actually be treated as 'husbands' in true sense? Perhaps not! As Radcliffe-Brown feels that

> 'It is not sexual intercourse that constitutes marriage' for 'marriage is a social arrangement by which a child is given a legitimate position in the society, determined by parenthood in the social sense' (1950 : 5, Introduction).

If that be so, if we agree to *what* Radcliffe-Brown has asserted, we may have to exclude many of the so called polyandrous societies from the list of the polyandrous societies of the world as in case of many of such societies, no marriage in true sense, is actually performed between the woman and 'all the male individuals' be they are brothers or otherwise related or not at all related, though there is socially approved sex relationship between them and the woman involved into the union.

Now let us examine the question of 'legitimate position of the children in the society' and 'parenthood in the social sense.' There cannot be any doubt that 'the bestowal and affirmation of legitimacy and affinity are key and possibly universal features of marriage' (Levine and Sangree, 1980 : 388). In all polyandrous societies in India a child born of the polyandrous union, gets acceptance in the society and therefore gets same 'position' in the society. Scholars who have worked in the polyandrous societies, have tried to show the importance of legitimacy of children which is also a distinguishing feature of polyandry, as they think, as it differentiates polyandry from cicibeism or other form of plural relationship of women (Barreman, 1978 : 18 ; Levine, 1980 : 289-294 ; Smedley, 1980 : 351-355; Muller, 1980 : 360-361 ; Prince Peter, 1980 : 372-373 ; Mandelbaum, 1938 : 575 ; Chanda, 1973 : 80-86).

Gough considering the Nayar marriage system as polyandry or 'group marriage,' which helps in establishing a relation,

> 'between a woman and one or more other persons.' Gough asserts that a child born to the woman under circumstances not prohibited by the rules of the relationship, is accorded full birth-status rights common to normal members of his society or social stratum' (1959 : 32).

But Tambiah (1966) in connection with the polyandry in Ceylone (Sri Lanka) thinks it 'as a customary form of marriage that establishes the inheritance rights of children,' and 'their full birth-status rights common to normal members' of the society or social stratum (1966 : 266). Donham (1912) considers it to be a domestic arrangement. Some other scholars have thought identically or a little differently. But the actual parenthood is not always certain. In each and every polyandrous society in this country, one of the husbands either through certain rites or by some social code, becomes the father of the child in the social sense but he may not be biologically responsible for the birth of this child. The child thus sometimes gets a 'social' father but not a 'biological' one always which he could get if he were born in the monogamous or polygynous societies. So, how far the child in such a situation, really gets actual 'position in the society' and an actual 'father' is the question.

One common but interesting point has been emerged out of all the definitions given by all the above scholars and that is in every polyandrous society one woman (or more than one sometimes) must be having more than one husband at a time. There is no much of controversy among the scholars as regards to the definition of polyandry as that exists in case of the definition of marriage. No doubt by the definitions given by different scholars, the polyandrous society can be identified. But *Encyclopedia Britanica* (1972 : Vol-18 : 194-195) has given more specific criteria for identifying polyandrous societies. It has prescribed the following criteria by which a polyandrous society can be identified:

(1) Children recognize more than one man as having the status of true father,
(2) A woman bears legitimate children to several different fathers in succession,
(3) A legitimately married woman regularly cohabits with several men, none of whom rate as father to her children and,
(4) A single legitimate husband allows other man for sexual access to his wife.

III

The earliest proof of the existence of polyandry is available from Sumer 'where relics of polyandry are apparent until the time of Uru Kaggina (1900 B.C.). The woman of that period were owned by two men' (Meissner Bruno, 1920 : 25 cf. Singh, 1978 : 48). In India this institution is in existence since Vedic period (1600-2000 B.C.). The case of the twin Asvins and their bewitching bride Surya, the daughter of Savita as stated in *Rg. Veda,* is a good example. The twin brothers married a common wife. Similarly the Maruts also had Rodasi who was their beloved, their young and radiant and their common wife. The Vishvadevas also had common wife (Singh, 1978 : 38-50).

In the post-Vedic period during the time of Mahabharata, the brightest example of polyandry was that of the Pandavas and their common wife, Draupadi. In Ramayana both Bali and Sugriva had their wives, Tara and Ruma in common (*op. cit.*, 108-153). Besides there are many such other cases as reported in many ancient Indian literatures and scriptures.

Alberuni, the Muslim scholar-traveller believed in the existence of polyandry in India in 11th Century A.D. (*op. cit.*, 161). Practices closely akin to polyandry or cicisbeism have been reported several times from parts of northern India in nineteenth and twentieth centuries. Different authors have mentioned about polyandry among the Jats of Punjab and also among the Gujjars.

Polyandry among the Tibetans and Bhotias of the border, the Kanets and lower castes of Kulu valley, inhabitants of Bushahar, the Thakkar and Meg of Kashmir, the people of Jaunsar Bower (U.P.), the Toda, the Kota and the Kurumbas of the Nilgiri, the Tolkolans of Malabar, Ishavans, Kaniyans and the Kammalans of Cochin, the Muduvas of Travancore, the Western Kallans and the Nayars has been reported in Census reports of 1911 and 1931.

IV

If the polyandrous societies are spotted in the map of India, we will find some definite distribution pattern. Here in India polyandry at present, is reported to be present among different ethnic groups inhabiting the Himalayas and a few in South India. In the Himalayan region this institution is present among the Bodh of Ladak, people of Lahaul and also of Spiti, the Kinnauras of Kinnaur, the Pangwala of Pangi valley (Himachal Pradesh), people of outer Siraj in Kulu, people of Sirmur district (Himachal Pradesh), Jaunsar Bower area of Dehra Dun District, and Rewain (Uttar Kashi) and Jaunpur (Tehri) areas of Uttar Pradesh, the Jats of Punjab and the

Bhotia and the Lepchas of Sikkim. In South India it is found among the Toda and the Kota of Nilgiri, the Nayars, Iravas and some other castes of South India. Iyer has reported polyandry among the Mannan, Panans, Vilkurpas, Kaniyans, Panikkams, Thandans and the Kammulans in South India (Kerala) (1909 : I : 161, 173, 182, 209, 301, 346). In Arunachal Pradesh some kind of polyandry, rather cicisbeism, is noticed among the Gallong, the Dafla, the Ramo, the Khampa and some other groups.

V

While in course of my own study under the research project, *Polyandry in the Himalayas*, I went through the literature on polyandry and the polyandrous societies of home and abroad, I came to know that polyandry has different types—somewhere the husbands are brothers, somewhere they are otherwise related (uncle-nephew polyandry in Ua-Da-la society of Indo-China or father-son or bigenerational polyandry in Tibet), somewhere they are clansmen but somewhere they are not even distantly related. In some other cases she leads a dual role - her role with her husbands in husbands' house and her role with her lovers in her paternal house. In some ethnic groups the wife cannot go beyond her husbands for a child, in some other communities she may seek co-operation of a stranger for begetting a child. In some case while the legislation forbade polyandry (the Ladakh case) in other case this institution was encouraged by the state legislation (the Kinnaur case). Further, polyandry has different reasons for its origin. While female infanticide or imbalance in sex ratio is the reason for polyandry in some cases, division of labour or avoiding fragmentation of land and other property, is considered as the cause for some other cases. Solidarity of the sibling group, high bride-price, prolonged absence of the husband from home, hard struggle for existence, physical inadequacy of man to produce child etc. are other reasons of polyandry. Population control for proper economic adjustment is thought to be still the other reason. It is also believed that the migrants who infiltrated into the Himalayas through Hindukush, were polyandrous and brought polyandry in India (Saksena, 1962 : 9-11). But Majumdar thinks that the polyandry is a resultant of superimposition of patriarchy over matriarchy (1944 : 63-64).

Thus it is seen that the diversity of reasons for the origin and occurrence of polyandry, is a special feature of polyandry. The reason for origin and development of polyandry may differ from one society to another living in the same or different geo-ethnic and geo-cultural situations.

> 'There is no reason to assume...that similar institutions must have the same function or need to be produced by the same concentration of causal factors' (Goldstein, 1978 : 336).

There is reason to believe that polyandry may be a product of a peculiar ecological condition, or peculiar ecological condition may have helped in the development and nourishment of polyandry. But it is at the same time true that a particular type of ecology can not compel all communities living within it, to adopt identical social trait or institution. It is thus interesting to note that all societies living in the same socio-economic and socio-ecological environment, are not polyandrous. Some may be polyandrous but others practise monogamy, of course, polygyny may exist in both with a weak strength.

In connection with the origin and distribution of polyandry, Berreman rightly asserts that,

> 'Polyandry, like polygyny is evidently not a sufficient unitary phenomenon to be explained in the same terms everywhere. It may have certain advantages or functionally related correlates in some areas and not in other areas. That they are not universal does not mean, of course, that they are not significant' (1962 : 72).

Many anthropologists and other social scientists who have worked among the polyandrous groups, have reported that this very interesting institution of the human society is rapidly vanishing. Singh thinks that,

> 'increasing contact with the non-polyandrous society of the plains is making serious inroads into their distinctive family organisation ; and their polyandry is perhaps on the way to comparative absolescence' (1978 : 172).

Parmar in connection with the polyandry of the Himalayas, found that,

> 'The attitude to polyandry also underwent a change, and it was no longer held in that esteem which it enjoyed two decades back....They (the polyandrous people of the Himalayas) now realise that they should discard it...where circumstances permitted the custom was given up and its place was gradually taken up by monandry.' (1975 : 170).

In Jaunsar Bowar areas also Majumdar marked that people particularly those who are educated and well informed, have started disliking polyandry and polygynandry (1963 : 134). Identically in Kinnaur also polyandry is gradually been disintegrating (Raha, 1978 : 101 ; Raha & Mahato, 1985 : 178). Same is the fate of polyandry in many South Indian castes and communities. The Nayars have almost become monogamous (Fuller, 1976).

VI

The study of polyandry is undoubtedly a very impressive study in the field of Anthropology. This interesting institution of human society is definitely a variant-quite distinct from all other social institutions and customs. The relation of one woman with a number of husbands and identically the relation of a child with his/her sociological father who may or may not be his/her biological father and his/her recognition for a number of 'fathers', reveal some interesting facets of human behaviour. The psycho-social analysis of this type of behaviour definitely proves that it is quite distinct from that prevalent in all other human societies. Disclosing the importance of the study of polyandry, Prince Peter remarked that,

> 'searching for something really at variant with our way of conducting family affairs, I eventually turned to polyandry. Here was something basically divergent. From child's point of view, there was a mother with a number of husbands, all of whom it looked up to as its 'fathers'. What could happen to the Oedipus complex in such a setting ? On which father, if any, would the infant be able to develop its identifications and rejections, such as children of our society do ?' (1963 : 14).

No doubt very little has so far been done on polyandry, on its structure, on its process and on its function. Though some ethnographic studies on some polyandrous societies have been done, but these have not dealt the analytical aspects of polyandry in any detail. In this respect polyandry is rather less known institution. Bhatt feels that,

> 'So far we have been solely occupied with the norm of sharing wives. That is why our studies of polyandry have tended to remain biotic, descriptive and lacking in depth, even unable to resolve that primary question : 'why polyandry?' No wonder, there has been the paucity in-depth studies of such structural aspects of polyandry as demography, kinship, economy, stratification, religion, polity and ideology. We have tended to concentrate more on the custom of polyandry and not on its formations vis-a-vis the ideals of the national social system.' (1981 : 56-57).

Being an anthropologist who undertook intensive studies in the Himalayas among the polyandrous people, I personally feel that detailed analytical study of this dying institution is urgently required as this has not been done properly as yet. To fill up this gap I have taken up a research project, *A Study of Polyandry in the Himalayas,* thanks to the Anthropological Survey of India. I have a plan to study and analyse the structure and function of this plural marriage system, and also to examine why and how people adhered to this custom and why and how polyandry survived and perpetuated in certain human societies till date. I hope my detailed analytical study of polyandry in India and abroad in general, and polyandry in the Himalayas in particular, will answer 'why polyandry'?. We will have to get this answer immediately as polyandry in human society may not survive long.

It is a fact that polyandry is interesting and less known custom. Prince Peter also found that,

> 'from the anthropological angle polyandry was equally of great interest. It was not very well known, because it has been reported from very few places on earth ; it had not been very much studied, probably for the same reasons, but also perhaps because it appeared as an aberrent and isolated example of family organisation with no serious bearing on this institution of human marriage in general.' (1963 ; 14).

On further examination on the importance of polyandry Prince Peter felt that,

> 'its very qualities of unusualness and rarity were worthy of scientific attention. There were possibilities, too, of making discoveries in this field, and the attraction of a novel research work exerted considerable fascination upon me' (*op. cit*).

No doubt this institution of human society is considered as very important and its detailed study requires urgent attention (Raha, 1981 : 101).

In 1973 in the Conference of Anthropologists Priority of Research organised by ICSSR, the study of polyandry was given priority along with other anthropological problems. Bhatt also feels that the polyandry in the Western Himalayas solicits topmost priority (1981 : 3).

Many eminent anthropologists feel the urgent necessity of keeping records of the endangered and degenerating cultural traits, customs and institutions as many of these are fast disappearing due to various factors. It is better to keep record of them now as in future we may not get the opportunity. Tomorrow may be too late.

VII

I have, in this book included twenty-two articles, which are so selected to cover three different polyandrous zones of India namely (I) North and Northwest India (II) South India and (III) East and Northeast India. Within our limitations, I have also tried to cover as many polyandrous people as possible. While I have covered most of the polyandrous groups of the North and Northwest India, I could not do so for South India or East and Northeast India. In North and Northwest India I have included articles on the polyandrous Bodh or Boot of Ladakh (Leh and Zanskar areas) in Jammu and Kashmir, the Lahaula of Lahaul and Spiti district, the Kinnaurese of Kinnaur and the Sirmurese of Sirmur districts, all from Himachal Pradesh, the Jaunsaries of Jaunsar Bower, Dehra Dun district of Uttar Pradesh and the Jats of Punjab. The coverage is quite wide though of course, I have not been able to incorporate articles on polyandry among the Pangawala of Pangi valley, Himachal Pradesh, and from Purola and Rewain (Uttar Kashi district) and Jaunpur (Tehri district) of Uttar Pradesh and also from a few more areas.

From South India I have got articles on the Nayars, the Illavans and the Kota and also on a few more castes. I have not got articles on some other polyandrous groups like the Mannan, the Panan, the Vilkurpus, the Kaniyans, the Pannikkar, the Iravas, the Thandans and others. I have included two interesting articles on the Kota polyandry, but inspite of my best efforts I failed to secure an article on the Toda polyandry though I have included an article on the bow and arrow ceremony of the Toda which determines the paternity of a newborn in the Toda polyandrous family system.

From East and Northeast India I have selected two groups among whom 'polyandry' is practised. These are the Gallongs of Arunachal and the Lepcha of Sikkim. Articles on polyandry among the Ramos, the Khampa and some other tribes have remained uncovered.

Besides the articles on polyandry on different people mentioned above, I have also included articles of some special nature like polyandry as was prevalent in ancient India, differential sex ratios in polyandrous areas, bow and arrow ceremony among the Todas and status and role of women in polyandrous societies etc.

I admit that this book has not included articles on polyandry and on various aspects of polyandry of all polyandrous societies in India. Could be, this book would have given better coverage and understanding of this unique but dying institution of India, had I covered all such articles, but everything has certain limitations. Inspite of my limitations and constrains, I firmly believe that this book will provide sufficient idea to our readers about the unique system of polyandry in India. We shall be able to know from this book what we want to know about polyandry and related matters of the polyandrous societies in India.

Of the twenty-two articles in this book, seventeen are on polyandry in certain polyandrous societies and the rest five articles are on some special issues relating to different aspects of the system of polyandry or the polyandrous society. Therefore I have divided this book into five parts. *Part one* : *Introduction* deals with polyandry and the related issues like the definitions, origin, development, distributions, characteristics, reasons of decline etc. *Part two* : *Polyandry in North and Northwest India* covers nine articles concerning polyandry prevalent among different communities of North and Northwest India including the Himalayas. *Part three* : *Polyandry in South India* includes five articles on this type of marriage prevalent among different ethnic groups of South India. *Part Four* : *Polyandry in East and North East India* consists of three articles on polyandry as prevalent in the East and Northeast India. *Part Five* : *Polyandry in India* (*special issues*) has housed five articles of special nature concerning some aspects of polyandry.

In Part Two out of nine articles all but one are on this type of plural marriage practised in the Central and Western Himalayas. The article by Prof. John H. Crook describes polyandry as prevalent among the Bodh or Bhot of Ladakh (Leh and Zanskar areas) in Jammu and Kashmir. In this very interesting article, Prof. Crook has made comparison of his data on polyandry in Leh and Zanskar areas collected in 1981 with the data collected by Prince Peter in 1938 from the same area and has tried to show the nature and extent of change in this system in time scale. Reference has also been made by him on polyandry in Nepal and Tibet.

The article by Shri T.K. Ghosh is on polyandry in Lahaul under Lahaul and Spiti district of Himachal Pradesh. Shri Ghosh, who has undertaken intensive research work in Lahaul area, has highlighted this unique system in this high Himalayan district and reasons for its gradual decline.

Through our (Raha & Coomar) article on polyandry in Kinnaur we have tried to analyse the structure of the institution of polyandry in Kinnaur, the north-eastern most district of Himachal Pradesh bordering Tibet and how it is functioning in different levels. We have also shown its adaptation to a particular eco-system and also stated probable reasons for its very development and decline.

Dr. Ramesh Chandra through his article, has shown how the polyandry system at present, is functioning both in Kinnaur and Sirmur districts of Himachal Pradesh. He has also shown the relevance of this type of marriage in the peculiar Himalayan ecology, factors responsible for its growth and development and also the nature and extent of changes in polyandrous system in these areas.

Part Two of this book has also housed four articles relating to the polyandry as practised in Jaunsar-Bowar and its contiguous areas. Berreman through his two articles, have shown the peculiar features of polyandry present in the Pahari speaking Jaunsar-Bowar and adjoining areas of Uttar Pradesh. In his first article Berreman has made a comparison between the polyandry in Jaunsar-Bowar and the monandry in Garhwal, and has tried to show that living in the same economic and ecological zone, the two societies do not have same system. Various factors 'as causal for, predisposing toward and correlated with polyandry' with reference to this society have also been highlighted by him. In his second article Berreman has shown how polyandry developed in the Jaunsari society and variations therein in time and due to circumstances.

Professor Goldstein's article is an interesting article in which he has made a comparison between the Pahari polyandry, as described by Professor Berreman and the Tibetan polyandry, his own work demonstrating the 'significant and often fundamental differences between such populations with respect to their marriage-family system'.

The paper on the Jaunsari polyandry by Dr. V. Sishaudia has attempted to show the structure and function of the polyandrous system among the Jaunsaries.

The last article under Part Two is on the polyandry of the Jat of Punjab. Dr. (Mrs.) Singh has very interestingly shown how this unique form of marriage still persists in the contemporary Jat society of Punjab, no doubt this plural marriage was also prevalent among them in the past (Kirkpatrick, 1878).

In Part Three of this book I have dealt with the system of polyandry, as prevalent in some communities of South India. There are five articles. The first one is on the Nayar polyandry. In this article Professor Gough has tried to show the polyandrous marriage system among the Nayar and 'thereby showing that in fact the notion of fatherhood is not lacking and that marriage does serve to establish the legitimacy of children'. He has also given a new definition of marriage vis-a-vis polyandry. Dr. Unni in his article has highlighted polyandry in Malabar regions among the Nairs/Nayars and some other caste groups after giving details of social system prevalent in the said areas.

The next article is of Professor Aiyappan who worked on polyandry in the Malabar areas and has presented his findings in this paper. He has shown how polyandry functioned in different societies in Malabar region, particularly among the Illavans.

The next two articles are on polyandry among the Kota. While Professor Mandelbaum has emphasised through his article what he meant by polyandry among the Kota among whom 'a man's brothers have free sexual access to his wife' though the Kota is not polyandrous in true sense. Dr. Verghese feels that it is not polyandry that is practised by the Kota, but some sort of cicibeism.

Part Four includes three articles of which first two are on the Gallong polyandry and the third one is on the polyandry among the Lepcha of Sikkim. In his article Dr. Das Gupta has emphasised that the Gallong practise polyandry which 'is not functioning as an obligatory prescriptive system. It is in their symbolic order.' Dr. Sarkar through his article has expressed his view that the polyandry as practised by these people is not polyandry in true sense of the term. Rather it may be said that this is some sort of permissible sex relation between the woman and her husband's brothers. It is rather 'monogamy with fraternal cicibeism...'

The third article of this part is on polyandry in Sikkim. In Sikkim polyandry is found to be practised by the Lepchas and the Bhotias. Here the author has described this form of marriage among the Lepchas which is fast dying out. Even though majority of them have become monogamous, still now younger brother is permitted to share elder brother's wife.

Part Five is meant for some special issues relating to the polyandry or polyandrous society. The first article of this part is on the polyandry as was prevalent in ancient India. Different ancient Indian scriptures have portraited this custom or such cases as prevalent among different period of time during the pre-Vedic, Vedic and post-Vedic times. This article is based on some such cases and has shown the nature and extent of this form of marriage as existed in India of bygone days.

The next article of this part is on the differential sex-ratios among the polyandrous societies in India. Dr. Pakrasi has shown through this article the sex-ratio among the polyandrous people of India on the basis of Census figures.

The next article is of Dr. Goswami who has described a peculiar ceremony of the Toda of Nilgiri hills which determines the paternity of the children born of the polyandrous union.

The two more articles of this Part Five are on the status of women in polyandrous societies. While in the first article Prof. Bhatt and Dr. (Miss) Jain have shown the role performed by the women in the polyandrous Jaunsari society, Dr. Nandi has described the status of the Lepcha women in Sikkim in the other.

The idea of compiling such a book cropped up in my mind when I started my research work in the polyandrous region of high Himalayas in early seventy. But due to my multifarious engagements, I could not proceed with this project. The idea got further impetus when I started my research work under the project, *A Study of Polyandry in the Himalayas.* But the urgency of preserving the records of this vanishing trait, compelled me to work on this book in later days. But there is other idea too behind compiling this book. I had in my mind before I started preparing the book, to publish a book on Indian polyandry for the students, particularly of post-graduate and under-graduate classes of the Departments of Anthropology, Sociology and allied disciplines in different universities and colleges. I further expected that such a book would be much beneficial to the research scholars engaged in studying the marriage system in general and polyandry in particular.

Now with the publication of this book, I hope that my ambition and expectation will be fulfilled if the students of both post-graduate and under-graduate classes and research scholars of Anthropology, Sociology and allied disciplines find this book useful to them. To those who are engaged in studying the structure and function of the Indian society, this book will, I believe, render some benefit.

REFERENCES

Berreman, G.D., 1962 Pahari Polyandry : A Comparison, *American Anthropologist*, vol. 64, No. 1.

——1975 Himalayan Polyandry and the Domestic Cycle. *American Ethnologist*, vol. 2.

——1978 Ecology, Demography and Domestic Strategies in the Western Himalayas. *Journal of Anthropological Research*, vol. 34, No. 3

——1980 Polyandry : Exotic Custom vs. Analytic Concept. *Journal of Comparative Family Studies*, vol. 11, No. 3.

Bhatt, G.S. 1981 Polyandry in Western Himalaya : Some Notes and Observations. *Journal of Social Research.* Special Number on Himalayan Studies. vol. 24, No. 2.

Briffault R. 1927 *The Mothers*, 3 vols. George Allen and Unwin, London.

Census of India 1911 *India*. vol. 1, Part 1, 1931 (ed.).

——1931 *India*, vol. 1, Part 1.

Chandra, R. 1973 The Notion of Paternity among the Polyandrous Kanet of Kinnaur, Himachal Pradesh. *Bull. Anthropological Survey of India*, vol. 21 No. 1&2.

Denham, E.B. 1912 *Ceylon at the Census of 1911*. Colombo : Government Printer.

Encyclopaedia Britanica, 1972, vol. 18. William Benten, Publisher, U.S.A.

Evans-Pritchand, E.E. 1978 *The Nuer : A description of the Modes of Livelihood and Political Institutions of a Nilotic Peddle* Oxford University Press, New York.

Fischer, H. Th. 1956 For a New Definition of Marriage. *Man*, vol 56.

Fuller, C.J. 1976 *The Nayars Today*. Cambridge University Press. Cambridge.

Goldstein, M.C. 1976 Fraternal Polyandry and Fertility in High Himalayan Valley in North-Western Nepal. *Human Ecology*, vol. 4.

——1978 Pahari and Tibetan Polyandry Revisited. *Ethnology*, vol. 17.

Gough, K.E. 1959 The Nayars and the definition of Marriage, *Journal Royal Anthropological Institute*. vol. 89.

Iyer, L.K.A.K. 1909 *The Cochin Tribes and Castes*. vol. 1&2, Madras.

Kapadia, K.M. 1984 *Marriage and family in India*, Oxford University Press, Calcutta.

Leach, E.R. 1955 Polyandry, Inheritance and the Definition of Marriage, *Man*, vol. 55.

——1961, Polyandry, Inheritance and the Definition of Marriage : With Particular Reference to Sinhalese customary Law. In *Rethinking Anthropology*, E.R Leach ed. The Anthlone Press, London.

Levine, N.E. 1980 Nyinba Polyandry and the Allocation of Paternity. *Journal of Comparative Family Studies*, vol. II, No. 3.

Majumdar, D.N. 1944 *The Fortunes of Primitive Tribes*, Lucknow.

——1963 *Himalayan Polyandry*. Asia Publishing House, London.

Mandelbaum, D.G. 1938 Polyandry in Kota Society, *American Anthropologist*, vol. 40, No. 4.

McLannan, J.F. 1896 *Studies in Ancient History*, London.

Muller, J.C. 1980 On the Relevance of having two Husbands : Contribution to the Study of Polygynous/Polyandrous Marital Form of the Jes Plateau. *Journal of Comparative Family Studies*, vol. II, No. 3.

Meissuer Brune 1920-25 *Babylonian and Assyrian* 2 vols. Heidelberg.

Needham, R. 1971 Remarks on the Analysis of Kinship and Marriage in *Rethinking Kinship and Marriage* (ed. Needham, R) A.S.A. Monographs, No. 11, Tavistock Publication, London.

——1971 *Notes and Queries on Anthropology* (6th edition). Routledge and Kegan Paul Ltd. London.

Parmar, Y.S. 1975 *Polyandry in the Himalayas*, Vikas Publishing House Pvt. Ltd. Delhi.

Peter, Prince 1955 Polyandry and Kinship group *Man*, vol. 55.

——1956 For a New Definition of Marriage *Man*, vol. 46.

——1957 For a New Definition of Marriage *Man*, vol. 35.

——1963 *A Study of Polyandry*. Mouton & Co., The Hague.

——1980 Comments on the Social and Cultural Implications or Variant

Systems of Polyandrous Alliances. *Journal of Comparative Family Studies*, vol. 11, No. 3.

Radcliffe-Brown, A.R. 1950 Introduction. In *African Systems of Kinship and Marriage*, ed. A.R. Radcliffe-Brown and D. Forde, Oxford University Press, London.

Raha, M.K. 1978 Stratification and Religion in a Himalayan Society, in *Himalayan Anthropology*, ed. James Fischer, The Hague.

——1981 Urgent Anthropology in the Himalayas, *Journal of Social Research*, Special number on Himalayan Studies, vol. 24 No. 11.

——S.N. Mopate 1985 *The Kinnaurese of the Himalayas*. Anthropological Survey of India, Calcutta.

——(*ed.*) 1987 *The Himalayan Heritage* Gian Publishing House, Delhi.

Saksena, R.N. 1962 *Social Economy of a Polyandrous People*. Asia Publishing House, London.

Sangre, W.H. and Levine, N.E. 1980 Introduction, Women with many Husbands : Polyandrous alliance and marital flexibility in Africa and Asia. *Journal of Comparative Family Studies*, vol. II No. 3.

Sarana, G. 1969 Some Observations on the definition of Marriage. *Ethnos*. vol. 33.

Singh, S.D. 1978 Polyandry in Ancient India. *Vikas Publishing House* Pvt. Ltd., Delhi.

Smedley, A. 1980 The Implications of Birom Cicibeism. *Journal of Comparative Family Studies*, vol. II, No. 3.

Spencer, H. 1921 *The Principles of Sociology*, New York.

Tambiah, S.J. 1966 Polyandry in Ceylon with Special Reference to the Laggala Region, in Furer-Haimendorf (ed). *Caste and Kin in Nepal, India and Ceylon*, Asia Publishing House, Bombay.

PART TWO

POLYANDRY IN THE NORTH AND NORTH-WESTERN INDIA

1

POLYANDRY IN LADAKH

JOHN H. CROOK

Introduction

The phenomenon of polyandrous marriage in Ladakh cannot be understood except in relation to the ecological, economic and demographic features of the cultural system of which it is an important traditional component. This system furthermore is in no essential feature different from that which has sustained the Tibetan culture of the trans-Himalayan area over many centuries (see De Fillippi, 1937) and, the local history of Ladakh has been linked with that of Kashmir throughout its history. It is therefore in terms of an understanding of a Tibetan rather than an Indian context that we must search for an explanation. We do not have here a local phenomenon attributable to some minor Himalayan tribe but one distinctive feature of a major world civilisation.

In the Tibetan cultural domain polyandrous marriage is intimately entwined with traditional patterns of land settlement and inheritance, household structure, taxation and obligatory service to rulers and the recruitment of young men for training in the extensive monastic system of Tibetan Buddhism (Goldstein, 1971).

The contemporary research worker will, however, encounter numerous frustrations in attempting field work on this topic.

Polyandry in Ladakh today is no longer a legal system of marriage although marriages so contracted in the past run no risk of prosecution. Where it exists, it is not frequently discussed and although in village communities it remains a frequent form of conjugal relationship, it now appears often in an informal or disguised form. A heavy weight of missionary and contemporary bourgeois opinion bears upon polyandry which suffers still from moralistic condemnation even though some comprehension of its valuable social functions in traditional society is beginning to appear. Since 1931 some contemporary Ladakhis, in addition to adopting quite untraditional moralistic positions, became aware of the relation between polyandry and low birth rate : they have criticised this form of marriage due to its lower contribution to the population than the systems of Islamic marriages practised by Moslem Ladakhis who are often seen as competitors in a struggle for influence. (Mann, 1978 ; Crook, 1980 b ; Grist, 1980).

These values and opinions are of recent origin. In 1938 Prince Peter of Greece, the first anthropologist to conduct field work on Tibetan polyandry, had a detailed conversation with a wealthy farmer who argued strongly in favour of the positive moral values then associated with this traditional marriage form.

> 'Lobsang Tok Tok complained bitterly of the immorality of young people in Leh. He said that polyandry was no longer desired by the younger generation and that this was all due to outside influence from India and Turki traders from Singkiang and from European missionaries and travellers who were perpetually speaking against the time-honoured custom... It seemed to him incomprehensible that one could stay rich while dividing up the family property with each monogamous marriage, as we do in our countries. It would be impossible to do this in Ladakh, he said, because there would never be enough to go round and everybody would be quickly reduced to famines' (Prince Peter of Greece, 1963).

This quotation reveals the association between ecology,

inheritance and polyandry which plays a major role in most interpretations of this phenomenon. It also reveals and explicts insight into these plausible relations by an intelligent member of the Ladakhi population.

Prince Peter sought out a number of polyandrous families in Ladakh (and also in Lahoul and Tibet) and provides detailed genealogies. In 1981, working with Tsering Shakya, I returned to this investigation by repeating the study on six families near Leh. The results show clearly how household organisation has changed since 1938 and thus reveals much concerning the function of polyandry (see below).

Unfortunately it has never been possible to make field studies on polyandry in actual Tibetan villages. Anthropologists have been forced to collect information from refugees living now in India. While such studies provide valuable insights (Aziz, 1978 ; Goldstein, 1971 ; Dargyay, 1982) they lack the precision of the few actual field investigations which have been made in the Indian Himalayas and in Nepal. The most useful of these are the researches of C. von Feurer Haimendorf (1964), Jest (1975) and Goldstein (1976) in Nepal and Grist (1980) in some villages of the Indus valley in Ladakh. Work by the Bristol University Expedition to Zanskar in 1980 now provides evidence from this area (Attenborough, Elford, in Crook in press). Due to the Gradual distortion and disappearance of polyandry in many of these communities, these studies rarely collect statistics from which calculated inferences can be drawn. Nonetheless a reasonably comprehensive account of this form of marriage can now be constructed. Other studies in the Himalayas (Majumdar, 1960 ; Parmar, 1975) are not primarily concerned with Tibetan people and do not therefore add anything specific to research material bearing on the Ladakhi system.

Traditional Land Inheritance and Polyandry in Ladakh

The key features of the relationship between polyandry and inheritance in Ladakh have been as follows :

(*i*) A farming estate is inherited upon marriage by a modified form of primogeniture. The eldest son of a generation together with one or more brothers takes over the big house (*khang chen*) and estate from the previous set of fathers. The eldest son is the head of the household and responsible for estate management. The estate is thus passed from one generation to another without subdivision between inheritors.

(*ii*) The parents of the managing generation move into the "small-house" (*Khang chung*, Zanskar) or (*khang gyu* (Indus-valley) which is supported by about a quarter of the estate land. Management of this plot usually still vests in the elder brother of the inheriting generation and upon the death of the old people the *khang chung* remains an unoccupied building on the estate until the next intergenerational transfer.

(*iii*) The actual details of inheritance on particular estates depend upon the ages, numbers and sex of the sibling group. Usually the eldest son takes a wife together with one of his younger brothers, who may still be a teenager at the time of the marriage. Often the second son becomes a monk and additional brothers marry out of the family into estates lacking sons. Table 1 shows the extent of polyandry in the six families near Leh studied by Prince Peter in 1938 and the reduced significance of polyandry today (Crook and Shakya, *loc. cit.*) It is however by no means always the cases that the second son becomes a monk. Table 2 shows the birth order position in the sequence of male siblings for monks in stongde and Phuktal *gompas* in Zanskar. Where the eldest brother chooses the life of a monk then the second becomes household head.

(*iv*) If there are no sons then the eldest sister, provided she has not married, inherits the estate. She may then take a *mag pa* husband from a family with excess sons. If she has a sister, she too may marry the same man thus establishing a polygynous household. The *mag pa* has little influence in the family but the estate will eventually pass to the sons resulting from his marriage. Thus whether by the note that for these sponsoring families the importance of sending sons to a monastery is such that the proportion of brothers sent, increases inversely with family size. 50 per cent of monks in these two *gompas* are second sons.

TABLE 1

Household membership and marital types. Six families near Leh (from Prince Peter 1963, Crook and Shakya, in press)

A. 1938 households							
	1	2	3	4	5	6	Total
males/females	9/5	5/3	5/5	5/6	5/5	8/5	37129 1:0.8
marital type							
Tetrandrous	—	—	—	—	—	1	1
Triandrous	—	1	1	1	—	—	3
Biandrous	2	1	—	1	1	1	6
Monogamous	2	—	2	—	1	1	6
Total	4	2	3	2	2	3	16
B. 1981							
males/females	18/6	14/9	9/3	8/7	12/7	6/9	67/41 1:0.6
marital type							
Tetrandrous	—	—	—	—	—	—	0
Triandrous	—	—	—	—	1	—	1
Biandrous	3	—	—	—	—	—	3
Monogamous	5	5	3	3	5	4	25

The estate is thus best viewed as passing from one generation of siblings to another rather than from an individual to another. So, long as they obey certain rules junior married brothers or sisters have *de facto* rights in the estate even if *de jure* the eldest is the prime inheritor.

(*v*) It follows that only one sex inherits the estate in any one generation. Furthermore, since the change-over

TABLE 2

Birth order positions among brothers of monks in sTong-de and Phuk. tal *gompas*, Zanskar

A. *sTong. de*

No. Brothers	No. Families (No. Men)	Birth 1	Order 2	Position of Monks 3	4	5	Total Monks (% of Brothers)
7	1(7)	—	—	1	—	—	1(14)
6	2(12)	—	—	—	1	1	2(17)
5	7(35)	—	5	3	1	1	10(29)
4	16(64)	2	6	5	9	—	22(34)
3	17(51)	1	11	7	—	—	19(37)
2	11(22)	—	11	—	—	—	11(50)
1	1(1)	1	—	—	—	—	1
Totals	55(192)	4	33	16	11	2	66(34)
B. *Phuk. tal*		1	2	3	4	5	
5	8(40)	3	2	5	2	1	13(33)
4	10(40)	2	6	3	1	1	12(30)
3	34(102)	1	22	13	—	—	36(35)
2	15(30)	5	11	1	—	—	17(57)
1	5(5)	5	—	—	—	—	5(100)
Totals	72(217)	16	41	22	3	1	83(38)
Grand Totals	127(409)	20	74	38	14	3	149(36)

occurs soon after the marriage, or at least as soon as a child is born, the parents quickly move into a *khang chung*. It is rare for an adult elder brother to be found elsewhere than in the *khang chen*. It follows that household heads are usually young men.

(*vi*) *Khang chung* inhabitants are thus usually parents or other older relatives (uncles, aunts, etc. of the estate owner). Grist (1980) remarks on a general rule against two couples of the same generation living under one roof and a lesser rule against two couples of different generations living together. However, as the polyandrous system changes these rules tend to break down (see Crook and Shakya, in press).

(*vii*) If a brother or uncle of the owner marries while living in a *khang chung* and has offspring, the house may then not revert to the estate but become a *khang chen* of a new family line. In Zanskar it appears that the entire village has to agree to the formal establishment of such a household as a new estate. This is mainly because it may involve changes in the distribution of cultivatable land, the allocation of water for irrigation.

(*viii*) If divorce occurs the wife or *mag pa* commonly returns to the natal home. In two of four cases known to Grist (*loc. cit.*) where the wife had children, she took all or some of them with her. A variety of arrangements are possible perhaps determined by negotiation in relation to the labour needs of.

(*ix*) Some times polygyny results from the addition of a second wife to a monogamous household. One case known to us at sTongde in Zanskar was explained to us by the husband. He said he had much land and, because he was unwell, not enough labour to work it. So he took a second wife and now has no less than 12 surviving children. Labour shortage will not be a problem in the next generation. The frequencies of marriage types in two Zanskar villages are shown in Table 3.

Examination of these details shows clearly how closely

associated are the marital and inheritance rules. The question may be put as to which of these is primary : is the inheritance rule contingent upon the marriage system or vice-versa ? The Ladakhi informants have always been quite explicit on this subject. Speaking of the functions of polyandry, they always say it exists in order to maintain the estates of the farmers intact. The Ladakhis do not usually mention population problems in connection with polyandry but old Lobsang Tok Tok, whom we quoted above, seems to have been quite clear about it. Multiple monogamous marriage in successive generations even when not associated with division of the ancestral estate would soon have led to its over-population. Polyandry evidently serves to ensure an adult labour force sufficient to manage a small estate but without incurring the burden of too many children.

Examples of polyandrous households in Ladakh

(*i*) *Six families near Leh*

Six families near Leh were originally studied by Prince Peter in 1938 because they contained polyandrous marriages. These were re-examined in 1981. It was expected that the contemporary situation would be different from that obtaining some forty years earlier and that an analysis of the contrasts would yield inferences concerning the functions of polyandry in the traditional society of farmers (Crook and Shakya in press, see also in Crook, ed. in press).

The six estates were unchanged as agricultural units but a major increase in the sizes of the families occupying them had occurred (mean household size in 1938 : 11.5 $\bar{X}$ in 1981 : 17.5). On these estates the number of *khang chen* remained the same but the mean number of *khang gyu* had gone up from 1.5 to 1.8. In 1938 63% of a population of 70 were accommodated in the *khang chen* while by 1981 only 50% of 105 persons were accommodated there. The number of *khang gyu* thus increased in relation to a larger per cent of the bigger families accommodated in them.

Table 1 shows that whereas in 1938 a married woman could have as many as four husbands in marriages of which 63% were polyandrous, by 1981 only one triandrous and three biandrous marriages still existed out of 25 marriages in total, a mere 16%. Furthermore in 1938 all *khang chen* families were polyandrous while by 1981 none were so ; polyandry being found in the older generation mainly in *khang gyu*.

One consequence of the disappearance of polyandry from *khang chen* has been that the transfer of the estate from father to elder son upon marriage now occurs in a much modified form. While *de facto* management is performed largely by the son, his father continues to reside in the *khang chen* until death. The old men thus exert a much enchanced influence and the rule whereby the younger generation of brothers comes to occupy the *khang chen* has broken down.

In 1938, with the exception of one sister, only wives and children of the reproductive generation lived in the *khang chen*. In 1981, a considerable number of grandchildren as well-as married monogamous brothers lived in *khang chen* as well as the elderly senior father. In addition, there was a great increase in the categories of kin to be found in the *khang gyu* (see Table 3).

TABLE 3

Kin categories in *k'hang gyu* of six families near Leh in 1938 and 1981 (data from Prince Peter, *loc. cit.*, and Crook and Shakya *loc. cit.*)

Kin household head	1938	1981
Grandparent	5	—
Uncle/Aunt	—	2
Parent	16	1
Brother (†spouse)	3 (—)	15 (6)
Sister (†spouse)	3 (—)	4 (1)
Nieces/Nephews	—	21
Children of Nieces/Nephews	—	5
Total persons	27	50

These changes in the occupancy patterns of the six households are linked to the appearance of gainful employment other than agriculture near Leh. In 1938, all adult males were engaged in farming. In 1981, only 50% were engaged in farming ; others

TABLE 4

Frequency of forms of marriage in Zanskar

sTongde	Total	Monogamous	Polygynous	Polyandrous
Bag. ma	48	34	4	10
Mag. pa	7	3	4	0
Totals	55	37	8	10
Kumik				
Bag. ma	56	23	1	2
Grand Total	111	50	9	12

(Data from Attenborough, in press, Elford, in press).

have jobs as teachers, soldiers, police, clerks. One was a professional civil engineer. Of the teenagers and young adults a proportion today will go on to University or other forms of higher education.

These six families do not seem to have contributed many monks to the local monasteries even in Prince Peter's time. Today only one elderly monk, a man of higher scholarly attainment, the eminent Lobon of Spituk Monastery, was found within this sample.

Generally speaking the household dwellings, whether *khang chen* or *khang gyu* are becoming separable units owned by monogamous couples. Although these couples remain associated in extended families at today's date, it is clear that subdivision of the original properties is gradually appearing. With the pressure on land for building around Leh and the new job opportunities which do not require a base in land ownerships, it is clear that a splitting up of these old farmsteads is highly likely to occur in the next generation. However, cooperative farming by group of monogamous couples may develop in at least one case.

Taking a retrospective look, at these changes reveals very clearly the functional significance of polyandry on these estates. The emphasis was on the reproductive fraternal group and their labour in common to produce the agricultural yield required for the family. The emphasis was on youth and strength so that the intergenerational transfer of an unbroken estate occured soon after one or two brothers were old enough to make socially acceptable marriages. Wealth depended not upon the area of land owned but, as we were clearly informed by villagers in Zanskar, upon the relations between land and labour available to work it. Between generations there could therefore be large changes in the wealth and attributed status of a family. The emphasis on reproduction is therefore significant and generates the dynamics whereby brotherless sisters may form polygynous relations with their *mag pa* husband.

(ii) Zanskar

In Zanskar today the ceremonial marriage of more than one brother to a wife appears to be a thing of the past ; even so in a number of households it appears to be the rule that the elder brother shares his wife with a younger. Such cases we consider at least functionally polyandrous as the household remains intact. In a survey of the village of sTongde (pop. 355) 65 men and 63 women were married while in neighbouring Kumik 29 males and 27 females enjoyed this status (Table 4).

In these two neighbouring villages 11% of marriages were polyandrous (one case of triandry, remainder biandrous), 8% polygynous and 45% monogamous. Over 6% were *mag pa* marriages. In sTongde Attenborough notes that a strikingly high proportion of *mag pa* marriages are polygynous. Thus in both types of polygamy it tends to be the single sexed spouse who marries into the land holding family rather than being an initial member of it. Kin relations between the co-spouses are high. In 9 cases at sTongde co-husbands were brothers and in the tenth patrilateral parallel cousins. Female co-spouses were always sisters in *mag pa* marriage but in two of four *bag ma* polygynous marriages the co-wives were not close relatives.

At sTongde of 41 reproductive marriages 10 were in *khang chung*. The rule that the reproductive generation occupies the *khang chen* is thus only generally true and exceptions clearly occur due to individual family circumstances.

Attenborough examined the natality differences between the types of marriage (Table 5). Compared with the standard

TABLE 5

Natality differences between marriage forms at sTongde (Medians for parous women, no cases in brackets)

Marital type	N. children standardised for age	Birth interval
Bag. ma monogamous	1.0 (37)	3.0 (117)
Mag. pa ,,	1.25 (3)	3.72 (12)
Bag. ma polygynous	1.35 (6)	2.0 (27)
Mag. pa ,,	0.75 (9)	2.5 (16)
Bag. ma polyandrous	1.0 (10)	2.0 (11)
Unmarried women	0.375(2)	4.0 (1)
Divorced	0.89 (1)	

pattern for monogamy, polygyny seems slightly more productive and has shorter birth intervals. Polyandry is not more productive in these figures (cf. Table 10) but there is a shorter average birth interval. A number of complicating factors (see Attenborough *loc. cit.*) could account for these differences and give the samples sizes no firm conclusions can be drawn.

Genealogies of 32 houses at sTongde were collected in 1980. From these it is possible to make some comparison between the present reproductive generation and that of the preceding one. The location of the *khang chen* owners' brothers in these generation is shown in Table 6.

If we exclude the boys from the present generation and compare the sets of reproductively aged males, the most striking feature here is that in each generation a large proportion of adult brothers of *khang chen* head become monks, 44% and 48%, 18% of the current reproductive generation are probably co-husbands. While in the preceding generation 15% held this status. The percentages for brothers separately married are 6 and 19 respectively. Only in the older generation do we find 15% *mag pa* although some as the boys of the present generation may become such. The figures suggest that polyandry *al beit* in its disguised form, is certainly not decreasing in this

TABLE 6

Location of Brothers of *khang chen* heads in two generations at sTongde

Number of Brothers additional to owner in family.	N. cases (No males)	Probable Co-husband	Mag. pa	Monk	Married	Unmarried or boy
A. *Current reproductive generation*						
3	5 (15)	3	—	6	1	5
2	6 (12)	1	—	6	—	5
1	7 (7)	2	—	3	1	1
Total	18 (34)	6	0	15	2	11
B *Father's generation*						
5	1 (5)	—	3	1	1	—
3	2 (6)	1	—	4	1	—
2	5 (10)	3	1	5	1	—
1	5 (5)	—	—	3	2	—
Total	13 (27)	4	4	13	5	0

highly traditional village and in 1980 the allocation of young brothers to the local monastery was as yet undiminished. We can note, however, that in this longer sample of estates (32) the percentage of polyandrously associated brothers is lower than in the six *selected* families examined by Prince Peter in 1938.

If we examine the 21 sisters of *khang chen* heads in a similar way we find that in the present generation 3 are married outside the village and 3 in it, 8 are unmarried and 7 are not of reproductive age. We have already noted the three cases of brotherless sisters marrying a *mag pa* in bigamy. In the fathers' generation 21 sisters married outside the village, there were two couples in *mag pa* marriages and one took a *mag pa* in the family *khang chung*. There were 6 unmarried sisters one of whom had been divorced and the others described as nuns resident in the household (*chos me*). These contrasts are doubtless largely due to the older age of the fathers' sisters giving them more time to have married outside the villages. The proportion of unmarried women in the fathers' generation is 6/32=19%.

At Kumik 50% of reproductive adults are married and 45% single, 5% are widowed. The single people are mostly the unmarried brothers and sisters of the present or retired heads of houses. Of these single men 14/21-67.1% are monks and the remainder are farmer or students. One man works in an office in the nearby town of Padum. Twenty-six of the twenty-nine unmarried women work on the land in their natal houses and two are elderly nuns. One is a student. Six of the seven single men who are not monks are less than twenty-five years old. Three will become owners when they marry. Three have neither joined their brothers in polyandry nor become monks. The decision as to whether they marry separately will be influenced by the availability of resources within the household for supporting a new family unit. 55% (16) of the single women are under the age of 25. Elford calculates that if the rate at which males become monks in Zanskar generally is as high as in Kumit, only about 70% of these women will marry. The practice of polyandry also increases the proportion of unmarried women. It seems likely that many of the considerable pool of unmarried young women at Kumik and sTongde will remain single like their aunts before them. As Elford comments it is unusual in Asia for such high proportions of people to remain unmarried (see for example the Nepal Fertility Survey Nepal F.P. and M.C.H. Project, Kathmandu 1977).

An analysis of the monks of sTongde and Phuktal monasteries also stresses the high percentage of non-reproductive males in Zanskar villages. The monks of sTongde *gom pa* are recruited from sponsoring families (*spyin dak*) in the villages of sTongde Kumik and Shillingkit. The monks of Phuktal are drawn from a rather larger number of villages and hamlets in the upper valley of the *Lingti chu.* The percentage of brothers from all monk donating families is shown in Table 2. On average no less than 36% of males from a sample of 127 Zanskari families are thus monks and excluded from the reproductive population. The effect of this on the demography of the valley must by very considerable indeed.

Villages in the Indus Valley

In general Grist's (*loc. cit.*) description closely parallels these from Leh and Zanskar. In addition to monogamous marriages polygyny and polyandry occurred but no reports of father and son marrying the same woman, as has been reported in Tibet, were heard. Nor did she hear of any case of *por jag*. an extra husband being brought in by a polyandrously married woman of her own choice. Prince Peter (1963) had some account of such marriage in Ladakh in 1938. Grist did, however, report one case of two brothers marrying two sisters, each member of one sex marrying the two of the other, in a complex variety of *bag ma* marriage also noted by Haimendorf as a rare marriage among the Sherpa.

As in Zanskar many polyandrous marriages are *de facto* rather than *de jure* today and comprise an elder brother with a younger one, often the third, who is commonly often away doing work elsewhere or in military service. Grist argued that she would expect polyandry to be most frequent in villages with large sibling groups where there should also be a few *mag pa* marriages. In several villages the percentage of all families, large enough to support polyandry was calculated and compared to the completed family size the incidence of *mag.pa* marriages and percentage of men in wage earning occupation. (Table 7)

TABLE 7

Polyandry and sibling group size (From Grist, 1980)

	Gompa	Mattho	Saspochey
% Polyandry/Possible cases	75	55	66
% *Mag pa*/all marriages	10	32	16
% Male wage earners	60	24	30
Completed family size	4.4	3.8	2.7

The expected association between sibling group size and polyandry is found when Gompa village is compared with Mattho Saspochey, where only 13 (50%) of households were examined does not, however, fit easily into this scheme. The village of Gompa is near Leh, has many males working there in non-agricultural jobs and has been fully aware of anti-polyandry propaganda. Yet a high percentage of marriages were *de facto* polyandrous. Grist suggests that on the rather large farming estates at Gompa, where polyandry can be assumed to have been traditionally as common as in Prince Peter's families in the valley below the villages, it has been found advantageous to include a wage owner as contributor to the family in which he lives as a sexual associate of his elder brother who is the 'official' husband. Such an arrangement would be entirely non-problematic to Ladakhi and Tibetan sentiment.

These research reports from a variety of village sites in Zanskar and the Indus valley regions of Ladakh show a very consistent pattern. The main points established are as follows:

(*i*) Fraternal polyandry has been a consistent form of marriage in Ladakh. As in Tibet, it is associated with the early transfer of agricultural estates between generations to an elder brother and co-husbands upon marriage. The institutions of *khang chen* and *khang chung* (or *khang gyu*) provide homes for the present and preceding reproductive generations respectively.

(*ii*) Polyandry may involve as many as four co-husbands but more usually only two. % marriages that are polyandrous range from 68 (1938) to 16 (1981) near Leh, 11% Zanskar (1980) and 55-70% of all families large enough to support it in three Indus valley villages. Today polyandry is *de facto* rather than *de jure*, is not marked by ceremonial group marriage of co-husbands, and the unofficial co-spouse additional to the elder brother is usually a brother who works outside the estate but contributes materially to it. His sexual rights are today conventional in this culture rather than forming part of contractual marriage.

(*iii*) Father-son polyandry is not reported from Ladakh, *porjag*, is probably rare but a wide variety of other marital arrangements result from varying sibling sex-ratios in sibling groups of differing size all of which follow the traditional rule of maintaining the agricultural estate intact.

(*iv*) Changes in household structure due to contemporary shifts in social organisation and economics are perhaps most marked in families living near the capital city—the town of Leh.

(*v*) The prime concomitants of polyandry are lowered birth recruitment in local populations associated with unusually large number of unmarried potentially reproductive males (monks) and females.

Studies of Tibetan and Himalayan villages outsdie Ladakh

In 1976, Goldstein published an important analysis of the effects of polyandry in Tsang village, Limi, Nepal based upon a detailed demographic survey. Usually 2-3 co-husbands were found in polyandrous families but as many as five were reported. Polyandry is in fact the rule whenever the sibling group contains more than one son. Although the sex ratio is about equal 33% of men do not seek a bride owing to polyandry and 31% of all potentially reproductive women do not bear children in marriage due to marital exclusion resulting from polyandry. The local people operate the rule of passing down undivided agricultural estates as inheritance between generations and interpret polyandry as a requirement enabling them to preserve the productive resources of the family estate. Goldstein argues that were monogamy to be suddenly established the population would rise by 16%.

Furer-Haimendorf (1964) provides an account of marriage and inheritance among the Sherpa population of the Khumba region of Nepal. The Sherpas originated in Tibet and emigrated into the Himalayan region in a manner and at a date which remains uncertain. Their mode of life is high alpine agriculture traditionally augmented by trade and porterage over the high passes. In recent years these latter skills have made them invaluable to mountaineers and trekkers alike.

Among 236 marriages recorded by Furer-Haimendorf only 19 were polyandrous and 5 polygynous. Polyandrous marriages were usually arranged by parents for the first and commonly the third brother with the intention, as elsewhere, of preserving a farming estate. In his 1964 account this author states that many girls preferred to marry two brothers for it improves her economic prospects and in her later years she enjoys the advantages of a younger husband. Some girls declined marriage with an elder brother if the younger were not included. However younger brothers sometimes leave a polyandrous marriage to set up on their own.

Furer-Haimendorf states that the woman's traditional attitude was based on an expectation of a higher standard of living in polyandry and since a husband may often be away trading or attending to herds the presence of second man, assures not only the effective maintenance of the home but also a continued sexual life. There were no prejudices against sexual relations with more than one man. Indeed women sometimes left a single husband in order to marry two brothers. Families tended in the past to have a tradition of polyandry and thus to ensure the integrity of their estates through several generations.

In 1964 Furer-Haimendorf reported that older people were complaining of the selfishness of young men who broke up a family estate in order to have wives to themselves. Polyandry was in no way detrimental to a family's prestige but rather a sign of fraternal solidarity. Any decrease in polyandry at that date was attributed to moralistic notions current in Darjeeling and hence of Indian and not local origin. In 1957 Furer-Haimendorf reported village polyandry to be still 12% of 39 marriages at one location but at a village open to "modernisation" it had disappeared.

The Sherpas do not, however, give the non-division of estates such pre-eminence as do the Tibetans or the Ladakhis. Furer Haimendorf (1964) describes how a father's inheritance is commonly divided among his relatives on death and a man may freely transform land into cattle or donate land as a religious act. There is thus some conflict between traditional values and an individual's right to dispose of his property as he pleases.

The Sherpas, like the recent Ladakhis, do not live under a system of aristocratic or monastic patronage so that taxation or social duties do not weigh heavily upon them. Furthermore the extensive involvement in trade rather than agriculture means that the unbroken inheritance of land may not have as great an importance for them as it did for traditional Tibetan farmers (see below). These factors may have been significant in relation to the lesser importance of polyandry among the Sherpas and the looseness of their inheritance rules. Unfortunately although we know from Furer Haimendorf that polyandry occurs among both rich and poor Sherpas, no study has been made of its relative significance to families respectively engaged predominantly in trade or farming.

In another region of Nepal, remote Dolpo, Jest (1975) found that polyandry was exceptional. The reason for this is not known.

Aziz (1978) collected accounts of polyandry and other aspect of the life of the southern Tibetan district of Ding.ri from refugees who had fled Tibet to live today in northern Nepal. She reports that 28% of marriages were polygamous. 66% of these were cases of polyandry where between two and six brothers might share a wife. Sororal polygyny accounted for a further 12%. There were also ten cases (N = 122) of mother and daughter sharing a husband and eight of father and son sharing a wife.

Aziz records a number of important links between the economic status and occupational role of a household and the occurrence of different types of marriage which are of the greatest theoretical interest. While polyandry is frequent in the rural farming population monogamy is practised by the merchants and government officials who live in Dingri. town. In these urban families, dependent on trade and salary rather than on the produce of the land, only the elder son inherits the father's house on his death and all sons can establish new households as they come of age and marry because the father's wealth is divided among his children. Landless rural labourers employed by others, the *du. chung* or "small smoke", do not show polyandrous marriage either.

Polyandry is thus revealed as a functional correlate of the *landed* farming way of life of the *mi. ser* peasant. The *mi. ser* usually hold the land inalienable from their overlord or directly from the government and must hand it down within the same family in each generation. In addition taxes, corvee and other services were traditionally due to the lord according to a very strict and enforceable contractual arrangement. *Mi. ser* furthermore were neither allowed to sell their land nor to leave it. Penalties for transgression were high. The population was thus locationally static although individuals could, under certain circumstances go on trading journeys or pilgrimage so long as the taxes were paid.

In Ding. ri there was almost no marital exchange between the rural *mi. ser* and the *Tsong pa* urban folk. In addition, to marry one of the "small-smoke" was to incur a loss of status. There was, however, a tendency for wives of polyandrous households to come from families of higher status and a wife retained a high status within the home. This involves a release of women from top ranking land owing households to those of middle rank in the society. Among the *du. chung* and poorer *mi ser* there is a reverse trend towards marriage of daughters up the social scale but this hypergyny is commonly restricted to those males starting a second marriage.

Dargyay (1982) has recently published her research on the villagers of a district of Gyantse in southern Tibet on the route from India to Lhasa who, as refugees, now live in India. Like Aziz's study this research relies on recalled information rather than on direct field study and refers to the period between

1925-59. The people of this district lived within a hierarchical rural estate system. At the top were government officials, the District Governor himself and both noble and monastic landlords. The *mi ser* were divided between these dependent upon monasteries and those who were subjects of the nobility. There was, however, a small but special class of more wealthy land holders who held the land from the government and paid tax directly to it.

Dargyay reports a correlation between marriage types and socio-economic status which resembles those described by Aziz (*loc. cit*) from Ding-ri (Table 8). The social strata of villager's ranged from the village headmen, treasurer and stewards of the local aristocrat's estate, through holders of independent farms who paid tax directly to the government, to the tenants of the

TABLE 8

Relation between social status, marriage, land holding and income near Gyantse, Southern Tibet. Simplified from Dargyay 1982

	Usual marital system	Land holding	Source of main income
Village headmen, treasurers, stewards of estates	Informal Polyandry Monogamy	Large	Employment by Aristocratic estate Farming
Private farmers, paying tax to government	Formal polyandry	Large	Self-employed farming
Tenants on estates	Monogamy Informal polyandry	Small	Work for land-lord plus farming own produce.
Farm workers on monastic estate.	Monogamy	Small	Individually engaged work. Some farming for family support
Share-croppers with small rented plots.	Monogamy	Very small	Employed by others.
Hired workers without plot.	Monogamy	None	Employed by others.

aristocratic estate, monastery or farmers and labourers of several sorts with contrasting contracts of service for which they received support, small plots of land or payment in cash or kind. Polyandry in which several brothers married in a joint ceremony, was only found among those farmers who cultivated land, held directly from the government and paid their tax directly to it. Here the stated function was to ensure the maintenance of an intact estate from generation to generation. About 10 persons per farm, per generation were believed to be essential for such an endeavour.

Dargyay contrasts this formal ceremonially contracted polyandry with casual polyandry in which younger brothers have sexual access to the wife. Her account correlates formal polyandry with the occupancy of large farms and direct payment of tax to the government. Tenants on the estate who mainly work for their lord and receive support from him, and the lords' estate officers may show informal polyandry but prefer monogamy. In the classes with least self-sufficiency in land ownership there is no formal polyandry and younger brothers try to marry better off women as *ma pa* husbands. They are said to succeed only with younger daughters but they increase their status by so doing.

The Functional Significance of Tibetan Polyandry

Studies have shown how the peoples of west central Asia are culturally adapted to specific natural habitats and that their agricultural economy and social life are direct expressions of that adaptation (Barth, 1956). The Tibetans are no exception and we can expect their life ways to be finely attuned to the arid, high altitude habitant in which they live and to the particular exigencies of a specific mode of production. Many explanations for Tibetan polyandry have been suggested (See Prince Peter, 1963 ; Heber and Heber, 1976 ; Mann, 1978) but none are sufficiently inclusive of the relevant associated social facts to merit much credibility.

The studies we have reviewed provide information about the occurrence of polyandry in the pre-1959. Tibet with its complex division into agricultural social strata and the economic division into rural and urban communities. A clear correlation exists between formal marital polyandry contracted between a group of brothers in a marriage ceremony and the holding of large farms from which payment of tax is made directly to the government. Less formal polyandry is evidently common in other tenanted land holders but monogamy is preferred among those sections of the community who are not dependent on self-sufficient agriculture but mainly upon employment by others. In urban life monogamy and inter-generational division of property is usual and the preferred life style. Among the aristorcrats, all types of marriage seem to have occurred (Taring, 1970).

Although Tibet is not an unproductive country, the areas of arable land are small and mostly dependent upon snow, melt for irrigation. The combination of small patchy production and limited irrigation of difficult land implies that competition for its exploitation may have been considerable and the loss of land a disaster to a family. Low yields and labour intensive farming also imply that the optimum farms will have a good labour force but not too many mouths to feed. Since estates are worked by families of a known average size the area for optimum production could be about the same in areas of similar agricultural potential but differ between areas. In ancient times, all such land belonged to the kings who distributed it among their people—and then charged tax and services for the privilege. From a king's perspective it would be desirable not to allocate farms too big for a family to exploit successfully not too small to sustain an average family unit. Maximum tax could only be obtained from farms, productive enough to yield a surplus beyond basic family maintenance.

We know that one ancient ruler (King Mune, son of the great ruler Trhisong Detsen circa A.D. 797-799) attempted to redistribute land in equal portions on several occasions and encountered great resistance to his plans—(in the end he was murdered by his mother). We may surmise that such attempted legislation was not merely based on grief at the disparity between rich and poor as the legend reports (Stein, 1972) but upon a need to regulate the taxation of an extensive empire. The 17th century King of Ladakh, Jam. dbyans, man, gyal is credited with similar legislation probably in relation to taxation. (Pelech, 1977). The world for tax (*khral*) also implied military service, so it is clear that land holding families would have been under considerable pressure to find labour sufficient to farm the land as well as to meet state obligations. Other laws required the estate to be handed down intact between generations of the same lineage. Furthermore peasants were not allowed to migrate because of their tax and other obligations to government or landlords appointed by the throne. The system in pre-1959 Tibet seems to have derived from these ancient regulations.

Given the rules preventing intergenerational partition of farms it follows that in successive generations sibling groups of very contrasting size and sex ratio would face the task of farming them. There were four problems. Firstly a sufficient adult labour force was required, secondly, there were heavy taxes to pay and other duties to fulfil as the price of a relatively independent farming existence. Thirdly, overpopulation would threaten the quality of the families' subsistence especially since emigration was not legal although extensive pilgrimage was commonly made. Lastly the need to maintain a strongly co-operative family work force necessitated a social system that was psychologically equable and not prone to fission.

Polyandry is not without psychological tension, although the Tibetan open system of relationships yields less conflict than people of other cultures expect. It seems certain that a group of monogamously married brothers each with his individual family and probably competitive wife may well be more fissiporous than a polyandrous system of fraternal co-operation with one carefully chosen and sexually fulfilling woman. Furthermore the rapid increase in family size in several monogamous units would impose pressures of a social, economic and ecological nature very rapidly, once the sibling group commencced reproduction. We know that elsewhere in the Himalayas such systems correlate with social tension, estate splitting to non-viable economic units, severe erosian and emigration. (Macfarlane, 1976).

It follows that polyandry achieves a sufficient labour force in units that are prone neither to overpopulation nor to social fission. Polyandry is thus a functional correlate of a state regulated system of land distribution which is itself a consequence of a patchy distribution of rich but size limited areas fit for farming. As a highly effective solution to population regulation and labour distribution in a difficult ecology it is hardly surprising that wise old men of former years ago extolled its moral value. If it were more widespread among the non-Tibetan peoples of the Himalayas many areas would be better off economically and ecologically than they are today.

In Ladakh a major component of the above is lacking. The kingly state of Ladakh was broken by invasion in the last century and since the conquest by the Dogras, the superstructure of king and aristocrats had disappeared as a functioning system. The farmer's relation to estates has thus been less rigorous lately than in traditional Tibet. In Zanskar indeed every farmer appeared largely independent of any overlord and the king of Zangla (Peissel, 1979) released his tenants from tax obligations some years ago. What remains is an extensive system of monastic patronage involving loans to farmers which are repaid in kind (Shakya and Crook in press) as an annual income for which the word *khral* meaning tax is still used. Nonetheless both formal and informal polyandry have continued to thrive in the farming community of rural Ladakh. In our documentation of change near the capital city of Leh, we can see the way in which the new employment opportunities and land values are rendering the old system less adaptive although through fraternal co-operation, a modified form of casual polyandry may still have a functional value in certain communities.

Our study of the consequences of polyandry and the history of its formal origin reveal its function in communities of agricultural Tibetans. The frequency of informal polyandry in less hierarchically organised communities and the general case with which Tibetans accept a variety of sexual and conjugal associations does, however, suggest an origin in an ecologically adapted culture prior to the legislation allocating a distribution of families to inalienable estates for effective taxation and national service. It seems likely that early tribal settlements on the same patchy resources may have evolved polyandrous tendencies as a way of solving their ecological problems. The attitudes and dispositions of Tibetans towards marriage may thus have a very ancient origin.

Socio-biologically inclined anthropologists will be concerned to know whether in addition to its ecological adaptiveness polyandry also maintains or enhances the inclusive genetic fitness of its practitioners. Beall and Goldstein examining the data from Limi, came to a negative conclusion based mainly upon the higher offspring survival experienced by monogamously mated females in their sample. They do note, however, that richer peasants (56%) opt for polyandry more when compared with poorer ones (33%)—findings resembling the studies of Aziz and Dargyay. They do not subject these categories to separate analysis.

We may propose for polyandry an extension of the explanation of marital polygyny in Asian societies put forward by Dickeman (1979 ; see Crook, 1980a : 218). She argued that polygyny occurred in the upper strata of societies where the rich could ensure greater economic stability. Women practising hypergamy, thus ensures an improved survival for the children and the reproductive success of the males is increased. These trends have profound effects on the cultures in which they occur. The Tibetan and the Himalayan estate holding farmers seek to secure agricultural viability in environments of extreme climatic harshness, a patchy distribution of irrigated land suited to farming and often, traditionally, in the context of an imposed structure of relations involving heavy taxation in kind and services. It seems plausible that the woman who marries into a polyandrous farming family secures on average an improved reproductive success when compared with the fecundity subject to the risks that would attend monogamy in such a community (above). Since few women marry her success can be seen as an example of intra-sexual competition, but the assistance given by unmarried female relations to their married brothers or sisters within an extended households is also a clear case of socio-biological 'altruism.' The co-operative brothers by providing the optimum economic adaptation to such an ecology likewise minimise the high risks to children that alternative systems of marriage would impose. Furthermore, as Crook and Crook (in press) demonstrate (and discuss further), only a small

TABLE 9

Family size in six households near Leh in relation to marital type. Data from 1938 updated to completed family sizes from research in 1981 (Bracketed figures). Data from Prince Peter (*loc. cit.*). **Crook and Shakya.** (*loc. cit*).

Households

Type of marriage	1	2	3	4	5	6	No.	X̄
Tetrandy	—	—	—	—	—	5(9)	1	9)
Triandry	—	5	0(3)	5(6)	—	—	3	4.7) 5.2
Biandry	2,2(7)	3(4)	—	7	4(6)	3	6	4.8)
Monogamy	2,5(8)	—	6.0	—	6	6	6	4.7)
No Families	4	2	3	2	2	3	16	5.0

In addition we have data from 9 other monogamous completed families (X̄.3) from the same source and one bigamous *mag.pa* marriage (7).

X̄ All polyandrous marriages= 5.2 (N 10. Total 52)

X̄ All monogamous marriages=3.66 (N 15. Total 55)

Not significant at 05. One tailed. Mann Witney U-Test.

increase in the fecundity of the wife would secure for them a genetic fitness measure as good as that for monogamy. As we have seen, there is some limited evidence that polyandrously married women have a shorter birth interval than those in monogamy (Table 5) and the mean completed family size for polyandrous households is suggestively higher than that of monogamous ones when relatively small samples from Leh were compared (Table 9). It can thus be argued that polyandrous marriage in the case of the Tibetan/subsistence farmer may not only be a "K selected" (Piankam, 1974) adaptation to an environment of limited carrying capacity but also a cultural device whereby reproductive fitness is maintained *per capita* as effectively as the ecology will allow. Unfortunately adequate da'a to test this viewpoint will not be easy to obtain.

REFERENCES

Attenborough, R.: In prep. The population of sTongde, Zanskar, Himalaya. In Crook, J.H. (ed.). In prep.

Aziz, B.N.: 1978 *Tibetan Frontier Families: Reflections of Three Generations from Ding-ri'* Vikas, New Delhi.

Barth, F.: 1956. Ecologic relationships of Ethnic Groups in Swat, North Pakistan. *Amer. Anthrop.* 58. 1079-1089.

Beall, C.M. and Goldstein, M.C.: Tibetan Fraternal Polyandry: A Test of Socio-Biological Theory. *Amer. Anthrop.*

Crook, J.H.: 1980a. *The Evolution of Human Consciousness.* Oxford.

——: 1980b. Social change in Indian Tibet. Soc. Sci. inform. 19.1.139-166.

——(ed.): In prep. *Himalayan Buddhist Villages: A Study of Communities in Zanskar, Ladakh.*

——and Crook, S. In Crook, J.H. (ed): In Prep. Function of Tibetan Polyandry. In press. *Loc. cit.*

——and Shakya, T.: In press. Six Families of Leh. In Proceedings of Conference on Ladakh Social Studies. University of Constance, 1982.

——and Shakya, T.: In prep. Monastic Settlements in Zanskar: Location, Social Organisation and Function. In Crook, J.H. (ed.) In press.

Dargyay, E.K.: 1982 *Tibetan Village Communities.* Aris and Philips, Warminster.

Defillipi, R. (ed.) : 1937 *An Account of Tibet : The Travels of Ippolito Desideri of Pistoia 1917-1927*, Routledge, London.

Dickeman, M. : 1979 The Ecology of Mating Systems in Hypergynous Dowry Societies. *Soc. Sci. Inf.* 18, 163-195.

Elford, J. : In prep. *Kumik : A Demographic Study*. In J.H. Crook. (ed) In prep.

Furer-Haimendorf, C. von. : 1964 *The Sherpas of Nepal*. John Murray, London.

——1975 *Himalayan Traders*. John Murray, London.

Goldstein, M. : 1971 Stratification, Polyandry and Family Structure in Tibet. *S.W. Journal of Anthropolgy*, 27, 64-74.

——1976 Fraternal Polyandry and Fertility in a high Himalayan Valley in N.W. Nepal. *Human Ecology*, 4, 223-233.

Grist, N. : 1980 Polyandry, Marriage and Land Tenure. In *Cambridge University Expeditions*, 1977-1979. *Reports on Ladakh. Social Studies in Mattro Village*. Typed MSS.

Heber, A.R. and Heber, K M. : 1976 *Himalayan Tibet and Ladakh*. Ess Ess, Delhi.

Jest, C. : 1975 *Dolpo : Communautes de lenge tibetiane du Nepal*. CNRS, Paris.

Macfarlane, A. : 1976 *Resources and Population : A study of the Gurungs of Nepal*. Cambridge University Press, London.

Majumdar, D.N. : 1960 *Himalayan Polyandry : Structure functioning and Culture Change. A field Study of Jounsar. Bawar* Asia Publishing House, New Delhi.

Mann, R.S. : 1978 Ladakhi Polyandry revisited. *Indian Anthropologist*. 8.1. 17.30.

Pamar, Y.S. : 1975 *Polyandry in the Himalayas*. Vikas, New Delhi.

Peissel, M. : 1979 *Zanskar. The Hidden Kingdom* Collins and Harvill, London.

Petech. L. : 1977 The Kingdom of Ladakh. c. 950 1842 A.D. *Serie Orientale Roma* 50 Rome.

Peter, Prince of Greece and Denmark : 1963. *A Study of Polyandry*, Mouton, La Hague.

Pianka. E. : 1974 Evolutionary Ecology. Harfew and Row, New York.

Shakya, T. and J.H. Crook : In pre. Monastic Economics in Zanskar.

Stein, R.A. : 1972 *Tibetan Civilisation*. Faber, London.

Taring, R.D. : 1970 *Daughter of Tibet*, John Murray, London.

2

PERSISTENCE OF LAHAUL POLYANDRY AND DECLINE

T.K. Ghosh

The peculiar feature of the Lahuli polyandry is that it is an economic arrangement, one established on the poverty of a barren country, whose inmates were and to an extent still are chiefly agriculturists, living in extreme climatic conditions. Hence, the system was, one can argue, economy oriented. Arable land in Lahaul was limited and need arose to prevent the land from sub-division and fragmentation, which would have led to social disarray and disintegration. To maintain the *status quo*, the means by which it could be achieved, was polyandry.

The Lahauli polyandry was a fraternal one. The eldest brother took a wife and simultaneously she became a wife to all the brothers, as well, in common. The family thus could never be divided, which spared the need of sub-division and fragmentation of holdings. Thus were they spared all the social and economic ills arising out of it. This in its turn, moulded their thinking and ends justified the means wherewith the elders vindicated the system by maintaining that there was greater harmony in the household with one daughter-in-law than many. The surplus girls who could never get married were either sent to the monasteries or stayed in their brother's household and made to undertake all the household chores and other jobs.

Sometimes residing with them would be their aged parents and unmarried or divorced sisters. For although the mother or the sister do not have the right to a share of the property, nevertheless, they have the right of residence preserved. The eldest brother is the head and the representative of the family and controls all family affairs. The younger brothers have a sub ordinate position, though the wife is held in common. The children, however, recognize all their fathers in the category of the descending order, elder or younger as the case may be, but pay more respect to the eldest. The property is held in common and never used to be divided. Today, however, when brothers have started to take separate wives for themselves, the residential premises may be divided but land may still be held in common and cultivated in common, the proceeds only being divided.

The economic criteria in the Lahaulian polyandry can be vindicated by the fact that in the changed circumstances of modern times, when they have no longer to depend wholly upon the land for their livelihood or survival, the system is falling apart. The main drawback of the system was the incompatibility of the mental adjustment between a common wife and the younger brothers of a large family who were years younger than the wife and who could, thus, not feel gratified with a woman much older than them in age and temperament and pretty soon unable to participate in the pleasures of sex wholeheartedly. For, it is common knowledge that women age far quicker than men. Moreover, sharing a wife in common was repugnant to them, they now feel, and the system was tolerated only due to economic compulsions and for social survival. No wonder, then, when this necessity took flight, the institution has and is being dispensed with.

Environment factors have effectively gone to show that the system of marriage in Lahaul is an economic arrangement. In such an extreme ecological set-up where arable lands are extremely limited, if at the death of the head of the family the property was to be divided among the sons, and, if each had a separate wife and family, there would not be enough to supply the wants of all of them. Therefore, a solution to meet the exigencies of the situation devised by the sons of a family was to have one common wife among them to ensure a joint family by means of which their property remained undivided and expenses on living economised. This has of necessity also controlled the growth of population i.e. the polyandrous system was needed also to control the growth of population and keep it at a minimum level, and, it is just as well for an economy which could only sustain a very limited number of people. The system was, therefore, necessarily conditioned by economic factors which helped in the persistence of polyandry.

This is supported by the fact that polyandry is prevalent more among the landholding classes like the Rajputs or higher classes, who had to depend upon the land for their livelihood whereas the incidence of polyandry amongst the menial classes, mostly landless, is much less, because they did not have to depend for their livelihood upon a limited factor of production. So, their adoption of polyandry, wherever found, was more in imitation of their masters and not economy-oriented, nor the demand of social compulsions, which in the later stages became a criterion with the former in the tussle for polyandry vs. monogamy. Hence, the more or less compulsive element was not present with their lower strata populace. However, since the whole thing was an economic arrangement, it was bound to decline with diversification of economic resources and sources of income, whereby the main dependancy on land came to an end.

Moreover, backward people are swift to emulate the more advanced ones, and so was the case with the Lahaula, who having all along practised the system for obvious reasons, was proved to the infection of monogamic institution with the first opportunity wherein economic compulsions no longer became imperative to adhere to polyandry. Hence, the extreme decision to change to the cultural values of the more advanced peoples was as swift to come and the change implemented inspite of social opposition from the more conservative elements who fought a losing battle. Prior to this economic necessity made him lack the confidence to take the risk. Economic compulsions deterred him from taking the drastic step.

Hence, the system or institution of polyandry did not make any compulsory or permanent impact on the Lahaula. Since the element of economy was greatly emphasised in the pursuit of the system, it was bound to decline, given the varied economic opportunities that have been opened out to them, as is the condition today.

In any case, while it was in vogue, polyandry in Lahaul served its purpose. But today, with changed economic conditions, due to development and growth as a result of an intensified contact with a growing economy, and especially where it did not have any religious sanction or conditioning as such, the institution, being no longer felt essential for human survival in the area, and having outlived its purpose, is dying a natural death.

Various factors have contributed to this decline. Apart from the feeling of sharing a wife in common, sometimes years older than the younger scions of the family, a feeling abhorred by these younger brothers, the tendency of individualism was also a major factor for this decay. Therefore, a major development today, where polyandry has persisted yet or is still persisting, but the incidence declining markedly, is the actual father of the child is being made recognizable. The actual father is named by the mother. This has been and is being made due to the tendency of personal possessiveness that had come to play upon the sentiments of the people of the valley and which in course of time, is leading them to more drastic changes in the family pattern and family structure in the shape of creeping monogamy and individual possession, resulting in sub-division and fragmentation of holdings, which is gradually engulfing the valley. Property is, therefore, being divided where the demand is being made among the brothers an equal share basis. And, even in the case where the demand is not being made of a division, and brothers are setting up individual families or households separately, without or within the same residential unit, the share of output from the cultivable lands is divided in the same proportion, provided the labour input and other input is joint. Sometimes, he may be provided according to his needs.

However, today, if any younger brother takes a separate

mate for himself, he generally separates from the main household and sets up his own household of which he becomes the head. He may continue holding landed property in common and farming in common, taking his share according to his needs. The tendency, nevertheless, is towards division of property, landed or otherwise, when brothers separate.

That polyandry in Lahaul was need-based, can also be vindicated from the fact that the system did not exempt the Hindus either. Again, the Pattan, which is the milder of the three Lahaul valleys, shows a lesser incidence of polyandry, further corroborating the economic orientation of the system.

One thing is certain that polyandry in Lahaul does not appear to be due to any disbalance in sex ratio in Lahaul. The Lahaulis themselves relate that economic necessities had made it imperative for them in the past to take recourse to polyandry. Today, when such imperatives do not exist, polyandry has outlived its purpose, and, hence, having not the popular support, is on the wane.

In a general review of the whole system, we can observe that in order to find out a clue to the practice of polyandry as a traditional trait of the people, we have to look into their ethno-cultural background.

The Buddhist Thakurs and Rajputs of the Gora, bordering Ladakh and western Tibet, are predominantly Mongoloid. It is among these people that the incidence of polyandry is the highest.

The Hindus of the Pattan, the Brahmins and the Rajputs, show predominance of Mediterranean physical features and even they have been diluted by admixture with the Mongoloids of Upper Lahaul, the incidence of polyandry in Pattan is reported to be much less in Gora and Rangloi. In the Pattan valley conditions are much better and sizeable section of the population are Hindus, therefore, and since economic compulsions are not so acute, many brothers have married separately and houses and lands have likewise been divided.

In so far as, the menial groups are concerned, such as the Lohars, the Sippis etc. the tendency of these peripheral groups are to follow the norms and practices of their benefactors or the dominant groups and hence some of them took to polyandry, although socio-economic factors did not demand such of them. Today, when the reverse trend is in process, they are retracting. Again, at the same time, of yore, these same groups serving Hindu masters, who were monogamous, strictly adhered to that practice in emulation of them.

It will, therefore, not be absolutely incorrect to identify polyandry in Lahaul as a trait of Mongoloid people, professing Lamaistic Buddhism, whether it be out of economic compulsion or not. The ruggedness and harshness of the terrain, wherever Lamaistic Buddhism has prevailed, may have given rise to this practice which in course of time became embedded in their society and culture. For, had it not been an economic compulsion, the case with which polyandry is being shun today, and abandoned, would not have been possible. And the resultant factors would not have been forthcoming.

It cannot, however, be generalized that polyandry is a by-product of or associated with Lamaistic Buddhism. It is by curious coincidence that wherever Lamaistic Buddhism has spread, conditions are hard and rigorous, which had given rise to the said custom, more out of compulsion, as a solution, to effectively face the circumstances; and, it has been condoned and sanctioned by the religious authorities, may be out of compassion to face a challenging situation. To this extent, Lamaistic Buddhism has been liberal enough to adjust according to prevailing conditions, so as to keep its faithfuls in tact.

The above contention can be corroborated by the independent findings of various other authors.

Nag states that 'in view of the heterogenous population of Lahaul, an attempt has been made to identify polyandry as a traditional practice of one of the ethnic groups of this region; and the author does not trace polyandry to the Mongoloids as a general rule,' (19 : 195) as this form of marriage is also prevalent among other races as well. Polyandry has strong pocket in the cis-Himalayas, where it is commonly practised in Dehra Dun district, in the Simla hills, in Jubbal (Himachal Pradesh) and the adjoining tracts by the people who are Indo-Aryans or mixed descent of the pre-Dravidians. This would go a long way to countermand the conclusive theory of Western-

TABLE 1

Polyandrous—Polygynandrous households and population in the Lahaula villages

Villages	Total Households	Total Population	Polyandrous/ Polygynandrous Households No.	%	Polyandrous/ Polygynandrous population No.	%	Ethnic groups involved
1	2	3	4	5	6	7	8
Sissu Koti	39	306	3	7.69	22	7.18	The Bodh
Kirting Shansha	22	204	2	9.09	23	11.27	The Swangha Pandit
Jaspa	24	191	5	20.83	52	27.23	The Bodh
Village Complexes around Jaspa	15	92	3	20.00	16	17.39	The Bodh
Tinnau	15	135	1	6.67	13	9.63	The Bodh

mark that polyandry is generally confined to Mongoloids and pre-Aryans. However, as is found, there are millions of Mongoloid people who are not polyandrous and there are others who are not Mongoloids are yet polyandrous. Therefore, Briffault has rightly stated that it would be a mistake to attribute the decay of polyandry in India among its Dravidians, and Mongolians to the conquering Indo-Aryans, for the latter had the same polyandrous institutions as the races they conquered, (1927 : 677).

Hence, the association of polyandry with Lamaistic Buddhism, which is the popular religion among the Mongoloid people of Ladakh, Tibet and Lahaul may be concluded to be incidental. It is unlikely that there is any link between this form of religion and polyandry, as the former is a later development in Lahaul, having entered Lahaul from India through the efforts of Padmasambhava in the 8th century A.D., whereas polyandry in this region appears to be of a greater antiquity.

Briffault is of the opinion, that the marriage institutions of Tibet are 'indefinitely old' and have a connection with Lamaistic Buddhism which was introduced at a comparatively later date (1927: 668). Rav. Francke, in his 'History of Western Tibet' states that polyandry was certainly not introduced by Buddhism, but religion never raised a finger against it (1907 : 112).

By all accounts, therefore, the economy criterion of polyandry in Lahaul is confirmed. Lamaistic Buddhism, as practised in Lahaul, is very accommodating and hence tolerated the practice as long as it served in sustaining the society. For the same reason, today when with changed conditions, the institution is crumbling down, religion is also accepting the inevitable in its stride.

REFERENCES

Briffault, R. 1927 *The Mothers*, 3 vols., MacMillan & Co. London.

Francke, Rev. A.H. 1907 *A History of Western Tibet.*

Nag, N.G. 1960 Family and Marriage in Lahaul Valley, *Eastern Anthropologist*, Vol-X III No. 4

Westermarck, Ed. *The History of Human Marriage*, MacMillan & Co, London.

3

POLYANDRY IN A HIGH HIMALAYAN SOCIETY : PERSISTENCE AND CHANGE

MANIS KUMAR RAHA
PALASH CHANDRA COOMAR

Polyandry was, sometimes, considered as an exotic and curious custom, in certain human societies in different parts of the world. But no doubt it is an arrangement by which a woman is married to more than one man at the same time. In India a major concentration of this type of marriage is found in the whole of the Himalayan regions particularly in the Western and Central Himalayas. From Leh district of Jammu and Kashmir to Jaunsar Bower of Dehra Dun district in Uttar Pradesh, polyandry in adelphic form, is found to be practised by different Himalayan societies. The people there believe that "*Khasni Khasbis, Man yek bap bis*" that means 'one Khasi woman and twenty husbands, one mother and twenty fathers'.

This proverb as mentioned in the Punjab District Gazetteer, Simla District, 1904, proves that polyandry was in vogue among the people (*khas*) particularly among the Kanets, of the Himalayas. (1906 : 30). The Kinnaurese society, like some other polyandrous societies in the Himalayas, also practise adelphic polyandry. Here in a household brothers, two and more in number, share a common wife, sometimes more than one wife. And the brother-husbands share the joint responsibility over the common wife and also on the children born of the union. However, we shall now enter into the polyandrous Kinnaura society to examine the system of polyandry prevalent there, and in the following pages the result of the analysis will be discussed. But before we come straight to the Kinnaura polyandry, we like to give our readers some idea about the Kinnaura society and also about the environment there.

Setting

In the previous unpublished (Raha, 1976 ; 1981 ; 1982 ; 1985 ; Raha & Mahato, 1975) and published articles (Raha, 1974 ; 1978 ; 1987 ; Raha et al, 1976 ; 1978 ; 1979) and in the book of the senior author (Raha & Mahato, 1985) the historical, ecological, environmental and ethnic settings of the district of Kinnaur and also social stratification, socio-economic and socio-religious conditions there have been discussed in detail. Therefore, we shall touch here only a little of it which we feel relevant for this article, so as to enable our readers to understand the situation in this high altitude society of the Western Himalayas located adjoining to the Indo-Tibetan border. This north easternmost district of Himachal Pradesh is situated on a vary difficult, inhospitable, undulating mountainous terrains. It has three administrative divisions, three distirct ecological zones and three different culture zones. The administrative divisions are Pooh, Nachar and Kalpa sub-divisions. The three eco-zones are (I) the arid zone covering the area adjoining Tibet border (Pooh sub-division) (II) the moist zone spreading over lower Kinnaur area (Nachar sub-division) (III) the central part of the district coming under the dry zone (Kalpa sub-division). The three culture zones are, Zone-I which includes most part of the Pooh sub-division and is dominated by Buddhism (Lamaism) Zone-II which covers Nachar sub-division and is dominated by Hinduism and Zone-III which has the co-existence of both Buddhism (Lamaism) and Hinduism and covers Kalpa sub-division. (Raha, 1978 : 84 ; Raha & Mahato, 1975: 11-13 ; Raha & Mahato, 1985:8). Thus it is seen that the administrative divisions, ecological zones and culture zones almost concide with one another. That means Pooh subdivision almost concide with Eco-Zone-I and Culture Zone-I,

Nachar sub-division mostly coincides with Eco-Zone-II and Culture-Zone-II and Kalpa sub-division almost covers Eco-Zone-III and Culture-Zone-III. The culture of these three areas of the district show distinct variations though of course, in many aspects their cultural commonness is also observed.

The Kinnaura with a population of 59,547 according to 1981 Census, have got 31,598 males and 27,949 females with a sex ratio of 885 females per 1000 males. They are divided into two distinct divisions—the *khosia* and the *beru* (Raha, 1978 : 88-89 ; Raha & Mahato, 1975 : 240-248 ; Raha & Mahato, 1985 : 135-139). The *beru* is further divided into three distinct categories, viz., (I) The Domang which includes the Lohar (iron and silver smith) and the Badhi (carpenter and mason) (II) the Chamang covering the Koli (agriculturists, leather workers, spinners and weavers) and (III) the Chanalas including the Nangalu (the basket makers). No further sub-division is noticed among these groups (except some very rudimentary formation of sub-groups in case of the Koli). Each of the groups is endogamous. These caste groups are the 'servants of the landowners from whom they receive food, and at harvest time a share of grains called *shikola*' (1911 : 33).

The *khosia* who includes the Rajput (Kanet), the most numerous among all groups (next comes the Koli), is divided into three status groups or *khels*, such as the Orang, the Maorang or Orang-Mech and the Waza, which are hierarchically arranged. Of the three *khels* the Orang is the superiormost and the Wazà, the earthen pot maker, occupies the lowest layer in the ladder of social hierarchy. Each of the *khels* is endogamous, but in recent years some relaxation in this rule is noticed between the former two *khels*.

> 'This *khel* system is not uniform throughout Kinnaur. The peculiarity of it is that it is in a rudimentary stage or absent in the areas where Buddhism prevails' (Raha & Mahato, 1985 : 139).

The *khel* system is thus present in full form in culture Zone-II and Zone-III areas but it is either rudimentary or absent in different areas under Culture-Zone-I.

Each of these *khels* is again divided into a number of exogamous lineages called *khandan* which are basically the marriage regulating units (Raha, 1987). These *khandans* are also hierarchically arranged. The *khandan* of the superior most *khel* are superior to those of other *khels* and again the *khandan* of the Waza *khel* have the lowest status. Some of the *khandan* have sub-*khandans*. But like the *khel* system, the *khandan* system is also developed in upper Kinnaur i.e. in Pooh sub-division. Particularly in the Hangrung valley areas, this is so much ill-developed that many of the households do not have any *khandan*, and the *khandan* there, where exists, does not perform all its functions properly. Finally comes the smallest social unit in the Kinnaura society, that is, *kim* or household which is patrilineal in nature.

The present day economy of the Kinnaura is based on agriculture, labour and livestok, particularly sheep and goat rearing. Of course, a few of them are engaged in service, business, cottage industry etc. Earlier (pre 1962 period) they had trade with Tibet when they used to bring from Tibet certain merchandizes in exchange of certain other items which they used to take from Indian side. At that time they used to take sheep and goats to Tibet as carriers and also for pasture.

The data for this paper have been collected from three intensively studied villages, one from each culture zone—Chango from Culture-Zone-I, Kongos from Culture-Zone-II and Rogi from Culture-Zone-III. Besides additional and confirmatory data have been collected from three more villages, one from each culture zone.

The Kinnaurese and the Himalayan Polyandry

In the Western and Central Himalayas polyandry was found to be in vogue in different areas (Stulpnagel, 1878 : 132-135). Thornton also observed the practice of polyandry in the Himalayas. (1862 : 518) It is at present found in Ladakh including Leh and Zanskar areas mainly and partly in Kargil district of Jammu and Kashmir. Polyandry is now found in districts of Lahul and Spiti, Kinnaur, Chamba, Kulu and Sirmur of Himachal Pradesh. Dasgupta reports that 'the system of polyandry' was in vogue in Kulu sub-division, the

Bushahar, Nahan, Mandi and Suket states of Himachal Pradesh (1921 : 147). Fraser also found that the people of different parts of Himachal Pradesh were practising polyandry. In Uttar Pradesh, it is found in Jaunsar Bawar (Dehra Dun District) and Rewain-Jaunpur areas (Uttar Kashi-Tehri districts).

In the Eastern-Himalayas polyandry is practised in Sikkim. In Arunachal Pradesh it (according to some it is cicibeism) exists among the Daflas, the Ramos, the Gallong and some other communities.

Polyandry is still prevalent in Ladakh. Prince Peter is reported to have found about 90% polyandry in Ladakh in early sixties. In his monumental work, *A Study of Polyandry* (1963) he writes,

> 'Asked what the proportion of polyandrous families was to the rest of the Buddhist population (the only one, naturally, among which polyandry is to be found) my informants told me that out of one hundred families, ninety of them lived in this form of matrimony' (1963 : 344).

But in 1978 Mann reports only 7.77% polyandry in this disolate high Himalayan area (1978:21). Both Prince Peter and Mann worked in and around Leh, the district Headquarter. But in Zanskar as referred to by Crooks, 11.0% are polyandrous. (1986 : 13).

In the Lahaul areas of the Lahaul and Spiti district 'polyandrous family...is of fraternal type where in a group of brothers share a common wife' (Nag, 1960 : 190). Here Nag reports about 48.57% of polyandry. Topdan a domicile of Lahaul, reports that 'about 20% of the total Lahaulian marriages are polyandric' (1979 : 6). Referring to polyandry in Lahaul, Ghosh (1986) writes,

> 'The Lahauli polyandry was a fraternal one. The eldest brother took a wife and simultaneously she became a wife to all the brothers as well, in common'.

Sharma (1986) also found that,

> 'From time immemorial polyandry is an honourable sacresanct and socially approved custom of marriage among the Lahaulea. The practice of polyandry, prevalent among the Lahula is of the adelphic fraternal type, in which only the eldest brother weds a woman ceremoniously and she becomes a *de facto* joint wife of all brothers having a common parentage'.

Polyandry also prevails in Sirmur district. Thornton (1884) in this regard opines that 'polyandry was universal in Sirmur state...' *The Sirmur Settlement Report* (1881) also confirms the presence of this form of marriage in Sirmur.

> 'It was found that women of all castes married more than one husband provided they were own brothers or sons of the same fathers and in special cases only could some other member of the family or an outsider hold a wife in common' (Parmar, 1975 : 87-88).

Chandra also found that, 'in the whole of the trans-Giri tract, in Rainuka *tehsil* polyandry is widely practised' (1975 : 120). The Gazetteer of Sirmur also confirms this (1969 : 14).

Polyandry is also found in some other areas of Himachal Pradesh. It is practised in the Pangi valley of Chamba district of Himachal Pradesh. It was prevalent in Kulu district, particularly in Outer Siraj area in Kulu district, Kotgarh, Mandi and also in erstwhile Suket and Jubbal States (Das Gupta, 1921 : 146-48 ; Stulpnagel, 1875 : 133), Crooke found this type of marriage among the Ahir and the Gujjar (1897 : 25). Fraser also observes that in the Himalayas "Three or four or more brothers marry one wife who is the wife of all..." (1920 : 134).

The most widely studied polyandry in the north and north-western India including the Himalaya is that practised in Jaunsar Bawar areas of Dehra Dun district, Uttar Pradesh. A large number of scholars, both anthropologists and non-anthropologists, became interested of this type of marriage prevalent in this hilly tract of Dehra Dun district and studied it. The existence of fraternal polyandry here has been reported by Walton (1911 : 89), Joshi (1929), Saksena (1962), Majumdar

(1944, 1955, 1963), Berreman (1962a, 1962b, 1972, 1975), Bhatt (1978, 1980, 1981), Jain (1948), Biswas (1963) and many others. The polyandrous people of Jaunsar Bawar have been studied in great details by many of the above authors. Polyandry also exists in the contiguous Rewain—Jaunpur areas of the Garhwal. Jain in this connection writes,

> 'In Jaunsar—Bawər people practise the fraternal form of polyandry. But several brothers, instead of having only one wife, have more wives than one and almost in all cases, the wives are held jointly' (1948 : 28-29)

Biswas considers Jaunsari marriage as,

> 'a complicated structure and amalgates the institutions of adelphic (fraternal) polyandry where brothers are common husbands of a wife or wives at polygamy, of combined polyandry and polygyny and of monogamy' (1953 : 10).

Saksena has also seen that polyandry is a common form of marriage in Jaunsar-Bawar and adjoining areas, 'where brothers are the common husbands of a wife or wives' (1953 : 94). Berreman also thinks that polyandry is preferred in this region (1962 : 61). Sishaudhia (1986) has very recently seen that fraternal polyandry is practised in five blocks of Uttar Pradesh i.e. Kalsi and Chakrata blocks of the district of Dehra Dun, Purula and Rewain of the district of Uttar Kashi and Jaunpur of the district of Tehri.

That polyandry existed in Punjab was reported over a century ago by Kirkpatrick (1878 : 86). 'I have ascertained that there exists *at this present time*, a system of polyandry among the Jats,' says Kirkpatrick (1878 : 86). Recently Dr. (Mrs.) Singh (1986) has shown how polyandry is functioning even in Punjab plains in recent days. According to her (1987), 'in some of the interior areas of Punjab state, it is being practised by some of the Jat Sikhs' though 'it is not an acknowledged form of marriage now'. Both Hershman (1981 : 176) and Pettigrew (1975 : 53) while acknowledging the practice of polyandry among the Jat of Punjab also found the wife of one brother, usually the eldest, is being shared by other brothers, usually younger.

In Sikkim polyandry was in existence (Earle, 1901 ; Stocks, 1975 ; Gover, 1938) and is still in existence (Nakane, 1966 ; Ghosal, 1986 ; Nandi, 1977). The polyandry is of fraternal type and husbands are usually brothers. Kotturan finds polyandry as common in Sikkim (1983 : 54).

In connection with the polyandry in Sikkim Earle states, 'If the eldest of a group of brothers marries a woman, she is regarded as the common wife of all the brothers' (1901 : XXVII). Ghosal (n.d) in his recent study, finds that 'the polyandry among the Lepchas of Sikkim is of adelphic or fraternal type where co-husbands are brothers. He also mentions that 'the Lepcha nuptial system includes true polyandry as well as polygyny which is called polygynandry...' (1986 : 3).

In Arunachal Pradesh polyandry is found among the Gallongs (Srivastava, 1962 : 74; Lal & Dasgupta, 1979:139-140; Das Gupta, 1986), the Ramos (Dhasmana, 1979:133), the Dafla (Dalton, 1872 : 41) and the Lhota Naga (Mills, 1922). In connection with the Gallongs Srivastava thinks that 'polyandry is the most prevalent form of marriage...' (*ibid*) and Das Gupta has also seen that 'among the polyandrous Gallongs brothers are allowed to have access to the wife/wives of other married brother/brothers' (*ibid*). But Sarkar thinks that it is fraternal cicibeism attached to monogamy (1963:134). Dhasmana has found the Ramos to practise polyandry but rarely (*ibid*).

It is important to mention here that in the whole of the Himalayan regions Tibet is considered to have 'best documented and most prevalent occurrence of fraternal polyandry' (Berreman, 1962 a : 61). Prince Peter also thinks Tibet as the most widespread and most flourishing polyandrous community in the world (1963 : 302). Polyandry is found to be practised in all parts of Tibet, particularly in U and Tsang areas with the greater proportion in the latter province. (Prince Peter, 1963 : 415). Goldstein also found that,

> 'Tibetan population practicing polyandry are found throughout Tibet and along most of the northern reaches of the Himalayas, such as the, Limi valley in north-west Nepal...' (1978 : 325).

Besides fraternal polyandry, another peculiar form of polyandry (bigenerational polyandry) in which father and son marry a common wife, is also found to be prevalent (Das, 1893 ; 1902 ; 1904 ; Prince Peter, 1952 ; 1963).

It is thus seen that this particular form of plural marriage, the fraternal polyandry, is found to exist or at least existed throughout the length and breadth of the Himalayas stretching from Ladakh in Jammu and Kashmir to Arunachal Pradesh covering parts of Himachal Pradesh and Uttar Pradesh hill districts, and Sikkim. It also prevails all through Tibet in purer form, and is widely practised.

The Marriage System in Kinnaur

The definition of marriage as given in *Notes and Queries in Anthropology* (6th Edition, Reprinted) does not always cover all types of marriages prevalent in this high Himalayan society because of the prevalence polygyny, polyandry and polygynandry along with monogamy. Identically the definition given in the 'Laws Relating to Social Reforms, Bushahar, Sambat 1889', for marriage that it is a *'relationship between a man and woman which is recognised by the law of the land in force or custom of the land'* also does not fit in. The Kinnaurese are polyandrous. They follow adelphic or fraternal polyandry in which the wife after marriage, becomes common to all brothers.

The Kinnaurese are basically endogamous. The two divisions of the Kinnaurese the *khosia* and *beru* are also endogamous. The further sub-divisions of these two divisions i.e. three *khel* or the status groups of the *khosia* which include the Orang, Maorang or Orang Mech, and the Waza, and the three sub-division of the *beru* including Domang, Chamang and the Chanalas are all endogamous (Raha, 1972 : 3-5; Raha, 1978: 88-89; Raha, 1986 : 2-4 ; Raha & Mahato, 1975 : 240-248 ; Raha & Mahato, : 1985 135-139).

In the olden days all these three status groups were strictly endogamous. The members of one status group were not allowed to marry into other status group. Marriage with the lower status group was considered as socially disgraceful and lowering of the status, but in recent years some relaxation is noticed in case of the first two *khels* i.e. the Orang and the Maorang (Raha,

1972 : 3-5 ; Raha, 1978 : 89-90 ; Raha, 1986 : 6 ; Raha & Mahato, 1975 : 252-253 ; Raha & Mahato, 1985 : 141-142). While all the above divisions are mostly endogamous, exogamy is prevalent in case of the *khandan* system. No one is allowed to marry in his or her own *khandan* as to marry in one's own *khandan* is considered as the heinous crime (Raha, 1986).

As already stated polyandry is the social norm in Kinnaur. But monogamy is the numerically most important marriage type. The gradual increase of interest and desire for monogamy leads to the gradual decline of polyandry. In fact, monogamy has already most numerous type of marriage in Kinnaur (see Table 1). Besides, polygyny-both sororal and non-sororal types, is also prevalent but only in a few cases. Polygyny coupled with polyandry leading to polygynandry is found only in a few cases.

Sororate though prevalent, is not common in Kinnaur. Levirate is non-existent as it cannot exist in a polyandrous society.

Cross-cousin marriage is not prohibited but practised only in rare cases, but the parallel-cousin marriage is not prevalent.

Marriage by exchange i.e. brother and sister of one household marrying sister and brother respectively of another household, is in practice in Kinnaur.

Sometimes sonless parents like to give marriage of their daughter to a man and bring the bridegroom to their house as household son-in-law. The son-in-law lives with his parents-in-law to look after them and to manage their property. This type of marriage prevalent in Kinnaur, is known as *makpa* type.

Two major types of marriage have been accepted by the Kinnaura : The regular form of marriage or marriage by negotiation is known as *zanekang*, *zan dung* or *zanchang* in local language. The other one is *dub-dub* or *khuchis* i.e. marriage by elopment (Raha & Mahato, 1975 : 284 ; 1985 : 158). Besides, love marriage is also present. The remarriage of divorced or by enticing away ones wife (*harri*) is quite frequent. According to Chandra,

> 'The prevalent types of marriage practised by the Kinnaurese are : (a) marriage settled by negotiation-*zanakang*

(b) marriage by elopment of a virgin-*dubdub* and (c) marriage by elopment of a married woman—*haari*' (1973 : 177).

Bajpai on the other hand, finds the Kinnaura recognizing four different types—*janetang* or *janekeng* form of marriage, *dumlongshis* or *benang-hachis* or *jushis* (love marriage), *dub-dub* or *khuchis* (marriage by capture) and the *har* (enticing away someone's wife) (1981 : 33-34). Chib is also of the view that (I) *Janakang* or *Janetang* is the common arranged marriage. Besides, (II) *Damchalshish* or *Damtangshis* or *bennang hachis* or *jushish* is the love marriage. (III) *Darosh* or *dub-dub* or *nyamsha depang* or *nymsha lemo* or *ashish* or *huchis* is the marriage by forceful or consented capture. (IV) *Har* is the marriage by enticing away one's wife (1984 : 111-112).

Types of Marriages in Kinnaur : Polyandry

Monogamy is no doubt the most dominant marriage type among the Kinnaura. But polyandry is no less important. The present data show that in Kinnaur polyandrous marriages count 26.38% of all marriages (See Table 1). Marriages which were previously polyandrous and polygynandrous but have turned into households with one husband-one wife combination, have also significant strength of 11.73%. Polygynandrous marriages, are of course, very low in number. Again, when we come down to individual ethnic groups we see polyandry has a significant strength. Identically marriages which were previously polyandrous and polygynandrous but not polyandrous and polygynandrous at present, have also important place in individual ethnic group level. That means if we combine polyandry, polygynandry and previously polyandrous and polygynandrous marriages together, we will find that such marriages had and even now have a dominant place in the marriage system in Kinnaur. For example from all villages combined together such marriages among all ethnic groups (AEG) are 40.39%. These are 40.09% among the Rajput, 42.25% among the Koli, and 35.72% among the other ethnic groups (OEG).

The village Chango follows almost same trend. Monogamy no doubt, edges over other types of marriage. But polyandry is

TABLE 1

Ethnic groupwise distribution of various types of marriage in Kinnaur

Type of	CHANGO							
	Rajput		Koli		OEG		AEG	
Marriage	No.	%	No.	%	No.	%	No.	%
Monogamous	76	58.91	6	50.00	2	33.33	84	57.14
Polygynous	1	0.78	—	—	1	16.67	2	1.36
Polyandrous	33	25.58	4	33.33	2	33.33	39	26.53
Polygynandrous	1	0.78	—	—	—	—	1	0.68
Previously (Polyandrous/ Polygynandrous)	18	13.95	2	16.67	1	16.67	21	14.29
Total	112	100.00	12	100.00	6	100.00	147	100.00

OEG=other ethnic group
AEG=All ethnic group

Contd.

Types of	KONGOS							
	Rajput		Koli		OEG		AEG	
Marriage	No.	%	No.	%	No.	%	No.	%
Monogamous	32	68.09	20	52.63	4	66.67	56	61.54
Polygynous	—	—	—	—	—	—	—	—
Polyandrous	8	17.02	12	31.58	—	—	20	21.98
Polygynandrous	—	—	1	2.63	—	—	1	1.10
Previously (Polyandrous/ Polygynandrous)	7	14.89	5	13.16	2	33.33	14	15.38
Total	47	100.00	38	100.00	6	100.00	91	100.00

Contd.

Types of Marriage	ROGI							
	Rajput		Koli		OEG		AEG	
	No.	%	No.	%	No.	%	No.	%
Monogamous	22	47.83	12	57.14	2	100.00	36	52.17
Polygynous	2	4.35	3	14.29	—	—	5	7.25
Polyandrous	17	36.96	5	23.81	—	—	22	31.88
Polygynandrous	4	8.69	1	4.76	—	—	5	7.25
Previously (Polyandrous/ Polygynandrous)	1	2.17	—	—	—	—	1	1.45
Total	46	100.00	21	100.00	2	100.00	69	100.00

Contd.

Types of	ALL VILLAGES							
	Rajput		Koli		OEG		AEG	
Marriage	No.	%	No.	%	No.	%	No.	%
Monogamous	130	58.56	38	53.52	8	57.14	176	57.33
Polygynous	3	1.35	3	4.23	1	7.14	7	2.28
Polyandrous	58	26.12	21	29.57	2	14.29	81	26.38
Polygynandrous	5	2.25	2	2.82	—	—	7	2.28
Previously (Polyandrous/ Polygynandrous)	26	11.72	7	9.86	3	21.43	36	11.73
Total	226	100.00	71	100.00	14	100.00	307	100.00

marked by its presence. In case of all ethnic groups (AEG) monogamy covers 57.41% and polyandry 26.53%. Polyandry is also important in case of the individual ethnic groups. It is above 25% in all ethnic groups. The marriages which were previously polyandrous and polygynandrous but now living with one husband-one wife basis, also have significant strength. Further if polyandrous, polygynandrous marriages and marriages which were previously polyandrous and polygynandrous are combined together, the frequency of such marriages in the total marriages becomes markedly high. Here in this village the incidence of such marriages is 41.50% for AEG, 40.39% among the Rajput, 50.00% each among the Koli and OEG.

Almost identical picture is found among the inhabitants of Kongos. Like Chango monogamy is most dominant type of marriage in this village. But here also polyandry is the next popular type of marriage. Marriages which were previously polyandrous and polygynandrous have also a significant place (15.38%) in case of AEG. And if all polyandrous and polygynandrous and previously polyandrous/polygynandrous marriages are put together, we find that these marriages have secured 38.46% for all ethnic group (AEG).

When we examine the cases of individual ethnic groups separately somewhat similar picture as we have found for Chango, is evidenced. The only difference is that the frequency of polyandrous marriages is lower here in comparison to that of Chango. In case of individual ethnic groups also monogamy is the most dominant type of marriage, and next in order comes polyandry and previously polyandrous/polygynandrous marriages. But in case of the individual ethnic group also polyandry is lesser in number in comparison to that of their congeners, living at Chango.

Following other two villages the village Rogi shows dominance of monogamous marriages, but here frequency of polyandry is much higher in comparison to that of other two villages. The number of polygynandrous marriages is also higher. But marriages which were previously polyandrous/polygynandrous, are significantly low in comparison to those prevalent in other two villages. Here the incidence of polyandrous, polygynandrous and previously polyandrous and polygynandrous marriages combined together form 40.58% for all ethnic groups (AEG) which is definitely quite high.

In case of individual ethnic groups one significant point is that polyandry is higher in number among the Rajputs than that among the Koli and combined polyandrous/polygynandrous and previously polyandrous/polygynandrous marriages among the Rajputs is as high as 47.82%.

Further data from three more villages, one from (Zone-I) second from Zone-II and the third from Zone-III, also reveal that out of a total of 226 unions 22.56% are polyandrous-polygynandrous unions and 18.58% are polyandrous marriages. And in these villages 31.42% unions which were polyandrous and polygynandrous earlier, have now given birth to nuclear households in due course and for many reasons. Zone-I village has 17.40% polyandrous marriages and no polygynandrous one, but at Zone-II village 17.40% are polyandrous marriages and 3.48% are polygynandrous marriage (i.e. 20.88% are polyandrous and polygynandrous marriages). At Zone-III village on the other hand, 21.53% are polyandrous and 7.70% are polygynandrous marriages. That means 29.23% marriages are polyandrous and polygynandrous. In case of Zone II and Zone III villages households previously polyandrous and polygynandrous have got over 30% in strength. Only in Zone-I village such type of households are 17.39% (Raha, 1978 : 93 ; Raha & Mahato, 1975 : 378-379 ; Raha & Mahato, 1985 : 210-211). But Chandra reports from a village in lower Kinnaur (Nachar sub-Division i.e. Zone-II) that polyandry holds 25.40% of the total marriages. Marriages which were earlier polyandrous but become monogamous in the later phase (poly-monogamy by Chandra) have a strength of 23.52%. In case of individual ethnic groups polyandry is highest (33.33%) among the Lohar followed by the Rajput (Kanet) with 29.76% of polyandry and the Badhi 23.08% (Chandra, 1973 : 181-186).

Another important point that has been emerged out the analysis, is that polygynandry has somewhat significant strength only at Rogi (7.25%) and Duni (7.70%) in comparison to other villages where it is less than 3.50%. It seems that polygynandry is somewhat significant in the villages near urban centre. Both Rogi and Duni villages are in the close proximity to the district

Headquarters, Kalpa. Rogi is about five kilometres and Duni within a kilometre. Out of other four villages, Chango and Namgia in Pooh and Kongos and Sungra in Nachar sub-division are far away from Kalpa. It may be inferred that urbanisation and modern forces may have something to do with polygynandry. In fact the urban and modern forces and many other factors as mentioned previously like modern education, modern legislations, cash and market economy, contact with non-polyandrous people, modern communication etc. prevalent particularly in urban centre, have developed a tendency among the present day Kinnaurese to adopt monogamy or singular marriage. Here in certain cases monogamy in traditional polyandrous system, has led to polygynandry as polygyny in polyandrous system has developed polygynandry in some polyandrous societies. The polygynandry in Kinnaur seems to be the outcome of the notional monogamy as practised by some Kinnaurese in the traditional polyandrous set up which they have failed to discard totally inspite of strong anti-forces prevalent in the present day Kinnaur particularly in the well communicated area like district Headquarters. That notionally one is married to the wife of ones brother, is still strongly imbeded in the mind of many Kinnaurese. But the idea that more wives will give better and more chances to fufil carnal apetite and will also help in developing a feeling among one to have 'own' wife, brothers started marrying more than once, resulting in the formation of polygynandry in polyandrous system. Polygynandry may in future lead to the development of monogamy and destruction of polyandry in Kinnaur.

Polyandry in Kinnaur

In Kinnaur polyandry was a social norm in the past and still that is in practice. That it existed in the past, is proved from the writings of the earlier authors.

'Polyandry as I have before observed, is frequent,' observed Gerard in the middle of last century in connection with the Kinnaura polyandry (Lloyd & Gerard, 1846 : 255). The Gazetteer for Simla Hill States of 1910 gives some details of polyandry practised in Kinnaur at least, in the beginning of this century. 'Polyandry prevails in the greater part of

Kanawar and in some places in Rohru tehsil...' (1911 : 15). Thornton in early sixties of last century also found polyandry as almost universal in Kinnaur (1862 : 518).

Andrew Wilson also found 'polyandry to exist commonly from Taranda in the Sutlej valley, a few marches from Simla upto Chinese Tibet' (1876 : 255).

Type of polyandry : The people of Kinnaur are practising fraternal or adelphic polyandry since time immemorial. Usually the brothers who are the sons of the same parents, same father/fathers but of different mother/mothers, and same mother/mothers but of different father/fathers come into a marital bond with a common woman. The non-fraternal type, where the husbands are not brothers, has not been met with during our study. But the Gazetteer of Simla Hill States of 1910, reported traces of non-fraternal polyandry practised in Kinnaur. It states 'There are two forms : (I) the higher, where joint husbands are brothers, and (II) the lower, where they are not brothers'.

> 'As a rule the former alone is found in Bushahr, but there are instances of the second. Occasionally two men, perhaps of different castes, and certainly not relations will become *dharm bhai*, and share the wife...' (1911 : 15-16).

But we have not come across a single case in Kinnaur where such a type of non-paternal polyandry has taken place.

In Kinnaur usually the eldest brother goes to the house of the bride to marry her in case of the *zanekang* or *zanchang* type of marriage. Usually other brothers do not accompany the eldest brother to marry her. But the newly wed bride becomes the wife of all the brothers through certain ritual. This ritual is known as 'turban tying ceremony.'

> 'In this ritual, which is considered as the most important ritual that symbolises polyandrous marriage, all brothers sit in a row. The bride sits before them. The grooms, i.e. brothers and their bride are garlanded....The maternal uncle of the bridegrooms then takes a piece of white cloth, makes *pagri* (turban) on the head of each brother with that piece of cloth, with accompaniment of music. This indicates the

> marriage of all the brothers with the common wife' (Raha & Mahato, 1985 : 252-253).

This 'turban tying ceremony' unites the brothers into the joint husbandhood to share a common wife. After this ritual each and every brother earns the right over their common wife. Only those brothers are considered as married to a wife/wives who have performed the turban tying ceremony (Raha, 1978 : 94).

The Punjab States Gazetteer, Simla Hill States, 1910 has also mentioned about this ritual.

> '...the marriage ceremony is completed by the bride washing the feet of the bridegrooms, and the bridegrooms tying round their caps pieces of muslim cloth called *paju*' (1911 : 16-17).

Gazetteer of Kinnaur also refers to a ceremony of putting on turban (*pag likshimu*) by each brother to get the status of a husband (Mamgain, 1971 : 95). Almost identical ceremony is also prevalent in Lahaul. (Nag, 1960 : 188).

Reasons for the Origin and Development of Polyandry

Ecology everywhere plays an important role in shaping the culture of the people. The case of Kinnaur is also no exception to this basic theory. The peculiar Himalayan ecology here, rocky and unfertile soil, insufficient farm productivity, extreme cold and lack of sufficient rain and many other factors have exerted influence on these people. The survival strategy in the midst of such inhospitable environmental conditions had compelled them to diversify their economy (Raha, 1976, 1982, 1983, 1985 : Raha & Mahato, 1975, 1985). Agriculture alone was unable to fill up their hungry mouths. They had to find out supplimentary sources. Animal husbandry and trade were the options, the supplimentary sources, which they readily accepted. And automatically to cope with the diversified economy division of labour among adult males came into being. Brothers divided among themselves the means of livelihood. No doubt the eldest brother for his previleged position in the household, took over the farm management meaning that he would be in the house. Other brothers had no option but to accept animal husbandry and trade for which they needed to travel a long hazardous difficult Himalayan terrains and to stay away from the natal household for a pretty long time. This peculiar condition definitely compelled them to think of their own family life. To take their wife and children along with them in their hazardous journey, was impossible and again to keep them in their village without any care, was a risk. Further the political situation of the area enhanced this risk much more. Kinnaur was in the past, subjected to the attacks of the soldiers of Kulu, the Tibetans, the Gorkhas and others ; so possibly the only solution left to them was to marry jointly and share the wife jointly. When the younger brothers would be away from home, the wife, common to all brothers and the children born of the union, would remain under the care of the eldest brother. Again when they would return, they would enjoy her as husbands. The Kinnaurese of the bygone days must have solved this crisis in this way resulting in the induction of polyandry in the society. To Llyod, people of Kinnaur gave the above reason.

> 'Polyandry as I have before observed, is frequent and the men assigned as a reason that their trading avocations often forcing them to be absent for a long period from their homes, it was requisite that females should have more husband than one' (Llyod and Gerard, 1846 : 225).

Punjab State Gazetteer, Simla Hill States, 1910 also supports this reason for polyandry.

> 'It enables a family of brothers to get the full benefit of several sources of livelihood, one can cultivate the joint land, another breed cattle, a third engage in trade, and so forth' (1911 : 16).

In one of his articles the senior author (Raha, 1986) has mentioned that the peculiar ecological conditions and the high altitude economy in Kinnaur had led to the formation of a definite system of division of labour, particularly among the adult males, which possibly was responsible, at least, partially for the development of polyandry there.

> 'If a household had three male members, the eldest usually looked after the land ; of the other two one remained engaged in trade with Tibet and other places, and the third one was meant for tending the animals in the alpine pastures and lower hills. This arrangement gave them a feeling of inconvenience and insecurity in running individual families ; so possibly institution of polyandry came into existence' (Raha, 1987 : 25).

So the division of labour among the Kinnaurese and the economic adjustment in a peculiar Himalayan ecology would possibly be the reasons or one of the reasons for the origin and development of polyandry. This no doubt, could possibly lead to polyandry and thereby causing surplus of unmarried adult women. To balance it they adopted *zomo* system so that these surplus women could be adjusted without causing any mal-adjustment in the society.

The origin and development of polyandry in Kinnaur may have another reason, and that is to prevent fragmentation of family property. They believe that if the brothers remain united, the family property will remain intact, and it will act as a good source of income in such an environmentally hostile country. And to have a common wife for all brothers, was thought to be the best way of keeping the family intact. Even they do not prefer polygynandry much (occurrence of polygynandry is very low--see Table 1) as that may lead to the break up of family and finally fragmentation of property.

Punjab States Gazetteer, Simla Hill States, 1910, reports in a similar way,

> 'The custom of polyandry is defended by those who practise it, on the ground that it prevents both over-population and sub-division of property in a country, where agricultural land is not sufficient for the needs of the country' (1911 : 15-16).

No doubt polyandry in Kinnaur perpetuated due to the direct encouragement of the State.

> 'Polyandry was in former days directly encouraged by the State through penalties exacted on partitions. When a set of brothers divided moveable property, one half share of the whole was appropriated by the State, and divisions of immoveable property were refused official recognition', reported Punjab States Gazetteer, Simla Hill States, 1910 (1911 : 16).

Not only that the state legislation helped them to retain and perpetuate this type of marriage, but the Kinnaurese also felt it convenient to accept this as their custom.

There could be another reason for the presence of polyandry in Kinnaur. The people of Kinnaur feel it to be an effective measure of checking the growth of population.

> 'As the Himalayan regions have inhospitable weather condition, limited resources, high altitude, lack of proper communication, limited cultivable land, less fertility of land, lack of industry etc. so the food supply is also limited. Naturally, the insufficient supply of food required the limitation of the growth of population, and the existence of polyandry has helped to solve these problems to great extent'. (Raha & Mahato, 1985 : 176).

Another system that may have helped the growth and perpetuation of polyandry in the Kinnaurese society is its rules of inheritance. According to these rules the eldest brother used to inherit the whole property after the demise of the father. As a result of this, the other brothers had to remain dependent on him for their maintenance. If any of the brothers wanted to get separated from the hold of the eldest brother, he would have to give up his claim over property and also on the maintenance. He would have no right to take any property from the core household. Rather he had to give compensation to the child born of the polyandrous union. The situation compelled him to depend on his eldest brother. Thus he used to refrain him from getting separated from the core household and went on living with other brothers and the common wife. From the common wife all brothers used to get the pleasure of sex life and other aspects of conjugal life. All brothers remained responsible jointly for the maintenance of the family and carrying out the livelihood.

Our informants feel that polyandry helps a family to run a healthy and happy life. They think that,

> 'If the brothers could live together in a single household and work hard they could make the family prosperous and thereby lead a happy and healthy life. The only way to do so was to marry jointly and lead a family life with a common wife. If all the brothers are tied up with a common wife, they would not be able to leave each other and would as such, lead a happy and healthy life.' (Raha & Mahato, 1985 : 176).

One of the important outcomes of polyandry is that there will be excess of unmarried women in any polyandrous society. The same is also true for the Kinnaur society. The centuries long existence of polyandry in this society might have resulted in the surplus of unmarried adult women. Now question is how this high Himalayan polyandrous society could manage with this surplus of unmarried adult women ? What was the mechanism which could effectively tackle and counterpoise this unusual growth and to get rid of the possible social maladjustment occurred from that growth ? Buddhism there gave a solution to it—a remedy. The system of *zomo* or nunhood was adopted by them which definitely counterbalanced the excess of unmarried adult women, at least partly.

But there could be a reverse possibility. Could be that with the advent of Buddhism in Kinnaur, *zomo* system was also introduced and,

> '...as a result of Buddhism some women renunciated the material world and became Buddhist nuns (*zomo*), instead of getting married and leading a family life. This institution of *zomo* gradually created a situation of the imbal-

anced sex-ratio, the number of marriageable women became less in number in comparison to the number of males in the society' (Raha, 1986 : 25).

This situation also could lead to the origin and development of the institution of polyandry in Kinnaur.

The polyandrous system among the Kinnaurese is definitely an outcome from the necessity of the adaptability of human beings to the most difficult ecological conditions. The main sources of the livelihood of the Kinnaurese were land and live-stock. Though land acted as the primary means of livelihood but in a natural way, it had limitation. It never was bountiful. Moreover, the fertility was less. Besides, there were many other diversities such as the problems of manure, problems of irrigation, insufficiency of rainfall and snowfall etc. Period of cultivation was also too limited, only seven months a year (April to October); during the rest five months of the year the area became very cold and often remained snow covered. As a result of these limitations, the limited area of cultivable land which was undoubtedly insufficient for the existing population of the district, could not produce a substantial quantity of foodstuff for the Kinnaurese. Rather, the yield that came out of their hard labour from that limited source, could barely meet their hunger and demand for greater part of the year. Similarly, for the animals there was definite limitation of the grazing land and also the fodder. At the same time the scope for increasing the area of cultivation and also for pasture was undoubtedly remote. Naturally under the circumstances, the Kinnaurese could not afford to expand their population, but to limit it. They could possibly think only to restrict the freedom for marriage, so that they could have limited number of children. To counteract the above alarming situation, they could only think of two things—firstly to marry one woman by several brothers instead of marrying separately, and secondly to prohibit marriage for certain boys and girls, and instead, sending them to the monastery to become *lama* and *zomo* respectively. These two methods adopted by the Kinnaurese and many other people of the high Himalayas, could definitely and effectively control the population growth to a great extent.

The people of Kinnaur knew that if different brothers in a household, could marry individually and thus having individual wife and family, they definitely would have begot more children than what they could get by adopting fraternal polyandry. As many boys used to take the path of celibacy and become *lama* who usually did not marry, they in another way, curbed their natural growth of population. Polyandry and *lamahood* resulted in the creation of surplus unmarried woman in the society and thus a new institution, the *zomo* system, started functioning in the Kinnaurese society. At least a major part of the surplus young unmarried Kinnaurese girls started dedicating their lives to the religion which forbade them from marrying.

It is believed that the imbalance in sex-ratio particularly when the male population far exceeds the female population, is possibly a reason for the origin and growth of polyandry in certain human societies. Could be, it is true for certain societies but definitely it is not so in case of Kinnaur. No doubt the female population here is always less than that of other sex except in 1951, but it does not seem to be so less that would lead to the formation of polyandry in this society. It is revealed in the table below where sex-ratio since 1901 has been given.

TABLE 2

Sex-Ratio in Kinnaur, 1901-1981

Year	Females per thousand males
1901	911
1911	935
1921	922
1931	941
1941	910
1951	1,070
1961	969
1971	885
1981	885

It is apparent that in earlier census decades (from 1901 to 1941) when incidence of polyandry was possibly more than that exists at present, the numerical position of the members of both sexes was almost balanced. The difference is not at all significant which could lead to the formation of a new social institution like polyandry. So this may be said that Kinnaur most probably, never had significantly less number of females and so it was not the cause for polyandry.

Further, it is also seen that some districts in Himachal Pradesh which at present do not have polyandry, have sex-ratio almost identical with Kinnaur, that is, number of women is less than that of men. For example, Simla district has a sex-ratio of 877, Solan 929, and Mandi 999. So it means that a little less in number of females in the society in comparison to the number of males, does not prove the existence of polyandry. Same type of sex-ratio is also met with in numerous other districts of India.

Identically history does not reveal that female infanticide was practised in Kinnaur. So the female infanticide, which is a cause for polyandry elsewhere, is definitely not so for Kinnaur.

It is thus seen that there may not be any single reason responsible for the origin and development of a particular trait or institution. There may be multiple reasons responsible. Similarly same reason or reasons may not hold good everywhere even in identical condition for every society having the same institution. Further, same conditions or reasons may not compel some other societies of the same area to have the same institution or trait. Polyandry does not exist in many Himalayan societies inspite of living in the same ecological, economic and socio-religious conditions.

Polyandry and the Kinnaurese Households

Now we will examine the different types and size of the Kinnaurese households and effects of polyandry on these. We will particularly examine the frequency of polyandrous and polygynandrous households and size of the same in order to highlight the characters of the polyandrous households.

In Kinnaur there are different types of households. The distribution of different types of households among different ethnic groups in three different villages under three culture zones have been discussed in Table 3 (Raha & Mahato,

TABLE 3

Distribution of different types of Household

Types of households	CHANGO Rajput No. of households	%	Koli No. of households	%	OEG No. of households	%	KONGOS Rajput No. of households	%
1	2	3	4	5	6	7	8	9
Nuclear	42	36.21	3	30.00	2	40.00	17	42.50
Extended	19	16.37	2	20.00	—	—	8	20.00
Polygynous	—	—	—	—	1	20.00	—	—
Polyandrous & Polygynandrous	32	27.59	3	30.00	2	40.00	7	17.50
Other types	23	19.83	2	20.00	—	—	8	20.00
Total	116	100.00	10	100.00	5	100.00	40	100.00

Contd.

Types of households	KONGOS						ROGI			
	Koli		OEG		Rajput		Koli		OEG	
	No. of house-holds	%	No. of house-holds	%	No. of house-holds	%	No. of house-holds	%	No. of house-holds	%
	10	11	12	13	14	15	16	17	18	19
Nuclear	8	26.67	2	66.67	14	35.00	4	18.18	2	100.00
Extended	8	26.67	1	33.33	3	7.50	3	13.64	—	—
Polygynous	—	—	—	—	1	2.50	2	9.09	—	—
Polyandrous & Polygynandrous	11	36.66	—	—	17	42.50	6	27.27	—	—
Other types	3	10.00	—	—	5	12.50	7	31.82	—	—
Total	30	100.00	3	100.00	40	100.00	22	100.00	2	100.00

1985 : 200-201).

The table shows that though nuclear households bear higher frequency among the Rajput of both Chango and Kongos, polyandrous and polygynandrous households have higher strength among the Koli of Kongos and among both Rajput and the Koli of Rogi. Among the Koli and other ethnic groups (OEG) of chango these two types of households (nuclear and polyandrous/polygynandrous) bear equal strength (30.00% and 40.00% respectively). In general it is seen from Table No. 3 that polyandrous and polygynandrous households (polygynandrous households are only a few in number) have significant position in the Kinnaurese society (These households are 27.59%, 17.50% and 42.50% among the Rajput of Chango, Kongos and Rogi villages respectively and 30.00%, 36.66% and 27.27% among the Koli of these villages respectively).

So far as the average size of the households is concerned, it is seen that the polygynous households scored the biggest average size when data for all villages are put together, but the polyandrous and polygynandrous households also follow the polygynous households very closely. The average size of polyandrous and polygynandrous households of all villages is as big as 7.91 (Table 4). In case of individual villages also these polyandrous and polygynandrous households are equally big (for Chango it is 6.95 and for Kongo 7.83) but in Rogi these types of households are unusually big (9.52), biggest in all villages (Table 4).

A major and interesting point becomes clear when we examine the number of population covered by these households. Over 40% population, rather 40.92% to be exact, of the total population of the three villages pulled together are covered by the polyandrous and polygynandrous households alone when polyandrous and polygynandrous households constitute 29.10% of the total household. That means quite a big chunk of population is included in the polyandrous households. These types of households alone cover much higher number of population than any other type of households do. And the same holds true for the individual villages also where polyandrous and polygynandrous households engulf biggest number of population if a comparison is made between different

TABLE 4

Size of different types of household in Kinnaur

Types of Households	CHANGO Total household	CHANGO Total population %	CHANGO Average size	KONGOS Total household %	KONGOS Total population %	KONGOS Average size %
1	2	3	4	5	6	7
Nuclear	47	194 29.48	4.13	27	119 29.53	4.41
Extended	21	112 17.02	5.33	17	107 26.55	6.29
Polygynous	1	9 1.37	9.00	—	—	—
Polyandrous+ Polygynandrous	37	257 39.06	6.95	18	141 34.99	7.83
Other type	25	86 13.07	3.44	11	36 8.93	3.27
Total	131	658 100.00	5.02	73	403 100.00	5.52

Contd.

Types of Households	ROGI			ALL VILLAGES		
	Total household	Total population%	Average size	Total household	Total population%	Average size
	8	9	10	11	12	13
Nuclear	20	100 22.37	5.00	94	413 27.39	4.39
Extended	6	43 9.62	7.17	44	262 17.37	5.95
Polygynous	3	23 5.15	7.67	4	32 2.12	8.00
Polyandrous+ Polygynandrous	23	219 48.99	9.52	78	617 40.92	7.91
Other type	12	62 13.87	5.17	48	184 12.20	3.83
Total	64	447 100.00	6.98	268	1508 100.00	5.63

types of households. But it would be worth to mention that at Rogi population constituting these households is significantly high (48.99%) i.e. almost half of the population of the village are covered by the polyandrous and polygynandrous households.

When we come down to the ethnic groups inhabiting different villages studied (Raha & Mahato, 1985 : 201-206) we find from the Table 5 that out of the total Rajput population (1,091) of all villages polyandrous-polygynandrous households cover 41.15% while nuclear households bear only 29.61%. Among the Koli also 41.23% of the total Koli population (367) have been grabbed by polyandrous-polygynandrous households. Similarly the polyandrous-polygynandrous households among the Rajput of Chango, Kongos and Rogi villages are composed of 39.32%, 23.47% and 55.81% of the total Rajput population of the three villages respectively. The same is true for the Koli of all three villages. In case of this, people also, the polyandrous-polygynandrous households cover 30.43%, 48.97% and 36.23% of the total Koli population of the three villages respectively. The peculiarity is that in Chango and Rogi villages population covered by the polyandrous-polygynandrous households among the Rajput is much more than that among the Koli of these two villages. But the condition is reverse in Kongos where polyandrous-polygynandrous households among the Koli are comprised of more population than that covered by the same type of households among the Rajput (Raha & Mahato, 1985 : 201-206).

Husband/Husbands-Wife/Wives Combinations in the Kinnaura Households

The number of husband (Hu) and wife (Wi) in different types of households in human societies varies. Whether there will be one or more wives for one or more husbands depends on what type of marriages they are involved in and what type of household unit they will form. And in a natural way, the Hu+Wi combination varies in nature and form-varies from nuclear household to polygynous household, thence to polyandrous to polygynandrous households, and so on. Here we shall particularly examine the Hu-Wi combinations and their variations and

TABLE 5

Distribution of population in different types of households

Types of households	CHANGO							
	Rajput		Koli		OEG		All ethnic groups	
	Population	%	Population	%	Population	%	Population	%
1	2	3	4	5	6	7	8	9
Nuclear	174	29.74	15	32.62	5	18.52	194	29.48
Extended	101	17.26	11	23.91	—	—	112	17.02
Polygynous	—	—	—	—	9	33.33	9	1.37
Polyandrous & Polygynandrous	230	39.32	14	30.43	13	48.15	257	39.06
Other types	80	13.68	6	13.04	—	—	86	13.07
Total	585	100.00	46	100.00	27	100.00	658	100.00

Contd.

Types of households	KONGOS							
	Rajput		Koli		OEG		All Ethnic groups	
	Population	%	Population	%	Population	%	Population	%
	10	11	12	13	14	15	16	17
Nuclear	78	39.80	33	17.01	8	61.54	119	29.53
Extended	48	24.49	54	27.84	5	38.46	107	26.55
Polygynous	—	—	—	—	—	—	—	—
Polyandrous & Polygynandrous	46	23.47	95	48.97	—	—	141	34.99
Other types	24	12.24	12	6.18	—	—	36	8.93
Total	196	100.00	194	100.00	13	100.00	403	100.00

Types of Households	ROGI							
	Rajput		Koli		OEG		All ethnic groups	
	Population	%	Population	%	Population	%	Population	%
18	13	14	15	16	17	18	19	20
Nuclear	71	22.90	19	14.96	10	100.00	100	22.37
Extended	25	8.06	18	14.17	—	—	43	9.62
Polygynous	8	2.50	15	11.81	—	—	23	5.15
Polyandrous & Polygynandrous	173	55.81	46	36.23	—	—	219	48.99
Other types	33	10.65	29	22.83	—	—	62	13.87
Total	310	100.00	127	100.00	10	100.00	447	99.98

(*Contd.*)

ALL VILLAGES

Types of Households	Rajput		Koli		OEG		All ethnic groups	
	Population	%	Population	%	Population	%	Population	%
	21	22	23	24	25	26	27	28
Nuclear	323	29.61	67	18.26	23	46.00	413	27.39
Extended	174	15.95	83	22.62	5	10.00	262	17.37
Polygynous	8	0.73	15	4.08	9	18.00	32	2.12
Polyandrous & Polygynandrous	449	41.15	155	42.23	13	26.00	617	40.92
Other types	137	12.56	47	12.81	—	—	184	12.20
Total	1091	100.00	367	100.00	50	100.00	1508	100.00

frequencies in polyandrous and polygynandrous households in Kinnaur.

In a polyandrous society

> 'a woman may have two or more husbands who are brothers. Further, in the polyandrous households, sometimes, the existence of polygyny can also be traced, and the polygynous marriage in the polyandrous households leads to the formation of polygynandrous households' (Raha & Mahato, 1975 : 373 ; Raha & Mahato, 1985 : 206) when one or more women may have two or more husbands'.

Besides there are a large number of monogamous marriages resulted in nuclear households and a few polygyny to form polygynous households. Now all these households have varied combinations of husband/husbands and wife/wives. In polyandrous and polygynandrous families,

> "In principle and in practice. all the brothers form an inseparable group of fraternal husbands in the name of eldest brother. The wives, on the other hand, join the union individually one after another, in the same way as it is usually found in the polygynous system except that the single husband is substituted by the polyandrous group of husbands". (Majumdar, 1963 : 72).

Saksena also found that in Jaunsar Bawar 'brothers may have one wife among them or they may have two or three wives, or even more, in common' which according to him leads to a peculiar combination of polygyny and polyandry (1962 : 21).

> "In Kinnaur also we get such peculiar combinations. Here also in the so called polyandrous-polygynandrous households two or more brothers may have one, two or more wives in common". (Raha & Mahato, 1975 : 373 ; 1985 : 207).

These husband/husbands and wife/wives combinationsvary

widely in different households. From our data we have here ten such combinations (Table 6). The frequency of each type of combinations varies culture zonewise, villagewise and even ethnic groupwise. Here we have tried to show such combinations culture zone, village and ethnic groupwise.

(i) *Hu-Wi Combinations* : *Culture Zone Level*

In order to show the strength of polyandry and polygynandry in Kinnaur we have compiled the husband/husbands and wife/wives combinations in the households distributed in three different culture zones of the district of Kinnaur. Data for each culture zone have been collected from two villages of that zone and the figures shown in the table (Table 6) are the combined figures from the two villages of that zone.

Table 6 shows that in Zone-I the frequency of polyandrous combinations (Hu_2+Wi_1 and Hu_n+Wi_1) is 18.95% whereas the same for two other zones are 19.42% (Zone-II) and 26.87% (Zone-III) respectively ; the figure for all villages combined together, comes to 20.92%. That means the highest frequency of polyandrous combination is in Zone-III. Identically the polygynandrous combinations (Hu_2+Wi_2 ; Hu_n+Wi_2 ; Hu_2+Wi_n ; Hu_n+Wi_n) is highest in Zone-III (7.47%) followed by Zone-II (2.43%) and Zone-I (0.81%) the figure for all zones combined together is 2.89%. It means that even though the incidence of polygynandry is quite low, but if both polyandrous and polygynandrous combinations are pulled together we find very significant and important frequency of these types of plural marriages in Kinnaur. Here Zone-III has the highest incidence of such marriage (34.34%) followed by Zone-II (21.85%) and Zone-I (19.76%), the figure for all zones combined together is 23.81%. Over and above if the figures for these nuclear combination (Hu_1+Wi_1 combination) which were previously polyandrous and polygynandrous (11.69% for Zone-I, 26.21% for Zone-II, 17.91% for Zone-III and 18.20% for all zones combined together) are added to the present day polyandrous-polygynandrous households, the frequency of the later types of households, will significantly increase. It clearly indicates that even today with all its modernizations Kinnaur still has quite a significant frequency of polyandrous-polygynandrous marriages and house-

TABLE 6

Nature & Distribution of Hu-Wi combinations in the households of three Culture-Zones

Combination of Hu-Wi in the Household	Zone-I		Zone-II		Zone-III		All Zones	
	No.	%	No.	%	No.	%	No.	%
1	2	3	4	5	6	7	8	9
Hu_1+Wi_1	168	67.74	105	50.97	58	43.28	331	56.29
Hu_2+Wi_1	28	11.29	24	11.65	25	18.66	77	13.10
Hu_n+Wi_1	19	7.66	16	7.77	11	8.21	46	7.82
Hu_1+Wi_2	2	0.81	2	0.97	6	4.48	10	1.70
Hu_2+Wi_2	2	0.81	1	0.49	3	2.24	6	1.02
Hu_n+Wi_2	—	—	4	1.94	4	2.99	8	1.36
Hu_1+Wi_n	—	—	—	—	—	—	—	—
Hu_2+Wi_n	—	—	—	—	—	—	—	—
Hu_n+Wi_n	—	—	—	—	3	2.24	3	0.51
Hu_1+Wi_1 (Previously polyandrous)	29	11.69	54	26.21	24	17.91	107	18.20
Total	248	100.00	206	100.00	134	100.01	588	100.00

Note : Hu=Husband ; Wi=Wife ; 1=one in number ; 2=two in number ; n=more than two in number.

TABLE 7

Nature and distribution of Husband (Hu)-Wife (Wi) combinations in Kinnaurese households

Combination of Hu-Wi in the Household	CHANGO						All ethnic groups	
	Rajput		Koli		OEG			
	No.	%	No.	%	No.	%	No.	%
1	2	3	4	5	6	7	8	9
Hu_1+Wi_1	76	58.91	6	50.00	2	33.33	84	57.14
Hu_2+Wi_1	18	13.95	4	33.33	2	33.33	24	16.33
Hu_n+Wi_1	15	11.63	—	—	—	—	15	10.20
Hu_1+Wi_2	—	—	—	—	1	16.67	1	0.68
Hu_2+Wi_2	1	0.78	—	—	—	—	1	0.68
Hu_n+Wi_2	—	—	—	—	—	—	—	—
Hu_1+Wi_n	1	0.78	—	—	—	—	1	0.68
Hu_2+Wi_n	—	—	—	—	—	—	—	—
Hu_n+Wi_n	—	—	—	—	—	—	—	—
Hu_1+Wi_1 (Previously polyandrous)	18	13.95	2	16.67	1	16.67	21	14.29
Total	129	100.00	12	100.00	6	100.00	147	100.00

(Contd.)

Combination of Hu-Wi in the Household	KONGOS Rajput No.	%	Koli No.	%	OEG No.	%	All ethnic groups No.	%
	10	11	12	13	14	15	16	17
Hu_1+Wi_1	32	68.09	20	52.63	4	66.67	56	61.54
Hu_2+Wi_1	5	10.64	8	21.05	—	—	13	14.29
Hu_n+Wi_1	3	6.38	4	10.53	—	—	7	7.69
Hu_1+Wi_2	—	—	—	—	—	—	—	—
Hu_2+Wi_2	—	—	—	—	—	—	—	—
Hu_n+Wi_2	—	—	1	2.63	—	—	1	1.10
Hu_1+Wi_n	—	—	—	—	—	—	—	—
Hu_2+Wi_n	—	—	—	—	—	—	—	—
Hu_n+Wi_n	—	—	—		—	—		—
Hu_1+Wi_1 (Previously polyandrous)	7	14.89	5	13.16	2	33.33	14	15.38
Total	47	100.00	38	100.00	6	100.00	91	100.00

(*Contd.*)

Combination of Hu-Wi in the Household	ROGI							
	Rajput		Koli		OEG		All ethnic groups	
	No.	%	No.	%	No.	%	No.	%
	18	19	20	21	22	23	24	25
Hu_1+Wi_1	22	47.83	12	57.14	2	100.00	36	52.17
Hu_2+Wi_1	10	21.74	5	23.81	—	—	15	21.74
Hu_n+Wi_1	7	15.22	—	—	—	—	7	10.14
Hu_1+Wi_2	2	4.35	3	14.29	—	—	5	7.25
Hu_n+Wi_2	1	2.17	—	—	—	—	1	1.45
Hu_1+Wi_2	2	4.35	1	4.76	—	—	3	4.35
Hu_1+Wi_n	—	—	—	—	—	—	—	—
Hu_2+Wi_n	—	—	—	—	—	—	—	—
Hu_n+Wi_n	1	2.17	—	—	—	—	1	1.45
Hu_1+Wi_1 (Previously polyandrous)	1	2.17	—	—	—	—	1	1.45
Total	46	100.00	21	100.00	2	100.00	69	100.00

(Contd.)

	ALL VILLAGES							
	Rajput		Koli		OEG		All ethnic groups	
	No.	%	No.	%	No.	%	No.	%
	26	27	28	29	30	31	32	33
Hu_1+Wi_1	130	58.56	38	53.52	8	57.14	176	57.33
Hu_2+Wi_1	33	14.86	17	23.94	2	14.29	52	16.94
Hu_n+Wi_1	25	11.26	4	5.63	—	—	29	9.45
Hu_2+Wi_2	2	0.90	3	4.23	1	7.14	6	1.95
Hu_1+Wi_2	2	0.90	—	—	—	—	2	0.65
Hu_n+Wi_2	2	0.90	2	2.82	—	—	4	1.30
Hu_1+Wi_n	1	0.45	—	—	—	—	1	0.33
Hu_2+Wi_n	—	—	—	—	—	—	—	—
Hu_n+Wi_n	1	0.45	—	—	—	—	1	0.33
$Hu_1=Wi_1$ (Previously polyandrous)	26	11.72	7	9.86	3	21 43	36	11.72
Total	226	100.00	71	100.00	14	100.00	307	100.00

(Contd.)

holds. It may further be added here that nuclear households with Hu_1+Wi_1 combination is no doubt the most dominant type in Kinnaur (67.74% in Zone-I, 50.97% in Zone-II, 43.28% in Zone-III and 56.29% belong to all zones put together) whereas frequency of polygynous type (Hu_1+Wi_2 and Hu_1+Wi_n) is quite negligible, highest (4.48%) being in Zone-III.

(ii) Hu+ Wi Combinations : Village and Ethnic Group Levels

When the data on such Hu+Wi combinations are examined in village as well as ethnic group levels, it is seen that variations and frequencies run in a close parallel to these of the culture zones.

In village and ethnic group levels the highest frequency, no doubt, goes to Hu_1+Wi_1 or nuclear combination resulted due to monogamous marriages and nuclear households, yet Hu_2+Wi_1 and Hu_n+Wi_1 combinations representing polyandrous marriages and households have quite a significant strength (26.39% in case of "All ethnic groups" (AEG) pulled together for all villages). The polygynandrous combinations (Hu_2+Wi_2, Hu_n+Wi_2, Hu_2+Wi_n and Hu_n+Wi_n) occupy only a very insignificant position (2.28%). But no doubt the incidence of Hu_1+Wi_1 combination which was earlier polyandrous and polygynandrous in character, is also significant in occurance (11.72%).

In case of individual villages the conditions are identical. In these villages Hu_1+Wi^1 combination has the highest frequency but Hu_2+Wi_1 and Hu_n+Wi_1 i.e. polyandrous combinations also have the significant strength. But ethnic groupwise and villagewise variations in the frequency of the Hu-Wi combinations are observed. For example while at Rogi such combinations among the Rajput bear the highest frequency (36.96%), at Kongos these have the lowest strength (17.02%) Chango secures the intermediate position (25.58%). Again in Chango and Kongos the frequency of polyandrous combinations (Hu_2+Wi_1 and Hu_n+Wi_1) among the Koli is higher than that of the Rajput, but at Rogi it is reversed. The incidence of polygynandrous combinations is insignificant among all the communities.

Number of Husband/Husbands/Per Wife/And Wife/Wives per Husband in the Kinnaurese Households

In the Kinnaura polyandry there is restriction on the number of brothers to become husband of a common wife. Usually a maximum of six brothers may have one common wife. But in most of the cases (64.20%) two brothers share a common wife. Only in one case of the villages studied six brothers are found to have married jointly to a common wife (Table 8). In individual villages also two brothers marrying a wife jointly, are the most common feature and have the highest numerical strength. It is 61.54% at Chango, 65.00% at Kongos and 68.18% at Rogi. Three brothers jointly sharing a common wife have also significant strength at Kongos (35.00%) and Changos (28.21%). Further while at Rogi six brothers are sharing a common wife, at Kongos a maximum of four brothers and at Chango, a maximum of five brothers are found to share two wives and one wife respectively in common. But these are of rare occurances. Further, it is also important to mention here that husbands usually do not go for more than three wives. We have not met with any case contravening this rule.

Further, brothers sharing more than one common wife (polygynandry) are only a few in number, and a maximum of three wives are shared by the common husbands. At Rogi there is only one case where three brothers have married three wives jointly whereas at Kongos four brothers have in only one case, married a second wife jointly. At Chango on the other hand, two brothers have always taken a wife in common. During our field work we came across only one case where seven brothers married two wives. In the village Rogi, some Samsher Singh's seven sons first married Chintamani. The marriage ceremony was performed by Jagdish, eldest son of Samsher Singh by *zanekang* system. After two years Samsher's second son Gangadhar eloped with the second wife (*dub-dub*). Thus the second wife became common wife of all the brothers. In this connection it may be said that Samsher Singh on the other hand, himself indulged in sororal polygyny by marrying two sisters.

In the same village six sons of Dilbar, a Rajput (Kanet)

TABLE 8

Number of Husband/Husbands per Wife and Wife/Wives per husband in the Kinnaurese Households

Number of Brothers Husbands	CHANGO			KONGOS		
	One wife No. %	Two wives No. %	Three wives No. %	One wife No. %	Two wives No. %	Three wives No. %
1	2	3	4	5	6	7
Two	24 (61.54)	—	—	13 (65.00)	—	—
Three	11 (28.21)	1 (100.00)	—	7 (35.00)	— —	—
Four	2 (5.13)	—	—	—	1 (100.00)	—
Five	2 (5.13)	—	—	—	—	—
Six	—	—	—	—	—	—
Seven	—	—	—	—	—	—
Total	39 (100.00)	1 (100.00)	—	20 (100.00)	1 (100.00)	—

(Contd,)

Number of Brother Husbands	ROGI			ALL VILLAGES		
	One wives No. %	Two wives No. %	Three wives No. %	One wie No. %	Two wie No. %	Three wives No. %
	8	9	10	11	12	13
Two	15 (68.18)	1 (25.00)	—	52 (64.20)	1 (16.67)	—
Three	3 (13.63)	1 (25.00)	1 (100.00)	21 (25.93)	2 (33.33)	1 (100.00)
Four	2 (9.09)	—	—	4 (4.94)	1 (16.67)	—
Five	1 (4.55)	1 (25.00)	—	3 (3.70)	1 (16.67)	—
Six	1 (4.55)	—	—	1 (1.23)	—	—
Seven	—	1 (25.00)	—	—	1 (16.67)	—
Total	22 (100.01)	4 (100.00)	1 (100.00)	81 (100.00)	6 (100.01)	1 (100.00)

married a common wife. The marriage was settled by negotiation. Dilbar has three more minor sons who have not married jointly with their brothers.

At Rogi Radhashyam, a Rajput (Kanet) had given marriage of his five sons by *zanekang* method. Later on his third son, Somnam fell in love with another girl, Rohini and finally married her. She became the common wife of all brothers.

There is an interesting case in Rogi village. Here three sons of Madhusudan have three wives in common. The first wife was married by negotiation but later on two wives were brought by two other brothers by *dub-dub* or *khuchis* method, who thereafter became common wives of all three brothers.

At Kongos four sons of Kishenchand were married to a girl. Later on one of the brothers married another girl by *dub-dub*, and finally both wives became common to all four brothers.

Five brothers (sons of Lendup) of a Rajput family of Change village married Sumit Dalma and she became their common wife. In the same village three brothers, Sherring, Bonchhing and Lendup who are sons of Rinchen, at first married Angmo, a Rajput girl. Later on second brother Bonchhing eloped with another girl, Rima, who also became common wife of all brothers.

Some idea about the number of brother-husbands sharing common wife/wives on the basis of 1901 census 'respecting the extent to which polyandry is practised in Bashahir' is generated from the table given in the above mentioned Gazetteer (1911 : 15).

The above table (Table 9) shows that of the total of 1240 cases majority (69.76%) of the wife/wives had two husbands. Cases where women having three life partners come next (19.11%). This condition prevails in case of all caste groups studied. In case of all caste groups women in majority of cases, are having two husband. The frequency of three husbands sharing common wife/wives have the next strength. Maximum of five husbands are reported to have common wives. It is thus seen that the trend that was prevalent at the begin-

TABLE 9

Number of Husbands having common Wife/Wives

Castes	No. of women having two Husbands		No. of women having three Husbands		No. of women having four Husbands		No. of women having five Husbands		Total	
	No.	%	No.	%	No.	%	No.	%	No.	%
1	2	3	4	5	6	7	8	9	10	11
Brahman	96	93.20	7	6.80	—	—	—	—	103	100.00
Koli	176	71.26	48	19.43	16	6.48	7	2.83	247	100.00
Jad	7	63.64	—	—	2	18.18	2	18.18	11	100.00
Kanet	521	64.80	173	21.52	68	8.46	42	5.22	804	100.00
Lohar	29	96.67	—	—	—	—	1	3.33	30	100.00
Rajput	13	100.00	—	—	—	—	—	—	13	100 00
Tarkhan	23	71.88	9	28.12	—	—	—	—	32	100.00
Total	865	69.76	237	19.11	86	6.94	52	4.19	1240	100.00

ning of this century (1901), is persisting in Kinnaur to a great extent.

As regards maximum number of brothers married a common wife, the Gazetteer of Punjab Hill States of 1910 states that the maximum of six uterine brothers, could have joint wife. In case of more than six brothers, two wives were married jointly (1911 : 15).

Differences of Age between Wi and Hu

In adelphic polyandrous and polygynandrous marriages, a wife cannot be of the same age with all her husbands and may not be junior or senior to all of them. In such marriages she may be junior to some of her husbands, could be of the same age with one of her husbands but may be senior by age with the rest of her husbands. The reason behind this is that the brother-husbands in such marriages have different ages, one senior or junior to the other. Accordingly, the wife may be junior to the eldest brother-husband, even could be junior to next brother-husbands, could be of the same age with the next husband, but could be senior to the rest of the brother-husbands. It is also seen that under such marriage system she has become the wife of a kid, even of the boy in the womb of her mother-in-law. The possibilities of the common wife (in case of polyandry only) having three husbands being junior, of the same age or senior to her husbands who are sons of the same parents have been formulated below :

(i) $Wi < Hu_1 < Hu_2 < Hu_3$
(ii) $Wi < Hu_1 < Hu_2 = Hu_3$
(iii) $Wi < Hu_1 < Hu_2 > Hu_3$
(iv) $Wi < Hu_1 = Hu_2 > Hu_3$
(v) $Wi < Hu_1 > Hu_2 > Hu_3$
(vi) $Wi = Hu_1 > Hu_2 > Hu_3$
(vii) $Wi > Hu, > Hu_2 > Hu_3$

The combinations would have been different in case the brother-husbands belong to different parents. They may belong to the,

(i) Same mother but different/fathers
(ii) Different mother/mothers but same father
(iii) Different mother/mothers and different father/fathers.

However, let us see what our data speak about the difference of age between wife/wives and husband/husbands.

In Kinnaur in case of polyandrous and polygynandrous marriages which are also adelphic, difference of age between the common wife/ wives and the brother-husbands is from no difference to a difference much over ten years. While in majority of the cases the first wife is junior to the first husband (eldest brother), she is senior to all other brother-husbands in majority cases (Table 10, 11 and 12).

In these cases where the first wife in Chango under Zone-I is junior to the first husband, she is junior to him by 0-4 years in majority of the cases (68.42 %) and in a good number of cases (21.05%) she is junior to him by 5 to 9 years. But where she is senior to her first husband, she is senior by 0-4 years in the vast majority of cases (90.00%). In 9.38% cases she is of the same age with her first husband.

In this village the first wife is junior to the second husband by 0-4 years in 50.00% cases. But she is senior to this husband by 5-9 years in 48.00% and 0-4 years in 36.00% cases. But the first wife is never junior to her third (except in one case) fourth and fifth husbands. In all these cases she is senior to her third (except one case), fourth and fifth husbands. In comparison to the age of her third husband she is senior to him in majority of the cases (53.85%) by ten years or more. In case of fourth husband she is senior to him by 5-9 years in half of the total cases while in the next 50.00% cases she is senior by 10 years or more. In case of her fifth husband she is senior by ten years or more in all cases. In a lone case the first wife is junior to her third husband by 13 years.

In Chango the second wife is also junior to her first husband in all cases and to her second husband in majority of the cases (66.67%). She is of the same age with her third husband by 50.00% cases while junior to him in rest 50.00% cases. In case of her fourth husband she is senior to him.

TABLE 10

Difference in Age between Wife and Husband in Polyandrous Households in Rogi

		Wife Junior to Husband by				Wife Senior to Husband by	
	Same age No. %	0-4 yrs. No. %	5-9 yrs. No. %	10+ yrs. No. %	Total No. %	0-4 yrs. No. %	5-9 yrs. No. %
1	2	3	4	5	6	7	8
W_1-H_1	2 6.90	15 62.50	3 12.50	6 25.00	24 100.00	3 100.00	—
W_1-H_2	1 3.57	5 55.55	4 44.44	—	9 99.99	11 61.11	6 33.33
W_1-H_3	1 8.33	—	1 100.00	—	1 100.00	3 30.00	6 60.00
W_1-H_4	—	—	—	—	—	1 25.00	2 50.00
W_1-H_5	—	—	—	—	—	—	2 100:00
W_1-H_6	—	—	—	—	—	—	—
W_2-H_1	—	—	2 100.00	—	2 100.00	—	—
W_2-H_2	1 25.00	1 33.33	2 66.67	—	3 100.00	—	—
W_2-H_3	—	3 100.00	—	—	3 100.00	—	—
W_2-H_4	1 100.00	—	—	—	—	—	—
W_2-H_5	—	—	—	—	—	1 100.00	—

	Wife Senior to husband by 10+yrs. No. %	Wife Senior to husband by Total No. %	Wife junior to husband No. %	Wife senior to husband No. %	Grant total No. %
	9	10	11	12	13
W_1-H_1	—	3 100.00	24 82.76	3 10.34	29 100.00
W_1-H_2	1 5.55	18 99.99	9 32.14	18 64,29	28 100.00
W_1-H_3	1 10.00	10 100.00	1 8.33	10 83.33	12 99.99
W_1-H_4	1 25.00	4 100.00	—	4 100 00	4 100.00
W_1-H_5	—	2 100.00	—	2 100.00	2 100.00
W_1-H_6	1 100.00	1 100.00	—	1 100.00	1 100.00
W_2-H_1	—	—	2 100.00	—	2 100.00
W_2-H_2	—	—	3 75.00	—	4 100.00
W_2-H_3	—	—	3 100.00	—	3 100.00
W_2-H_4	—	—	—	—	1 100.00
W_2-H_5	—	1 100.00	—	1 100.00	1 100.00

TABLE 11

Difference in Age between Wife and Husband in Polyandrous Households in Kongos

	Same age No. %	Wife junior to husband by 0-4 yrs. No. %	5-9 yrs. No. %	10+ yrs. No. %	Total No. %	Wife senior to husband by 0-4 yrs. No. %	5-9 yrs. No. %
1	2	3	4	5	6	7	8
W_1-H_1	1 6.25	9 60.00	5 33.33	1 6.67	15 100.00	—	—
W_1-H_2	3 14.29	4 80.00	1 20.00	—	5 100.00	5 38.46	6 46.15
W_1-H_3	—	—	—	—	—	2 40.00	3 60.00
W_1-H_4	—	—	—	—	—	1 50.00	—
W_2-P	1 12.50	1 16.67	4 66.67	1 16.67	6 100.00	1 100 00	—
W_2-H_2	—	4 100.00	—	—	4 100.00	—	—
W_2-H_3	—	—	1 100.00	—	1 100.00	—	—
W_3-H_1	—	2 100.00	—	—	2 100.00	—	—
W_3-H_2	—	—	—	—	—	2 100.00	—
W_3-H_3	—		—	—	—	1 100.00	—
W_4-H_1	—	—	—	—	—	—	—

	Wife senior to Husband by		Wife junior to Husband	Wife senior to Husband	Grant total
	10+ yrs. No. %	Total No. %	No. %	No. %	No. %
	9	10	11	12	13
W_1-H_1	—	—	15 93.75	—	16 100.00
W_1-H_2	2 15.38	13 99.99	5 23.81	13 61.00	21 100.00
W_1-H_3	—	5 100.00	—	5 100.00	5 100.00
W_1-H_4	1 50.00	2 100.00	—	2 100.00	2 100.00
W_2-H_1	—	1 100.00	6 75.00	1 12.50	8 100.00
W_2-H_2	—	—	4 100.00	—	4 100.00
W_2-H_3	—	–	1 100.00	—	1 100.00
W_3-H_1	—	—	2 100.00	—	2 100.00
W_3-H_2	—	2 100.00	—	2 100.00	2 100.00
W_3-H_3	—	1 100.00	–	1 100.00	1 100.00
W_4-H_1	1 100.00	1 100.00	—	1 100.00	1 100.00

TABLE 12

Difference in Age between Wife and Husband in Polyandrous Households in Chango

		Wife Junior to husband by				Wife senior to husband by	
	Same age	0-4 yrs.	5-9 yrs.	10+ yrs.	Total	0-4 yrs.	5-9 yrs.
	No. %	No. %	No. %	No. %	No. %	No. %	No. %
1	2	3	4	5	6	7	8
W_1-H_1	3 9.38	13 68.42	4 21.05	2 10.53	19 100.00	9 90.00	1 10.00
W_1-H_2	2 6.45	2 50.00	1 25.00	1 25.00	4 100.00	9 36.00	12 48.00
W_1-H_3	—	—	—	1 100.00	1 100.00	—	6 46.15
W_1-H_4	—	—	—	—	—	—	2 50.00
W_1-H_5	—	—	—	—	—	—	—
W_2-H_1	—	2 33.33	2 33.33	2 33.33	6 99.99	—	—
W_2-H_2	—	2 50.00	2 50.00	—	4 100.00	2 100.00	—
W_2-H_3	1 50.00	1 100.00	—	—	1 100.00	—	—
W_2-H_4	—	—	—	—	—	1 100.00	—

	Wife senior to husband by 10+ yrs. No. %	Wife senior to husband by Total No. %	Wife junior to husband No. %	Wife senior to husband No. %	Grant total No. %
	9	10	11	12	13
W_1-H_1	—	10	19	10	32
		100.00	59.37	31.25	100.00
W_1-H_2	4	25	4	25	31
	16.00	100.00	12.90	80.65	100.00
W_1-H_3	7	13	1	13	14
	53.85	100.00	7.14	92.86	100.00
W_1-H_4	2	4	—	4	4
	50.00	100.00		100.00	100.00
W_1-H_5	2	2	—	2	2
	100.00	100.00		100.00	100.00
W_2-H_1	—	—	6	—	6
			100.00		100.00
W_2-H_2	—	2	4	2	6
		100.00	66.67	33.33	100.00
W_2-H_3	—	—	1	—	2
			50.00		100.00
W_2-H_4	—	1	—	1	1
		100.00		100.00	100.00

The trend is almost similar in case of the people of Kongos under Zone-II. Here the first wife in polyandrous and polygynandrous marriages, is in most cases (93.75%) junior to the first husband. But she is definitely senior to her second, third and fourth husbands in most of the cases. In the majority of the cases (60.00%) the first wife is junior to the first husband by 0 to 4 years ; but only in 23.81% cases she is junior to her second husband, and in these cases she is junior to him by 0 to 4 years in majority of the cases (80.00%). But where she is senior to her second husband, she is senior by 5 to 9 years in a highest number of cases (46.15%). She is senior to him by 0 to 4 years in 38.46% cases. In a good number of cases (14.29%) she is of the same age with her second husband. In case of her third husband she is senior to him by 5 to 9 years in 60.00% cases and by 0 to 4 years in rest 40.00% cases. But in equal number of cases she is senior to her fourth husband by 0 to 4 and 10 years or more respectively.

The second wife is always junior to her first, second and third husbands except in one case (12.50%) where she is senior to her first husband and of the same age in equal number of cases. She is junior to her first and third husbands by 5 to 9 years in majority of the cases ; but in case of second husband she is junior by 0 to 4 years in cent percent cases. In a lone case she is senior to her first husband by 0 to 4 years.

The third wife is always junior to her first husband but also senior to her second and third husbands in all cases. And in all cases whether she is junior or senior to her husbands, she is junior or senior by 0 to 4 years.

At Rogi under Zone-III the condition agrees with that prevalent in other two villages. Here also the first wife is in most of the cases (82.76%) junior to her first husband. But in majority of the cases she is senior to her second, third, fourth, fifth and sixth husbands ; particularly in cases of fourth, fifth and sixth husbands she is senior to them in cent percent cases. Only in a few cases she is of the same age with her first, second or third husband. Where first wife is junior to first husband, she is junior by 0 to 4 years in majority of the cases (62.50%). And in all cases where she is senior to him, she is also senior by 0 to 4 years. But when the difference of age between the first wife and her second husband is calculated it is seen that in majority of the cases (61.11%) she is senior by 0 to 4 years. She is senior by 5 to 9 years from her third, fourth and fifth husbands in majority of the cases. And in cent percent cases she is senior to her sixth husband by over ten years.

Here in the village Rogi the second wife is found to be junior to her second and third husbands while in majority of the cases (66.67%) she is junior to her second husband by 5 to 9 years, in cent percent cases she is junior to her third husband by 0 to 4 years. But she is senior to her fifth husband by 0 to 4 years only.

It is thus a general trend in the polyandrous households in Kinnaur that the first wife is in most of the cases junior to her first husband but senior to her other husbands. Again the second wife is junior to all her husbands in most of the cases. The difference of age in most of the cases is between 1 to 4 years and in some cases between 5 to 9 years. Only in a few cases the difference is 10 years or more.

Conflict and Break up of the Polyandrous Household

In the Kinnaurese polyandrous households all brothers are supposed to have chance to share the common wife, yet it is seen that the eldest brother enjoys more privileges than other brothers. All brothers know it and admit it ; it is not that they do not get jealous sometimes. But in most of the cases they agree to it. Usually the eldest brother goes to bring the bride from the latter's household. Further, eldest brother after the death of the father, inherits the property. He stays in the house throughout the year to look after the household and thus naturally gets maximum chance to satisfy his sexual urge over his wife. Moreover, being the head of the household, he allots the duties to his brothers and naturally he allots such duties so that other adult brothers remain away from the house for a considerable length of time. Actually in the polyandrous union the rights and the privileges of different brother-husbands are well defined. Again when the eldest brother dies the next elder brother takes over the charge of the head of the household and enjoys same rights and privileges as enjoyed by his deceased eldest brother. And this process is continued till the last brother takes over the charge.

It is not that the brothers do not develop conflict between them over the common wife (sometimes, severe conflicts lead to the break up of the polyandrous households in Kinnaur). Sometimes the common wife, due to humanly urge, shows more interest to a particular brother. This often leads to conflicts among the brothers and ultimately unless the wife restrains herself, this conflict separates the brothers. It is also seen that inspite of the polyandrous marriage, the eldest brother, or any other brother claims absolute right over the common wife and disallows other brothers from enjoying her. This also has a fatal result leading to the break up of the polyandrous household.

In Kinnaur many of the households which are nuclear now, were polyandrous and polygynandrous earlier. In some cases these polyandrous households broke up into nuclear households because of the conflict among brothers for the common wife. Particularly during the present decades the educated and somewhat modernized Kinnaurese youths desire for monogamy and want to have their own wife. They sometimes break up the polyandrous unit and form nuclear unit of their own. In olden days also when the younger brothers used to return home from trade or from pasture after a long absence from the core household, they were eager to get the company of their common wife. At that time if the eldest brother did not get liberal, he had to invite conflict.

Of course at present for break up of the polyandrous and polygynandrous households there are some other reasons too. Now many young persons go to different cities of India for higher education. Many of them after completing education, prefer to have their own wife and own households, and so ultimately marry separately. Similarly, on getting service outside Kinnaur, a polyandrous Kinnaurese again marries separately, thus breaking the core polyandrous household. Some members of the polyandrous household are also found to live outside Kinnaur, preferably in some non-polyandrous areas, in order to get rid of polyandry, thus breaking up of the core polyandrous household. The difference in age between the younger brother-husband and the common wife also sometimes leads to the break up of the polyandrous households of Kinnaur. The younger-brother husband considering himself incompatible in sex game with the much elderly common wife, seeks to have his own wife, and finally settles up in separate establishment with his own wife. The present day cash and market economy is also another reason for the break up of the polyandrous household. In many cases it is seen that after accumulating some cash by rendering labour in developmental projects or by business, a Kinnaurese wants to have his own wife and declines to share the common wife or to allow his wife to be shared by his brothers.

Thus it is seen that in the present day Kinnaur the polyandrous households are gradually breaking up for many reasons.

Decline of Polyandry in Kinnaur : Reasons

As already stated polyandry in Kinnaur as it is everywhere in India, is declining. Various factors are responsible for this. Modern education, cash and market economy, better communication and transport system, new legislation, immigration of the non-polyandrous people from the plains and lower hills etc. are the factors responsible for the decline of this type of marriage. The present-day younger generation particularly the educated ones, does not favour polyandry. Rather they feel ashamed of this system. They want to discard it. Besides education and other factors, another important reason is the influence of the political parties. Due to the influence of the at least one of the political parties in Kinnaur, the younger generation is openly expressing their disliking for polyandry. The immigrant people also do not like it ; and this has got impact on the people of Kinnaur.

As a result of their liking for monogamy, the polyandry in Kinnaur is fast disappearing. Their liking for monogamy developed not only for the various causes as mentioned above, but also for their contact with the people from non-polyandrous societies, particularly from plains and lower hills who have come to this high Himalayan district for varied purposes. A large number of Government officials, teachers, businessmen, members of the military and para-military organisations, labourers and others, who are the members non-polyandrous monogamous societies, have come to Kinnaur. They may have their disliking for this custom which they often express openly. During the field work the senior author had seen how non-polyandrous people from plains and lower hills, rediculed the Kinnaurese for their polyandry and also condemned this practice. Obviously the local people get worried and ashamed of stating that they practise it. And gradually they start discarding the system. Moreover when the young people go to different cities and towns for education and/or service or business or for some other purposes, they too become victims of the redicules of the over-whelming non-polyandrous people with whom they come in contact. Gopal Surag of a village who was a student of B.Sc. (Agriculture), intimated us that he would never rocognise her elder brother's wife who was much elder than him, as also his wife. He had recognised her as his *bhabi* i.e., sister-in-law (elder brother's wife). He said that he would marry separately and his wife would be his wife only and would never be the wife of his elder brother. The same opinion was expressed by a number of the members of the *Tarun Kinnaur*—a youth organization in Kinnaur. Many of the political party members also decried against polyandry. When the senior author took interview of some businessmen and also teachers who came from outside Kinnaur where there was no polyandry, they clearly stated that polyandry undoubtedly a 'dirty' custom without knowing the relevance of polyandry in the high altitude areas.

Cash and market economy is no doubt another important factor responsible for the decline and degeneration of certain customary cultural traits. Polyandry is one of such unfortunate traits. With the opening of road communication and mechanised transport, new legislation and education, immigration and closure of the trade with Tibet, the market economy developed in Kinnaur. Cash economy has also replaced the traditional barter system. These have made Kinnaurese to become self centred and the concept of 'individual family' or 'own family' has been infused in them. Many people became eager to have their own families. Identically the service holders also started liking to have their 'own families' with 'own wife' and 'own children' instead of 'common wife' and 'common children.'

Concluding Remark : Polyandry in Kinnaur : Persistence and Change

From the above analysis it is seen that polyandry which was the traditional institution of Kinnaur, has perpetuated to the contemporary Kinnaurese society. Even in these days too the people of Kinnaur practise polyandry to a considerable extent, though no doubt it is shrinking at a very fast rate. This cultural trait perpetuated because it got the encouragement from the erstwhile Bushahar State authority. The encouragement from the King definitely boosted the desire of the Kinnaurese to remain united under the polyandrous hold with a common wife for all brothers. This system continued functioning in the Kinnaurese society for a pretty long time as the Kinnaurese accrued definite gain out of it. It helped them not only to remain united in the polyandrous household with the common wife but also to save fragmentation of property, to yield better crop, to have a suitable division of labour, to cope in a better way with the barter system developed in the peculiar Himalayan ecology and so on. But this century old system is gradually loosing its grip with the advent of the various modern forces. With the opening of the district to easy communication system when the Kinnaurese started coming in contact with the non-polyandrous people from outside Kinnaur more and more, the changes in their culture occurred, and the system of polyandry started decaying. The process of gradual degeneration of polyandry in Kinnaur has been quickened because of the various forces in the post-independence are acted on these areas—the forces like modernization, execution of various development and constructional projects, modern education, modern Land Reform Acts, modern communication, cash and market economy etc. have enticed the people of Kinnaur, like many other Himalayan polyandrous societies, to discard this unique institution. Thus the century old polyandry in this high Himalayan society has been left at deaths' door.

REFERENCES

Bajpai, S.C. 1981 *Kinnaur in the Himalayas*, Concept Publishing Co., New Delhi.

Berreman, Gerald, D. 1962a Pahari Polyandry : A Comparison, *American Anthropologist*, vol. 64.

———1962b Caste and Economy in the Himalayas, *Economic Development & Culture Change*, vol. 10.

———1972 *The Hindus of the Himalayas : Ethnography and Change*, Univ. of California Press, Berkeley.

———1975 Himalayan Polyandry and the Domestic Cycle, *American Ethnologist*, vol 2.

Bhatt, G.S. 1978 from Caste Structure to Tribe : The Case of Jaunsar Bawar, *The Eastern Anthropologist*, vol. 31.

———1980 Constrains of being Polyandrous Tribe : The case of Jaunsar Bawar, in *Family, Marriage and Social Change on the Indian Frings*, Ed. S.M. Dubey & others, Cosmo Publications, Delhi.

———1981 Polyandry in Western Himalayas : Some Notes & Observations in *Jn. Social Research* vol-XXIV No. 11 Special Number on Himalayan Studies.

Biswas, P.C. 1963 Polyandry among the Hill Tribes of Jaunsar Bawar, *Vanyajati*, vol. I, No. 1.

Briffault, R. 1927 The *Mothers*, 3 vols, George Allen & Unwin Ltd. London.

Chandra, R. 1973 Types and Forms of marriage in a Kinnaur Village, *Man in India*, vol. 53, No. 2.

———1975 Report on the project : Polyandry in a Himalayan Village, *Bull An S. I.* vol-XXIV No. 384.

Chib, S.S. 1984 *Caste, Culture & Economy of Kanauras of the Trans-Himalayas*, Ess Ess Publications, New Delhi.

Crooke, J.H. 1987 Polyandry in Ladakh in *Polyandry in India* Ed. M.K. Raha & P.C. Coomar.

Crooke, W. 1896 *The Tribes and Castes of N.W.F.P. and Oudh*, vol. III Superintendent, Govt. Printing, Calcutta.

Dalton, E.T. 1872 *Descriptive Ethnology of Bengal*, Calcutta.

Das, S.C. 1893 The Marriage Customs of Tibet, *Jn. of Asiatic Society of Bengal*, vol-LXII, pt. II.

———1902 *Tibetan-English Dictionary*, Calcutta.

———1904 *A Journey to Lhasa and Central Tibet*, John Murry, London.

Das Gupta, B.K. 1987 A Note on Polyandry among the Gallong : An Analytical Appraisal in *Polyandry in India* Ed : M.K. Raha & P.C. Coomar.

Das Gupta, H.C. 1921 A Short Note on Polyandry in the Jubbal State (Simla), *Indian Antiquity*, vol. 50.

Dhasmana, M.M. 1979 *The Ramos of Arunachal : A Socio-Cultural Study*. Concept Publishing Co., New Delhi.

Earle, A 1901 Polyandry in Sikkim and Tibet, *Census of India*, 1901 Appendix-V.

Francke, A.H., Rev 1907 *A History of Western Tibet*, London.

Frazer, J.B. 1920 *Journal of a Tour Through Part of the Snow Ranges of the Himalaya Mountains and to the sources of Jamuna and Ganges*, Londan.

Ghosal, S. 1987 Polyandry among the Lepchas : A Dead or Dying Institution ? in *Polyandry in India* Ed. M.K. Raha & P.C. Coomar.

Ghosh, T.K. 1987 Persistence of Lahaul Polyandry and Decline in *Polyandry in India* Ed. M.K. Raha & P.C. Coomar.

Goldstein, M.C. 1978 Pahari and Tibetan Polyandry Revisited, *Ethnology* vol-XVII No. 3.

Government of Punjab 1906 *Punjab District Gazetteer, Simla District*, 1904 Lahore.

———1911 *Punjab States Gazetteer*, vol. VIII, Simla Hill States 1910, Lahore.

Gover, G. 1938 *Himalayan Village*, Michael Joseph, London.

Hershman, P. 1981 *Punjabi Kinship and Marriage*, Hindustan Publishing Corp. (India) Delhi.

Jain S.C. 1948 Some Features of Fraternal Polyandry in Jaunsar Bawar, *Eastern Anthropologist*, vol-I.

Joshi, L.D. 1929 *The Khasa Family Law in the Himalayan Districts of the United Provinces of India*. The Supdt. Govt. Press Allahabad.

Kirkpatrick, C.S. 1878 Polyandry in the Punjab, *The Indian Antiquary* vol. 7.

Kotturam, G. 1983 *The Himalayan Gateway : History and Culture of Sikkim*, Sterling Publishers Private Limited, New Delhi.

Lal, P.N. & Das Gupta B.K. 1979 *The Lower Siang People*, Memoir no. 50, Anthropological Survey of India, Calcutta.

Lloyd, W. & Gerard, A. 1846 *Narrative of the Journey from Counpore to Boorendo Pass in Himalaya Mountains*, vols. I & II, London.

Majumdar, D.N. 1944 *The Fortunes of Primitive Tribes*. Universal Publishers, Lucknow.

———1955 Family and Marriage in a Polyandrous Village. *The Eastern Anthropologist*, vol. 8 No. 3.

———1963 *Himalayan Polyandry*, Asia Publishing House, Bombay.

Mamgain, M.D. 1971 *Himachal Pradesh District Gazetteer Kinnaur*, Govt. of Himachal Pradesh, Simla.

Mann, R.S. 1978 Ladakhi Polyandry Reinterpreted, *Indian Anthropologist*, vol. 8 No. 1.

Mills, J.P. 1922 *The Lhota Nagas*, London.

Nag, N.G. 1960 Family and Marriage in Lahaul Valley. *The Eastern Anthropologist*. vol-XIII No. 4.

Nakane, Chie 1966 A plural Society in Sikkim—A Study of the Inter relations of Lepchas, Bhotias and Nepalis in *Caste & Kin in Nepal*,

India & Ceylon Ed. C. von Furer-Haimendorf, Asia Publishing House, Bombay.

Nandi, S.B. 1977 Status of Women in Polyandrous Society, *Man in India*, vol. 57 No. 2.

Nagi, T.S. 1969 *Himachal Pradesh District Gazetteers, Sirmur*, Govt. of Himachal Pradesh.

Parmar, Y.S. 1975 *Polyandry in the Himalayas*, Vikas Publishing House, Delhi.

Pettigreed, J. 1975 *Robber Nobleman : A Study of the Political system of the Sikh Jats*, Routledge & Kogan Paul, London.

Prince Peter HRH 1955 Polyandry and Kinship Group, *Man*, vol. 55.

———1963 *A Study of Polyandry*, Mouton & Co. The Hague.

Raha, M.K. 1972 Society and Religion in Kinnaur (Unpublished article presented in the workshop on the Himalayan Border Area Studies.

———1974 The Highlanders of the Western and Central Himalayas, *Vanyajati* vol XXII No. 3.

———1975 Religion and Politics in Kinnaur (Unpublished article).

———1976 Changing Economy in a Himalayan Society (Paper presented in the Seminar on Tribal Economy in India Unpublished).

———1978 Stratification and Religion in a Himalayan Society, in *Himalayan Anthropology* Ed. James F. Fisher, Mouton & Co., The Hague.

———1981 Urgent Anthropology in the Himalayas in *Jr. Social Research* Sp. number on the Himalayan Studies, vol. XXIV No. 11. Also in the *Transaction of the Centre for Himalayan Studies*, Univ. of Ranchi.

——1983 Subsistence Economy, Environmental involvement and Survival Strategies in a High Himalayan Society (Unpublished paper presented in the Seminar on Cultural Ecology and Human Adaptation).

———1984 Education in Kinnaur (Unpublished Report).

———1987 The Khandan System among the Kinnaura of the Western Himalayas in *The Himalayan Heritage* Ed. M.K. Raha, Gian Publishing House, Delhi.

———(n.d.) Economic Strategies, Religious Dualism and Change in Diverse Cultural and Ecological Setting : A Case from the Western Himalayas in *The Himalayas and the Himalayans*. Ed. M.K. Raha (in press).

———(n.d.) Environmental Diversities and Polyvalent Economy in the Western Himalayas (Paper presented in the Seminar on Environmental Anthropology).

Raha, M.K. & S.N. Mahata 1975 The Kinnaurese of the Himalays (Unpublished report).

———1985 *The Kinnaurese of the Himalayas* Memoir no. 63, Anthropological Survey of India, Calcutta.

Raha, M.K., S.N. Mahato & R.S. Negi 1976 The Kinnaurese Kinship System : A Terminological Analysis, *Bull. Anthropological Survey of India*, vol. XXV No. 3 & 4.

Raha, M.K., J.C. Das & R.S. Negi 1978 Tribal Women of the Western and Central Himalayas in *Tribal Women in India*, Indian Anthropological Society, Calcutta.

Raha, M.K., J.C. Das & S.C. Mondal 1980 Village structure in Kinnaur, *Journal of Social Research*, vol-23, No-1.

Saksena, R.N. 1958 *Social Economy of Polyandrous People*, Agra University House, Bombay.

Sarkar, N. 1973 The So-called Polyandry among the Gallongs, *Man in India*, vol. 53 No. 2.

Sharma, D.D. 1987 Kinship Organisation of the Polyandrous Lahaula in *The Himalayan Heritage*, Ed. : M.K. Raha, Gian Publishing House, Delhi.

Singh, K.P. 1987 Polyandry among the Jat Sikhs of Punjab in *Polyandry in India*, Ed. M.K. Raha & P.C. Coomar.

Sishaudhia, V.K. 1987 Polyandry in a Cis-Himalayan Community in *Polyandry in India*, Ed. M.K. Raha & P.C. Coomar.

Srivastava, L.R.N. 1962 *The Gellongs*, NEFA Secretariat, Shillong.

Stocks, C.D.B. 1975 *Sikkim Customs and Folk-lore*, Cosmo Publications, Delhi.

Stulpnagel, C.R. 1878 Polyandry in the Himalayas, *India Evangedical Review*, vol. 5, *Indian Antiquary*. vol. 7.

Topdan, N. 1979 Polyandry : A Form of Marriage in Lahaul, *Himalaya : Man & Nature*, vol. 3, No. 1.

Thornton, E. 1862 *A Gazetteer of the Territories under the Government of the East India Company*, London.

Walton, H.G. 1911 *Dehra Dun : A Gazetteer* (District Gazetteer of the United Provinces of Agra & Oudh, vol-1) Govt. Press, Allahabad.

Westermarck, E. 1921 *The History of Human Marriage*, London.

Wilson, A. 1876 *Abode of Show*, Edinburgh.

4

POLYANDRY IN THE NORTH-WESTERN HIMALAYAS : SOME CHANGING TRENDS

RAMESH CHANDRA

Polyandry has drawn attention of anthropologists to understand it from various viewpoints since not very long. It is only for about one and a half century that it became a topic for research among those having concern for social institutions like that of marriage. McLennan (1896), Herbert Spencer (1904) and Briffault (1927) have dealt with polyandry directly or by alluding it with reference to the institution of marriage. Some specific field studies concentrating on the problem of polyandry began perhaps with elaborate study of the Toda done by Rivers (1906). And in the Himalayan area, studies mentioning about polyandry, in somewhat lucid manner, could be regarded that of Fraizer (1820), Gerard (1846) and Wilson (1870) and some others. However, Westermark in his three volume on *History of Human Marriage* has discussed about polyandry at length taking sample across the world, talking much of Indian polyandry—polyandry of the south among the Nairs of Malabar and Tibetan polyandry—along with sporadic cases of north-western Himalayan societies. Intensive studies on polyandry in the north-western Himalayas are made available by Majumdar (1940;1968), Saxena (1955), Prince Peter (1963), Chandra (1975a ; 1978) and others.

Polyandry as understood in anthropological literature is the custom or practice 'by which a woman is permitted to have more than one husband at the same time' or 'as the system under which a woman is married to several men at the same time' (*Notes and Queries on Anthropology*, 1953 : 113 ; *Encyclopaedia Britanica*, 1969 : 194). Often to recognise polyandry emphasis is laid on 'co-existant union of a woman with two or more men'. It generally signifies the plurality of husbands to a woman. Some scholars believe that in actuality

> Polygyny is the preferred male strategy in man, polyandry is adopted, according to socio-biologist, as a last resort in severe ecological circumstances or at the bottom of stratified hypergamous systems with polygyny prevailing at the top (Hiatt, 1980).

Further, might be after following evolutionary norms, polyandry is divided into : (1) Fraternal or adelphic polyandry and (2) non-fraternal polyandry basing on the fact if woman's husbands are brothers or different unrelated men respectively. While talking of group marriage Briffault viewed the stage of fraternal polyandry to be 'the complement of the rule of sororal polygyny' (in Taylor, 1959 : 129).

Polyandry, on the world's face, is rather a rare practice, as perhaps it is less than 1% societies of Murdock's world ethnographic sample of 565 societies that follow polyandry of one kind or the other (cf. Hiatt, 1980). It is said to have its existence in Africa, America, Asia and Australia among various tribes. Some of them like the Avanoes and Maypurese of Orinico, Zapro of Equador, Eskimos of Green land, Cree Indians, Chuckchees, Gylaks and the Ainus of Japan are the examples. The Shoshoni and the Pivisto Indians have also been alluded to be polyandrous by Stewart (1936) and Park (1937) respectively. In Asia Tibet, India and Sri Lanka (erstwhile Ceylone) are the main pockets for polyandry to have flourished. Some of the Indian societies living in the lofty Himalayan range viz. the Khasas of Jaunsar Bawar, Dehra Dun, the Sirmurese, Kinners, Lahulians, Spitians—all in north-western Himalayas—and some in north-eastern Himalayas like the

Gellong and some others are the known polyandrous people. Besides a few more viz. the Toda and the Kota of Nilgiris, Tamilnadu and some groups living in Kerala, of whom Nayars are well known for having polyandry atleast until recent past, have been listed as polyandrous societies in India (Rivers, 1906; Aiyappan, 1932; Majumdar, 1962; Prince Peter, 1963; Chandra, 1974, 1979).

For Indian polyandry Majumdar divided it into two (1) Polyandry of the north based on Patriarchy, patriliny and patrilocal characteristics and (2) Polyandry of the south where he alluded polyandrous groups of Malabar casst of Kerala—which has bearing on matriarchy, matrilocal and matrilineal features. The north-western Himalayan societies are fraternal polyandrous where 'husband unit' is composed of brothers. Fraternal polyandry and hills seem to have some interdependent relationship so far the distribution pattern of the former is concerned. All such societies having fraternal polyandry e.g. the Sirmurese, Kinners, Khasas, Lahulians, Spitians and even the Toda in Nilgiris, all of them dwell at height above 1500 metres in altitude. The polyandry got such an imminent place in these societies that for long it could achieve the status of an institution or at least a derivative of the institution of marriage. It projects a specific environment, geo-economic and ecological perspective of the area where it is practised by the inhabitants. Or vis-a-vis most of the north-western Himalayan societies have taken polyandry as a countervail to the environmental, geo-economic and ecological conditions prevailing in the area of their habitation for their survival and perpetuity.

The present paper is based on my field research conducted in two districts of Himachal Pradesh mainly, Kinnaur and Sirmur, for four years (1970-74). Kinnaur is a high altitude area situated in the north-east direction while Sirmur is located in the south and south-west direction in the map of Himachal Pradesh. Kinnaur is in interior of western Himalayas whereas Sirmur is on the foot hills; however practice of polyandry in both the districts is in area above 1500 metres in height. As such the polyandrous area of the two districts resembles in many respects viz. their ecology, economy and socio-religious set up, mountainous region, housing pattern, material culture and economic life. Small landholdings varying from low lands to high slopes, hard agricultural conditions, domestication of milch animals, sheep rearing etc. are also some common points for these two regions. Some of the ethnic group are common to both districts. Kinnaur is a scheduled area where inhabit five ethnic groups viz. the Rajput (Kanet), Koli, Badhi, Lohar and the Nangalu. The Rajput (Kanet) and the Koli dwell in all the villages of Kinnaur while the latter three ethnic groups are found only in some villages in central and western part of the district. Putting all these five ethnic groups together Kinnaur forms scheduled tribe (the Kanet) and the scheduled castes (rest all the four ethnic groups); which are often alluded as godly tribe. The Kinners have faith in two religions the Hinduism and Buddhism. Hinduism has its domain in western and central part (partially) while in entire eastern Kinnaur people profess their faith in Buddhism. However, all the people practise fraternal polyandry irrespective of their religion.

In general Kinners have mixed economy. They practise agriculture, tend domestic animals and have sheep rearing. Until recently they had trade links with Tibet which has ceased for the last score of years. Demographically speaking Kinners are not very large population. According to Census 1971, there are some 49673 people with sex ratio of 89 females per hundred males. Incidentally in the villages of study (some three villages were studied intensively) they have shown an equal ratio between the sexes (Chandra, 1978).

Sirmur as described is situated in outer range of the north-western Himalayas at a comparatively lower height. However, the polyandrous zone falls only in the area above 1500 hundred metres in altitude thus having many of the ecological, economic and socio-cultural features common as compared to Kinnaur. In Sirmur, polyandry is practised in Trans-Giri tract of Renuka tahsil and in Shillai area of Paonta tahsil. In these polyandrous areas ethnic groups inhabiting are the Kanet, Brahmin, Koli, Lohar and the Dom besides some smaller groups like Sunar and Vaisya (cf Chandra, 1981b : 205). Although the Kanet who are scheduled tribe in Kinnaur, do not enjoy the same status in Sirmur as they have a caste status and not the tribe status. However, the Koli have been scheduled as caste in both places. In general, both the Sirmurese and Kinnars present some similarity at the regional level in their cultural matrix.

Since our discussion centres round the practice of polyandry, I will refer and allude the material from both the areas of research from that viewpoint only. I propose to deal with the problem in the manner that I demonstrate, basing on the literature available, polyandry in the classic form, rise and form of polyandry, causes held responsible for polyandry ; and after I have done all this, I shall present the changing scene, i.e., emerging trends in polyandry, if any. While presenting my viewpoint, based on field data, I shall try to give some clue about the future of polyandry as well under the prevailing circumstances. Before we further any argument, it is desirable to bear in mind the concept of polyandry in terms of plurality of husbands who are brothers partaking in marriage ceremonies and rituals as well. More so idea of *ipso facto* and *de jure* is also to be kept alive as it promotes the idea of polyandry and helps men to share the common wife.

The north-western Himalayan societies consider polyandry as the normative form of marriage to be followed by their members. As the tradition holds it polyandrous form of marriage is the societal profile and at least once (first time) sons should be given marriage following polyandrous form. In the classic form of polyandry prevalent in the north-western Himalayas, husbands are necessarily related as uterine brothers. Moreover, often the norm is relaxed in case of half brothers (sons born of at least one common parent, in most of the cases mother). Ideally speaking, sons born to a set of parents, irrespective of their mode of alliance, are included in polyandry. Above all, it is an economic corporate group in a particular generation which is recognised as polyandrous unit rather than any other criteria being attributed as who would constitute the fraternal polyandrous unit and under what circumstances ? The case of Kinners is little different than the Sirmurese and the Jaunsaris who often relax to the extent of allowing their cousins as well to join the polyandry (Chandra, 1975a ; Saxena, 1955). The Ladakhi polyandry and the Tibetan polyandry are also said to have varied forms of relaxation in the classic form as allowing an outsider in the fraternal polyandrous union in

Ladakh (Drew, 1877) and sharing the common wife by two different generations viz. uncle-nephew and father-son sharing same wife (Prince Peter, 1963 : 476) are known cases. The Todas also have no rigid rule of fraternal polyandry as a wife may be shared by men who may not belong to same fraternity (Rivers, 1906). The Kinners and Sirmurese consider fraternal polyandry as the ideal form of marriage. However, much variation in marriage form is observed in these societies and different stages and forms of polyandry are practised by these people. A detailed discussion about these would follow little later after a mention about the polyandry in the classic form is made.

Polyandry in Classic form

In India that polyandry is supposed to have once been a trait of Brahminic culture is available from classic instance of Draupadi having the five Pandavas (of Mahabharata fame) as her husbands. Also, some allusions regarding polyandry made in the vedic mythology are available. However, instance of Draupadi sharing five brothers as husbands and thus enjoying plurality of husbands has been more often than not questioned as the whole incidence occurred in a peculiar circumstances of Pandavas mother Kunti having said to divide the 'alms' they had brought, among themselves, without knowing what alms they (sons) referred to. But after seeing the 'alm' in form of a woman-Draupadi, Kunti was taken aback (cf. Kapadia, 1955; 52-63). While justifying the marriage of Draupadi with five Pandavas Rishi Vyasa tried to show five Pandavas to be five Indras, who because of the curse of Lord Siva for some of their mischiefs, were born on the earth as men ; and Draupadi is goddess Sri or Laxmi who took birth in form of woman and married those five Indras (born as Pandavas) Udhishthira, eldest of the Pandava brothers, also upheld this marriage and cited cases of Jatila marrying with seven *rishis* and of Varksi who married ten brothers in support of righteousness of the instance of five brothers marrying Draupadi. Further

> "It is elsewhere said that Narada advised the Pandavas to accept Draupadi as the legal wife of all and to prevent

dissension among the brothers. He strengthened argument by quoting the narrative of two demon brothers, Sunda and Upsunda of yore, who had fought for a woman and had died." (Kapadia, 1984 : 54).

This leads to think that even in earlier times in vedic ages polyandry was not heard of. Nevertheless, it is also disputable that whether polyandry had any place during the Brahmanic traditions as Panchal king, Druapada is said to have protested against the polyandry. Some Indologists even do not consider Pandavas to be of Aryan stalk. In Rigveda some astray references do reveal some significant relationship between the women and her husband's brothers ; at least this was not unknown to vedic Aryans. However, having liberal relations even based on intimacy for a woman with her husband's brothers or as incited in Rigveda' as a widow invites her brother-in-law to her bed do not clearly give any concrete support to the clue that polyandry was societal practice in that period; as these happen to be cases of occurrances only rarely, and then do not befit the framework of polyandry as understood by the social scientists as 'practice of a woman having more than one husband simultaneously and not in succession'. For most of the fraternal polyandrous societies instance of 'Pandavas sharing Draupadi' works as source to which they can trace the origin of their practice of polyandry. North-western Himalayan societies also believe in this and upheld the Pandavas as the source for their being polyandrous. In Kinnaur, some relics like fort at Morang and *bhairav ka talab* in village Kothi support the view that Pandavas had lived in this area during their shelter in secrecy. In "Jaunsar-Bewar among the Khasas polyandry has been reinforced by the mythology of Pandavas, from whom the Khasas trace their origin" (Majumdar, 1962 : 77). Among the Sirumese also citation of Draupadi having being shared by five Pandava brothers in common, thus giving rise to the practice of polyandry is commonly known. Besides, another evidence is seen in their religious pursuits. They held Pandavas in veneration and

"the reminiscence of this is seen among the people in terms of *shatha* and *pasha* systems according to which two groups of people (usually Rajput Kanet and Brahmin at *bhoj* level) cannot live in the same village as each of the group considers itself to belong to either Pandavas or Kauravas who had some differences among themselves. The *shatha* stands for the Kauravas and the *pasha* for the Pandavas". (Chandra, 1975a : 87).

Rise of Polyandry

There are different types of marriage followed by the people in north-western Himalayas—each giving rise to a distinct form of marriage. Though different terms are used in different areas yet basically they refer mainly to five forms of marriage. In Kinnaur *zanakaong* or *zanthung* or even *phaglin* type of marriage gives rise to polyandrous form of marriages as they are traditionally upheld types giving full sanctity and legality to polyandrous form. A common term *mashtarka shaadi* is also often used to devote such form. *Dubdub*, *hazri*, *kuiya* or *reja* form of marriage usually give rise to poly-monogamy, monogamy and rarely polygyny. While alluding these types, it is also kept in mind that these are only vague categories as under special circumstances these may not provide satisfactory answer to already set notion about them. Illustration in this regard will follow little later while each type of marriages is dealt with. In Sirmur, *jhajhra* or *bara shadi* are the types giving rise to polyandry. *Reet* is another very common way of inducting women as wives in the polyandry and its allied forms. Infact, it is a quick way of divorcing a wife thereby allowing her to re-marry a new set of husbands or man after he pays back double the amount incurred by the woman's husband (former) at the time of their marriage. This money is called *reet*. By way of *reet* women are inducted in polyandry, polyandry and polygyny, monogamy and polygyny forms of marriages. Thus there is no distinct type of marriage which can be held responsible for giving rise to polyandrous marriage in Sirmur. *Zanakang* type of marriage gives rise to polyandry in Kinnaur. The type is the socially recognised way of acquiring wife for sons in the household; and at least once i.e. first time (subsequent marriages may take place afterwards) parents arrange *zanakang* for their sons. This type of marriage is negotiated by the parents in which Fasihu (Father's sister's husband) and/or Mo.Br (mother's brother) take active role to negotiate the marriage. During negotiations they are known as *bistu* while negotiating *zanakang* lineage status, hierarchy etc. are also considered significantly. Finally concurrence from village god is sought before approving such negotiation. *Barni*, customary bride-price which traditionally used to be Rs. 5 and has now gone up, is an essential feature of *zanakang* which is paid by the father or patri-kin of the grooms. What symbolizes polyandrous union is tying of *pagri* (by mother's brother or father's sister's husband) by one and the same piece of cloth on all would-be husbands who are brothers ; and offering of garlands of *neoza* and walnut seeds by the bride to all her prospective husbands who are brothers, at the same ceremony. These two rituals signify the rise of polyandry in the Kinners' society. However, in astray cases when there is only son in the house obviously *zanakang* will give rise to monogamy under circumstances and not polyandry as expected. Grand feasting, rejoicing and participation of kin group and people of other social groups is almost a necessary part of *zanakang*. This may be treated as an expensive device of acquiring mate as it entails heavy expenditure in terms of bride-price and marriage expenses. Many people who cannot afford to spend heavy amount, go for *dubdub* and mutual consent type of marriage. In this types boy elopes with the girl and after sometime declares his intention of marrying the girl. When *dubdub* is done within the knowledge of girl's patri-people, expenses are usually small as *izzet* money remains the main item of expenditure. *Izzet* is the money given by groom's side as compensation to the girl's people for the loss of prestige they suffered in *dubdub*. When the concerned parties mutually agree to *dubdub* type of marriage in the interest of small economic investment generally polyandrous form of marriage is observed among the brothers. In cases where boy elopes with the girl without taking her parti-people into confidence, *izzet* money charged is quite high and this types of marriage gives rise to monogamy, sometimes to poly-monogamy and often to polyandry or polyandry-polygyny forms of marriage as well. Marriage by mutual consent are those where both boy and the girl mutually agree to marry. Such type of marriage also gives rise primarily to monogamy or 'poly-monogamy.'

Haari is yet another type of marriage rarely practised by the Kinners to acquire a mate. In this type of marriage a married woman elopes with the man of her choice after developing fancy for him, thus deserting her 'husband unit'. It is of course very rare in occurrence as it involves much complications, sense of prestige and morality on ethical grounds etc. More so Kinner women do not enjoy much relaxed standard of morality as is seen in case of the Jaunsaris and the Sirmurese women who have double standard of morality as *dhyanti* (daughter of the house) and *ryanti* (wife or woman of the house) in Jaunsar Bawar and as *dhyain* and *rewain* in Sirmur respectively. An important feature determining (most of the time) the form of marriage is the element of the money and mode of payment. The payment of *barni, izzat* of even *reet* determine the fact whether the marriage is going to be polyandrous, poly-monogamous or monogamous. To illustrate this, if the money has been paid from the common household purse, the 'marriage is ought to be polyandrous'. This is based on the simple rule of 'sharing the joint estate' by the brothers. In *zankang* since *barni* is paid by the father, all his sons will have equal right over the bride/wife and perhaps on this account, the brother born even after the marriage ceremonies have been performed, has right to enjoy the wifehood of the woman brought in by marriage at that time, and is included in the husband unit when he comes of age. Similar is the case with subsequent marriages when if money paid as *izzet* or *reet*, is from the common household purse, all brothers will share the woman in common as wife on assumption that they also have their equal potential claim on the money paid for her. However, if some of the brothers pays money earned by him, i.e. from his individual earning, he will have sole possession of the women, and this type will give rise to poly-monogamy. Thus, money invested in marriage and marriage types usually determine the form of marriage in these societies. These forms of marriage, however, give some clue to the evolutionary scheme and developmental stages in marriage system itself if examined carefully with some serious thought. This respect of discussion I would deal after I explain the marriage forms.

Polyandry and its Allied Forms

The north-western Himalayan societies having polyandrous form of marriage as societal profile also have some other forms prevalent either under circumstances or in wake of developmental/progressive stages. Some transitional stages in the marriage forms have also appeared on the scene and need special attention of anthropologists and social scientists. A brief mention illuminating each form seems alright here.

Polyandry form of marriage involves plurality of husbands and fraternal polyandry form (in context of north-western Himalayan societies) necessarily involves brothers to form the 'husband unit'. In this form of marriage, their economic, ritual, social and sexual aspects are involved. Each of these aspects is shared and exercised in partial possession of the common wife. The sense of partial possession, control and share yields cooperation, mutual trust and cementing factor—affection—among the brothers within the interest of household unit.

Poly-monogamy is another form emerging out in the Kinners society. This form of marriage takes rise in cases where man after being in polyandry form of marriage desserts the polyandrous union on some account or the other and marries another woman to be shared exclusively by him and him alone, and leads to monogamy. Thus in his initial stage he would have shared, along with his brothers, the common wife but later on goes for monogamous union. Reasons attributing to this situation resulting in this form of marriage may be like :

(1) Dissatisfaction from the common wife in area of her wifehood tasks and sexual displeasure.
(2) Change in economic condition of the man who might be able to earn livelihood single hand like wages etc.
(3) Ability to procure wife for himself exclusively.

(4) Fission of the household and property division taking place among the brothers.

A stage falling prior to poly-monogamy as evident from the case of the Sirmurese and which is significantly important in the light of varying marriage forms is the *joridar*. The *joridar* form of marriage as practised by the Sirmurese restricts the number of husbands from many (as in polyandry) to two. Thus, ideally speaking, for each set of two brothers a separate wife is thought to be alright by the society; however in *modus operandi*, some relaxation with regard to extension of relationship between other units within the household, if any, is also conveniently allowed. Of the total sample of 37 marriages based on polyandry and its allied forms some 12 (32.43%) marriages were found to be of the *joridar* form. This may not look very significant for its being high lighted at the moment as an element needing further research and analysis in terms of statistics and interpretation. However, it is socially upheld norm that makes it important to be viewed as a social event happening in the light of changing scene in marriage forms. The sense of 'reducing the number of husbands' is clearly indicative of a set trend in the direction of changing marriage forms from polyandry to monogamy and ultimately to polygyny. The Sirmurese's case of the *joridar* is just a step in transition leading to the final goal; and this cannot be ignored by the scholars having concerned for marriage and its evolutionary/progressive stages.

'Polyandry and polygyny' to which Majumdar referred to as polygynandry (cf Chandra, 1973) is another form found in existence in north-western Himalayan societies. This is an allied form of polyandry yielding more scope of physical relationship between a set of wives (women who may not necessarily be sisters) and a set of husbands (men who are necessarily brothers). Thus it could be treated as group marriage in the restricted sense of it as several women and men form the unit based on conjugal dyad (Adams, 1971). Briffault while talking of group marriage mentioned :

"The complement of the rule of sororal polygyny is that of

> fraternal polyandry, i.e., when a woman contracts a marriage with a member of another family she marries all the marriageable males of that family. The simultaneous observance of both these rules constitute a marriage between the two groups, irrespective of the relations between the members composing them. However, the one sided observances of sororal polygyny, and perhaps also fraternal polyandry, are much more common today than the combination of two practices as complete group marriage. The reason for this is plain. The combination of the two practices is an unstable arrangement, and can only operate in a modified form where sexual relations do not entail permanent cohabitation. As soon as marriage involves economic interdependence the arrangement becomes impracticable, for economic association can only take place when the labour of the woman or women is in some degree specially allotted to the husband, and it necessarily breaks up into the one or another of its aspects—that is, into sororal polygyny or fraternal polyandry...." (Briffault, in Taylor, 1959 : 129)

In case where besides association of woman's labour to the husband, it is also associated to the household unit in terms of working hands as a countervail to ecological setting yielding much pressure on economy, as is found in case of most of the hilly societies of north-western Himalayas, breaking of the practice in favour of fraternal polyandry is rather imminent and must.

Monogamous form of marriages is also in consistent degree practised in these societies. As earlier said that this form of marriage takes rise under special situation like the male spouse being the only son in the household or could be he is the only surviving husband of the husband unit of polyandrous union. There could be no denial to the fact that an increasing trend towards monogamy is evident in north-western Himalayan societies.

Polygyny is yet another form of marriage which also gets some place in these north-western Himalayan societies. If well off economic condition is any criterion to establish the argument in favour of polygyny, it should hold its ground in case of the Kinners and the Sirmurese as whatever incidence of polygyny was noticed in all such cases, economic condition of the households was much more than being merely satisfactorily. Distribution of marriage forms as evident from the two societies—the Kinners and Sirmureses—is given in Table-1.

Factors/Reasons associated with Polyandry

It may look exclaimatory that majority of the north-western Himalayan societies are fraternal polyandrous societies. Many social scientists and anthropologists looked at the problem of polyandry from different viewpoints to arrive at some concrete point of understanding with a historical context as well. The most common argument put forward in favour of polyandry is the disparity in sex ratio and shortage of women. Parmar in his book *Polyandry in the Himalayas* dealt with this aspect at length basing on census data of Sirmur and his own data collected among the Sirmurese. The sex ratio at the district level in Sirmur is 84 females per hundred males whereas it was somewhere 77 females per 100 males and 68 females for 100 males as the ratio found in polyandrous tract of the district studied by Parmar; that is decidedly a low ratio. However, during my research investigation the sex ratio was found to be 81 women for each hundred men. Jaunsar-Bawar area also presents somewhat similar picture in this regard as there are 789 females/1000 males in comparison to 922 at the state level of Uttar Pradesh (Berreman, 1962 : 68). The idea of female infanticide, as it has been a practice among the Rajput once, is also associated with the disparity in sex ratio. It is believed that the hill Rajputs are those who took shelter in the Himalayas at sometime or the latter during various wars which broke and posed danger to their lives. Practice of female infanticide has also been alluded by some researchers as a case for shortage of women in these areas. Kapadia (1955) believes that 'sex disparity is likely to perpetuate though it does not necessarily give rise to a polyandrous pattern'. However, my personal research does not concur much to this it. On the basis of my research among the Sirmurese "I

TABLE 1

Distribution of forms of marriage in two north-western Himalayan societies

	Total No. of marriages studied*		Polyandry		'Polyandry and polygyny		Poly-mono-gamy		Monogamy		Polygyny		not specific	
	No.	%	No.	%	No.	%	No.	%	No.	%	No.	%	No.	%
Kinners	372	100	97	26.88	7	1.08	72	19.35	160	43.01	10	2.69	26	6.99
Sirmurese	98	100	20	20.40	17	17.35	—	—	52	53.06	9	9.18	—	—

*Total sample for Kinners is based on three villages while sample for Sirmurese has been collected from one village only.

concur with Parmar's viewpoint over this issue only to some extent as it is interesting to point out that all polyandrous societies do not have too much of disparity sex ratio...." (Chandra, 1979). I hasten to submit my viewpoint in this direction as another sample society—The Kinners—have altogether different picture with regard to sex ratio which shows a balanced sex ratio in case of some villages studied intensively and in general nearing all India picture of sex ratio as well. In most of the decinial population figures the ratio is more than 90 females per 100 males. In 1961, Kinnaur had the sex ratio of 96 women per 100 men and in 1971 it came down to 89 per 100 males against all India picture of 92 women per 100 men. Therefore it could be argued substantially that, though no denial to the possibility of disparity in sex ratio as one of possible factor for polyandry, there are several other factors viz. economic, ecological, geo-economic and psychological, working intently in favour of polyandry. Of these economic factor having bearing on geo-economy (cf. Majumdar, 1963) and ecology is perhaps the most important factor in favour of polyandry to have flourished in these north-western Himalayan societies.

The economic factor has widely been suggested as vital catalyst in promoting polyandry in the north-western Himalayas (Chandra, 1974 ; Majumdar, 1963 ; Prince Peter, 1963 ; Saxena, 1955). In fact in these societies social and the economic systems are quite dependent on each other, thus having complimentary and supplementary rules to play in the cultural pattern of the region. In general

> "Life in the north-western Himalayan areas is very tough. Though agriculture forms the basis of economy for the dwellers of this region, no single economic pursuit alone can satisfy the need of the people for landholdings are small and of low fertility hence many working hands are required to produce a moderate yield ; domestic animals are small and yield little milk, wool and other products. Recently introduced horticulture needs orientation, skill and scientific knowledge to produce good results. . . . ." (Chandra, 1981 : 203-4).

Some of the 'people' like the Kinners were also having trade and for that they used to move between lower hills and plains—Rampur, Simla and Hardwar etc. and across the border in Tibet with the trading items like sheep, goat, wool, salt, vessels and dry fruits etc. At present with the cessation of trade, the Kinners have now almost forgotten this aspect of economic life. The agricultural lands owned in small units are well scattered over a vast area right from high level lands on mountains to low level lands often situated much below the village level. Sheep rearing, muleteering, keeping of milch cattles, apple orchards etc. are some of the subsidiary economic pursuits of these societies. All occupations put together make these people self sufficient. Thus to meet the requirement of these various economic fronts a joint venture is required at the household level with an increasing lust for mutual help, cooperation and 'being together' to attend all such needs. More working hands are always welcome, but to the extent that the 'joint ventured' economic yields can feed them sufficiently well. The total situation at the household level remains that it has land to cultivate—spread in vast area, domestic animals and goat and sheep herds to look after, orchard for its management and besides all these several other pursuits of incidental occurrence are also there to be attended to in the interest of household economy. This all cannot be properly handled unless these is a well united corporate group having concern for such matters and common interest for the entire unit of the household. To meet the demand brothers in these societies join hands together and share their labour and rewards in the area of vividly diversified economic fronts and there by remain united to help solve the problems emerging out from the economic system. While doing so, they find a good solution in the practice of polyandry. Further,

> "sense of avoidance of fragmentation of land in the larger interest of household units is felt by these people. With the fragmentation of land there is a danger of loss of productivity of land due to shortage of man-power and then the land size becomes unviable because of the division of land ; other property, animals and equipments etc. are also

> divided. As a result it becomes almost impossible for the concerned members to run their economy smoothly at the household level for the want of manpower, animals and tools etc." (Chandra, 1981).

An intent effort is made to maintain the household estate undivided and pass it onto the next generation as such, just in the interest of survival and perpetuity. Prince Peter also believed that 'economic function of polyandry intensifies the unity and solidarity of the sibling group' (1955 : 181). The notion of property and economic contracts are so much pervasive in the minds of these people that they seek a solution to their economic problems in polyandry. This led to Stulpnagel to say that

> "in Himalayan hills polyandry is in reality nothing more than a more custom of community of wives-among brothers who have a community of other goods" (1878 : 135).

Environment and ecology are yet other dimensions considered very important from the viewpoint of the prevalance of the practice of polyandry. It provides a fresh look at the whole problem since both environment and ecology play vital determinantal role in this aspect. It remains beyond doubt that human beings, both as individuals as well as a group, have an intrinsic quality of responding to environmental conditions however harsh they may be, in the best suited manner as countervail to the situation just in the interest of their survival thus perpetuating their lot. The environmental factors or ecological setting causes its impact on organizational relationships. A reflection of man's adaptation to ecological conditions can easily be seen, as it is evident as well, in the socio-cultural institutions that operate in a particular setting and the response or behaviour of the people towards it. For fraternal polyandrous societies the environment or ecological conditions working are almost similar if we take the north-western Himalayas as a 'region' or unit for our consideration. Even other societies viz. the Toda of Nilgiris also face similar ecological conditions to a great extent. Both areas of study, Sirmur and Kinnaur, share many environmental factors in common*, conspicuous features of environment or ecological settings could be the altitude above 1500 metres, cold climate, harsh, tough and challenging surroundings, snowfall, heavy or no rainfall, agricultural produce, kind of habitation and types of domestic animals etc. I have made a case for the role of environment elsewhere citing the case of Kinners where it has been attempted to demonstrate how best the Kinners have found out solution, to the problem of harsh environment and tough ecological setting, in the practice of polyandry to repell any danger to their society (Chandra, 1982). In brief the ecological conditions have forced these north-western Himalayan societies to go for these marriage forms which help them in maintaining the joint extended—vertical or horizontal—household where everything is shared in common, wife and children remaining at the foci of the unit, plurality of economic pursuits is followed, an intent check on population growth is attempted in the interest of keeping population size low which otherwise, would bring disaster as it would cause heavy pressure on land and other resources. And of course in this effort these societies "keep the members of' domestic unit' united....ratio of working hands or adults to children high...." (cf. Chandra, 1981). While describing these situations with reference to the Jaunsari polyandry and ecological and economic conditions Majumdar (1962) tried to combine these two, economy and ecology, together as promoting factor for the prevalance of polyandry among the Khasas and termed the situation as geo-economic factor.

Other factors said to be responsible for the existence or continuance of polyandry are tradition, social and psychological. In establishing some ideals, tradition of any society plays some significant role and perhaps people follow those ideals in

---

*(It is to be noted that though Sirmur is a low lying area in altitude even then the trans-Giri tract, where polyandry has found its existence, presents similar conditions or atleast meets the required conditions for polyandry as found in Kinnaur and other polyandrous areas in the region).

the wake of their 'cultural heritage' as well. However, tradition remains the part of cultural treasure. Tradition gives support and strength to the practice in the interest of continuance of any custom or practice so long it is required for survival and smooth running of the life.

Social and psychological factors take their position only as aftermath of economic and ecological factors. What is accepted as a model by the people becomes socially approved and works as promoting factor for any practice as it enhances prestige of the people. Psychological factor comes into being only when people start evaluating or rationalising their act. A common notion that 'since the practice has been there for long, it should be practised' prevails in the minds of people. Personality formation has a role to play in the make up and working of institutions. It is believed by the people that polyandry teaches men to live with love, affection and mutual help and cooperation and share all what is available in the 'house'. Members of these societies inherit the very idea of polyandry from their surroundings. Men learn to live in harmony and share their wives with brothers while women get knowledge about their role and right to share their 'wifehood' with several husbands, and thus a sense of change in 'sexual partners' strictly in terms of husbands develops in them. It could be one of the reasons for frequent changes in spouses as is evident from the case of the Sirmurese. Change in 'husband unit' is not so uncommon in the Sirmurese society and this gives rise to *reet* type of marriages (Chandra, 1974).

Changing Trends in Polyandry

So far we have viewed polyandry from the view point of its being a societal profile, a necessity coming out as a countervail to economic and ecological conditions prevailing in the region when it is practised at large in a given somewhat static set of framework. Maintaining every thing as constant I tried to show how best polyandry works favouring peoples' interest and their survival and perpetuity. In the wake of changing conditions, and circumstances society has the capacity to mould its behaviour strategy to cope up with the situation ; there are some changing trends emerging out in polyandry as well.

The entire north-western Himalayan area is passing through the stage of economic development (Parmar, 1970). Economy of the people is also facing some changes. With the cessation of trade the Kinners had to divert their attention towards other sources for their livelihood. Cash oriented salaried jobs and skill oriented occupations have yielded opportunities to the people to get detracted from the traditional 'joint ventured' mixed economy to such occupations and pursuits that can be run single handed and from the earning of that one can think of establishing his household and can afford to have a wife exclusively for himself. Such cash oriented economy and single handed occupations viz., labour jobs, service in offices and jobs like craftsmanship etc. have given rise to some allied forms of polyandry which could be viewed as traditional stages heading towards monogamy and might be at sometime to polygyny as is believed to be at the top in the evolutionary scheme. In the changing economic conditions the Kinners have shown their inclination from polyandry to monogamy through the stages of 'polyandry and polygyny' and poly-monogamy. Concept of *joridar* falls somewhere in between these two stages and concurs with the idea of improving or better economic considerations of those following it. Polyandry is the stage where all members of the husband unit pool their resources together and share their labour and property along with their brothers and common wife in the interest of household economy. This situation might have taken its shape where people found it extremely difficult to survive in the prevailing severe ecological circumstances and where joint venture and sharing of any thing and every thing (in terms of social and physical property and possession) became a must for them. Need and desire for more working hands or adults in the joint estate and of course little ease and improvement in economic condition gave rise to the form of 'polyandry and polygyny'. In this form also men virtually shared all their assets or community of goods along with community of wives with a little eased situation that wifehood tasks and role were relatively easier to be had by the husbands. Some sense of relaxation in terms of pressure on women to oblige their husbands in regard to their wifehood tasks and roles was felt as they could devote relatively more time and attention in attending their duties. However, main advantage of such form of marriage was realised from the improvement of household economy. And to emphasize this form itself takes rise only in improved economic situations as payment of *izzet*, *haari*, or *reet* money is involved besides other day-to-day miscellaneous expenses for each addition in the household. In the wake of improving economy another advanced form of polyandry is seen in case of the Sirmurese. This is called *joridar* system where a wife is shared only between two brothers. We see a marked sense of 'progress' or advancement from the stage of polyandry where all the uterine brothers share the common wife to 'polyandry and polygyny', where more women are inducted as wives to all the members of polyandrous union, and from there to the stage of *joridar* where sharing is restricted among two brothers. If the number of brothers is more, then a separate marriage is arranged for them after the notion of *joridar* system

> "Wherein polyandrous communities the number of brothers is too large ; more wives than one may be shared by the brothers. The event that a set of brothers share particular common wife, is called *joridar*. This is easier when the number of brothers is even. In case the number is odd, the odd brothers is *adjusted* (italics mine) to any one of the *joris*. A bride once assigned to one group of brothers will not be allowed to seek a change in that household, although she can abandon the household and can marry somebody else. Nor is any brothers belonging to one *jori* allowed to poach or encroach upon any other *joridar*" (District Gazetter of Sirmur, 1969 : 114).

This system of *joridar* (English equivalent—Biandry) also indicates an attempt of the practitioners of polyandry to restrict or decrease the number of sharers of wife—from many to few and may be ultimately to one sometimes in future, if conditions permit them to do so.

A further improvement in the changing trends is once again shown by the Kinners in terms of poly-monogamy form of marriage. As described earlier, this form of marriage takes rise after man's desserting the polyandrous union and going for a wife exclusively for himself in monogamy. Obviously while going for poly-monogamy man severs his relations from the 'joint estate' and 'joint venture' in the economic pursuit. This leads us to assume that he has established his livelihood on some single handed economy or cash oriented job needing no he'p from 'others' in that matter. He can sustain the handships and challenges bestowed from the ecological and environmental conditions with the resources pooled all by himself. In nut-shell, after achieving capability and capacity to maintain own nuclear household the Kinners, more often than not, dessert the polyandrous union and switch over to monogamy : since they have shared polyandrous union before entering into monogamy, this stage is referred to as 'poly-monogamy' which is an indication of transitional form.

Monogamy takes rise further as in the wake of contact with the 'outside world', exposure to media, awareness of 'other cultures'. Of course, improvement in the ability to cope up with the environmental challenges monogamy is being preferred at large by the north-western Himalayan societies. As evident from the table furnished, it is seen that in both societies listed here frequency of monogamy surpasses all other forms of marriage if taken singularly. However, it is no less significant even if all the allied forms of polyandry are put together. Conclusion could be as simple as :

> "it is worth while to mention that the change in marriage forms is directly linked with changes in the occupational pattern. This is supported by the facts that the persons involved in the polyandrous form of marriage are engaged in complex set of occupation...while those involved in monogamous unions tend to have an economy based mainly on labour, service or other means where joint efforts at family level are not necessarily needed. The people engaged in the intermediary forms...tend to combine an economy based on individual endeavour with sharing the joint economy with their brothers. Thus, it may be presum-ed that with the changing patterns of the developing

economy...the forms of marriage may take a different shape and dimension in course of time ; the prevailing trend being monogamy" (Chandra, 1973).

About polygyny it would be alright if I mention that though the Kinners or other polyandrous societies are not completely ignorant of polygyny, yet it is of rare occurance in these societies. As a strategy, 'polyandry and polygyny' form might be fulfilling the requirement in these societies to a considerable extent. Trends in polyandry in the north-western Himalayan societies do give some cue to foresee some definite changes in marriage forms in the 'progressive' direction.

ACKNOWLEDGEMENT

I express my sense of indebtedness to the Director, Anthropological Survey of India, Calcutta from whom I received two research fellowships (Junior & Senior) during the years 1970-74 to carry out research in Himachal Pradesh.

REFERENCES

Adams, R N. 1960 (1971) The Nature of family in *Kinship* ed. Jack Goody. Penguin Books Ltd., Middlesex.

Aiyappan, A. 1932 Nayar polyandry. *Man* vol. XXXII : 99.

Berreman, G.D. 1962 Pahari Polyandry : A Comparison. *American Anthropologist*, vol. 64 : 1.

Briffault, R. 1927 (1959) *The Mothers*. Abridged vol. ed. Taylor, George Allen and Unwin, London.

Census of India 1969 *District Gazetteer of Sirmur*, Simla.

Chandra Ramesh 1972a "Socio-economic study of Kinnaurese of Himachal Pradesh" Report A.S.I., Calcutta (Unpublished).

———1972b The Notion of paternity among the polyandrous Kanet of Kinnaur, *Bulletin Anthropological Survey of India*, Calcutta, vol. XXI : 3-4.

———1973 Types and forms of marriage in a Kinnaur village, *Man in India*, vol. 53 : 2.

———1975a Report on the Project : Polyandry in a Himalayan Village ; in *Bulletin Anthropological Survey of India*, Calcutta. vol. XXIV : 3-4.

———1975b Impact of changing Economy on Tribal marital Institution : A case from Himachal Pradesh, Proceedings of 1st Annual conference of Ethnographical and Folk Culture Society, Lucknow.

———1978 Kinners : A study in their Society and Religion ; Ph. D. Dessertation, Lucknow University, Lucknow.

——1979 Need for urgent research on the vanishing trait of polyandry in South India. *Review of Ethnology*, vol. 7 : 3 Wien.

———1981a Sex role arrangement to achieve Economic security in north-western Himalayas in *Asian High Land Societies* ed. C. von Furer Haimendorf. Sterling Pub. Delhi.

———1981b Ecology and Religion of Kinners : Mountain dwellers of the north-western Himalayas in *Nature Man Spirit Complexes in Tribal India* ed. R.S. Mann, Concept Pub. Co., Delhi.

———1982 Quest for Environmental adaptation among the Kinners of north-western Himalayas (in process).

Fredric Drew 1877 *The Northern Barvier of India,* Edward Stanford London.

Fortes, M. 1971 The Developmental cycle in domestic groups in *Kinship* ed. Jack Goody. Penguin Books, Middlesex.

Frazer, J.B. 1829 *Journal of a tour through part of snowy ranges of the Himalayan-mountains*. London.

Garard, A & William Lloyed 1846 *Narrative of Journey from Kanpur to the Borando Pass in the Himalayan mountain*. London.

Hiatt, L.R. 1980 Polyandry in Sri Lanka : A test case for parental investment theory *Man* vol. 15 : 4.

J.R.A.I 1953 *Notes and Queries of Anthropology*. London.

Kapadia, K.M. 1955 *Marriage and family in India*, Oxford Uni. Press, London.

Majumdar, D.N. 1940 'Marriage customs of cis-Himalayan tribes', Madras (special lecture).

———1962 *Himalayan polyandry,* Asia Publishing House, Bombay.

Mc Lennan 1896 *Studies in Ancient History.*

Murdock, G.P. 1949 *Social Structure.* Macmillan & Co., New York (Reprint 1965).

Park, W.Z. 1937 Pavisto Polyandry. *American Anthropologist.* vol. 39.

Parmar, Y.S. 1970 Strategy for Development of Hill Areas. D.P.R. Simla.

———1971 Himalayan Polyandry its sccial, Economic and Political background (Thesis unpublished).

———1975 *Polyandry in the Himalayas* Vikas Publishing House, Delhi.

Prince Peter, H.R.H. 1955 Polyandry and the kinship group. *Man* vol. 53 : 198.

———1963 *A Study of Polyandry,* The Hauge.

Rivers, W.H.R. 1906 *The Toda.* London.

Saxena, R.N. 1955 *Social Economy of a Polyandrous People,* Agra.

Spencer, H. 1904 *Principles of Sociology*, vol. I., Williams and Norgate Pub.

Stewart, J.H. 1936 Shoshoni Polyandry. *American Anthropolagist*, vol. 38.

Stulpnagel, G.R. 1878 Polyandry in the Himalayas. *The Indian Antiquary*, No. 7.

Westermarck, A. 1922 *The History of Human marriage.*

Wilson, A. 1870 *Abode of snow,* Edinburgh.

5

PAHARI POLYANDRY : A COMPARISON*

GERALD D. BERREMAN

Polyandry has long been a popular subject for speculation and occasionally for research by anthropologists.[1] Recently efforts to explain the origin and functioning of this rather unusual institution have been supplemented by attempts to define it (Fischer, 1952; Leach, 1955; Gough, 1969; Prince Peter, 1955a). It can be most simply defined as that form of marriage in which a woman has more than one husband at a time.[2] In fraternal polyandry which is by far the most common kind, a group of brothers, real or classificatory, are collectively the husbands of a woman (or women).

This kind of polyandry has been reported from many parts of the world (Westermarck, 1922 : 107 ff.), but its best-documented and most prevalent occurrence is in Tibet, described by Prince Peter (1955c : 176) as "the largest and most flourishing polyandrous community in the world today," and in India. Mandelbaum (1938 : 581 f.) notes that

> "in South India polyandry is of especially frequent occurrence. Six polyandrous tribes have been reported for Cochin; the Nayars of Travancore and the Irava of British

*Reproduced by Permission of the American Anthropological Association, from 'American Anthropologist', 64/(1) : 60-75, 1962.

Malabar have this form of marriage ; while the Todas are the classic example of a polyandrous people in the text books of anthropology."

The Singhalese are known to practice polyandry to some extent (Leach, 1955). In North India the Jats of the northern Punjab, and especially those who are Sikhs, have been repeatedly reported to practice polyandry (Briffault, 1959:137; Kirkpatrick, 1878 : 86; Prince Peter, 1948 : 215). The most consistent practitioners of polyandry in India today are probably the residents of certain sub-Himalayan hill areas in Himachal Pradesh, the northern Punjab, and north-western Uttar Pradesh. It is the polyandry of this relatively little-known region which I propose to discuss in this paper.

Non-Tibetan, Indo-Aryan-speaking Hindus inhabit the lower ranges of the Himalayas from south-eastern Kashmir across northern most India and through Nepal. These people are collectively termed *Paharis* ("of the mountains"). They constitute a distinct culture area bordered by the peoples of Tibet to the north and by those of the Indo-Gangetic plains to the south. With the latter peoples, they share historical origins as well as linguistic and cultural affinities (Berreman, 1960). Among the Paharis, polyandry has been reported in several districts (cf. Das-Gupta, 1921) and has been studied in some detail in Jaunsar Bawar, a subdivision of Dehra Dun district in north-western Uttar Pradesh (Majumdar, 1944; Saksena, 1955). All of the Pahari areas in which it occurs are in the western Himalayan hills and are inhabited by people who share the Western dialect of the Pahari language (Grierson, 1916 : 101). There are no reliable reports of Pahari polyandry east of Jaunsar Bawar and its immediate vicinity, i.e., in the Central or Eastern Pahari-speaking areas.[3]

This paper is based on a study carried out among Central Pahari-speaking people in Garhwal, a hill area adjacent to, and east of, Jaunsar Bawar.[4] The people of Garhwal, though they have not previously been studied, have frequently been cited as non-polyandrous by those who have written on polyandry in Jaunsar Bawar. One goal of the research which led to this paper was to study marriage in its total cultural context among the non-polyandrous people of Garhwal in order to compare that system with the polyandrous system of neighboring Jaunsar Bawar as reported in the literature. The general hypothesis with which the investigation began and which this paper will discuss was that economic, demographic, or social-structural differences would be found which would correlate with the occurrence of polyandry in Jaunsar Bawar and its absence in nearly Garhwal. Further, some of the features found in Jaunsar Bawar would correspond to those reported by people who have studied polyandrous societies in other parts of the world.

The peoples of Jaunsar Bawar and Garhwal live under virtually identical physical conditions and their populations and cultures are very similar, having derived from a common source (Berreman, 1960). Conditions for a comparative study with polyandry as the dependent variable therefore seemed ideal. In both areas the economy of the majority high-caste population is primarily agricultural, with a secondary dependence on animal husbandry, while the low-status artisan castes live by their craft specialities. Land is valuable but not as scarce as in most of North India. All property is owned jointly by male members of the patrilineal, patrilocal extended family. If property is divided among brothers, they usually receive equal shares. Normally, however, brothers continue to hold the patrimony in common and division occurs in the next generation, among patrilateral parallel cousins. The eldest active male dominates in the joint family but cannot compel younger men to remain within it. Marriage takes place within the caste group and outside the clan and mother's clan. It involves a payment of bride-price which must be returned if the marriage is dissolved unless the husband is clearly at fault. Where dowry is used, it is exceptional and evidently of recent origin, having diffused from the plains. Levirate is the rule upon a husband's death and payment must be made to his family if his wife wishes to go elsewhere. These are general features of Pahari culture as I know it and as it is reported in the literature.

Polyandry in Jaunsar Bawar

In Jaunsar Bawar, fraternal polyandry has been described as "the common form of marriage". Indeed, it does seem to be the preferred, but not the exclusive, form. Monogamy, polygyny and fraternal polyandry, including a combination of polyandry and polygyny approximating fraternal "group marriage," appear in the same villages and even in the same lineages (Majumdar, 1944 : 167 f.). Non-fraternal polyandry is not reported. In one village for which figures are available. Majumdar (1955b : 165) reports that of 57 families, 39 % are polyandrous with more husbands than wives, 10% are polyandrous with an equal number of husbands and wives, 12 % are polygynous, and 39 % are monogamous.[5]

In this society, a polyandrous union occurs when a woman goes through a marriage ceremony with the eldest of a group of brothers. This man represents the group of brothers, all of whom thereupon become the woman's husbands. Subsequent wives may be taken, especially if the first one is sterile or if the age differential of the brothers is great. If so, the wives are individually married in a ceremony with the eldest brother and are shared by all, unless one or more brothers wish to break away from the joint family. No brother can remain a member of the joint family and claim exclusive rights to a wife. The eldest brother dominates with respect to the wife or wives, but he has no exclusive sexual or reproductive rights. A woman considers all of the brothers to be her husbands. Children recognize the group of brothers as their fathers; they call all of them "father" and inherit from all as a group without regard to paternity or maternity within the polyandrous family (Majumdar, 1944 : 178; 1953 : 179). In cases of division of the family, paternity may be assigned by lot, by mother's designation, or by order of birth (Majumdar, 1944 : 144 f.). This is "true" fraternal polyandry similar to that reported among the Iravas of Central Kerala by Aiyappan (cf., Aiyappan, 1935 : 114 ff. ; Leach, 1955 : 182 ; Gough, 1959: 34).

Monandry in Garhwal

Majumdar (1944 : 168) has pointed out that "the Garhwalis do not observe polyandry but the Jaunsaris do." While people of Jaunsar Bawar acknowledge their polyandry quite readily and defend this custom, the idea of polyandry is rejected by Garhwal residents. I neither found nor heard of any case of polyandry in the area of my work. Of a total of 300 marital unions for which I accumulated complete information in one Garhwal village, 85 % were monogamous and 15 % were polygynous. There every family is careful to secure a wife for each of its sons, and each son normally goes through the marriage ceremony with his own bride.[6]

Although there are strong negative feelings about polyandry in this region, sexual relationships within the family are not greatly different from those among fraternally polyandrous families of Jaunsar Bawar. The situation is very similar to that among the Kota as reported by Mandelbaum (1938). Brothers have the right of sexual access to one another's wives. Despite these rights of fraternal ciscisbeism, every man has own wife and each child its own father. There is never ambiguity on this point. Brothers share their wives' sexuality but not their reproductivity. As long as a wife fulfils her sexual obligations to her husband and does not indicate a preference for another, she is normally available to all of her husband's brothers, but her children are the children of her husband only.

In assessing the hypothesis with which this study began I will look briefly at some of the factors which have been advanced in the literature as causal for, predisposing toward, or correlated with polyandry and consider them with reference to the societies being described here.

Factors Associated With Polyandry

Economic factors

Contemporary discussions frequently emphasize economic factors in accounting for polyandry.

E.R. Leach (1955 : 183 ff) believes that polyandry "...is intimately associated with an institution of dowry rights," and has hypothesized that

> "...adelphic polyandry is consistently associated with systems in which women as well as men are the bearers of property rights".

In such systems, as distinguished from those in which property is exclusively in the hands of males, each marriage "establishes a distinct parcel of property rights."

> If two brothers share one wife so that the only heirs of the brothers are the children born of that wife, then, from an economic point of view, the marriage will tend to cement the solidarity of the sibling pair rather than tear it apart, whereas, if two brothers have separate wives, their children will have separate economic interests, and maintenance of the patrimonial inheritance in one piece is likely to prove impossible (Leach, 1955 : 184).

Polyandry thereby also serves "to reduce potential hostility between sibling brothers". Without polyandry there would be a tendency for children of brothers to break up the joint family in order that each group of siblings might pursue its own economic interests.

The Pahari evidence contradicts this hypothesis. Dowry is not part of the traditional Pahari marriage transaction which is, in fact, dependent upon bride-price for validity (Joshi, 1929 : 50f). Moreover, and more importantly, a woman has no property of her own except in most unusual circumstances and she forfeits even her jewelry if she divorces her husband. Children remain with their father or his family when a marriage dissolves. Therefore, in the Himalayan hills, children of brothers who share a wife have no different economic interests as a result of that fact than do children of brothers each of whom has his own wife.[7]

A widely cited economic advantage of fraternal polyandry is that it keeps family property, especially lands, intact in a patrilineal, patrilocal group (Westermarck, 1922 : 185 f.). It accomplishes this by restricting the number of heirs and by keeping them together around a common wife. This virtue of polyandry is cited for Ceylon (Prince Peter, 1955b), Tibet (Prince Peter, 1955c), and the Himalayan hill area (Saksena, 1955 : 33 ; Stulpnagel, 1878 : 133).[8] It is an advantage that is claimed by Jaunsar Bawar people themselves (Majumdar, 1944 : 168). Where this economic function is served by polyandry, it is attributed to the desire to keep intact the property of the wealthy, to the necessity to keep the property of the very poor from dropping below the subsistence level, or to both (cf. Prince Peter, 1955b : 169 ; Stulpnagel, 1878 : 103 ff.).

If fraternal polyandry were practised consistently, there would be no patrilateral parallel cousins, and it is they who generally divide land in the Himalayan hills. If the number of wives were appreciably less than in non-polyandrous societies this would reduce, absolutely, the number of offspring and hence heirs. Either or both of these would theoretically tend to reduce fragmentation of property, especially if, as will be discussed below, polyandry were to reduce the frictions which lead to break-up of joint families.

The over-all effect of polyandry for family property retention in Jaunsar Bawar is tempered by the fact that not all marriages are polyandrous ; of those that are, many involve a plurality of wives. While in the Jaunsar Bawar village cited 49% of the families are polyandrous, 61 % have as many (or more) wives as husbands and hence no reduction in the number of heirs. Occasional polygyny or monogamy among brothers in a lineage might wipe out the advantage, for property retention, of generations of polyandry. On the other hand, in the non-polyandrous Garhwal village three of 16 land allotments have remained intact in the joint families to which they were assigned nearly 150 years ago. Unfortunately, land fragmentation figures for Jaunsar Bawar are not available to compare with those of the Garhwal village. My guess is that they would not show significant differences.

Polyandry has often been attributed to economic hardship which necessitates cooperative work among brothers for survival (Kapadia, 1955 : 71 ; Majumdar, 1944: 168). The expense of obtaining and/or maintaining a wife and of supporting a family has been cited as an important factor in contributing to polyandry in several contexts. Stulpnagel (1878 : 133) and Kapadia (1955 : 71) mention the difficulty of raising a sufficient bride-price and the consequent necessity for several brothers to combine to purchase a single wife. Majumdar (1955a : 95) notes the similar difficulty of providing the costly jewelry which a Pahari woman requires.

Bride-price marriage, though it is the rule in Jaunsar Bawar as elsewhere in the Himalayan hills, is not a likely motivation for polyandry since the amount is proportional to the wealth of those involved. Moreover, permanent unions may be established without payment at all. In the non-polyandrous areas men do not often go unwed because of bride-price. Precisely the same points are applicable with regard to the bride's jewelry.

Heath (1955) has suggested that polyandry is related to "...sex specialization in which the woman makes only an insignificant contribution to subsistence." This explanation could not be farther from the facts found in the Himalayan hills, including Jaunsar Bawar.[9] There women contribute as heavily as do men to subsistence, and a wife is an economic asset (Majumdar, 1944 : 171). In the Garhwal village which I studied, need for additional field labour was cited as a reason for securing *an additional wife* in eight of twelve current cases of polygyny. As one villager remarked, "Here two wives are better than one because they do much of the work. In your country and on the plains the husband has to support his wife so a second wife is a hardship and a luxury." In polygynous families the agricultural and pastoral labour is divided among wives just as in polyandrous families it is divided among husbands except that in both cases ploughing is reserved for men and certain household tasks for women. Saksena (1955 : 33) notes that in the difficult economic circumstances of Juansar Bawar it often takes several men to support a single wife and family : "In order to make life successful a system of life in keeping with the demand for joint labour within a village had to be evolved. The wide practice of polyandry seems to be the outcome of this demand." However, polyandry is only one means of enlarging the work force of the family. In Garhwal (and in many families of Jaunsar Bawar) the same end is achieved by polygyny, by adoption of sons, by hiring agricultural servants, or preferably by having several sons.

An advantage of polyandry may be that it tends to keep the ratio of working adults to children high in the family, just as it keeps the number of heirs low. In the polyandrous village mentioned above, this would apparently not be true for the 61% of all families who have one or more wives per husband. However, in that village about 20.5 % of the population is ten years of age or under, while in the non-polyandrous Garhwal village which I studied about 28 % of the population is in this age bracket. This sample is far too small to yield significant conclusions, but it does not contradict the contention that there are fewer children in polyandrous communities than in non-polyandrous ones—an advantage in an economically hard-pressed area.

It must be noted in respect to all of the economic arguments for polyandry, that polyandrous Jaunsar Bawar is no more hard-pressed than non-polyandrous Garhwal, and that the Paharis in general are economically more secure than many people of North India, despite their reputation for poverty (Berreman, 1959 : 102).

Social factors

Security of wife and family in the prolonged absence of the husband has been noted as an advantage of polyandry among such martial peoples as the Jats of the northern Punjab and the Nayars of South India (Prince Peter, 1948 : 223 ; 1955b : 169 ; Westermarck, 1922 : 193). Likewise, it has been cited as an advantage to the Paharis who travel considerable distances to tend lands and cattle and are therefore absent from their homes for extended periods (Kapadia, 1955 : 72). Brothers can arrange to protect a common wife in such circumstances where an individual could not. This advantage accrues equally in formal polyandry and in wife-sharing. In Garhwal a man may be sent to accompany his brother's wife on a trip or while she works in the forest or even to live with her in the absence of her husband to insure that she will have no liaisons with men outside the family.

A more fundamental social function of polyandry, and one of the benefits most widely acclaimed by both observers and practitioners of polyandry, is the maintenance or intrafamilial amity, i.e., it reduces quarrels among brothers (Aiyappan, 1937; Carrasco, 1959 : 36 ; Leach, 1955 : 185 ; Prince Peter, 1948 : 224 ; 1955a : 181 ; 1955b : 170 ; Saksena, 1955 : 33). In India, joint family dissolution is frequently attributed to friction among wives who enlist the support of their respective husbands, with resultant fraternal strife.[10] Polyandry is said to minimize fraternal conflict by eliminating this source, though jealousy over the common wife or wives is also reported (Mukherji 1950). As was indicated above, Leach attributes decreased friction in fraternally polyandrous families to the identity of economic interests among their members. Reduction of friction might be achieved in part by the simple reduction in number of heirs which polyandry theoretically accomplishes and the consequently decreased number of potential disputants in the family. Unfortunately, no data such as frequency of joint family dissolution are available with which to test this alleged advantage of fraternal polyandry.

Socio-economic factors

Radcliffe-Brown defined the unity of the sibling group as "its unity in relation to a person outside it and connected with it by a specific relation to one of its members," and he said that "it is in the light of this structural principle that we must interpret...adelphic polyandry..." (Radcliffe-Brown, 1941 : 7f.). Prince Peter (1955a : 181) has suggested that "the economic function" of polyandry "intensities the unity and solidarity of the sibling group".

The missionary Stulpnagel (1878 : 135) commented that in the Himalayan hills "polyandry is... in reality nothing more than a mere custom of community of wives among brothers who have a community of other goods." Majumdar (1944 : 172) has made the same point with regard to property and polyandry in both Tibet and the Himalayan hills where he has described marriage as a "group contract." This corresponds closely to the explanation for fraternal wife-sharing among the Kotas given by Mandelbaum (1938 : 575 ff.), who describes it as one manifestation of a general principle of "equivalence of brothers" which shows itself in the sharing of labour and property, and which is maintained because (and as long as) it is economically worth while. Leach refers to similar "corporate polyandry" among the Iravas of Central Kerala as described by Aiyappan. (Leach 1955 : 182)

In Jaunsar Bawar and Garhwal, a group of brotherc has the kind of unity to which Radcliffe-Brown referred. It is expressed prominently in economic matters, but also in ritual and social relations. The unity is especially apparent in the relationship between a group of brothers and their wife or wives. Marriage in these areas is in a sense a group transaction in which the family pays collectively for a woman and acquires her economic, sexual, and reproductive services. All three kinds of services are shared by a group of brothers in Jaunsar Bawar. In Garhwal, the first two services are shared by the brothers while the third, reproductive capacity, is granted to one brother exclusively during his lifetime and is passed to another on his death by the practice of levirate. Kapadia (1955 : 66) has discussed in some detail the Pahari woman as the "property" of her husband(s) and the implications of this concept.

The economic arrangement helps explain the community of interest in the wife, but it leaves unexplained the difference in marriage pattern between Jaunsar Bawar and Garhwal, and it leaves unanswered the question of why groups in other parts of India with a similar community of property among brothers do not tolerate either fraternal polyandry or wife sharing.

Psychological factors

Psychological functions of polyandry have been little discussed in the literature and I have no new data on this subject. Prince Peter's suggestion (1955a : 181) that polyandry satisfies repressed incestuous desires seems tenuous at best.

Traditional factors

Most people attribute their customs to tradition. In India, polyandry is widely attributed to specific traditions, notably those embodied in the religious epic, *Mahabharata* which tells of the exploits of the five Pandava brothers and their common wife Draupadi. Almost every group that practices fraternal polyandry in India attributes the practice to that precedent, and usually to an intimate association between themselves and the deities of that epic (cf. Kapadia, 1955: 52f., 75, 92f.; Prince Peter, 1948 : 223). Paharis are well known as devotees of the Pandavas who roamed these very hills in their legendary travels. This tradition in the Himalayan hills has led to such statements as that of Munshi (1955 : i) who says that Jaunsar Bawar culture represents "a fossil of the age of the *Mahabharata*".

The historical origins of polyandry in the Himalayan hills have been speculated upon at some length by Saksena. Mayne is quoted as having suggested that polyandry was adopted by the Indo-Aryan invaders of India from the aborigines or neighbouring polyandrous people, and Majumdar seems to share this view (Saksena, 1955 : 30). Among neighbouring people most often cited as possibly influential are the polyandrous Tibetans with whom the Paharis have long been in occasional contact. Saksena holds the widespread view that polyandry in this area is a remnant of the culture of early Indo-Europeans who came to India via the Himalayan hills. Support for this opinion is found by its proponents, not only in the polyandry of the *Mahabharata*, but in other Hindu classics and ancient records wherein polyandry and other traits characteristic of the hills, such as animal sacrifice, meat-eating, freedom of women, widow remarriage, and lack of caste rigidity are mentioned without disfavour (cf. Briffault, 1959 : 138 f). Saksena summarizes his view in the following words :

> "...A polyandrous belt can be traced extending from Jaunsar Bawar through Kangra valley to Hindu Kush and even beyond. This led Briffault to remark, "The practice of polyandrous marriage is among the Indo-Aryans of the Punjab associated with other survivals of a more archaic and tribal order of society, which are culturally identical with the usages of the polyandrous people of Hindu-Kush, whence the invaders came to India" (Saksena, 1955 : 30).

It is, therefore, evident that polyandry was an institution not unknown to the early Aryan settlers in the Western Himalayas from where it gradually spread southwards, and is even now the accepted form of marriage among the Rajputs and Brahmans of Jaunsar Bawar.

To quote Briffault again :

> "The highland regions of the Himalayas are but a residual cultural island which preserves social customs that had once a far more extensive distribution. The institutions which are found there were once common throughout the greater part of Central Asia" (Saksena, 1955 : 32).

Thus, it is possible that polyandry was an acceptable form among the ancestors of the Central Asian invaders who are presumed by many to be ancestral to present-day high-caste Paharis. It is also possible that it was adopted by Paharis, or some groups of them, from aborigines (often thought to be the ancestors of low-caste Paharis) whom they presumably met and culturally absorbed in this area. It may have been adopted as a result of contacts with the polyandrous Tibetans. It could well have been a regional development, probably in the Western Himalayan hills. Its precise origins have been obscured by time and are not now a fruitful subject for inquiry. More promising is the subject of the present functioning of polyandry and its economic and social structural implications among those who practise it.

Demographic factors

In most discussions of polyandry, the possible influence of the sex ratio has been mentioned (Aiyappan, 1935 : 118 ; Majumdar, 1944 : 168 ; Prince Peter, 1955b : 173 f. ; Westermarck, 1922 : 158 ff.), along with explanations to account for any disparity of the sexes found in association with it (e.g., Rivers, 1906 ; 520 f.). Heath (1955) has suggested that polyandry is generally related to a shortage of women. The consensus of most modern writers is typified by Kapadia (1956 : 1970) when he states that "sex disparity is likely to perpetuate, though it does not necessarily give rise to, a polyandrous pattern."

Data on this subject from the Himalayan hills are suggestive but inconclusive. While North India shows a general surplus of males over females, polyandrous Jaunsar Bawar has an unusually great shortage of females : 789 per 1000 males as compared to the Uttar Pradesh state ratio of 922.[11] Adjacent non-polyandrous Garhwal has a striking and very unusual (for India) surplus of females : a ratio of 1110 in one district and 1149 in the other. These contrasting sex ratios extend back as long as census figures have been available. The two small sub-districts of Garhwal (both adjacent to Jaunsar Bawar) for which polyandry has been reported are the only parts of

Garhwal in which there is a relative shortage of women, with ratios of 942 and 965.

Thus, in the areas of immediate interest here there is a gross correlation between polyandry and a shortage of women and conversely, between monandry and a surplus of women. From the point of view of explanation, the significant fact is that in the Himalayas there is not an equal distribution of the sexes among both polyandrous and monandrous groups as those who reject the sex ratio as an explanation would expect. Neither is there a simple shortage of women in the polyandrous areas in contrast to an equal distribution in the monandrous areas, as those who consider polyandry to be an adaptation to an unusual sex ratio might expect. Instead there is an unusual and unequal sex ratio among *both* the polyandrous and monandrous groups, with the inequality in each case apparently favoring the marriage system of that group. Under these conditions one system cannot be considered *prima facie* to be "natural" and the other deviant.

Figures for larger regions are more ambiguous. The entire Western Himalayan area, throughout which polyandry has a scattered distribution, shows a consistent though (for North India) not an unusual surplus of males, while the Central Himalayan region, where no polyandry has been reported, shows a more nearly equal distribution of the sexes. The latter may be a relatively recent trend, however, as the proportion of women has increased quite steadily from a ratio of 955 in 1901 to a ratio of 1019 in 1951.[12].

Conclusions

In describing and attempting to account for differences in the marriage rules of Jaunsar Bawar and Garhwal, a most important feature has been overlooked by previous commentators : that within the family, sexual and interpersonal connotations of the two systems are very similar, as described above. In view of this fact and of the non-universality of polyandry even where it is practised, the systems are not as different in their functioning as might be expected. Polyandry and monandry in the Himalayan hills appear not to be polar types of marriage systems as has been implied in the literature and as was supposed at the initiation of this research. They are, in fact, relatively minor variations on a central theme, namely : that a wife brings common benefits to a group of brothers who have acquired her by common payment and who share other rights and property in common. The brothers are equivalent, and show their unity as a group, relative to the wife. In one case her reproductive capacity (i.e., the "title" to her offspring) is shared in the other it is not. In both groups any one of a family of brothers may be the biological father of a particular offspring. In Jaunsar Bawar the role of social father is shared ; in Garhwal it is exclusive. That is the main difference between polyandry and monandry in this area. It represents a significant difference in values but a less drastic difference in the functioning of the systems than had been anticipated.

In view of the over-all similarity of Pahari cultures, contrasts between polyandrous Jaunsar Bawar and monandrous Garhwal have not appeared as clearly as was expected when the research began. However, some conclusions pertaining to the original hypothesis can be stated :

> Features of polyandrous societies reported in other parts of the world correspond only partially with those found in Jaunsar Bawar. The Pahari case contradicts the hypotheses that virtual economic uselessness of women, and dowry or property rights held by women, are universal correlates of polyandry.

As evidenced by a comparison of marriage and family relations in Jaunsar Bawar and Garhwal, fraternal polyandry may be advantageous but is not inevitable when there is a shortage of woman and when a low proportion of children in the family is economically advantageous.

"Equivalence of brothers" in economic matters and in relation to the sexuality of their wives may be advantageous when, in a patrilocal society, husbands leave their wives for extended periods, but there is no evidence to show the superiority of polyandry over wife-sharing in such circumstances.

It seems logical, but could not be demonstrated by this

comparative study, that fraternal polyandry would be advantageous when cost of obtaining or maintaining a wife is high, and also when in a patrilineal society property upon which livelihood or wealth depends is unusually scarce and limited. The latter is an advantage frequently cited by people of South Asia who are fraternally polyandrous.

No evidence was adduced with regard to the psychological implications of polyandry nor the value of polyandry as a means toward intra-family cooperation and consensus. The latter is, however, widely held to be an adjunct of polyandry and is a necessary one if the economic advantages of unity of family property in such societies are to be fully realized.

Characterization of polyandry as an extension of the principle of equivalence of brothers, especially in economic matters, is valid for Jaunsar Bawar as well as for other Himalayan hill areas and probably for Tibet. It does not, however, characterize formal polyandry in contrast to fraternal wife sharing. This is evidenced by its applicability to the Garhwal Paharis and to the South Indian Kotas, neither of whom allow a woman a plurality of husbands or endow a child with more than one social father. Both polyandrous and non-polyandrous Paharis share a favourable attitude toward the sharing of wives and property among brothers. This equivalence of brothers may be a predisposing but not sufficient precondition for formal polyandry. Certainly this attitude characterizes most fraternally polyandrous people in South Asia.

The question of why Jaunsar Bawar people are polyandrous and Garhwal people are not has not been answered. The answer undoubtedly lies in a combination of cultural-historical factors, including the advantages which one system may have relative to the other in a particular context (cf. Cooper, 1941 : 55). Without going too deeply into conjectural history, some possibilities may be considered.

The Pahari culture functions satisfactorily under either polyandry or monandry. Whatever the history of polyandrous and monandrous institutions of Pahari marriage, they likely proved differentially advantageous among their practitioners or potential practitioners. Each would presumably have persisted most among those groups to which it proved most advantageous or least disadvantageous. Advantages could take the form of the approval of neighbours, economic well-being, social integration, etc.

Accurate historical data on the origins and contacts of Himalayan peoples are lacking, and according to my evidence the distribution of polyandry as contrasted with wife sharing in this region cannot be explained in terms of associated economic or social structural features. It is therefore not unreasonable to seek a partial explanation in the one apparently significant difference which does appear between polyandrous and monandrous groups of the area : the sex ratio. The sex ratio could have been a potent factor in the acquisition and/or retention of one system or the other. For example, when external pressure for abandonment of polyandry grew as a result of increasing administrative, religious, and social contacts with people of the plains of India, polyandry, persisted most in Jaunsar Bawar, the area in which the sex ratio favoured it to the greatest extent.

Of the several advantages which can be cited for polyandry or monandry, a crucial one could have been the social and economic advantage which derives from insuring the availability of family life for every adult. These are societies in which it is difficult as well as almost unheard of to subsist without a family. The sex ratio might tip the scale toward polyandry or monandry on the basis of this advantage.

The weakness in this argument is that it depends on a disparity in the sexes as an antecedent condition, and this cannot be demonstrated. Some observers claim that male Garhwal residents emigrate in great numbers to work as servants on the plains. It is extremely doubtful that this occurs frequently enough to account for the sex ratio, but no data are available with which to verify or disprove the suggestion.[13] The same can be said of military service as a possible explanation. Some claim that selling of Jaunsar Bawar women to plains people has resulted in the shortage of women there, but this, too, doubtless occurs too infrequently to account for the sex ratio. Moreover, in Jaunsar Bawar, the ratio of the sexes among children is as uneven as that of adults. This suggests as "causes" of the paucity of females, female infanticide, for which there is no evidence ; or neglect of female children, which is less unlikely (cf. Majumdar, 1944 : 171). Rivers (1906 : 520 f) was among the first to point out that such practices can as satisfactorily be attributed to the effects of polyandry as they can be described as its causes.

To explain the origin or distribution of polyandry and monandry in the area would therefore require data which are not available : cultural history and census data from earlier eras. The futility of seeking causes without knowledge of the attendant conditions is well known.

Why there is polyandry in Jaunsar Bawar and not in Garhwal is therefore not a question that is likely to be answerable now, or that in this context is very relevant. A comparable question would be that of why Jaunsar Bawar people speak Western Pahari while Garhwal residents speak Central Pahari. These are relatively minor differences ; the culminations of culture history, contacts, and of drift from a common base. They have resulted from many choices over considerable periods of time. The choices have taken place within the cultural context of economic and social equivalence of brothers and of the contractual nature of marriage where in a bride is "purchased" by the family into which she marries. Both of these conditions are compatible with fraternal polyandry. The choices which have led to regional differences in marriage patterns have been made in response to conditions (limitations and opportunities) within and without the groups involved directed in over-all pattern, perhaps, by certain advantages which followed from them. But the particular conditions which influenced them are now largely unknown. According to this research there are in the Himalayan hills no simple functional correlates of polyandry as contrasted to monandrous wife-sharing except in so far as the sex ratio is so correlated. The important correlations are those of specific cultural content : polyandry is one feature of an over-all cultural pattern of the Western Himalayas which contrasts in a number of details with the over-all pattern of the Central (and probably the Eastern) Himalayas, one feature of which is the absence of formal polyandry. The present distribution of these patterns is apparently the result of regional divergence from a common and relatively homogeneous culture; a divergence made possible in part by relative regional isolation.[14] The same processes which resulted in divergence of such features as language, dress, and worship facilitated the present distribution of marriage regulations (Berreman, 1960). Therefore, regional variation in marriage regulations is no more fundamental nor surprising than other cultural differences in these hills and is to be understood as being of approximately the same order.

Observers feel compelled to question and explain polyandry wherever it occurs because it is unusual. One might equally fruitfully question the occurrence of polygyny. The factors leading to one are probably no more consistent and compelling than those that lead to the other. Polyandry, like polygyny, is evidently not a sufficiently unitary phenomenon to be explained in the same terms everywhere[15]. It may have certain advantages or functionally related correlates in some areas and not in others. That they are not universal does not mean, of course, that they are not significant.

There may be conditions which correlate with fraternal polyandry on a widespread cross-cultural scale. However, these probably take the form of effects of the functioning of polyandry, or prerequisites for polyandry, rather than specific causes which inevitably lead to polyandry.

NOTES

1. This paper was read in abbreviated form before the Fourth Annual Meeting of the Kroeber Anthropological, Society, May 21, 1960, at Berkeley. The research was carried out in India during 1957-58 under a Ford Foundation Foreign Area Training Fellowship and is reported in full in : Berreman 1959. I would like to thank David Mandelb aum for his helpful comments on the manuscript.
2. Following the recent definition of marriage put forth by Gough (1959 : 32), as a husband may be defined as a person who is in a relationship to a woman such that a child born to her under circumstances

not prohibited by the rules of the relationship is or may be publicly acknowledged to be that person's child and is accorded full birth-status rights common to normal society members of the society or social stratum into which it is born.

3. Polyandry has been reported in the Rawai and Jaunpur sub-districts of Tehri-Garhwal, immediately adjacent to Jaunsar Bawar (Kapadia, 1955 : 63). These portions wherein polyandry is found are doubtless the western border areas which fall into the Western Pahari sub-culture area, or on its peripheries.
4. By Garhwal, I mean the districts of Tehri-Garhwal, Garhwal and the hill sections of eastern Dehra Dun district (other Central Pahari districts are Almora and parts of Naini Tal). The research reported here was in a hill area of western Garhwal, overlapping Tehri-Garhwal and Dehra Dun districts (Berreman, 1960). The area can legitimately is lumped with Garhwal because its residents are culturally of Garhwal. Their ancestors came from interior Tehri-Garhwal, they consider themselves to be Garhwalis and are so considered by others. Generalizations in this paper about Garhwali marriage and family relationships are valid for western Garhwal and only inferentially for the rest of Garhwal.
5. Note that a plurality of husbands constitutes polyandry and the number of wives is considered irrelevant in the definition implicit here. Most discussions of the advantages of polyandry imply either that only one wife is involved or at least that husbands outnumber wives.

   The incidence of polyandry reported by Majumdar for this village is high if, as seems probable, he is referring to conjugal family units. If *all* sets of adult real brothers currently living in the Garhwal village I studied had formed fraternally polyandrous conjugal families, then 43 % of all conjugal families in that village would have been polyandrous. This is comparable to the proportion of polyandrous families reported by Majumdar. Fraternal polyandry would therefore seem to be preferred pattern of marriage in Majumdar's village, with an incidence about as high as possible. Monogamy probably occurs most often among men with no brothers. Plural wives are probably secured in either case primarily to remedy a shortage of labour or heirs in the family, as they are in Garhwal.
6. I witnessed one Garhwal marriage in which an elder brother substituted for the groom. This arrangement was devised to avoid the consequences of incompatibility in the horoscopes of the intended bride and groom rather than to effect a polyandrous union. The intended husband took over after the ceremonies. One might speculate upon a polyandrous precedent for this device but I could find no evidence to support such a speculation. More probably this incident reflects the general equivalence of brothers in Pahari culture. David Mandelbaum has pointed out that it illustrates

not only the ritual and social equivalence of brothers, but also their personal non-equivalence in relation to the supernatural. Nothing could be more personal than the horoscope and in that respect the brothers were significantly not equivalent.

7. Majumdar (1944 : 173 ff.) and Kapadia (1955 : 73, 83), have argued rather unconvincing that high-caste Paharis were once matrilineal or heavily influenced by matrilineal people, evidently in the belief that this is more compatible with polyandry than is a purely patrilineal tradition. This is in line with the belief of McLennan and others that polyandry is associatcd with matrilineality. Leach (1955 : 183), who hypothesizes that inheritance of property through females as well as through males is consistently associated with polyandry, implies that only patrilineality of "an ambiguous and rather uncertain type," and not "patrilineal systems of the more extreme type," can be associated with polyandry. Although Pahari patrilineality is not extreme, it is so with regard to inheritance of property. Leach's hypothesis is not supported by my research nor by the evidence presented by Majumdar or Kapadia.
8. An exception, according to Prince Peter (1955b : 171 f.), are the Todas. He asserts that they share no property in the family. However, Rivers (1906 : 558 ff.) describes the house as specifically belonging to a group of brothers who share a wife, and he mentions that although buffaloes are largely individual propety, "in practice, owing to the fact that brothers usually live together a herd of buffaloes is treated as the property of a family of brothers but whenever the occasion arises there are definite rules for the division of the buffaloes among them." Such rules are undoubtedly to be found in all polyandrous societies, as they are among the Paharis.
9. The Tibetan evidence, too, contradicts this as a general explanation of polyandry. Carrasco (1959 : 35, 68) describes the important and productive economic role of women in Tibetan society. It also seems doubtful, according to his data (Carrasco, 1959 : 36 f.), that Tibetan women are invested with property rights frequently enough to support Leach's hypothesis concerning the relationship between such rights and polyandry.
10. This explanation undoubtedly contains a large element of rationalization. It serves to preserve an ideal of fraternal amity in the face of a good deal of actual fraternal strife by blaming it on wives who are essentially outsiders in the family and who most often come from alien villages.
11. Sex ratios given here are figured as they are in the Census of India, i.e., number of females per 1000 males. This is the reciprocal of the usual ratio given in the United States Census.

    All figures are for rural areas, i.e., excluding towns of over

5000 population in most cases, and are drawn from various volumes of the 1951 Census of India.

12. In non-polyandrous and almost entirely non-Pahari Dehra Dun district adjacent to both Jaunsar Bawar and Garhwal, the shortage of women (ratio of 759) is even greater than in Jaunsar Bawar, and in non-polyandrous Naini Tal to the east the sex ratio is only 728. These two areas border on the hills, but their populations are largely derived from the plains. Dehra Dun, at least, has been relatively recently settled and the sex ratio is affected by the presence of tea plantations and other innovations a typical of the hill areas.

13. In the immediate area of my research there was neither a surplus of women nor a significant amount of out-migration by men.

14. This divergence may have been of polyandry from a monandrous base in the Western Pahari area, or of monandry from a polyandrous base in the Central and Eastern Pahari areas. The change need not have been a difficult or disorganizing one in view of the over-all similarity of the cultures involved and the apparent compatibility of both polyandry and monandry in these cultures.

    Gough (1952 : 86) records a case of significant structural change without discontinuity in South India : "the Nayar system has, over a period of two hundred years, changed from a very extreme form of matriliny into a 'bilateral' system with only a weak tendency to matriliny ; but the latter system developed imperceptibly out of the former."

    Prince Peter (1955 : 183) notes that in Ladakh, Muslim converts dropped polyandry almost overnight, apparently without seriously affecting other aspects of their culture.

15. The following parallel comment by Westermarck (1922 : 206) was discovered by the author after this article was in Press : "To explain in full why certain factors in some cases give rise to polyandry and in other cases not is as impossible as it often is to say exactly why one people is monogamous and another people polygynous."

REFERENCES

Aiyappan, A. 1935 Fraternal Polyandry in Malabar. *Man in India* 14 : 108-18

——1937 Polyandry and Sexual Jealousy. *Man* 37 : 104.

Berreman, G.D. 1959 Kin, Caste and Community in a Himalayan hill village, Doctoral dissertation. Cornell University.

———1960 *Cultural varia and brift in the Himalayan hills, American Anthropologist* 62 : 774-94.

Briffault, Robert 1959 *The Mothers*. London, George Allen & Unwin Ltd.

Carrasco, Pedro 1959 *Land and Polity in Tibet.* Seattle, University of Washington Press.

Cooper, John M. 1941 *Temporal sequence and the marginal cultures.* The Catholic University of America Anthropological Series, No 10.

Dass Gupta, H.C. 1921 A short note on Polyandry in the Jubbal State (Simla). *The Indian Antiquary* 50 : 146-48.

Fischer, H.T. 1952 *Polyandry.* International Archives of Ethnography, 46 : 106-15.

Gough, Kathleen 1952 Changing kinship usages in the setting of political and economic change among the Nayars of Malabar. *Journal of the Royal Anthropological Institute of Great Britain and Ireland* 82 : 71-87.

———1959 The Nayars and the definition of marriage. *Journal of the Royal Anthropological Institute of Great Britain and Ireland* 89 : 23, 34.

Grierson, George A. 1916 *Linguistic Survey of India* vol. IX, part IV. Calcutta, Superintendent of Government Printing.

Heath, Dwight B. 1955 *Sexual division of labor and cross-cultural research.* Paper read at the Fifty-fourth Annual Meeting of the American Anthropological Associations Boston. Reference in The World of Man, by J.J. Honigmann, New York, Harper and Brothers (1959), p. 374.

Joshi, L.D. 1929 *The Khasa family law in the Himalayan districts of the United Provinces of India.* Allahabad, The Superintendent, Government Press.

Kapadia, K.M. 1955 *Marriage and family in India.* London, Oxford University Press.

Kirkpatrick, G.S. 1878 Polyandry in the Punjab. *The Indian Antiquary* 7 : 86.

Leach, E. 1965 Polyandry, inheritance and the definition of marriage. *Man* 55 : 182-86.

Majumdar, D.N. 1974 *The Fortunes of Primitive Tribes* Lucknow, The Universal Publishers Ltd.

———1953 Children in a polyandrous society. *The Eastern Anthropologist* 6 : 177-89.

———1955a Family and marriage in a polyandrous society. *The Eastern Anthropologist* 8 : 85-110.

———1955b Demographic structure in a polyandrous village. *The Eastern Anthropologist* 8 : 161-72.

Mandelbaum, D.G. 1983 Polyandry in Kota society. *American Anthropologist* 40 : 574-83.

Mukherji, Anima 1950 The pattern of polyandrous society with particular reference to tribal crime. *Man in India* 30 : 56-65.

Munshi, K.M. 1955 Foreword. In Social economy of a polyandrous people, by R.N. Saksena, Agra University Press.

Prince Peter of Greece and Denmark 1948 Tibetan, Toda, and Tiya polyandry : a report on field investigations. *Transactions of the New York Academy of Sciences*, Series II, 10 : 210-25.

———1955a Polyandry and the kinship group. *Man* 55 : 179-81.

———1955b The Polyandry of Ceylon and South India. Acts due IV Congress International des Sciences Anthropologiques at Ethnologiques Vienna (1952) 2 : 167-75.

———1955c The Polyandry of Tibet. Acts due IV, Congress International des Sciences Anthropologiques at Ethnologiques, Vienne (1952) 2 : 176-84.

Radcliffe-Brown, A.R. 1941 The study of kinship systems. *Journal of the Royal Anthropological Institute of Great Britain and Ireland* 71 : 1-18.

Rivers, W.H.R. 1906 *The Todas.* London, Macmillan and Company Ltd.

Saksena, R.N. 1955 *Social economy of a polayandrous people* Agra, Agra University Press.

Stulpnagal, C.R. 1878 Polyandry in the Himalayas. *The Indian Antiquary* 7 : 132-35.

Westermark, Edward 1922 *The History of Human Marriage.* vol. III, New York, The Allerton Book Company.

6

HIMALAYAN POLYANDRY AND THE DOMESTIC CYCLE[1]

GERALD D. BERREMAN

Polyandry has fascinated and challenged anthropologists from the early evolutionists to contemporary structural-functionalists[2]. Nowhere in the world, save perhaps Tibet, does this form of marriage and family organization occur more consistently than among the people of the mountains (the *pahari*) in certain regions of the Western Himalayas of North India, especially in Himachal Pradesh and north-western Uttar Pradesh. I have elsewhere described and analyzed the polyandry of this area with reference to the general literature on polyandry, focusing on the people of the mountainous subdivision of Dehra Dun District known as Jaunsar Bawar, in the north-western corner of Uttar Pradesh (Berreman, 1962). That account contrasted the fraternally polyandrous system of Jaunsar Bawar, as reported in published accounts and by people who had worked there (cf. Majumdar, 1944, 1953, 1955a, 1955b, 1962 ; Jain, 1948 ; Saksena, 1955), with the marriage and family system of the nearby and culturally and ecologically similar monandrous

---

Reproduced by permission of the American Anthropological Association, from *American Ethnologist*, 2 (1) : 127-138, 1975.

(non-polyandrous) people of Garhwal, among whom I had done intensive research (Berreman, 1972). My aim was to examine, by reference to these data, various factors which had been proposed as causal for polyandry or as in one way or another accounting for its occurrence. I concluded that none of these explanations was convincing and that, moreover, "polyandry...is evidently not a sufficiently unitary phenomenon to be explained in the same terms everywhere" (Berreman, 1962 : 72). Pahari polyandry seems not to be significantly similar to number of other systems also called "polyandry" in the literature, although it may well be significantly similar to *some* such systems. That is, it may be useful to discuss the origin, function and consequences of polyandry$_1$, polyandry$_2$, polyandry$_3$, etc., but not polyandry *per se*.

My intention in the present paper is to further describe the fraternally polyandrous family of Jaunsar Bawar and its variations in time and circumstance. I do so in order to describe and account for the high degree of intra-cultural variation in family type that has been noted for Jaunsar Bawar. I do so also to throw additional light on the nature of this "polyandrous" system of domestic organization and its implications for general and theoretical statements that have been made about both Himalayan polyandry and polyandry in general[3]. Such statements have failed to take into account the temporal factor in family composition and organization—the life-histories of families—which Fortes (1971) has called the developmental cycle of the domestic group. Yet, as I shall show, the temporal factor—the developmental cycle—largely explains the apparent diversity in family organization in this region. As Fortes warned : "the developmental factor is intrinsic to domestic organization and to ignore it leads to serious misinterpretation of the descriptive facts". (1971 : 3) Such misinterpretation includes the assertion that Pahari polyandry is like some quite dissimilar instances of polyandry and that it inevitably implies significantly fewer married (and reproducing) women than men and hence fewer children and heirs than other domestic arrangements—an assumption which underlies virtually all attempts to explain the phenomenon in functional terms (cf. Berreman, 1962). By following the developmental cycle of "polyandrous" Pahari families, one can achieve a more realistic understanding of the structure and functioning of the family in this society, its intra-cultural variety, its existential reality and its theoretical and practical implications.

A brief general description of polyandry in Jaunsar Bawar is necessary in order to provide a context for that which follows. In this society a polyandrous union occurs when a woman goes through a marriage ceremony with the eldest of a group of brothers, all of whom thereupon become the woman's husbands. Subsequent wives may also be taken, and in fact usually are. If so, each wife is individually married in a ceremony with the eldest brother, or, if the woman has been previously married, she simply moves in with the brothers (after necessary arrangements regarding bride-price have been made with her previous husband(s) or with her family of orientation). The new wife is shared, along with her co-wives by all of the brothers unless one or more brothers wish to break away from the joint family. No brother can remain a member of the joint family and claim exclusive rights to a wife. Nor can he do so and claim exclusive rights to land, houses, cattle, clientele, etc., for in all of these respects, as in the case of their relationships with wives, children, and parents, brothers are regarded as equivalent (cf. Mandelbaum, 1938). The eldest brother dominates with respect to the wife or wives, as he does in other domestic matters, but he has no exclusive rights, sexual, reproductive or otherwise. A woman considers all of the brothers to be her husbands. Children recognize the group of brothers as their fathers : they address all of them as "father" and the sons inherit from all as a group without regard to paternity or maternity within the polyandrous family (Majumdar, 1944 : 178 ; 1953 : 179 ; 1962 : 101)[4]. In cases of division of the patrimony, special portions may be given to the eldest (and sometimes the youngest as well) of the brothers. If the family is divided while the children are young and unmarried, paternity may be assigned by lot, by mother's designation (she is supposed to assign paternity to the first husband who had sexual relation with her after her last menstruation prior to the child's conception), or by order of birth (whereby the eldest child is attributed to the eldest father, second child to next-eldest father, and so on in a sequence which rotates back to the eldest father to begin again if the number of children exceeds the number of fathers) (cf. Majumdar, 1944 : 144f). Physical resemblance between a child and a particular father may also be a basis for assigning paternity. In cases of familial fission, wives are assigned their husbands by preference and agreement wherein affection, relative age, and marriage sequence, as well as maternity (i.e., trying to keep mothers together with their young children) are likely to be taken into account. This latter factor also affects the designation of children's paternity in that the child of a favoured wife may be assigned the paternity of the husband who favours her. Such familial fission among brothers is, however, rare and is rarer still after children have been born.

In other respects, the ethnography of the region is very similar to that of nearby Garhwal as described in *Hindus of the Himalayas* (Berreman, 1972 ; cf. Majumdar, 1962). In both areas, the economy of the majority high-caste population is primarily agricultural, with a secondary dependence on animal husbandry while low-status artisan castes live by their craft specialities serving a largely high-caste clientele. Land is valuable but not as scarce as in most of North India. All property is owned jointly by male members of the patrilineal, patrilocal extended family. If property is divided among brothers, they usually receive equal shares, although in some regions (as indicated above) the eldest and sometimes the youngest may receive special shares. Normally brothers continue to hold the patrimony in common, and among non-polyandrous groups division occurs in the next generation among patrilateral parallel cousins. The eldest active male dominates in the joint family but cannot compel younger men to remain within it. Marriage takes place within the caste and outside the sib and mother's sib. It entails payment of a bride-price which must be returned if the marriage is dissolved, as it can be by either party, unless in the dissolution the husband is clearly at fault. Where dowry is used, it is exceptional and evidently of recent origin, having diffused from the plains as an aspect of status emulation of plains people. A man's initial marriage should always be to a previously unmarried woman selected by his parents in consultation with a priest. The initial marriage of a man or a woman should always be effected through a formal marriage ceremony, and rules of exogamy and endogamy must be scrupulously observed. Subsequent marriages for both sexes need not be ceremonialized, and rules of exogamy and endogamy are occasionally contravened. In monandrous Garhwal, levirate is the rule upon husband's death, and repayment of the bride-price must be made to his family if his wife wishes to go elsewhere.

Although in Jaunsar Bawar, fraternal polyandry is the ideal and, as described by Majumdar, is also "the common form" of marriage, it is not a system wherein a group of brothers necessarily or even usually shares a single wife. Neither in the history of any particular family or individual, nor at any given moment in any community, is classic fraternal polyandry, such as that described for the Iravas of central Kerala by Aiyappan (1935 : 114ff), likely to be the only form of the domestic group.

> "Monogamy, polygyny and fraternal polyandry, including a combination of polyandry and polygyny approximating fraternal 'group marriage', appear in the same villages and even in the same lineages" (cf. Majumdar, 1944 : 167f ; Berreman, 1962 : 61)

Moreover, as Majumdar observed more recently,

> "the types of family referred to are not stable and there is a constant shift from one type to the other due to frequency of divorce and of taking multiple wives, and even a polyandrous and polygynous family may be reduced to monogamous unions" (Majumdar, 1962 : 80).

"shift from one type to the other due to frequency of divorce and of taking multiple wives, and even a polyandrous and polygynous family may be reduced to monogamous unions"

(Majumdar, 1962 : 80). In the two Jaunsar Bawar villages for which figures are available, *Lohari* (Majumdar, 1955b : 165) and *Baila* (Majumdar, 1962 : 78), it is reported that of a total of 146 domestic units, 44% are polyandrous, 20% are polygynous, and 36% are monogamous. For one of the villages (Lohari), Majumdar gives figures showing that while 49% of the families are "polyandrous," 61% of those unions had as many (or more) wives as husbands. (Note that a plurality of husbands constituted "polyandry", and the number of wives was considered irrelevant in Majumdar's terminology at that time, except in the case of "polygyny" where there was only one husband). Comparing the figures for Lohari with the demography of a similar village I had studied in adjacent, monandrous Garhwal, I concluded, in 1962, that the incidence of fraternal polyandry reported by Majumdar was about as high as was demographically possible (Berreman, 1962 : 73n) suggesting that it was indeed the "common" and preferred domestic arrangement.

Subsequent to his report on Lohari, Majumdar (1962 : 73) coined the term "polyandry" to refer to any marital union involving a multiplicity of both husbands and wives, (Theretofore he, like his students and colleagues, had called all multiple-husband unions "polyandrous" regardless of the number of wives). Applying this newer terminology to the village of Baila, Majumdar reported eighty nine marital unions, of which 30% were polygynandrous, 9% polyandrous, 25% polygynous, and 34% monogamous (Majumdar, 1962 : 78).

The only other precise figures available for marital arrangements in Jaunsar Bawar are those provided by Jain (1948), based on a sample of 593 married woman comprising all of the currently married women in three families in each of three villages in each *Khat* or administrative sub-division of Jaunsar Bawar. Of these, 57% had multiple husbands ranging in number from two to nine, and 43% had only one husband. However, of the 43% recorded as monandrous, one-fourth (12% of the total) were partial widows who had previously had multiple husbands. The remaining three-fourths of the monandrous women (31%

TABLE 1

Marital arrangements in Jaunsar Bawar Villages.*

Source	Polygynandry (multiple wives & husbands)	Polyandry (multiple husbands only)	Polygyny (multiple wives only)	Monogamy	Number of Units
Village Baila (Majumdar, 1962 : 78)	32.6%	9.0%	24.7%	33.7%	89
Village Lohari (Majumdar, 1955b : 165)	49.0%		12.0%	39.0%	57
District sample (Jain, 1948)	47.0%		43.0%		593

* In the cases of village Lohari and the District sample, the authors lumped all marital arrangements involving multiple husbands under the term "polyandry," regardless of the number of wives. In the District sample, the calculations were made with reference to the number of married women rather than to domestic units as such. Thus, in that sample the only factor distinguished is the number of husbands per wife.

of the total) were monandrous, as the author notes, "mostly because the husband had no other brother" (Jain, 1948 : 31).[5] In short, few were monandrous by choice. These figures provide further evidence that fraternal polyandry with multiple wives, i.e., polygyandry, is the common and preferred domestic arrangement in this region. This being the case, how then does one account for the reported presence of "monogamy" and "polygyny" in this "polyandrous" society, and how does one account for the variable ratio of married men to women even in the "polyandrous" unions ? The reasons are to be found in developmental, circumstantial and optional factors of domestic organization rather than simply in a tolerance for diverse social forms.

Developmental factors

"Developmental factors" in the domestic cycle are those structural features with emerge as characteristic phases in the life histories of particular domestic groups in society—as distinguished from the distinct structural types which they may resemble. Fortes (1971) has noted that the papers which his essay introduces describe societies in each of which a variety of types of domestic organization and residence could be cited, with results that would be confusing. "But when it is recognized that these so-called types are in fact phases in the developmental cycle of a single general form for each society, the confusion vanishes" (Fortes, 1971 : 3). I will demonstrate that the polyandry, polygyny, polygyandry or group marriage, and monogamy of Jaunsar Bawar are variations (many of which are attributable to developmental factors) on a single general form rather than distinct coexistent types of structures, and that moreover they are so regarded by the people who comprise them. Their coexistence seems to the latter no more puzzling or complicated than the coexistence in the community of families including three, two and one generations, or of families with no children, few children, and many children, or with widely differing proportions of the sexes or widely differing age-distributions among their children.

In order to describe developmental factors in Jaunsar Bawar, I have constructed an ideal-typical hypothetical family. I have done so because I want to use an illustrative example, and I do not have precise data on an actual Jaunsar Bawar family through time. However, this case accords with the structural and demographic facts of family life reported synchronically for two villages by Majumdar (1955b ; 1962 : 78), for a sample of villages by Jain (1948), and with those recorded over time for families in Sirkanda, the monandrous Garhwal village I know best, some thirty-five miles to the east. This case accords also, I believe, with the experienced reality of the lives of the people of Jaunsar Bawar ; that is, they would find it true to life.

For simplicity I will describe only a single generation in a single family, ignoring the co-resident parental generation and the emergence of children, both of which would be expectable in such a family. For illustrative purposes, I have invented an agricultural (land-owning) family with more spouses than the average, but well within the expectable and reported range in any agricultural village of Jaunsar Bawar. I think that the total number of working adults (hence spouses) in agricultural families in Jaunsar Bawar, as in nearby Garhwal, is more or less proportional to the amount of cultivable land held by the family (cf. Berreman, 1962 : 64-65 ; 1972 : 150ff ; Majumdar, 1962 : 76). Women are as productive in agricultural work as men, and with the exception of ploughing and other activities involving draft animals, they do virtually the same farm work. Thus, a family of three or four brothers with modest land-holdings (four to five acres) might be most likely to have one or two wives, while a family of one man or two brothers with an equal amount of land might have two to four wives. Families with less land would generally have fewer wives. Families without land at all would have less incentive to acquire multiple wives, for in such cases women's work is primarily household work that can be handled by one or two women. For similar reasons, such families have little incentive to adopt male household members or to hire servants. They also have less incentive than the landed to retain the common patrimony through joint-family organization among brothers. In the absence of land, there is little for the brothers to share and little work that can best be done in common. The result is that family size is smaller among the landless, and multiple marriage is somewhat less common. This is the case in the Garhwal village of Sirkanda (Berreman, 1972 : 146f), and is reported to be the case in the village of Lohari in Jaunsar Bawar (Majumdar, 1955b : 170 ; 1962 : 75). This principle is illustrated most graphically in the distribution of family size, polyandry and multiple wives among the low castes, most of whose members are landless. Thus, Majumdar notes for village Lohari :

> "the Kolta who do not own land and live as agrestic serfs, have a lower incidence of polyandry (than do the land-owning Rajputs), viz., 36.36% as contrasted with 68.96% among the Rajput. The incidence of joint

family among the Kolta is 45.45% while it is 62% among the Rajput" (Majumdar, 1955b : 168).

It is clear, however, that the "polygynandrous" union described by Majumdar is found in all castes (cf. Majumdar, 1962: 78), as are monogamous, polyandrous and polygynous unions. Table 2, a summary of caste-specific data on marriage types in village Baila (the only such data available), illustrates caste differences in domestic organisation, which in turn reflects landed-landless differences.

TABLE 2

Marital arrangements in village Baila, by caste groups (after Majumdar, 1962 : 78)

	Polygy-nandry	Poly-andry	Polygyny	Mono-gamy	No. of unit
High castes* (*Brahmin* and *Rajput*)	40.0%	6.0%	28.0%	26.0%	47
Low castes* (*Badi, Sunar, Bajgi, Kolta*)	24.0%	12.0%	21.0%	43.0%	42
Total	32.6%	9.0%	24.7%	33.7%	89

*High castes (*khas*) are landed castes and low castes (*dom*) are for the most part landless.

In order to describe and understand the coexistence of these arrangements of marriages and family, it is useful to observe one family over time. Let us assume that in a Jaunsar Bawar village in the year 1910, there were three young brothers in a moderately prosperous Rajput farming family, age 18, 15, and 12. (Since all sisters will marry and reside patrilocally, none will be included here). In that year, the eldest brother underwent a marriage ceremony with a fifteen-year-old girl of the same caste and of an unrelated sib, as is prescribed by custom. She thereby became the wife of all three of the brothers in common, as is also prescribed by custom. The domestic group in this generation then became, structurally, a typical fraternally polyandrous one (although, of course, in fact the youngest brother-perhaps both of the younger ones-did not begin to have sexual relations with the wife until they reached about sixteen years of age) :[6]

Five years later, a second wife, sixteen years old, was married in the same manner as the first, becoming the second common wife. The domestic group was thereby transformed into one which Majumdar would term "polygyandrous" (1962 : 72), and which might be described structurally as comprising fraternal group marriage. If there had been only one husband (i.e., if he had, had no brothers, as is not infrequently the case), the same event would have created a typical polygynous household. A number of reasons might be cited by the brothers for adding another wife-all within the context of the general fact that polygyny (a multiplicity of wives) is as common and a legitimate, although not as remarked in the region, as polyandry. Additional wives may be sought : (1) in order to produce children (especially sons), if the first wife (or wives) is barren, has only daughters, or has few sons ; (2) in order to increase the adult labour force in the family (e.g., if there is more land or other work than the adults already present can effectively handle) ; (3) to provide increased or improved social and sexual companionship within the family.

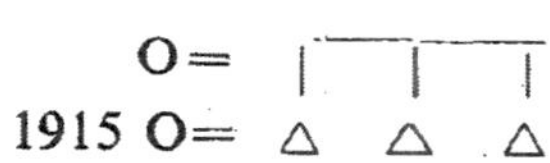

Note that at this point our data contradict the common assertion that group marriage nowhere exists. Bohannan, for example, says :

"There has never been discovered a kinship group that contains within it all of the ten basic kinship relationships (wife, co-wife, husband, co-husband, mother, father, daughter, son, brother, sister). A family based on the group marriage of Morganian tradition would have contained all" (Bohannan, 1963 : 72).

The "polygynandrous" family of Jaunsar Bawar frequently does contain all of these relationships although the children who are acknowledged by all of the men, are not acknowledged by all of the women in the group as Morgan postulated they would be in group marriage. That is, the paternity of the children is regarded as shared by the "fathers," unless some unusual circumstance of family fission requires that they be apportioned among the men (at which time a child is likely for the first time to be associated with a particular father). In contrast, the biological mother of each child is known and socially recognized as such even within the family and despite the fact that a child addresses and refers to all of its fathers' wives as "mother" (*iii*) (cf. Berreman, 1962 : 62 ; Majumdar, 1944 : 144f ; 1953 : 179 ; 1962 : 101, 122).

Returning to the example, we might find that five years later a third wife was acquired. Inquiry would reveal similar reasons for this marriage as for the second. This wife, however, might well have been a widow or divorced of, say twenty-three years of age (as might have been, in fact, any but the initial wife), in which case no ceremony would have marked the marriage—she would simply have moved into the household. (If she had left a previous husband in order to do so, he would be reimbursed by the new husbands in the amount of the bride-price). Thus, in 1920, the domestic group in this generation comprised three brothers, ages 28, 25, and 22, with their three common wives, ages 25, 21, and 23. This arrangement has been most frequently called simply "polyandry" (Jain, 1948 ; Majumdar, 1944, 1955a ; Saksena, 1955). and in one instance, more precisely, "polyandry with an equal number of husbands and wives" (Majumdar, 1955b : 165). From the point of view of structure, it could as well have been termed "polygyny" or "polygyny with an equal number of husbands and wives." In the terminology of the time it might better have been called "fraternal group marriage with an equal number of husbands and wives." In the terminology of his 1962 book, Majumdar would have called it "polygynandrous", to which one might add his earlier modifying phrase, "with an equal number of husbands and wives." This seems to be the most precise and descriptive terminology. In any case, this marriage was a turning point in the demography of the family in our example because the number of husbands no longer exceeded the number of wives. This precluded the oft-cited unique consequences of polyandry for fertility, reproduction, and demography.

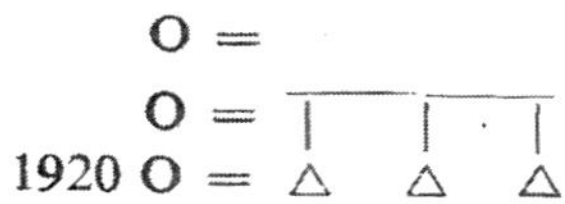

In another five years, a brother might have died—let us say the middle one—and an additional wife of twenty years of age might have been acquired with the thought of replacing the labour of the dead brother. Then the women in the family would outnumber the men four to two, with obvious reproductive implications. This large a plurality of wives is unusual but not improbable. Such families Majumdar earlier termed "polyandrous with unequal number of hushands and wives" (1955b : 165), and more recently simply "polygynandrous" (1962 : 72), neither of which is very illuminating about the sex ratio in the family or its reproductive implications.

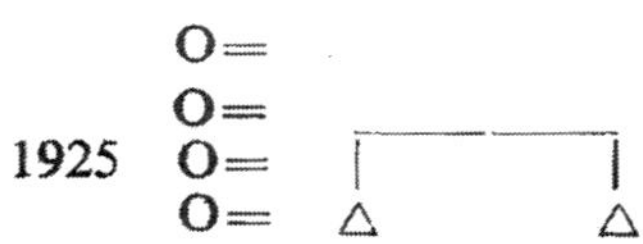

In the course of ten years, a wife—perhaps the third one-might have departed (since divorce and remarriage are commonplace), and another—perhaps the first—might have died, leaving two wives of ages 36 and 30 and two husbands of ages 43 and 37, returning the spouses to sexual parity.

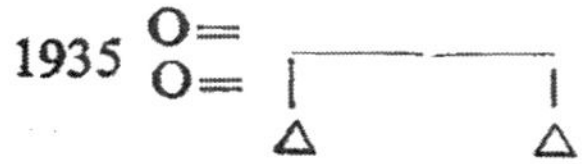

In the passing of another decade, the first brother might have died, leaving a "typical" polygynous family (wives of ages 46 and 40, husband of age 47).

1945 O=
O= Λ

Following the death of the first wife during the next ten years, a "typical" monogamous household would be created, in this case one beyond the age of reproductivity.

1955 O = Λ

The remaining wife might have survived her remaining husband for a few years.

1965 O = Λ

Upon her death that generation of the domestic unit would have disappeared and their children and grand-children would be well along in similar cycles. This, then, describes the rise and fall—the domestic cycle—of a "polyandrous" or "polygynandrous" family of Jaunsar Bawar. The family looked quite different at various times in its cycle, yet the same structural principles and the same processes were operative throughout and the same value system supported it in every phase. A static account of the structure of family, lineage, village or region would immortalize and fossilize these variations, giving them the artificial appearance of discreate formal types.

Circumstantial and optional factors

Variation in the composition of the domestic group also results from factors which are not primarily developmental, temporal, cyclical or the product of the familial life-cycle. Those which are beyond intentional control, might be termed "circumstantial"; those which are matters of choice can be called "optional" factors. Some of the variations described in the above example are of these kinds while others are not.

For example, there might have been only one male in the generation under consideration—a man without brothers. In that case, circumstances would have prevented polyandry from being either a possibility or an actuality ; monogamy, polygyny and the developmental cycles characteristic thereof would have been the structural possibilities (the unmarried state occurs only in cases of the severally physically or mentally handicapped). This lone husband might have chosen to have only one wife in his lifetime (as a result of economic or affectional considerations, for example), or only one wife at a time, or he might have taken a second wife late in life, on the other hand, he might have taken more than one early in life. These are optional factors which determine the composition of the domestic group, the structural form it takes, and the developmental cycle it follows.

In the hypothetical group of brothers there might never have been more than one or two wives acquired. A plentitude of sons, paucity of land, or the preferences of the initial wife or wives might have led them to opt for only one or two wives. Also, of course, different individuals in the domestic group might have survived and died, stayed and left-circumstances which would alter the proportions of the sexes and the reproductive potential of the group.

Other circumstantial and optional variations come to mind and appear in the data as possibilities. A much younger brother might have been born, fifteen to twenty years after his siblings. When he reached maturity he would have been likely to demand an additional wife appropriate to his age. If he had also demanded exclusive sexual access to her, then he would have had to separate economically from his brothers, for no brother can have an exclusive relationship with a wife and still share in other aspects of the joint family. This would have established another, monogamous domestic unit. Similarly, any one (or more) of the brothers might have formed a separate household in order to live separately with one (or more) of the wifes, or in order to work a share of the land independently (cf. Majumdar, 1955b : 164f).

Like the developmental factors which are inherent in social organisation with the passage of time, such circumstances of fate and choice as those described here—non-cyclical but prevalent-affect the composition of domestic units and must be taken into account if one is to understand Pahari polyandry and Pahari domestic organisation.

Conclusion

In Jaunsar Bawar, an individual may experience in his or her lifetime a single spouse, a multiplicity of spouses (serially or simultaneously or both), a co-spouse or a multiplicity of co-spouses. Through time he or she may experience any or all of these marital states. At any moment a single village is likely to include all of these arrangements. Viewed statically, these appear to comprise a high incidence of intra-cultural variation in marriage and family organization—a wide variety of structural types —the most unusual of which are polyandry and polygynandry or group marriage. Both the fact of formal variety and the occurrence of unusual forms are likely to excite our anthropological "exotic bias" (Naroll and Naroll 1963), disorting our theoretical understanding by focusing attention on those features while ignoring others that are equally significant in what proves to be a coherent and unified pattern of domestic organization based on a single set of rules or assumptions about marriage and the family. Among the most significant of these assumptions are that : (1) the family is patrilineal, patrilocal, extended, and joint ; (2) sons live and work with their parents, and, as they become adult, brothers share equally in the property and labor of the family, with the eldest exercising primary authority ; (3) marriage is a contract between a group of brothers and a woman (generally effected through arrangements by their respective families of orientation, entailing a "bride-price" (4) married women live with the group of brothers who are their husbands and contribute their labor, sexuality, and reproductivity collectively ; (5) any number of marriages may be contracted by men without terminating previous ones ; (6) only one marriage may be contracted by a woman unless the previous one is terminated ; (7) any marriage contract can be broken by either party, but children remain with their father(s), and the wealth given in exchange for a woman must be returned to any husband(s) whom she leaves ; (8) brothers who are unwilling to share equally in their common patrimony, labor, wives, and children must divide all of them as equally as possible—they cannot share some aspects of joint family life while dividing others. The domestic unit can assume any form permitted by these rules. Thus, in the course of time, and according to circumstances and choice, families occur which take the forms commonly described as monogamy, fraternal polyandry, polygyny, and fraternal polygynandry or group marriage, with the number of wives and husbands varying.

No account of Pahari polyandry and its implications can ignore these facts, and no comparative or theoretical discussion of polyandry can include Pahari polyandry without attending to them.

The variables and processes of domestic organization in Jaunsar Bawar described here have been demonstrated by reference to a hypothetical but realistic example. Their consequences for the incidence and duration of the various forms of domestic units and for fertility await statistical documentation. As Fortes (1971 : 13) points out, quantitative data are essential for the complete analysis of the developmental cycle. The qualitative facts, as the people of Jaunsar Bawar experience them, however, are clear and are prerequisite to the interpretation of the quantitative data which describe their incidence.

As a rule—that is, other things being equal-Pahari polyandry can be described as a group of brothers married to one or more women. But as in all human affairs, other things are rarely equal. We cannot claim to understand or explain the rule unless our understanding and explanation comprehend also its exceptions and variations. The developmental cycle and the circumstantial and optional variants in Pahari polyandry are crucial to its understanding and explanation, for they are as important as the rule itself—in fact, they too are the rule.

NOTES

1. I have developed this material over a number of years, for use in teaching. I am indebted to my students and to Irven Devore and John Rowe, whose interest inspired me to write it up.

2. Polyandry can be defined simply as that form of marriage wherein a woman has more than one husband at a time. If the husbands are necessarily brothers, the polyandry is fraternal. (See Fischer 1952 ; Leach, 1955 ; Gough 1959 ; Prince Peter 1963).

   The fascination with polyandry is no doubt partly because it is unusual, appealing to our exotic bias (Naroll and Naroll 1963). However, one cannot overlook the possibility also of an androcentric bias. Most anthropologists have been men and/or trained by men. Polyandry has seemed to them puzzling and challenging, while its sexual mirror-image, polygyny, is not only more common, but also evidently seems more plausible, expectable, and perhaps agreeable to them. The former has elicited innumerable and often tortured attempts at explanation (cf. Berrema 1962 : 63-69), whereas the latter attracts little attention, creates little curiosity and generates only the most casual explanation. I have difficulty dispelling the suspicion that this article and its predecessor might be manifestations of this same phenomenon.

3. I base what I have to say primarily on published accounts, supplemented by data and explanations derived from colleagues in India who have worked in the western Himalayas (notably M.K. Raha, Ramesh Chandra, and their colleagues in the recently established North-Western Branch of the Anthropological Survey of India, in Dehra Dun)—and my own work in adjacent Garhwal together with my acquaintance with a few Jaunsari people and two very brief excursions of my own into Jaunsar Bawar.

4. Terms of reference for the fathers (*baba*) are often prefixed to indicate the senior-most and the junior-most, while if there is more than one intermediate "father," they may be specified with prefixes indicating their occupational sub-specialties within the family (Majumdar, 1962 : 101).

   Majumdar (1962 : 101) also reports that a common term (iii) is used in addressing one's mother and her co-wives. When used in reference, it is prefixed with the woman's village of Origin. Nevertheless individual maternity is clearly recognized within the family as individual paternity is not.

5. Note that Jain (1948) records only the number of husbands per wife. He does not record or make any mention of the number of wives per husband or per family. Therefore his figures do not distinguish polygyny from monogamy nor polyandry from "polygynandry," nor the number of women in any multi-husband marriage. This is another frustrating artifact of the preoccupation, among authors of accounts on this region, with polyandry to the virtual exclusion of broader interests in marriage and family organization.

6. This group and their subsequent offspring would doubtless live as a joint family with the brothers' parents so long as they lived.

REFERENCES

Aiyappan, A. 1935 Fraternal Polyandry in Malabar. *Man in India* 14 : 108-118.

Berreman, Gerald D. 1962 Pahari Polyandry : A Comparison. *American Anthropologist* 64 : 60-75.

——1972 *Hindus of the Himalaya : Ethnography and Change.* Berkeley ; University of California Press.

Bohannan, Paul 1963 *Social Anthropology,* New York : Holt, Rinehart and Winston.

Fischer, H.T. 1952 Polyandry, *International Archieves of Ethnography* 46 : 106-115.

Fortes, Meyer 1971 Introduction. *In The Developmental Cycle in Domestic Groups,* Jack Goody, Ed. Cambridge Papers in Social Anthropology, No. 1. Cambridge, Eng. : The University Press. pp. 1-14.

Gough, Kathleen 1952 Changing kinship Usages in the Setting of Political and Economic Change among the Nayars of Malabar. *Journal of the Royal Anthropological Institute of Great Britain and Ireland* 82 : 71-87.

Jain, S.C. 1948 Some features of Fraternal Polyandry in Jaunsar Bawar. *The Eastern Anthropologist* 1 (3) : 27-33.

Leach, E.R. 1955 Polyandry, Inheritance and the Definition of Marriage. *Man* 55 : 182-186.

Majumdar, D.N. 1944 *The Fortunes of Primitive Tribes.* Lucknow, India : The Universal Publishers.

——1953 Children in a Polyandrous Society *The Eastern Anthropologist* 6 : 177-189.

——1955a Family and Marriage in a Polyandrous Society. *The Eastern Anthropologist* 8 : 85-110.

——1955b Demographic Structure in a Polyandrous Village. *The Eastern Anthropologist* 8 : 161-172.

——1962 *Himalayan Polyandry* : Structure, Functioning and Culture Change, A Field Study of Jaunsar-Bawar. New York : Asia Publishing House.

Mandelbaum, D.G. 1938 Polyandry in Kota Society. *American Anthropologist* 40 : 574-583.

Naroll, Raoul, and Freda Naroll 1963 On Bias of Exotic Data. *Man* 63 : 24-26.

Peter, Prince of Greece and Denmark 1963 *A Study of Polyandry.* The Hague : Mouton.

Saksena, R.N. 1955 *Social Economy of a Polyandrous People.* Agra, India : Agra University Press.

7

PAHARI AND TIBETAN POLYANDRY REVISITED[1]

MELVYN C. GOLDSTEIN

Throughout the years the various behavioral complexes involving multiple males in union with a female have intrigued anthropologists seeking to understand them. Yet, a universal explanation for polyandry, as these are called, has eluded us. This lack of success raises the question of whether these behavioral complexes are really as similar as observers assume. Gerald Berreman (1975 : 127-128), in discussing Pahari polyandry, has cogently argued that "polyandry is not a sufficiently unitary phenomenon to be explained in the same terms everywhere," and that it might be more useful to discuss the origin, function and consequences of polyandry[1] polyandry,[2] etc. I concur with this position. The obvious similarity between polyandrous groups—the fact that multiple males maintain unions with females—has diverted attention from significant and often fundamental differences between such populations with respect to their marriage-family system. In this paper I shall demonstrate this by comparing the Tibetan and Pahari forms of polyandry.

Reproduced by permission of the authority of *Ethnology* from *Ethnology* XVII (3) : 325-337, 1978.

Tibetan populations practicing polyandry are found throughout Tibet and along most of the northern reaches of the Himalayas, such as the Limi Valley in northwest Nepal where the author undertook field research trips in 1974, 1976, and 1977. The Pahari (lit. of the mountains) people are Indo-Aryan language-speaking Hindu hill farmers living mainly in the middle and lower sections of the Himalayas in India, Nepal and Bhutan. While most Pahari speakers are not polyandrous, there are several such polyandrous Pahari groups in the Indian Himalayas from whom data are available.

On the surface, the Pahari and Tibetan marriage systems seem very similar. Both have polyandry of the fraternal variety and a household survey of either group would demonstrate the existence of a similar range of marriage types : monogamy, polygyny, fraternal polyandry, fraternal polygyny-polyandry, or polygynandry (two or more male siblings in union with two or more females), although, as we shall see, the frequencies of these types would be rather different.

Berreman (1975) accounts for much of this ground level diversity in the Pahari context as the natural consequence of the family development cycle. For example, two brothers initially take a bride together and then after some years take a second bride producing a fraternal polygynandrous family. Still later, one brother dies resulting in a polygynous family and then one wife dies leaving a monogamous nuclear family type unit. This is obviously an important element in any explanation of the diversity of "ground level" marriage types but it clearly does not explain all diversity. To do this, it is necessary to focus on and attempt to understand the goal-oriented factors underlying marriage and family decisions. While Berreman does not exclude this dimension, discussing it briefly in a section on "circumstantial and optional factors," he does not place sufficient importance on it, although these factors are central to understanding the differences between these two seemingly similar systems of marriage and family, the Pahari and the Tibetan.

I will argue in this paper that the underlying principles generating the surface patterns of marriage and family in these two societies are very different and that this accounts for the statistical differences in types between the two systems. I will also argue that the Tibetan form of polyandry is a functional analog of other wealth conserving kinship mechanisms such as primogeniture and that it is intimately intertwined with the system of stratification, the distribution of the means of production and social status.

Tibetan Polyandry

Tibeten society is basically patricentric in that polyandry is normally fraternal, residence is normally patrilocal, and inheritance is normally patrilineal.[2] Since Tibetans have a considerable variety of marriage and family options, why then do some marry polyandrously and others monogamously? What objectives underlie the selection of these and other alternatives? What needs do they satisfy?

The Tibetans' own explanation of their preference for polyandry is highly materialistic[3]. They choose fraternal polyandry to preserve the productive resources of their corporate family unit intact across generations. Polyandry is perceived and consciously selected primarily as a means of precluding the division of a family's estate among its male coparceners and secondarily as a means of concentrating labor. They consider the maintenance of the family estate intact a critical factor in sustaining the quality of life associated with families of substance and social standing. Fraternal polyandry is the mechanism they use to accomplish this.

Tibetans believe that families having two (or more) conjugal units in a given generation (i.e., two or more married siblings with different brides) are unstable. Demographic anomalies in the number of children (heirs) from each conjugal pair, unequal allocation of resources to such conjugal units, and interpersonal animosities between the unrelated spouses, are among the common factors considered likely to precipitate serious internal discord and eventually fission of the family and division of its property. Polyandry is selected because it precludes such inherently unstable situations by producing only one set or stem of heirs (i.e., the children of the wife) per generation.

Polyandry produces, therefore, a family type which is functionally analogous to the stem family characteristic of parts of Europe and Japan. Kitaoji's (1971 : 1050) description of this family type in Japan illustrates this isomorphism :

> Because two or more siblings may not stay in the same family after marriage, only one married couple is selected to the senior positions. The institution of the selection may be presented by such rules as ultimogeniture, primogeniture, etc. By this systematic process of positional succession and selection, the stem family perpetuates itself generation after generation. In this sense, the stem family is, in principle, a "*perpetual social organization*".

The Tibetan "polyandrous" stem family also perpetuates itself along one stem. However, it does so by retaining all the sons in the natal unit but linking them in marriage to a single bride. The set of male siblings acts as a single jural entity vis-a-vis the wife. Not only does this reduce the risk of the family estate being divided (as does the classic stem family) but it also possesses one of the advantages of joint families ; i.e., the concentration of labor in the family unit.

This functional isomorphism with the classic stem family, however, results in a very important structural contradiction. Goldschmidt (1971 : 1069), in comparing peasant family structures, found patrilineal stem families to be associated with land scarcity and impartible inheritance. The Tibetan situation fits this in terms of land scarcity but not single-heir inheritance. While Tibetans value impartibility in inheritance, they have a normative system which permits partition of the family patrimony by males on demand.

Inheritance in Tibetan society is primarily patrilineal in the sense that males have demand rights to the immovable property of their natal family corporation whereas females do not.[4] Thus, the great emphasis Tibetans have in minimizing intra-familial conflict via the polyandrous stem family is understandable. Since all males in a family have rights to equal shares of land, intra-familial strife and conflict could result in one or more of the male heirs claiming this right and splitting the family corporation. In fact, one wonders why younger brothers do not split from their polyandrous alliances more often than they do.

The traditional answer to this goes back at least to the Jesuit Desideri who lived in Lhasa in the early eighteenth century and wrote a fascinating account of his experiences. He contended that it was necessary to marry polyandrously in Tibet because of the difficulty of eking out a subsistence existence in the harsh and infertile wasteland of the Tibetan plateau.

> One reason for this most odius custom is the sterility of the soil, and the small amount of land that can be cultivated owing to the lack of water. The crops may suffice if the brothers all live together, but if they form separate families they would be reduced to beggary (De-Filippi, 1937 : 194).

While arable land is certainly scarce in Tibet and the Himalayan areas of the Tibetan culture, the real ty of the situation seems to argue against this. All cases where there are multiple brothers do not result in polyandrous stem families, and all or even most instances where fission occurs do not result in "beggary" for the individuals concerned. Younger brothers splitting from their polyandrous natal family can survive even if they receive no land since labor shortages in Tibet provided an economic alternative, *albeit* not a highly profitable one. Similarly, very poor families (i.e., those with little or no land and few if any animals) characteristically do not marry polyandrously but undergo fission each generation. Such poor families derive their subsistence primarily from wage labor, crafts, or servitude. Since they have no estate of substance to conserve and since individuals are as competitive individually as they are in sets of male siblings, there is little advantage to marrying polyandrously. Fraternal polyandry, therefore, is actually characteristic of the landholders, including both the aristocracy and the serfs[5].

In Tsang village, Limi, for example, the thirteen high stratum (*thongchen*)[6] peasant families had seventeen potential polyandrous situations (i.e., more than one son in a given generation) and only four splits (23.5%) whereas the lower stratum (*mire*)[7] families had a 50% fission rate (six out of twelve potential situations). Of the six *mire* polyandrous marriages (actually involving only four families), in four instances the families are extremely wealthy, in one it is moderately wealthy, and one is clearly upwardly mobile.

Tibetans do not consider fraternal polyandry a highly valued end in and of itself; e.g., something to be encouraged because of a fundamental belief in the value of sibling solidarity. They can articulate quite clearly the negative aspects inherent in it as well as what, for them, are its overriding advantages. Fraternal polyandry, therefore, is not seen to be without problems. Because authority is customarily excercised by the eldest brother, younger male siblings have to subordinate themselves with little hope of changing their status. When these younger brothers are aggressive and individualistic, inter-sibling tensions and difficulties often occur. Similarly, tension in polyandrous families may derive from the relationship between the wife and her husbands or from the brothers' relationship concerning access to the wife. While the cultural ideal in Tibet calls for symmetrical treatment in terms of affection and sexual access, deviations from this idea occur and generate intra-familial tensions if not outright conflict. Such deviations are particularly common when there is a sizeable difference in age between the partners in the marriage. Thus, while polyandry provides an answer to one type of culturally perceived problem (*albeit* one which the subjects see as critical), it does generate other types of problems. Deviation from the polyandric ideal, therefore, is manifested not only by the very poor landless but also by those younger brothers who feel their intra-familial conflicts are unbearable.

More significant than these categories, however, are those cases where individuals could— in terms of interpersonal relations—remain together with their brothers yet individually might prefer more personal freedom and independence.

All polyandrous societies offer actors options other than polyandry and in comparing such societies it is essential to understand the decision-making structure underlying surface distributions of marriage types.

The choice facing all younger male siblings is whether to

trade-off personal freedom for real or potential economic security, affluence and social prestige. Young siblings who are not forced by interpersonal conflict to initiate fission must, before splitting, assess their potential for attaining satisfactory income and social status within some reasonable period. They must examine the opportunity cost of fraternal polyandry vis-a-vis going it alone.

Understanding actual Tibetan inheritance patterns is essential to this question. Although Tibetan inheritance norms permit the partition of the family estate among its male members and although each male in the corporation theoretically have demand rights to an equal share of land and animals, on a *de facto* level the system operates almost as if there is impartible inheritance.[8]

Let us take a hypothetical family consisting of a father, a mother, and three sons where one son decides to separate. Ideally, this son should receive a share equal to one-fourth of the estate with the rest of the members retaining three-fourths of the property and the corporate identity. The matter of corporate identity is important in Tibetan society since it governs not only access to resources and obligations but also defines social status.

Tibetan society is organized into a number of hierarchically ranked strata.[9] Although status crystallization was incomplete, there was a strong tendency for the higher strata to control wealth and power in addition to prestige. Membership to these strata was basically ascriptive, it automatically devolved on all offspring of a legitimate female spouse in a family. On the other hand, one's initial status was retained only so long one remained a member of such a family unit. Females who marry out assume the status of their spouse's family. Similarly, when fission occurs, one segment of the natal family unit (that including the father and elder brother) retains the name and identity (as well as rights and obligations) of the initial unit, while the separating unit or units revert to a lower strata if one exists. In Tibet, for example, on the serf-peasant level, "taxpayer" serfs who separate from their families become dujung[10] serfs and in Limi, the *thongpa* or *thongchen* who do so, become *mire.*

Furthermore, in contrast to the expressed partible ideal, the covert assumption and behavioral reality is that those members staying with and maintaining the initial family corporation, get the major share of the estate. In a case such as that mentioned above, the departing son might receive only one-eighth or one-tenth of the land, and then mostly land of poorer quality. If the father and elder brothers were antagonistic toward him or were short of land and animals, they might well give him even less. Litigation, while theoretically possible, requires ready capital, political skills and support networks normally not possessed by younger brothers and is rarely initiated. Consequently, the actual operation of inheritance in Limi and Tibet results in a system in which the maintenance of the economic integrity and viability of the perennial corporate family takes precedence over the theoretically equal demand rights of males.

Polyandry in Tibet, therefore, while clearly related to economic factors, is oriented primarily toward the social consequences of economic productivity rather than toward subsistence *per se*. Mary Douglas (1966 : 268), in talking about the motivation for regulating population, noted that individuals "are more often inspired by concern for scarce social resources, for objects giving status and prestige" than for concerns about population, and the same can be said for polyandry in Tibet. Polyandry is primarily selected not for bread and butter motives---fear of starvation in a difficult environment-but rather primarily for the Tibetan equivalent of oysters, champagne, and social esteem.

Fraternal polyandry's economic advantages maximize the likelihood of generating income over and above caloric subsistence, replacement funds, ceremonial funds, and rent (tax) funds. Polyandry in Tibet maximizes the potential for attaining (or sustaining or increasing) an individual's quality of life in terms of the material markers of affluence, as well as social advantage and prestige. Taxpayer serfs lose their higher ascribed status in the social hierarchies as well as economic productive potential when they split and the small household serfs (*dujung* or *mire*) minimize their chances for attaining the good life.

Since the inheritance a younger brother receives is not likely to generate a resource base adequate for economic independence, what other alternatives might be available to a son/brother contemplating fission? The obvious avenues for acquiring wealth and status, such as opening new fields, building up sheep and yak herds, and entering into traditional trade, are unlikely to be perceived by actors as highly viable options. Yet, resource availability is an important factor and Tibetan fraternal polyandry, as I have argued in other papers (Goldstein, 1976, 1977a, 1977b) is part of a cybernetic system regulating population to certain types of low-capital resources. When resources of economic opportunities requiring little or no capital were scarce, fraternal polyandry was more strictly adhered to, but when such opportunities arose defections from polyandrous unions were common. This, in turn, produced an increase in overall fertility since unmarried females previously excluded from the reproductive pool now married and were brought back into a status of high conception risk.[11] This increased fertility and generated population pressure on the nonelastic resources finally leading to the reassertion of the conservative view of the opportunity costs of fission and stricter adherence to the fraternal polyandry alternative. The key to this process is the availability of profitable economic resources requiring little or no capital.

Most of the plateaus and valleys of Tibet are extremely arid and require adequate and reliable sources of irrigatable water for the sustenance of agriculture. In many areas this is not available and only pastoralism is possible, but even in areas such as Limi, where farming is practiced, opening new agriculture fields is still a dubious alternative. The soil in Limi and Tibet is extremely rocky and boulder-strewn and requires an immense effort to clear even a small plot, let alone construct permament terracing. Moreover, such newly cleared land has far lower fertility than established fields and is difficult to work since it is inevitably further from the main village's core field area.

Animal husbandry also presents difficulties. To make herding profitable, an individual or neolocal couple has to devote virtually full time to husbandry activities during both summer and winter, virtually precluding other income generating activities via agriculture, wage labor, crafts or trading. More critical, however, is the fact that animal herding is extremely risky. Animal mortality does not operate "on the average" and it would not be unusual for a couple's initial (inherited) herd to die, or be decimated during the first winter. A recurrent saying in Limi, for example, is that "land doesn't die the way animals do." Yearly fluctuation in animal mortality due to climatic and disease vagaries is great and it is the small herders who are obviously most vulnerable.

Under what circumstances, then, might younger males perceive the opportunity costs of fission as not prohibitive ? Traditionally, there are very few indeed. The most important would be when arable land and animal herds became available at minimal or no cost. That is, situations where natural catastrophes (such as epidemics, floods and landslides) eliminated the membership of one or more family corporations. But, since these are few and far between it seems highly unlikely that there would have been frequent occasions when sizeable defections from the polyandrous model occurred over and above those prompted by unbearable intra-familial discord and those initiated by the poor and landless.

As a result, the estates of corporate family units of the higher peasant strata and the wealthier units of the lower stratum were preserved intact to a larger degree than among the poor and landless. Thus, over generations, a land-to-people ratio was maintained by them that is higher since they had fewer offsprings per male (due to polyandry) and thus higher productivity on a *per capita* basis. In Tsang village in Limi, for example, the hereditary higher status peasant families (*thongchen*) comprise only 25% of the total families and slightly more than 40% of the population but possess upwards of 60% of the arable land.

Recent political events in the Himalayas, however, have created new economic options and a very different evaluation of opportunity costs regarding fission and fraternal polyandry. The Chinese take-over of Tibet in 1959 and the resultant flight of tens of thousands of Tibetans to India has had a major impact on Tibetan peoples such as Limi in the non-communist Himalayas. While the effects of these international events on areas like Limi are too complicated to discuss here, some discussion is necessary because one consequence of these changes has been an increase in fission which, in turn, has produced an increasing rate of population growth that threatens both the economic and environmental stability of that area.

Traditional trade in Limi was oriented to Tibet and the Nepalese and Bhotia people living in the east-west Humla Karnali River Valley just south of Limi. There was no pattern of trade with India and Kathmandu. Post-1959 Chinese policies in Tibet changed this by ending the laissez-faire policy of the traditional Tibetan Government under which Limi people could trade when, where, and with whomever they pleased. The Chinese restricted trade to officially designated Trade Marts and then only with government personnel in government shops. Concomitantly, a new market emerged in India. The presence of thousands of Tibetan refugees in India triggered an upsurge of interest in Tibetan culture and, as an offshoot, a demand for Tibetan jewelry and artifacts among Westerners. It also opened a new market for the beautiful wooden eating and drinking bowls traditionally made in Limi but previously sold in Tibet.

As this trade developed, it very quickly became apparent that the sale of artifacts and jewelry not only was very profitable but required relatively little initial capital. Such items could be purchased in Tibet at low prices during the summer and then carried to India and Kathmandu by human transport during the winter. Parallel to this, the post-1959 years saw the Limi wooden bowls increase significantly in value as the wealth of the Tibetans in India and Kathmandu increased. In 1976, for example, the profit from the yearly bowl output of one person, when converted to the amount of grain it could purchase, was equal to the grain yield from the average amount of land held by the lower strata Limi families (the *mire*). The development of winter trade networks in North India and Kathmandu also facilitated Limi participation in the lucrative musk trade.

The changing political situation in Tibet affected Limi in another way. After the flight of the Dalai Lama and his government to India, thousands of Tibetans similarly sought refuge in India and the other contiguous Himalayan states such as Nepal. In north-west Nepal, many of the nomads from the Lake Mansarovara region just across the border fled with their herds into Limi. Since Limi is the end of the Tibetan type alpine steppe ecozone, these nomads could not take their sheep and could not remain in Limi. They were forced, therefore, to sell their herds to the Limi inhabitants at extremely low prices. Many animals, furthermore, were simply abandoned and rounded up by whomever wanted them. It is said, although I have no verification, that some animals were simply spirited off during this chaotic period. In any case, this sudden and inexpensive supply of sheep and yaks also encouraged fission by younger brothers.

Given such new opportunities, it is not surprising to find that roughly, 25% of the younger brothers "in-risk" actually left their natal family corporations and established neolocal independent family units during the period from 1960-1970. This defection has decreased the fertility-reducing consequence of fraternal polyandry since it brought females into the reproductive pool who otherwise would have been excluded, and is playing a major role in stimulating noticeable population growth. Similarly, it can be argued that the increased income in Limi resulting from these activities and the large sheep and yak herds that were created, has improved the amount and quality of diet. This, as has been shown for western Europe in the eighteenth and nineteenth centuries (McKeown, 1976), could very likely have reduced mortality rates. If this pattern continues (as seems likely) or becomes exacerbated, Limi will undergo sustained population growth which could severely alter its delicate economic-environmental balance and result in serious environmental degradation. There is already some question as to whether this is not now occuring with respcct to the pasture and forest area. The real question concerning the future of Limi, then, is whether a temporary expansion of population due to the short term emergence of new resources and opportunities has occurred, or whether recent trends mark the beginning of new patterns of marriage, family and reproduction—the beginning of a demographic and social transition.

Pahari Polyandry

Like Tibet, the Pahari society is patricentric in terms of inheritance and residence. Females move to the households of their husbands and all males are co-parceners with respect to their family's estate ; i.e., brothers have demand rights to a share of property.

Marriage practices are also similar in that a variety of options are available ; viz., monogamy, fraternal polyandry, polygyny and fraternal polygyny-polyandry (polygynandry).

In fraternal polyandrous (and fraternal polygynandrous) unions, the wife is shared by all the brothers. No brother can claim exclusive rights to a wife or to any portion of the family land unless he formally splits off from his natal family and additional wives added to polyandrous unions are considered the wife of all the brothers. Also, like Tibet, the eldest male dominates but cannot compel younger males to remain in the family unit.

The Pahari system of marriage unions differs, however, from the Tibetan in terms of the frequency of the various types of unions and with regard to the strategic principles underlying their selection.

Although initial studies reported high frequencies of fraternal polyandry, later work revealed that most what was called polyandry among Pahari was really polygynandry. Berreman (1975 : 130) summarized the data for two Jaunsar Bawar villages and showed that fraternal polyandry is much less common than previously thought. In Lohani village, for example, the majority of the 49 % of unions initially reported as polyandry end up to be cases of fraternal polygynandry (61 %). Of the 89 unions in Baila village, 33 % were polygynandrous, 25 % polygynous, 34% monogamous and only 9% fraternal polyandrous.

These figures clearly illustrate the preference so-called polyandrous Pahari groups have for unions with more than one wife via either polygyny or polygynandry. They also indicate the presence of very different strategic values among the Pahari ; i.e., that the Pahari actually prefer or find advantageous, unions with more than one wife per generation. Unfortunately, ethnographies on these groups do not analyze the decision-making strategies underlying the multiplicity of family-marriage types. They do, however, contain data which are supportive of this contention. Majumdar (1955a), for example, writes that family prestige rises with its numbers but poor families can afford only one wife shared among brothers. Elder brothers are responsible for providing wives for their younger brothers (and would themselves like to have a second wife) but can only do so when economic conditions improve. Similarly, Parmar (1975) points out that while poor men must share a wife, prosperous men will have more than one. Saksena (1956) indirectly supports this when he writes that "A husband can have many wives and if marries a young girl, the expenses incurred in the marriage are not much. So polygyny combined with polyandry is increasingly practiced".

Although no systematic information is available on how Pahari evaluate the opportunity costs of the various marriage options, this type of data suggests strongly that it is a lack of wealth (due in no small part to the traditional practice of paying bride-price rather than dowry) that forces Pahari brothers to marry polyandrously and not, in sharp contradiction with Tibetans, the perceived and intended "estate conserving" advantage.

Berreman (1977), in a recent discussion of the high frequency of polygynandry among polyandrous Pahari, reasserts his earlier view that there is no factor, e.g., ecology, sex ratio, inheritance rules, or population pressure, which can be shown to determine polygynandry (or polyandry) among Pahari. He (Berreman, 1977 : 12) argues that while polygynandry is "one of a number of cultural forms unique to the Western Pahari area whose origins are lost in unrecorded antiquity," it does provide synchronically a useful economic option in that it is a means of managing the ratio of workers and consumers to resources. There is little doubt that this is one relevant factor that Pahari consider strategically but, based on the primary value considered.

While the lack of appropriate first hand data on these polyandrous Pahari groups restrains further analysis, it is clear that a fundamental dichotomy exists between the Tibetan and Pahari types of fraternal polyandry. Whereas the Tibetan marriage system is oriented toward the minimization of wives, the Pahari marriage system is oriented toward the maximization of wives. Social status, esteem and wealth are associated with maximizing the number of wives among Pahari, whereas among polyandrous Tibetan populations it is associated with a corporate family's ability to minimize the number of brides per generation ; i.e. to maintain fraternal polyandrous stem families.

Fraternal polyandry, while present in both Pahari and Tibetan society, is the product of very different underlying values and strategies and thus, not surprisingly, is found in very different frequencies in these societies. Fraternal polygynandry and polygyny typify the Pahari context but are considered the least advantageous options in Tibetan society and occur with the least frequency there.

Tibetan Fraternal Polyandry and Other Wealth Conserving Kinship Mechanisms

As indicated earlier, not only are there very significant differences between so-called polyandrous societies but there are also striking similarities between the marriage and family systems of societies heretofore considered very different. It is my contention that Tibetan fraternal polyandry is a functional analogue of other wealth conserving mechanisms such as the primogeniture generated stem families of various parts of western Europe and Japan. In all of these, primary valuation is placed on the minimization of wives for each corporate family unit and the production of only one set or stem of heirs. In the European and Japanese situations this is achieved by restricting the stem to one male, whereas in the Tibetan system it is restricted to a group of siblings acting as a single jural entity. Although space does not permit discussion here, I think it is possible to show that in each of these situations, the adaptation derives from an isomorphic combination of political, economic, demographic and environmental factors. Interestingly, it is also apparent that these systems have the unintended consequence of reducing overall fertility and seem to fit the general cybernetic model briefly outlined for Limi. For example, let us examine the situation for Ireland.

The introduction of the potato in Ireland increased the yield per unit of land greatly and thereby facilitated the fragmentation of land holdings since a relatively small plot could support a family. This led to easy and early marriage, and a significant increase in the population growth rates. The potato famine ended this shift and led to the reassertion of old European patterns of marriage and inheritance. D.V. Glass, as cited in Lorimer (1969 : 173) writes that after the catastrophic famine :

> The fragmentation of holdings went no further. Instead it became customary, *as it had before the potato era* (italics added by Lorimer) for the farm to be passed intact to one child. A father would, during his own lifetime, arrange the marriage of the chosen son and hand the farm to him, retaining certain rights to support during old age. The dowry brought in by the bride would be used partly to compensate the father for giving up the farm, partly to satisfy the claims of the other children. Other sons might receive a professional or business training. And if the sum of money brought by the bride was sufficient, the daughters might be given dowries and marry farmers in their district. The alternative was to move into town and find jobs, or to emigrate. Women often went abroad to save money for a dowry ; with that they might marry into a farm on their return home. Men also sometimes returned with their savings to re-establish themselves in their homeland . . . . Because of this total combination of demographic and social factors, Erie . . . has tended to become a nation of elderly bachelors. In 1841, 10% of the men between the ages of 45 and 54 years were unmarried,

Blake and Davis (1956 : 216) argue similarly :

> Later, during the sixty years before the Famine, when the potato became the staple food and the economy shifted from pastoralism to cultivation, couples could get property at marriage by subdivisions of the land, thus removing temporarily the main obstacle to early marriage. But with the crisis of the Famine, the futility of progressive subdivision led to the Land Purchase Acts stipulating that the loans which transformed tenants into owners were granted only on condition that no subdivision would take place. Since the annuities ran for 35 years, this represented some restraint on subdivision. A more powerful restraint was the fact that, once the tenants became owners, they grew unwilling to subdivide on behalf of their sons. The tendency was to retain only one son on the paternal land, the remainder of the children being dispersed, partly through migration abroad. The independent nuclear family was maintained, but the son who remained at home could not establish such a family until the father was willing to resign both authority and property. As a result the average age at marriage in Ireland came extremely advanced, reaching 29.1 for women by 1926.

Ireland, therefore, went through a series of changes that parallel roughly those discussed for Limi. From scarce land preserved intact across generations via stem families, impartible inheritance and lowered fertility due to late marriage and high rates of celibacy, a pattern of early marriage and fragmentation of land holdings emerged when a new resource—the potato—greatly increased the productivity of land and permitted economic independence with only small plots of land. The terrible potato blight that began in the 1840s ended this phase replacing it with the traditional wealth preserving patterns that predated the introduction of the potato as a subsistence crop. A similar situation seems to have occured in the Sherpa (Tibetan) area of Khumbu in Nepal.

Before the opening of Nepal to Westerners in 1950, this area was known to have been one in which traditional

Tibetan fraternal polyandry was practised. Today it is a rarity. Not surprisingly, the Sherpa population has been growing substantially and there is a great deal of seasonal and permanent out-migration to Kathmandu and Darjeeling. A major cause of this was the new economic opportunities presented by mountaineering and tourism. Like the trade opportunities discussed for Limi, these required little or no capital, and, as they developed, would have offered younger brothers both satisfactory income and social standing. It is not surprising, therefore, to find that fraternal polyandry ceased to be selected in this area and has virtually vanished from the scene. Obviously, all population growth cannot be attributed to tourism and mountaineering alone for excellent medical facilities have also been established there. Similarly, while no hard data are available, it is not unlikely that the introduction of tourism may simply have exacerbated an earlier shift in the introduction of tourism may simply have exacerbated an earlier shift in the perception of the opportunity costs of marriage alternatives caused by the introduction of potatoes—the current staple—to the area.

Conclusion

This paper has, very cursorily to be sure, tried to illustrate the manner in which two societies commonly considered to be fraternal polyandrous differ fundamentally. It also suggests in a preliminary fashion that Tibetan fraternal polyandry is a functional analogue of other wealth conserving kinship mechanisms such as primogeniture, which operate to reduce the frequency of, or preclude, division of family patrimonies and, in an unperceived and unintended manner, also reduce fertility levels in their respective societies. In the metaphor of transformational grammarians, the two polyandrous societies have different deep structures with the same surface structure whereas the Tibetan and the non-polyandrous wealth conserving societies have different surface structures with the same deep structure.

While the perennial anthropological quest for universal explanations of institutions such as polyandry will undoubtedly continue, there is no reason to assume, as Merton (1949) chided many years ago, that similar institutions must have the same function or need be produced by the same concatenation of causal factors. The Tibetan-Pahari case indicates the desirability of examining both the different functions of fraternal polyandry in different environments and the causal and functional similarities it shares with other non-polyandrous institutions.

NOTES

1. The data on Tibetan marriage used in this paper were collected by the author in Nepal and India under grants and fellowships from the Population Research Institute, NICHHD, of N.I.H., American Council of Learned Societies and the American Institute of Indian Studies. I wish to thank Dean P.R. Sharma of the Center for Nepal and Asian Studies, Tribhuvan University, Kathmandu, Nepal for his advice and help, and the many Nepali and Tibetans who have so kindly assisted me. In particular, I want to express my gratitude to the people of Limi who showed me—and on my second expedition my son—so much friendship and warmth.
2. There are however, no patrilineal descent groups. As I have indicated in earlier articles on Tibetan social organization (Goldstein, 1971b ; 1971c), the largest kinship group is the family, although bilateral kindred are important and are used to define exogamy. Clans have been reported for parts of eastern Tibet, northern Nepal and northern Tibet, where they seem to function solely as marriage-exogamy definers but as yet there are no firm data on how these function, if in fact they really exist.
3. See Goldstein (1971a, 1976a, 1977a, 1977b) and Prince Peter (1963).
4. Inheritance is discussed further later in the paper.
5. A more extensive examination of the relationship between feudalism serfdom and Tibetan polyandry is found in Goldstein (1971a) and a detailed analysis of Tibetan serfdom is found in Goldstein (1971b, 1971c).
6. Tibetan terms are cited in the standard phonemic transcription used in Goldstein 1975b. The written Tibetan transliteration will be presented in footnotes. *Thongchen=grong chen* sometimes simply called *thongpa - grong ba*).
7. *Mire=mi re.*
8. Jack Goody (1976) has recently linked female inheritance with the plough agriculture and social stratification characteristic of Eurasian

societies. Tibetan society would fall under this rubrick but only in a marginal way. Females in Tibet inherit from their natal family corporations in two ways :

(a) In the absence of brothers (i.e., male heirs), a female is sometimes kept in her natal family and an adoptive bridegroom brought (in-uxorilocal marriage).
(b) Females who marry out (the normal situation in Tibet) receive a portion of their family corporation's wealth at the time of marriage in the form of what is usually called a dowry but which in Tibetan actually means a share (*qela* ; *skal ba*) of some property or estate. This share, however, does not include immovable property such as land. For example, a daughter in an aristocratic family might have received one or two sets of jewelley and an assortment of clothes as her dowry. Occasionally a maid-servant would also be sent with her. In the villages, among the higher status peasant—serfs and the wealthier lower status ones, similar norms prevailed although the amount and value of the clothes and jewelley were much smaller. In Limi, a higher status girl usually gets a set of jewelley, clothes, one or two female bovines, and on rare occasions usufruct rights to some of the land of the natal corporation (with the land reverting to the latter on the bride's death).

9. The political-economic hierarchy in village Tibet (excluding the aristocracy) typically consisted of three strata :
taxpayer or *theepa* (*khral pa*) serf (also called *thongchen, thongpa*), small householder or *dujung* (*du chung*) serfs (also called *mire*) *morang* or *phorang* serfs (*mo rang, pho rang*).
All of these could include inherently unpolluted, inherently polluted, and priestly lineage (*sngags pa*) serfs.
10. dujung=*dud chung*
11. For example, in Tsang village, Limi, more than 30% of the females over twenty are unmarried (see Goldstein, 1976).

REFERENCES

Berreman, G. ; 1962 Pahari Polyandry : A Comparison. *American Anthropologist* 64 : 60-75.

———1975. Himalayan Polyandry and the Domestic Cycle. *American Ethnologist* 2 : 127-139.

———1977 Ecology, Demography and Social Strategies in the Western Himalayas : A Case Study. Proceedings of the C.N.R.S. International Conference on the Ecology of the Himalayas : *The Life Sciences*. Paris.

Davis. K. and J. Blake ; 1956 Social Structure and Fertility : An Analytic Framework. *Economic Development and Cultural Change* 4: 211-235.

De Filippi, F. (ed.) 1937 *An Account of Tibet* : *The Travels of Ippolito Desideri of Pistoia, 1712-1727*. London.

Douglas, M. 1966 Population Control in Primitive Groups. *British Journal of Sociology* 17 : 263-273.

Goldschmidt, W. and E.J. Kunkel 1971 The Structure of the Peasant Family *American Anthropologist* 73 : 1058-76.

Goldstein, M.C. 1971a. Stratification, Polyandry, and Family Structure in Central Tibet. *South-western Journal of Anthropology* 27 : 65-74.

———1971b. Serfdom and Mobility : An Examination of the Institution of 'Human Lease' in Traditional Tibetan Society, *Journal of Asian Studies* 30 : 521-34.

———1971c. Taxation and the Structure of a Tibetan Village. *Central Asiatic Journal* 15 : 1-27.

———1974 Tibetan Speaking Agro-pastoralists of Limi : A Cultural Ecological Overview of High Altitude Adaptation in the North-west Himalayas. *Objects et Mondes* 14 : 259-268.

———1975a Report on Limi Panchayat, Humla District, Karnali Zone. *Contributions to Nepalese Studies* 2 : 89-101.

———1975b Tibetan-English Dictionary of Modern Tibetan. *Biblioteca Himalaya*, Series II, Vol. 9. Kathmandu.

———1976 Fraternal Polyandry and Fertility in a High Himalayan Valley in North-west Nepal. *Human Ecology* 4 : 223-233.

———1977a Culture, Population, Ecology and Development : A View from North-west Nepal, proceedings of C.N.R.S. International Conference on the Ecology of the Himalayas : *The Life Sciences*. Paris.

———1977b. Population, Social Structure and Strategic Behaviour : An Essay on Polyandry, Fertility and Change in Limi Panchayat. *Contributions to Nepalese Studies*. 4 : 47-52.

Goody, J. 1976 *Production and Reproduction*. Cambridge Studies. in Social Anthropology, No. 17. Cambridge.

Kitaoji, H. 1971 The Structure of the Japanese Family. *American Anthropologist* 73 : 1036-57.

Lorimer, F. 1969 *Culture and Human Fertility*.

Majumdar, D.N. 1955a Family and Marriage in a Polyandrous Society. *The Eastern Anthropologist* 8 : 85-110.

———1955b Demographic Structure in a Polyandrous Society. *The Eastern Anthropologist* 8 : 161-172.

MoKeown, T. 1976 *The Modern Rise of Population*. New York.

Merton., R.K. 1949 Manifest and Latent Functions. *Social Theory and Social Structure* ed. R. Merton, pp. 21-81. Glenoor.

Parmar, Y.S. 1975 *Polyandry in the Himalayas.* Delhi.

Prince Peter of Greece and Denmark 1963 *A Study of Polyandry.* The Hague.

Saksena, R.N. 1956 *Social Economy of a Polyandrous People.* Agra.

8

POLYANDRY IN A CIS-HIMALAYAN COMMUNITY

V.K. SISHAUDHIA

The Himalaya is the youngest mountain system in India. It extends from Nanga Parbat (8126 m.) in Kashmir to Namcha Barwa (7756 m.) in Arunachal Pradesh in the shape of a big arch from west to east. According to Hindu mythology it has been the abode of various ethnic groups such as the Apsaras, the Yakshas, the Gandharvas and the Khasas etc. Even today the variety of different ethnic groups inhabiting the Himalayas have literally made it anthropologist's and sociologist's paradise. These various ethnic groups are scattered all over the Himalayas from foot hills to the high altitude areas as high as 14000 ft. Among the various ethnic groups inhabiting the Western Himalayas, the Jaunsaris occupy an important place both in their numerical strength as well as in typical cultural practices. These people well known in the annals of Indian anthropology and sociology for their practice of fraternal polyandry, have been included in the list of Scheduled Tribes by the Government of India in 1967.

Jaunsar Bawar, the abode of the Jaunsaris, lies in the foot hills of the cis-Himalayan region forming the Chakrata tehsil in the district of Dehra Dun, Uttar Pradesh. It constitutes the hilly part of the district of Dehra Dun and is roughly oval in shape with its major axis lying north and south. It is bounded on the north-east, east and south-east by the district of Tehri Garhwal, on the west and north-west by the district of Sirmaur of Himachal Pradesh and in south by Doon valley. The term Jaunsar Bawar denotes once two distinct parganas and three natural sub-divisions (Walton, 1911). One of the three natural sub-divisions is Jaunsar, comprising the whole of the Kalsi block. This portion acquires a triangular shape with its apex at Kalsi. The second is Lokhandi, locally known as Kand-march which means the 'rugged hillock', with a length of 78 kms. and running from west to east. The Lokhandi ranges from a transitional zone between Jaunsar and Bawar. Third is Bawar covering the northern part of the Chakrata Tehsil.

The whole area is composed entirely of a succession of hills and mountains. It has the characteristic of being one of the wildest and most rugged tracts, offering very little levelled ground for agricultural purposes. The hills are rough and precipitous. The revines are, as a rule, deep and sudden in the descent. The altitude of any part of the area is not less than 2,000 ft. and at certain places it has almost reached 10,000 ft. (Kharamba, 10,075, Deeban 9,331 and Lokhandi 8,000 ft. respectively). It is a region of sparse population, sparsely scattered small nucleated villages and very small and laborious agriculture. (Majumdar, 1963).

Despite attaining the tribal status for themselves, the Jaunsaris represent the traditional Hindu caste structure with a very little difference. As compared to innumerable castes elsewhere in India here

> 'One comes across only a few stereotyped castes whose relative statuses are well defined and manifested in the rules of endogamy, social intercourse, distances, rituals of pollution and purity and different life styles of various castes'. (Bhatt, 1978).

All the caste groups present in the region can be classified into three groups based on hierarchy. On the top of this system there are the dominating groups of 'high castes', including the

Brahmins and the Rajputs. Having lions's share in the available agricultural land, the Brahmins and the Rajputs claim themselves as zamindars, landowner-cultivators. In the middle there are 'shilpkars, or artisan castes' such as the Badi, the Bajgi, the Sunar, the Lohar and Nath and the others. At the bottom of this three tier caste hierarchy there are 'low castes', such as the Koltas and the Doms. They occupy the lowest rung in the social ladder. Most of them are agricultural labourers working for their masters of 'high castes'. The Koltas are the most exploited landless untouchables in the region. They are not allowed to enter temples or to see the image of the local gods. They are not allowed to enter the houses of their master but their approach is confined to the ground floor of cattle quarters (Hasnain, 1982). The story of their life and living is of human endurance and fortitude against constant sufferings, perpetual persecution and all embracing exploitation (Hasan, 1971). Between the two 'high castes', there are thin barriers to endogamy and a considerable social interaction is observable.

Polyandry as a form of marriage sounds peculiar in modern times but it is no doubt prevalent in many parts of the world as well in some areas in India. Like the Kinnars, the Lahulis and the Bodhs of the North-Western Himalayas, the people of Jaunsar-bawar also practise fraternal or adelphic polyandry associated with patrilineal system of inheritance. Polyandry is not confined to this region only but it has been present, in the past in the whole of the Western Himalayas extending from Jaunsar Bawar through the Kangra valley to the Hindu Kush and even beyond. At present this polyandrous tract forms a part of wider polyandrous area covering five blocks i.e. Kalsi and Chakrata of the District of Dehra Dun, Purola and Rawa-in of Uttarkashi and Jaunpur of Tehri districts.

The entire socio economic structure of the Jaunsari community revolves round the principle of 'joint living and joint agriculture', (Sishaudhia, 1981a). This is the main axis of their economic system. This system of joint living is maintained through the custom of fraternal polyandry prevalent among them. Although this custom has been reduced considerably on account of the growth of individuality and the changed outlook, but in whatever amount it prevails it is not confined to any particular caste or group but it extends to all castes and groups in Jaunsar Bawar. This custom of polyandry runs parallel to the other forms of marriage such as monogamy and polygyny.

Polyandry or to be more exact fraternal polyandry is the common form of marriage in this region. Here all the brothers are the common husbands of a wife or wives. The actual marriage rites are performed with the eldest brother and all others *ipso facto* become her husbands. The younger brothers automatically gain the rights over the common wife/wives. They have not to under go any type of specific ceremony as among the Lahulis the younger brother accompanies the party at the time of *maklaba* (*gauna*) and presents Re. 1 to girl's mother which establishes his rights as the second husband on the girl or the distribution of sweets to the brothers of the husband among the Kaniyans and Panikans of Cochin (Parmar, 1975). In Jaunsari community all the brothers are co-husbands to the wife or wives brought in the family. Thus this society sanctions marital unions comprising any combination of numbers of the two sexes, provided that the men are brothers born to the same set of father/fathers and mother/mothers. Majumdar (1962) considered the term polyandry inappropriate for this institution and suggested more descriptive neologism 'polygynandry' for it, which is further modified by Berreman (1975) to 'fraternal polygynandry'.

The marriage ceremony is quite simple and different from their neighbours of plains. The offer for the marriage goes from the side of the boy. The talks are initiated through an intermediary till the matter is finalised. Thereafter the father of the would-be bridegroom goes to the village of the prospective bride and settles the marriage by giving one rupee as bride-price and a pair of gold or silver bangles for the bride. Often the date of marriage is decided by the priests of both house-holds. After this the father of the bride decides the number of *barati* (people that accompany the bride to bridegroom's place). In contrast to the neighbouring plains here the *barat* (marriage party) goes to the place of bridegroom with the bride.

One day before the auspecious day of marriage the father

of the bridegroom along with one or two other persons comes to the village of the bride to accompany her to his village. When he comes a lavish feast of home brewn liquor. thee, multon and rice, is hosted to all the near and dear ones by the father of the bride. After the feast singing and dancing. Next morning the bride along with the persons from her in-law's place and her father or brother leaves for the bridegroom's village. She generally reaches the bridegroom's village in the morning and has to cross the thrashold of her in-law's house at an auspecious hour. She is welcomed in the house by the mother of the groom. The sister of the bridegroom washes her feet along with her brother's feet. Bride's *pallu* is tied to that of groom's and he then leads her into the main hall of his house where they exchange garlands and sweets before the priest and the marriage is over. Here marriage is free from the intricacies of classical rituals as prescribed by the *Shastras*. The marriage party reaches the village in the evening with the dowry of the bride. They are received into the village by the father and other members of groom's family. Drums and other traditional instruments are played by the Bajgis to welcome them. On their arrival they are offered tea and tobacco in 'huccka' or cigarette. After this they are led to their place of stay where their feet are washed by the girls of their village but married in groom's village, before their entrance to the room. Here they are served liquour and lavish dinner. After the drink and dinner, they dance and sing for the whole night. In the morning they are again served tea or liquour and after it curd and rice in breakfast. Before their departure for their own village they are provided lunch consisting of mutton, rice, *chapati*, *halwa* and *dal*. The total expenditure of marriage exceeds Rs. 4,000 in case of the Kolta, Rs. 3,000 in case of the Bajgi and Rs. 8,000 to 10,000 in case of the Rajputs and the Brahmins.

After the marriage ceremony the bride also goes back to her parental village either with the marriage party itself or only after one day as she is generally very young. She comes back after a considerably long time to stay permanently with her husband/husbands. But in case of *chootar* (divorcee) she stays back in bridegroom's house just after the marriage.

As it has been mentioned that the marriage is solominised with the eldest brother and all other brothers and even those born after the marriage *ipso facto* become the husband of common wife/wives. Younger brothers though husbands of the same wife, cannot have sex relations under the same roof in the presence of the eldest brother. They follow her (them) in the fields or wait for the eldest brother to be absent from home (Khairwal, 1975; Berreman, 1962). The multiplicity of domestic and economic engagements mostly keep the eldest brother away from the home. In these circumstances the determination of biological fatherhood of the children born to the wife/wives is rather impossible; so it is socially determined. All the children are named after the eldest brother, and he is the head of the family.

In patriarchal fraternal polyandrous families of Jaunsar-Bawar the eldest brother occupies the most important place. He is the owner of the house, husband of all the wives and father of all the children born. In matters of inheritance the eldest brother is entitled to get the house in which they live and some more land as *jethang*.

The children address the eldest brother as *bara baba*, other brothers are also called *baba* but with a prefix of their work in household economy such as the brother engaged with cattles is called *gorawa-baba*. There is no term of address in Jaunsari kinship system for husband's brothers as they all are co-husbands and are called *khawind*. This absence of kinship terminology for father's brother and husband's brother indicate the presence of polyandry in the region since long.

Regulation of sex life in a polyandrous family is a complicated process. Although in the presence of eldest brother no other brother can take liberty with the wife, but she has to satisfy the sex needs of other brothers too. In fact, a wife in polyandrous marriage carries a much greater responsibility than in a monogamous marriage. Giving equal treatment and emotional satisfaction to all husbands at the same time is a delicate task. Her exclusive favours to any one of the husbands may create trouble for her and some times may result in dissolution of marriage (*chhoot*). The interpersonal relationships among spouses, co-husbands and co-wives are of cooperation and mutual help. The interpersonal or sex jealousy is completely absent in these families (Majumdar, 1962).

The institution of marriage is most fragile and easily dissolvable. Marriages are fixed and broken at any time at the desire of partners. Divorce is locally known as *chhoot* and can be initiated by either of the party. The high frequency of divorce and remarriage without any social stigma is a significant feature of the Jaunsari community. When a marriage is dissolved the wife's parents or the would-be husband have to pay her former husband a compensation known as *chhoot* money or *kheet*. There are no prescribed rules and strict regulations for dissolution of marriage. The divorces are obtained on flimsy grounds. A woman may be divorced by her husband due to her having committed adultry in her husband's village (Saksena, 1953) but the more frequent cause of divorce is the inability of woman to bear children or sterility. The motherhood is considered a virtue of woman. A woman of advanced age who has given birth to children may fetch more bride price than a younger virgin. On the other hand, a woman may divorce her husband/husbands for the failure on his/their part to provide her with adequate ornaments. Cases have been found when women of neighbouring Sirmaur area have divorced their husbands in Jaunsar Bawar on account of the difficult conditions of communication and some differences in the dialect (Majumdar, 1962). Bhatt (1978) found in his study that of all the married women in the villages studied about 50% were married as *chhootarh* (divorcees). This itself speaks of the extent and frequency with which the marriages are dissolved and resolemnized.

Like the grounds for divorce the process of divorce is also quite simple but prolonged. A woman desiring a divorce, goes to her father's house and refuses to return to her husband's house. When she does not return to husband's house despite requests from her husband's people, it is assumed that she will not come back. In the meantime a prospective husband may approach her father and the later goes to her first husband's house to negotiate the divorce. Her husband or father-in-law settles the *chhoot* money which may extend to even thousands of rupees. When this amount is paid either by the father of the woman or the prospective husband the divorce is completed and she is free to marry the second husband. All her relations with the previous husband and his family are terminated. For the high frequency of divorce and lack of any stigma to it, divorce does not create bitter or strained relationships between the two parties and is taken as a routine matter.

The prevalence of polyandry associated with a freedom to divorce and their importance in local economy has given complicated shape to the status of woman. In this community, the status of woman is governed by the dichotomy of *dhayanti* and *rayanti*. *Dhayanti* means daughter of the family. In polyandrous joint family, father's sister, sister, daughter and grand-daughters are termed as *dhayanti*. *Rayanti* means wife in particular but in general it stands for woman's position in her in-law's house.

The rights and privileges enjoyed by woman as *dhayanti* and *rayanti* are quite different and contrary to each other. As *rayanti* she is subjected to strict control of her husband(s) or in-laws in regard to discipline and rules of chastity, "slightest disloyalty or the slightest slip on her part may result in divorce" (Saksena, 1953). As *rayanti* she is not allowed to enter the temple, she does not keep her husband's purse not even ornaments she is allowed to use (Jain, 1980). In contrast to this the woman as *dhayanti* is allowed many liberties and previleges. Whenever she comes to her parental village, even after her marriage, she is treated as *dhayanti* and is allowed group dancing and free mixing with her age mates of both sexes. *Dhayantihood* goes with "culturally tolerated extra marital relationship, casually not usually" (Jain, 1980). On her visit to her parent's house "she may well relapse into her old alliances" (Sinha, 1980).

Due to her importance in household and agricultural economy woman is considered as prized possessions. But the presence of bride-price has reduced her status to a chattel which can be purchased, possessed and even disposed whenever required. Her standing in household is weak, she dare not hold her opinion even in household matters.

A variety of causal explanations has been forwarded for the origin, development and continuation of polyandry in this region. The origin of this institution in this area is lost in 'unrecorded antiquity'. There are diverse views regarding its origin, the Jaunsaris themselves trace the origin of polyandry to the Pandavas whose discendants they claim to be. It is believed by the local population that the Pandavas spent a considerable time of their exile in this region, and the temple in Lakhamandal is considered the main centre of their activities in Mahabharatas period.

Commenting on the development of polyandry Saksena (1953) mentioned,

> "It might have developed among the Rajputs and Brahmins as a result of culture contact with the Doms, who were the aborigines of this region, further helped by the forces of geographic isolation ane economic hardships".

But Biswas (1953) is of the opinion that this assumption is contrary to the general principles of acculturation i.e. the superior culture always prevails upon the inferior one. Here the Rajput and the Brahmins are definitely culturally superior to the Doms, so it is not possible for the Rajputs and the Brahmins to copy such an important custom like polyandry from the Doms rather the Doms may have taken it from them. He further argues that perhaps during the migration of these people to their present locale they had only a few women with them and polyandry was the only answer to their marriage problem at that time.

A complex and deep rooted institution like polyandry cannot be attributed to a single factor, howsoever important it may be. Its continuation can only be attributed to a multiplicity of factors such as the combination of demographic, psychological and economic factors. Among these various factors the first are demographic i.e. an excess of males over the females, and it is certain that there is such an excess in Jaunsar-Bawar. The area suffered from disparity in sex ratio since long. There were only 814 females for 1,000 males in 1900 (Parmar, 1975) which further detoriated to 720 females for 1000 males in 1971 (cf. Table 1). In a field survey conducted in 1979 the sex ratio in the area comes as 784.64 females per 1,000 males

(Sishaudhia, 1981). This disbalance in sex ratio combined with instances of polygyny is one of the important factor for the continuation of the practice of polyandry in Jaunsar-Bawar. Polyandrous sex behaviour of males and females coupled with culturally tolerated extra-marital relations, as the unvarified hypothesis goes, produces more male children. Thus polyandry and sex disbalance create a vicious circle making each other cause and effect, When the females are fewer and bride-price is high fraternal polyandry is a good solution to the need for a wife. Therefore, peculear demographic situation (structure) may contribute to the continuation of polyandry, whether or not it had any role in its origin (Berreman, 1962b).

The psychological desire and the economic requirement to keep the family in well-knit form to prevent its fragmentation has been advanced by many anthropologists-sociologists as the factors responsible for the continuation of polyandry in the region. Psychologically the sharing of common wife/wives developes a feeling of unity and solidarity among brothers. The remarkable absence of sex jealousy among brothers (co-husbands) and the unlimited rights vested in the eldest brother keeps the polyandrous family a wellknit unit. Radcliff-Brown (1941) had also suggested that adelphic polyandry is to be interpreted in the light of structural principles of the solidarity of the sibling groups.

The scarcity of land associated with hard working conditions and the desire to retain the landed wealth, whatever is available, intact by preventing the divisions of assets among independently settled brothers, has played no less significant role in sustaining the institution of polyandry. The divisions of family property has been discouraged in the region by the customary law i.e. Dastur-ul-Amal, which reads :

> 12 (2nd.) Goods are divided in the following manner viz. after deducting one thing of each kind, and one field for pitants, viz. rights on account of seniority and half of that field viz. kanchoo for the youngest, and the rest are divided equally among them.
>
> The sayana distributes the shares and receives one sheep,

> one goat, one dish, one weapon and five rupees. The panchayat receive five rupees and the villagers two rupees.

This unequal distribution of family property among the brothers has indirectly encouraged the continuation of polyandrous joint families in the region. Majumdar (1960) has termed these factors as 'geo-economic' causes of polyandry. The scarcity of agricultural land compels the people in the area to take to other secondary occupations such as sheep rearing and cattle rearing. This multiplicity of occupational engagement necessitate the long term absence of male members of the family, which may also be one of the factors for polyandry in the region. To Roy Burman (1981) also this fraternal polyandry seems to be a demographic solution for the difficult economic problems where every household has to depend simultaneously on agriculture, sheep rearing and allied activities.

At present the people of Jaunsar-Bawar are relactant to accept the prevalence of polyandry in the area. Although the spread of education, urban contacts and modern means of communication have created an awareness among the people in the area about the stigma attached to the institution of polyandry elsewhere in the plains of the country but in the niche of socio-economic circumstances it has not been possible for them to completely do away with this institution. The practice of polyandry is on decline. In 1953 Sak ena (1954) observed 74.7% of the total married females living in polyandrous families. The incidences of polyandry as calculated by Majumdar (1955) comes to 49.40 % which are further reduced to merely 19.67 % in 1981 (Sishaudhia, 1981). In contrast to the general trend of decline Bhatt (1978) has observed the reinforcement of the cultural norms of fraternal polyandry to preserve the politically achieved status of a tribe by the Jaunsaries.

Despite persistant outside pressures and forces for assimilation and conformity to dominant alien cultural norms in the name of 'progress and modernization' this institution of polyandry still survives strongly. The demo-economic structure of the region has been playing an important role in counter-balancing the forces and means of induced changes. If polyandry were merely a social evil not having any thing to do with demo-economic structure and forces, its eradication would not have been so difficult. The social factors are so complexly interwoven with demo-economic considerations that in spite of widened social outlook as a result of spread of modern education and communication as well as the presence of external forces of change in the area the practice of polyandry still continues among the Jaunsari community.

ACKNOWLEDGEMENT

I am very thankful to Sri G.S. Bhatt, Head Dept. of Sociology, D.A.V. College, Dehradun and Sri D. Tyagi, An. S.I., Dehra Dun for their comments and valuable suggestions on the paper.

TABLE 1

Population and Sex-ratio of Jaunsar-Bawar

Year	Total Population	Males	Females	Sex-ratio
1881	45117	25400	19717	1000 : 776
1891	50697	28435	22262	783
1901	51101	28349	22752	803
1911	54812	30518	24294	796
1921	55623	31567	24056	762
1931	56774	31922	24857	778
1941	57650	32345	25305	782
1951	58469	32704	25765	788
1961	66674	37650	29024	771
1971	77609	45495	31755	720

REFERENCES

Bhatt G.S., 1978 "From Caste Structure to Tribe : The Case of Jaunsar Barar", *The Eastern Anthropologist*, vol. 31 No. 3.

——1980 Constrants of Being Polyandrous Tribal : The Case of Jaunsar-Bawar, in *Family, Marriage and Social Change on the Indian Fringe*, Eds. Dubey, S.M., Bordoloi P.K. & Borthakur B.N., Cosmo Publications, New Delhi.

—— Berreman G.D. 1972 *Hindus of Himalayas : Ethnography and Change*, University of California Press, Burkley.

1977 Demography, Domestic Economy and Change in the Western Himalayas, *The Eastern Anthropologist*, vol, 30, No. 2.

Biswas P.C. 1953 Polyandry Among the Hill Tribes of Jaunsar-Bawar, *Vanyajati*, vol. 1 No. 1.

Hasnain Nadeem 1982 *Bonded for Ever : A Study of the Kolta, a cis-Himalayan Tribe* ; Hornam Publication, New Delhi.

Hasan Amir 1971 *A Bunch of Wild Flowers and other Articles*, Ethnographic And Folk Culture Society, Lucknow.

Joshi L.D. 1929 *Khasa Customary Law*, Government Press, Allahabad.

Jain S.D. 1980 Women's Status in Marriage and Family in a Polyandrous Society, in *Family, Marriage and Social Change on the Indian Fringe*, Eds. Dubey S.M., Bordoloi P.K. and Borthakur B.N., Cosmo Publications, New Delhi.

Khairwal C.S. 1975 Customs and Traditions in Jaunsar-Bawar, *Journal of L.B.S. National Academy of Administration*, vol. XX, No. 3.

Majumdar D.N. 1954 *Rural Profile*, Ethnographic and Folk Culture Society, Lucknow.

Majumdar D.N. 1962 *Himalayan Polyandry*, Asia Publishing House, Bombay.

Parmar Y.S. 1975 *Polyandry in the Himalayas*, Vikas Publishing House, New Delhi.

Roy Burman B.K. 1981 Population and Society in the Himalayas, in *Himalaya—Aspects of Change*, Eds. Lal J.S. and Moddie A.D., Oxford University Press, New Delhi.

Sinha Raghuvir 1980 *Family to Religion*, National Pubiishers, New Delhi.

Saksena, R.N. 1953 Marriage and Divorce in Jaunsar-Bawar, *Vanyajati*, vol. 1, No. 1.

——1954 *Social Economy of a Polyandroue People*, Asia Publishing House, Bombay.

Sishaudhia V.K. 1981 Demographic Structure of a Tribal Village : A Priliminary Study, *Vanyajati*, vol. XXIX, No. 3.

——1981 Ek Bahu Patiya Janjati Ki Jananki, *Manav*, vol. 9, No, 3.

—— 1982 Jaunsar-Bawar : Bahupati Pratha avam Mahilayan, *Uttar Pradesh*, Year 11, No 2.

9

POLYANDRY AMONG THE JAT SIKHS OF PUNJAB

K.P. SINGH

Courtship, love and mating in any society are influenced by "the way the sexes face one another in public and in private as well as the economic cooperation that is demanded of them" (Majumdar, 1961). The institution of marriage plays a major role in the regulation of sexual relations. Thus polyandry as mentioned in the Encyclopedia of Social Sciences (1968) is a marital union of two or more men, in which there is cultural endorsement of sexual intercourse between the partners of opposite sex and generally the expectation that children will be born of the relationship.

It is not possible to determine at what stage this institution made its appearance in India but according to Parmar (1975) it is mentioned in the Vedic and post-Vedic literature. Kapadia (1962) mentioned that the polyandrous union was once practised by the people of Cis-Himalayan tract in Northern India and among some tribes of pre-Dravadian groups in South India. It exists even today in the transgiri territory of Sirmur, Jubbal and Kulu and it has been practised there for a long time (Parmar, 1975).

Polyandry of the fraternal type is more or less frequent in vast districts of the Himalayan region; and it is also found, though more or less concealed, among various communities of the North Indian plains (Westermark, 1926). He further mentioned that polyandry of the fraternal type was practised in various parts of Punjab, and it was not unusual arrangement among the Sikhs ; for the brothers of a family to have a wife in common. And even today, the Jat Sikhs in some of the eastern Punjab districts are stated to have continued with the same practice, though without full recognition.

Large number of studies have been conducted in various parts of the country to understand the working of this institution In recent years it has been seen that it is only in the interior areas that one finds polyandry. In most of the places where it existed, it is giving way to monogamy because of the spread of education and modernization. It is interesting to note that even today, in some of the interior areas of Punjab state, it is being practised by some of the Jat Sikhs. It is not an acknowledged form of marriage now, still it is being practised. The present study is the outcome of some of the observations made by the investigator in village Bhurthala Mandar, District Sangrur in Punjab.

Therefore, the main objective of the study is to examine the extent of polyandry in the village Bhurthala Mandar and investigate some of the reasons for its existence even in the present times. An attempt would also be made to see whether it is different than the polyandrous unions found in other parts of the country or not.

Methodology :- The present study being an exploratory one, case study method was adopted so that fairly exhaustive information could be gathered.

A census survey of the whole village was undertaken and a list of families having polyandrous unions was prepared. According to 1971 census, the village consisted of 342 households. Of these households, 198 of them belonged to the Jat Sikhs, the dominant caste. Further, of these 198 Jat Sikh households, polyandrous unions were found in 41 households. In terms of percentages, it came out to be 21% of the Jat Sikh families. For the present study, only 31 households could be contacted and the remaining 10 were not available due to various reasons,

Thus the present study is limited to these 31 cases. The case histories of these families were prepared by interviewing the ritually married man, his unmarried brothers and the common wife.

Although it is not pertinent to make any broad generalizations on the basis of limited number of cases, but as already pointed out that with the economic development and with the spread of education, this institution is fast disappearing and giving way to monogamy; hence there are very few people who practise it now. Nevertheless within the limitations of small number of cases, the generalizations would hold good for Punjab as similar practise is being followed by limited number of people in the other remote villages of the state also.

Socio-Economic Characteristics of the Cases Under Study

Although literacy level in the rural areas is very low but it is much lower in the present study. All the brothers, i.e., the married man and his unmarried brothers, with a few exceptions were either illiterate or just literate whereas all wives were just illiterate. The main occupation of the respondents was agriculture although their land holdings were quite small. In ten cases, they owned 4 or less than 4 acres of land, in 16 cases, the land owned was between 5-15 acres and in the remaining five cases it was between 15-20 acres. The women were confined to the household works and not engaged in any gainful employment.

So far income is concerned, it was not possible to get monthly income very accurately because of the nature of their occupation, hence annual income was recorded. In nine cases, the yearly income was upto Rs. 3000 which is very low but which corresponds to the fact that they have small land holdings. In 16 cases the income was between Rs. 3000 to Rs. 8000 and in the remaining 6 cases it was above Rs. 8000. On the whole majority of these respondents belonged to lower middle or low socio-economic status.

Another important point to be noted was their age at marriage. Of the total number of cases, two men were married below the age of 20 years and another nineteen of them were married between the age of 21-29 years and the remaining ten were married after the age of 30 years. The average age at marriage was 28.3 years and that was much above the average for the Punjab State (22 years in 1971). Comparatively average age at marriage was much lower for women as it was only 17.5 years. Average size of the household was found to be 6.3 although average number of children was 3.1 only.

Findings of the Study

The data reveals that only one brother was ritually married to the woman irrespective of the number of brothers in the family. It is not preplanned as to which one would be married. It all depends upon the particular circumstances of each case. Still in most of the cases the determining factor is the age of the man, his educational level, physical abilities and his ability to manage household affairs.

Thus out of the total number of cases, in 25 cases (80%) two brothers were sharing one wife, in five cases (16%) three brothers had one wife and in one case five brothers shared one wife. Since only brothers can share a wife, therefore, the number of brothers or husbands is limited by the number of brothers in the family. In the absence of any specific criterion as to which brother would be married, it is interesting to note that of the 25 cases, where two brothers share one wife, in fifteen cases, the elder brother was ceremonially married whereas in the remaining ten cases the younger brother was married. Further of the five cases where three brothers shared one wife, in two cases, the eldest brother was married and in the remaining three cases the middle one was ritually married. Lastly in one case where five brothers lived with one woman, second in order was married. Thus on the whole in 17 cases (55%) the eldest brother was married, in four cases (13%) middle one was married and in the remaining 10 cases (32%) the younger or the youngest as the case may be, was ceremonially married to the woman. The age of the unmarried brother or brothers, at the time of present survey, was nowhere less than 35 years, indicating thereby, their remote possibility of getting married now.

It was observed that in all these cases, the unmarried brothers whether younger or older had an equal right of access to the married man's wife with his full consent. Since our societal norms do not permit sharing of one's wife with others, the ritually married men, i.e. the real husbands were quite reluctant to disclose this fact in a direct and open manner. They were hesitant to discuss it as they felt ashamed to admit that they allow their brothers to share the wife with them. But it was interesting to note that the unmarried brothers in almost all cases had no such inhibitions and openly admitted that their sexual needs were being satisfied in the family only and the woman was obliged to accept them. In case of women, some of them who were older in age, i.e. above the age of 35 years were also reluctant to disclose this fact openly as they felt ashamed of it. But indirectly these women stated that they had no choice but to entertain the husband's brothers. Some of the younger women took it easy and openly admitted that this practice was their in the family. All of these married women revealed that the mental make up which was necessary for the adoption of this practise, was not there when they were married as there was no indication that they would have to share the bed with their husband's brothers, although it was known to them that the husband's unmarried brothers live in the same family.

Causes of Polyandry

The question arises as to what could be the reasons which have given rise to this practice or which are responsible for its continuation even in the present times.

Although origin of polyandry cannot be traced to any single factor, some of the writers have traced its origin to the numerical disproportion between the sexes. The polyandrous people are said to be more men than women, and there polyandry has in several cases been directly attributed to this fact. In many parts of the Himalayan region in which polyandry is practised the women are distinctly said to be in a minority. In Punjab also, greater disparity between the sexes could be an important reason for the prevalence of polyandrous relations. The state of Punjab has very high sex ratio, rather the highest in the country. According to 1971 census, the number of females per 1000 males in rural areas of Punjab is 879 but in the rural areas of Sangrur district where the present study was taken up, the number of females per 1000 males was 839, and this was the lowest in the state. Thus it could partly be the effect of an excess of males over females.

Among various people polyandry has also been traced to economic reasons. Under economic motives it may be the small and difficult land holdings in hilly areas or the difficulty of raising the sum to be paid for a wife, that induces brothers to have a common wife. It has been reported that among the Jat Sikhs ownership of the land is the most important basis of mate-selection and absence of it or small land holdings are a major obstruction in marriage. In the present study with the exception of six cases where the land owned was more than 10 acres, the land holdings were considered to be quite small for negotiating any marriage proposals. Out migration from the village was very little, and men preferred to remain as helpers in the household rather than go out of the village. Further, of the six cases which the land owned was more than ten acres, in five cases, they did not have this land when they were of marriageable age and it was acquired only recently. In addition to this in four of these cases, the fathers of these men also had the problem of getting a mate and when they could not arrange it, they brought women from outside the Punjab state, and since then a stigma is attached to these families and no one from the Jat Sikh families is willing to give them their daughters.

It has also been reported that it is not customary among the Jat Sikhs to go around and ask for a girl for their sons. They consider this as below their dignity. They feel proud to have sons and are expected to be approached by the girl's family. In most of these cases, it was reported by the men that they never received any marriage proposals because of their small land holdings and low economic status. Further in many cases, irrespective of the customary practices, parents, friends and relative of these men tried through various indirect sources and in some cases, were even prepared to pay bride price, still they could not arrange to find a mate for them. Of the seven cases only one son was married with great difficulty and they had to pay bride price. In two other cases they had to be married in a lower caste. Many of them also reported that there was shortage of young girls of marriageable age in their community.

Thus the very fact that these men could not arrange their marriages even though they were willing to pay bride price, corroborates the fact that their low economic status alongwith the disproportionate sex ratio, have given rise to polyandrous relationships.

In some of the studies, it has also been mentioned that it is due to the difficulties which surround a woman left alone in her home during the prolonged absence of her husband. This has also been reported by Westermark (1926) about Jat Sikhs who worked in the army. But in the present study this could not be an important reason as only two men (one as a driver and the other in the army) were found to be outside the village and all other brothers were living within the village.

Thus in short the two most important factors which have caused this practice and which are also responsible for its continuation by the people are scarcity of women and low economic status due to small land holdings and perhaps indirectly a desire to transmit the land undivided.

Having discussed the causes of polyandrous unions, it becomes essential to understand the kinship network among these people and whether it is different from the polyandrous unions prevalent in other parts of the country.

In most of the polyandrous societies, the usual custom is that one of the brothers, usually the eldest one performs the marriage ceremony, and after this the bride's right hand is held by all brothers who are deemed to have married her or some other ceremony is performed to indicate that all brothers are the husbands of the woman. In the present study, the woman is ceremonially married to only one brother and no other ceremony is performed to indicate that she is the joint wife of all brothers. She neither addresses them as her husband nor gives them the treatment of a co-husband but only considered them as husband's brothers. She uses the kinship terminology of 'Dever' or 'Jeth' as the case may be while addressing them. On the other hand husband's brothers also do not address her as their wife but as 'Bhabi' or 'Bahu' indicating a brother's wife.

In polyandrous unions as mentioned by Parmar (1975) every

male child right from the beginning, develops the attitude that he is the virtual husband of the joint wife of his brothers, and it is done as a matter of routine and is noticed by no body. But in the present situation, unmarried brothers had no such attitudes and understanding. They as well as the woman did not have the mental make up to accept this practice as customary. They infact are not socialized to accept this as the normal practice.

In polyandrous societies, conventional methods exist for ascertaining the social paternity of a child. But in the present study, sociological fatherhood is more important than the biological one. As all the brothers live together and have access to the wife, nobody knows by whom the child has been begotten. Therefore, only the brother who performed the ceremonies of marriage, is recognized as the father of the child. Moreover, apart from having sex relations with the woman, the other brothers have no right over the children born to her.

It was also observed that there was no difference between the kinship terms used by the children for father and father's brother in these polyandrous unions and those of a monogamous marriage. The term 'father' is used only for the ritually married man, no matter that he is in fact a sociological father. The brothers of the married man are addressed differently and a distinction is made between the elder and the younger. The elder one is addressed as 'Taya' and the younger one as 'Chacha'. These brothers in turn address the children as nephews and nieces and not as sons and daughters.

Lastly in a polyandrous society, it is generally maintained that a woman gains long married life and hence becomes immune from widowhood. As long as any one of the brothers is alive, she cannot become a widow. But here a woman becomes a widow after the death of her ritually married husband. After the performance of the last rights of her husband another ceremony called *kareva* takes place and then she becomes the wife of that brother who performs that ceremony.

Thus there was no difference in the use of kinship terminology and the manner of address in these polyandrous unions and those of the monogamous marriage.

In the end with a view to understand the perceptions of these respondents regarding the functioning of this institution and the justifications, if any, they were asked to give their own impressions about it as well as the reactions of the other villagers towards them.

It was interesting to note that all the married men looked upon this practice with disfavour and considered it as a necessary evil. They feel ashamed in disclosing it to the outsiders. They have tolerated it and have allowed it to continue because of their fraternal feelings and also to pervent subdivision of landholdings which are already very small. Since their brothers could not be married and they have no other way by which they could satisfy their sex needs, they feel helpless. On the other hand, the unmarried brothers did not look upon it with much disfavour although they are well aware of the fact that attitude towards polyandry was no longer held in esteem. But they defended it on the ground that they worked for the family and contributed to the family finances and their share of property would go to the children of this union. They considered it a matter of right to have access to the brother's wife and expected her to render all services to them. The most unhappy person in the family was the woman who had to satisfy more than one man. This is clear from the statement made by one of the women that she leads an animal's life as it is difficult to satisfy one man whereas she has to satisfy three of them. They did not mind cooking, washing and rendering all other services for the husband's brothers on the consideration that they contribute to the family finances. Added to that is the consideration that since they are not married their share of property would go her children. But at times they resent the sexual liberties taken by the other brothers.

It may thus be pointed out that all these respondents who practise polyandrous relations, today are well aware of the fact that other people in the community do not approve of their relations and consider them immoral. Their contact with other people has convinced them of their own degraded condition. This is one of the reasons that they are reluctant to acknowledge it. But they defended it on the ground that their land holdings are too small, and it is not possible for all brothers to be married.

Thus it was observed that those who practise these polyandrous type of relations, do so not because they are backward and their social outlook has not changed, but because their social and economic conditions are such that they cannot afford to give it up under the present circumstances.

Discussion

After having discussed the functioning of this institution among the Jat Sikhs the question arises as to whether we can really call this as polyandry. Polyandry has been defined as the marriage of one woman to more than one man. But if there is no marriage, then a group of men or brothers living with one woman, having sexual relations with her and even procreating children, cannot strictly be called polyandrous. It is simply a convenient arrangement suitable to all the members of the household due to certain considerations. Moreover, all the mates of a woman even if they are brothers, are by no means at par neither in terms of relationships nor in kinship terminology. Only the man who goes through the marriage ceremony, is the legitimate husband. So it is nothing but monogamy, with mutually agreed cohabitation by the wife with the husband's brothers.

Another important question which needs further probe is why it is practised only by the Jat Sikhs and not by other land owning people who also possess small land holdings ? Is it a practice among the Jat Sikhs rooted in some remote past where the cultural pattern of the society sanctioned it or is it some thing else?

REFERENCES

Census Commissioner 1972 *Census of India*, 1971 paper I

Kapadia, K.M. 1962 *Marriage and Family in India*, Bombay, Oxford University Press.

Kirk Patrick, S.C. 1878 Polyandry in the Punjab *The Indian Antiquery*, vol. VII, Bombay

Majumdar, D.N. 1962 *Himalayan Polyandry*, Bombay, Asia Publishing House.

Majumdar, D.N. *Races and Culture of India*, Bombay, Asia Publishing House.

Nandi, S.B. 1977 Status of Women in Polyandrous Society, in *Man in India*, vol. 57, No. 2.

Parmar, Y.S. 1975 *Polyandry in the Himalayas*, Delhi, Vikas Publishing House.

Sarkar, Niranjan 1973 The Socalled Polyandry among the Gallongs in *Man in India*, vol 53, No. 2.

Sills, D.L. (Ed.) 1968 International Encyclopedia of Social Sciences, the Macmillan Company and Free Press, U.S.A.

Westermark, Edward. 1921 *The History of Human Marriage*, vol. III London, Macmillan and Co.

10

THE NAYARS AND THE DEFINITION OF MARRIAGE*

E. KATHLEEN GOUGH

The problem of a satisfactory definition of marriage has vexed Anthropologists for decades and has been raised, but not solved several times in recent years.[1] Over time it became clear that cohabitation, ritual recognition, definition of sexual rights or stipulation of domestic services each had too limited a distribution to serve as a criterion for all the unions anthropologists intuitively felt compelled to call 'marriage'. For good reason therefore the '*Notes and Queries*' definition of 1951 makes no reference to any of these : 'Marriage is a union between a man and a woman such that children born to the woman are recognized legitimate offspring of both parents.'

Admirably concise though it is this definition too raises problems in a number of societies. The Nuer institution of woman-marriage-to-a woman would be a case in point. Here, both parties to the union are women yet, as Evans-Pritchard (1951 : 108-9) has shown, the legal provisions of the union are strictly comparable to those of simple legal marriage between a man and a woman. Few therefore would questions Evans-Pritchard's logic in calling this union a marriage.

* Reproduced by permission of the Royal Anthropological Institute of Great Britain and Ireland from *Journal of the Royal Anthropological Institute of Great Britain Ireland* 89 (I & II) : 23-34-1959.

The *'Notes and Queries'* definition contains two criteria : that marriage is a union between one man and woman, and that it establishes the legitimacy of children. Nuer woman-marriage does not conform to the first criterion but it does to the second. At this point the problem therefore becomes : is a definition feasible which would insist only on the second criterion, that of legitimizing children ?

In Europe[2] Dr. Edmund Leach initiated the most recent chapter in this discussion (Leach, 1955), and rather than review its whole history it is pertinent for me to take up the argument where he and others have left it. In effect, Dr. Leach answered 'no' to the question posed above. He argued not only against the vagueness of the pharse 'legitimate offspring' but also against any use of potential legal paternity as a universal criterion of marriage. He concluded in fact that no definition could be found which would apply to all the institutions which ethnographers commonly refer to as marriage. Instead he named ten classes of right which frequently occur in connection with that we loosely term marriage, added that 'one might perhaps considerably extend this list', and seemed to conclude that since no single one of these rights is invariably established by marriage in every known society, we ought to feel free to call 'marriage' any institution which fulfils any one or more of the selected criteria.

There is, surely, a quite simple logical flow in this argument. For it would mean in effect that every ethnographer might extend at will Dr. Leach's list of marital rights, and in short define marriage in any way he pleased. This may be legitimate in describing a single society. But I would argue that for purposes of cross-cultural comparison, we do need a single, parsimonious definition, simply in order to isolate the phenomenon we wish to study

In support of his argument against using the legitimizing of children as a universal criterion of marriage, Dr. Leach cited the Nayar case. On the basis of two my papers on the Nayars (Gough, 1952 ; 1955a), he stated that the Nayars traditionally had 'no marriage in the strict (i.e. Notes and Queries) sense of the term, but only a "relationship of perpetual affinity" between linked lineages (Gough, 1955a). 'The woman's children, however they might be begotten, were simply recruits to the woman's own matrilineage. He stated further, "The notion of fatherhood is lacking. The child uses a term of address meaning "lord" or "leader" towards all its mother's lovers, but the use of this term does not carry with it any connotation of paternity, either legal or biological. On the other hand, the notion of affinity is present, as evidenced by the fact that a woman must observe pollution at her ritual husband's death (Gough, 1955a). Later Dr. Leach concludes that 'among the matrilineal' matrilocal Nayar, as we have seen, right (to establish a socially significant "relationship of affinity" between the husband and his wife's brothers) is the only marriage characteristic that is present at all' (Leach, 1955: 183)

This paper has two objectives. It will begin by analyzing traditional Nayar marital institutions and thereby showing in fact that the notion of fatherhood is not lacking and that marriage does serve to establish the legitimacy of children. My analysis will, I hope, not only dispose of a misinterpretation on Dr. Leach's part, but will in general clarify what has always proved a crucial but difficult borderline case for theorists of kinships. The paper will conclude with a new definition of marriage which will again make the status of children born to various types of union critical for decisions as to which of these unions constitute marriage. The ultimate aim is not of course to re-define marriage in a dogmatic way to suit a particular case, for definitions are tools of classification and not aims of research. The aim is to show that there is a common element not only in the institutions anthropologists have confidently labelled 'marriage' by the Notes and Queries definition, but also in some unusual cases to which that definition does not apply. Whether we call the element 'marriage' does not much matter provided it is made explicit, but it would probably be convenient to do so.

Nayar Marriage in Central Kerala

This account will refer to Nayars in the former kingdoms of Calicut, Walluvanad, and Cochin in the centre of the Malabar Coast or Kerala. In the northernmost kingdoms (Kolattunad,

Kottayam) and probably also in the southernmost kingdom of Travancore, Nayar residence appears to have been avunculocal even before the period of British rule, marriage was optionally polygynous but not polyandrous, and individual men appear to have had definite rights in and obligations to their children. Full information is not available for these northernmost and southernmost kingdoms in the pre-British period. But it seems probable that in the northern kingdoms at least, even the Notes and Queries definition of marriage wasapplicable to the Nayars. It was certainly applicable in the latter half of the nineteenth Century for which I have accounts from informants.

My account of marriage in the central kingdoms is a reconstruction of a State of affairs which appears to have been general before 1792 when the British assumed government of the Coast. As I have shown elsewhere (Gough, 1952) Nayar kinship was slowly modified in the nineteenth century and more rapidly in the twentieth. But in remote village the traditional institutions persisted until towards the end of the nineteenth century and were remembered by a few of my elder informants. Their reports are not contradicted and are substantially corroborated by writings of Arab and European travellers of the fifteenth to eighteenth centuries.

In this account I shall use the terms 'marriage', 'husband' and 'wife' without definition. My reasons for doing so will appear later.

In each of the three central kingdoms the Nayar caste was divided into a number of ranked subdivisions characterized by different political functions. Chief of these were (a) the royal lineage, (b) the lineages of chiefs of districts, (c) the lineages of Nayar village headmen and (d) several sub-castes of commoner Nayars. Each of these last either served one of the categories (a) to (c) or else served patrilineal landlord families of Nambudiri Brahmans. I shall deal first with the commoner Nayars of category (d).

There were present in each village some four to seven exogamous matrilineages of a single sub-caste of commoner Nayars. These owed allegiance to the family of the head of the village, which might be a patrilineal Nambudiri family, a Nayar village headman's matrilineage, a branch of the lineage of the chief of the district, or a branch of the royal lineage. The commoners held land on a hereditary feudal-type tenure frcm the headman's lineage and, in turn, had authority over the village's lower castes of cultivators, artisans and agricultural serfs. Each retainer lineage tended to comprise some four to eight property-owning units which I call property-groups. The property-group formed a segment of the total lineage and was usually composed of a group of brothers and sisters together with the children and daughter's children of the sisters. The members owned or leased property in common, lived in one house, and were under the legal guardianship of the eldest male (*karanavan*) of the group. Both the property-group and the lineage were called *taravad*.

Nayar men trained as professional soldiers in village gymnasia and for part of each year they tended to be absent from the village in wars against neighbouring kingdoms or for military exercises at the capitals. Only the *karanavan*, the women and the children of the property-group remained permanently in their ancestral homes.

The Nayars of one village or of two adjacent villages formed a neighbourhood group (*kara* or *tara*) of some six to ten lineages. Each lineage was linked by hereditary ties of ceremonial co-operation with two or three other lineages of the neighbourhood. These linkages were reciprocal but not exclusive, so that a chain of relationships linked all the lineages of the neighbourhood. The lineages linked to one's own were called *enangar* ; the total neighbourhood group, the *enangu*. At least one man and one woman of each linked lineage must be invited to the house of a property-group for the life crisis rites of its members. Its linked lineages were also concerned if some member of a lineage committed a breach of the religious law of the caste. It was their duty at once to break off relations with the offending lineage and to call a neighbourhood assembly to judge and punish the offence. Its linked lineages thus represented the neighbourhood group as a whole to the offending lineage and were special guardians of its morality. Sometimes in small neighbourhoods to commoner Nayar lineages were all *enangar* to each other, but in larger neighbourhoods this was not feasible, for the heads of property-groups would have too many ceremonial obligations to fulfil.

The linked lineages played their most important role at the pre-puberty marriage rites (*tālikoṭṭukalyāṇam*) of girls (Gough, 1955 b). At a convenient time every few years, a lineage held a grand ceremony at which all its girls who had not attained puberty, ages about seven to twelve, were on one day ritually married by men drawn from their linked lineages. The ritual bridegrooms were selected in advance on the advice of the village astrologer at a meeting of the neighbourhood assembly. On the day fixed they came in procession to the oldest ancestral house of the host lineage. There, after various ceremonies, each tied a gold ornament (*tāli*) round the neck of his ritual bride. The girls had for three days previously been secluded in an inner room of the house and caused to observe taboos as if they had menstruated. After the *tāli*-tying each couple was secluded in private for three days. I was told that traditionally, if the girl was nearing puberty, sexual relations might take place.

This custom began to be omitted in the late nineteenth century, but from some of the literature it have been essential in the sixteenth and seventeenth centuries. At the end of the period of seclusion each couple was purified from the pollution of cohabitation by a ritual bath. In Calicut and Walluvanad each couple in public then tore in two the loin-cloth previously won by the girl during the 'cohabitation' period, as a token of separation. This rite appears to have been omitted in Cochin. In all three kingdoms however, the ritual husbands left the house after the four days of ceremonies and had no further obligations to their brides. A bride in turn had only one further obligation to her ritual husband : at his death, she and all her children, by whatever biological father, must observe death-pollution for him. Death-pollution was otherwise observed only for matrilineal kin. In Cochin, even if their mother's ritual husband never visited his wife again, her children must refer to him by the kinship term *appan*. Children in the lower, patrilineal castes of this area used this word to refer to the legal father, who was presumed also to be the biological father. In Walluvanad and Calicut I did not hear of this verbal usage and do not know by what term, if any, Nayar children referred to their mother's ritual husband.

The pre-puberty *tali*-rite was essential for a girl. If she menstruated before it had been performed, she should in theory be expelled from her lineage and caste. In fact, however, my informants told me that in such a case the girl's family would conceal the fact of her maturity until after the rite had been performed. But it was a grave sin to do so and one which would never be publicly admitted.

The *tali*-rite marked various changed in the social position of a girl. First, it brought her to social maturity. She was now thought to be at least ritually endowed with sexual and procreative functions and was thenceforward accorded the status of a woman. After the rite people addressed her in public by the respectful title *amma* meaning 'mother', and she might take part in the rites of adult women. Second, after the *tali*-rite a girl must observe all the rules of etiquette associated with incest prohibitions in relation to man of her lineage. She might not touch them, might not sit in their presence, might not speak first to them and might not be alone in a room with one of them. Third, after the *tali*-rite and as seen as she become old enough (i.e., shortly before or after puberty) a girl received as visiting husbands a number of men of her sub-caste from outside her lineage, usually but not necessarily from her neighbourhood. In addition she might be visited by any Nayar of the higher sub-castes of village headmen, chiefs or royalty, or by a Nambudiri Brahman. All of these relationships were called *sambandham*. Among commoner Nayar women, however, the great majority of unions were with men of commoner sub-caste.

Relations between any Nayar women and a man of *lower* Nayar sub-caste or between any Nayar woman and a man of one of the lower, non-Nayar castes, were strictly prohibited. If a woman was found guilty of such a relationship her lineage's *enangar* carried the matter to the neighbourhood assembly. This temporarily excommunicated the woman's property-group until justice has been done. In the nineteenth century and early this century the property-group was re-accepted into caste only after its *karanavan* had dismissed the woman from her household and caste, never to return. In pre-British times a woman so dismissed became the property of the king or chief and might be sold into slavery with foreign traders. Alternatively, however, the man of her property-group had the right, sometimes exercised, to kill both the woman and her lover and thus preserve the good name of their lineage.

After the ritual marriage the bridegroom need have no further contact with his ritual wife. If both parties were willing, however, he might enter into a sexual relationship with his ritual bride about the time of her puberty. But he had no priority over other men of the neighbourhood group. There is some uncertainty as to the number of visiting husbands a woman might have at one time. Writers of the sixteenth and seventeenth centuries report that a woman usually has some three to eight regular husbands but might receive other men or her own or a higher caste at will. Hamilton in 1727 states that a woman might have as husbands 'twelve but no more at one time' (Hamilton, 1727 : 310). As late as 1807 Buchanan reported that Nayar women view with each other as to the number of lovers they could obtain (Buchanan, 1807 : I ; 411). A few of my older informants could remember women who had had three or four current husbands, although plural unions were being frowned upon and had almost died out by the end of the last century. There appears to have been no limit to the number of wives of appropriate sub-caste whom a Nayar might visit concurrently. It seems, therefore, that a woman customarily had a small but not a fixed number of husbands from within her neighbourhood, that relationships with these men might be of long standing, but that the woman was also free to receive casual visitors of appropriate sub-caste who passed through her neighbourhood in the course of military operations.

A husband visited his wife after supper at night and left before breakfast next morning. He placed his weapons at the door of his wife's room and if others came later they were free to sleep on the varandah of the woman's house. Either party to a union might terminate it at any time without formality. A passing guest recompensed a woman with a small cash gift at each visit. But a more regular husband from within the neighbourhood had certain customary obligations. At the start of the union it was common although not essential for him to present the woman with a cloth of the kind worn as a skirt. Later he was expected to make small personal gifts to her at the three main festivals of the year. These gifts included a loin-cloth, betel-leaves and arecanuts for chewing, hair-oil and bathing-oil, and certain vegetables. Failure on the part of a husband to make such a gift was a tacit sign that he had ended the relationship. Most important, however when a woman became pregnant it was essential for one or more men of appropriate sub-caste to acknowledge probable paternity. This they did by providing a fee of a cloth and some vegetables to the low caste midwife who attended the woman in childbirth. If no man of suitable caste would consent to make this gift, it was assumed that the woman had relations with a man of lower caste or with a Christian or a Muslim. She must then be either expelled from her lineage and caste or killed by her matrilineal kinsmen. I am uncertain of the precise fate of the child in such a case, but there is no doubt at all that he could not be accepted as a member of his lineage and caste. I do not know whether he was killed or became a slave ; almost certainly, he must have shared the fate of his mother. Even as late as 1949, over a hundred and fifty years after the establishment of British rule, a Nayar girl who became pregnant before the modern marriage ceremony was regarded as acting within the canons of traditional religious law if she could simply find a Nayar of suitable sub-caste to pay her delivery expenses. But if no Nayar would consent to this she ran the danger of total estracism, with her child, by the village community, I heard of several cases in which such a girl was driven from her home by her *karanvan* at the command of the sub-caste assembly. Her natal kinsmen then performed funeral rites for her as if she had died. In each case the girl took refuge in a town before or shortly after her child was born.

Although he made regular gifts to her at festivals, in no sense of the term did a man maintain his wife. Her food and regular clothing she obtained from her matrilineal group. The gifts of a woman's husbands were personal luxuries which pertained to her role as a sexual partner-extra clothing, articles of toilet, betel, and areca-nut the giving of which is associates with courtship, and the expenses of the actual delivery, not, be it noted, of the maintenance or either mother or child. The gifts continued to be made at festivals only while the relationships lasted. No man had obligations to a wife of the past.

In these circumstances the exact biological fatherhood of a child was often uncertain, although, of course, paternity was presumed to lie with the man or among the men who had paid the delivery expenses. But even when biological paternity was known with reasonable certainty, the genitor had no economic, social, legal, or ritual rights in nor obligations to his children after he had once paid the fees of their births. Their guardianship, care and discipline were entirely the concern of their matrilineal kinsfolk headed by their *karanavan*. All the children of a woman called all her current husbands by the Sanskrit word *acchan* meaning 'lord'. They did not extend kinship terms at all to the matrilineal kin of these men. Neither the wife nor her children observed pollution at the death of a visiting husband who was not also the ritual husband of the wife.

In most matrilineal systems with settled agriculture and localized matrilineal groups, durable links are provided between those groups by the interpersonal relationships of marriage, affinity and fatherhood. The husbands, affines, fathers, and patrilateral kin of members of the matrilineal group have customary obligations to and rights in them which over time serve to mitigate conflicts between the separate matrilineal groups. The Nayars had no such durable institutionalized interpersonal links. This does not mean that man did not sometimes form strong emotional attachments to particular wives and their children. My information indicates that they did. I know for example that if a man showed particular fondness for a wife, his wife's matrilineal kin were likely to suspect the husband's matrilineal kin of hiring sorcerers against them. For the husband's matrilineal kin would be likely to fear that the husband might secretly convey to his wife gifts and cash which belonged rightfully to his matrilineal kin. This suspicion was especially rife if the husband was a *karanavan* who controlled extensive property. Informal emotional attachments did therefore exist between individuals of different lineages. But what I wish to indicate is that among the Nayars, these interpersonal affinal and patrilateral links were not invested with customary legal, economic or ceremonial functions of a kind which would periodically bring members of different lineages together in mandatory forms of co-operation. Four special kinship terms did apparently exist for use in relation to affines acquired through the *sambandham* relationship, although, as I have said, there were no patrilateral terms for kin other than the mother's husbands. All men and women currently engaged in *sambandham* unions with members of ego's property group, and all members of the property-group of these individuals, were collectively referred to as *bandhukkal* ('joined ones'). A current wife of ego's mother's brother was addressed and referred to as *ammayi*, and a wife of the elder brother as *jyeshtatiamma* (lit. 'elder-sister-mother'). Finally the own brother and the sambandham husband of a woman employed the reciprocal term *aliyan* to refer to each other but used no term of address. All the current *bandhukkal* of a property-group were invited to household feasts, but as individual affines they had no ceremonial or economic obligations and were not obliged to attend. As representatives of *enangar* lineages, however, some of these same individuals might be obliged to attend feasts and to fulfil ceremonial obligations as *enangar*. But as particular affines they had no obligations. In place therefore, of institutionalized interpersonal patrilateral and affinal links, the Nayars had the hereditary institution of linked lineages. Whether or not, at a particular time, sexual relationships existed between individuals of linked lineages, the linked lineages must fufil their obligations at household ceremonies and give neighbourly help in such emergencies as birth and death. In the patrilineal and double unilineal castes of Kerala precisely the same obligations are fulfilled by the matrilateral kin and affines of individual members of the patrilineal group. The linked lineages of the Nayars must therefore, I think, be regarded as having a relationship of 'perpetual affinity', which carried the more formal functions of affinity and persisted through the making and breaking of individual sexual ties.

In view of those facts, it is convenient to mention here that Dr Leach's statement that Nayar marriage served to establish a socially significant relationship between the husband and his wife's brothers' is not strictly speaking, correct. The *sambandham* union did not establish 'a socially significant relationship' between brothers-in-law for in spite of the reciprocal kinship term, these persons had no institutionalized obligations to one another by virtue of the particular *sambandham* tie. Further, the *tali*-rite did not *establish* a relationship between the ritual husband and the brothers of his ritual bride. The ceremony set up no special obligations between these persons ; it was merely that their lineages were, hereditarily, *enangar*, both before and after any particular *tali*-rite. What the rite did *establish* was a ritual relationship between the *tali*-tier and his ritual bride, and, as I shall try to show later, a relationship of group marriage between the bride and all men of her sub-caste outside her lineage. But a particular *tali*-rite in no way modified the hereditary relationships between male *enangar*. It is for this reason that I call the *enangar* relationship one of perpetual affinity, *between lineages*, which though it carried the ceremonial functions of affinity, persisted irrespective of particular *sambandhams* and *tali*-rites.

The Nayars of this area were thus highly unusual. For they had a kinship system in which the elementary family of father, mother and children was not institutionalized as a legal, productive, distributive, residential, socializing or consumption unit. Until recent years, some writers have thought that at least as a unit for some degree of co-operation in economic production and distribution, the elementary family was universal. This view has been put forward most forcibly by Murdock (1949 : chapter I). Radcliffe-Brown, however, was one of the earliest anthropologists to observe that if the written accounts of the Nayars were accurate, the elementary family was not institutionalized among them.[4] My research corroborates his findings.

I turn briefly to marital institutions among the higher Nayar sub-castes of village headman, district chiefs, and royalty. At various times during the pre-British period these lineages were accorded political office one set themselves up as of higher ritual rank than the commoner Nayars. The ritual ranking between these major aristocratic sub-divisions was fairly stable, but the mutual ranking of lineages within each sub-division was in dispute. Most village headmen acknowledged the ritual superiority of district chiefs, and most chiefs of the royal lineage. But some village headmen disputed among themselves for ritual precedence and so did many chiefs. As a result, each of these aristocratic lineages tended to set itself up as a separate sub-caste, acknowledging ritual superiors and inferiors but acknowledging no peers. In the course of time, moreover, following the vicissitudes of political fortune, such lineages could rise or fall in the ritual hierarchy. It was in these lineages therefore that hypergamous unions became most highly institutionalized, for most of these lineages refused to exchange spouses on equal terms. Instead, most of them married all their women upwards and all their men downwards. Women of village headman's lineages entered *s mbandham* unions with chiefly, royal or Nambudiri Brahman men. Men of these lineages had unions with commoner Nayar women. Chiefly women had unions with royals or Nambudiris ; chiefly men, with the women of village headmen's or commoner Nayar lineages. Royal women for the most part had unions with Nambudiri Brahmans of the highest rank. A few, especially in Calicut, however, had unions with men of older and ritually higher ranking royal lineages which had through conquest become politically subordinate to their own. Among Nambudiri Brahmans, only eldest sons were permitted to marry Nambudiri women and beget children for their own families. Younger sons of Nambudiri households might have *sambandham* unions with Nayar women of any sub-caste.

In all these hypergamous unions the visiting husband owed the same periodic gifts to his wife as in the case of equal unions between persons of the same commoner sub-caste. The husband in a hypergamous union was also held responsible for payment of delivery expenses at the birth of a child to his wife. Hypergamous unions differed from 'equal' unions in that in the former, the husband being of higher ritual rank, might not eat in the house of his wife. The husband was also prohibited from touching his wife, her children, or her other kinsfolk during the daytime while he was in a state of ritual purity. Finally, although children called their mother's higher caste husband by the term *acchan* plus the caste title, Nayars as a whole were not permitted to use affinal terms toward the Nambudiri of their womenfolk, nor did the Nambudiris address or refer to their Nayar wives' brothers as a affines. Nayars insist, however, that a *sambandham* union with a Nambudiri Brahman was of the same character as *sambandham* union with a Nayar of equal sub-caste. It seems that from the legal point of view we must also judge it to be so, since the Brahman husband, like the Nayar was responsible for payments at the birth of a child to his Nayar wife. During my field work, the three Nambudiri Brahmans whom I was able to question closely on this subject told me that from *their* point of view only marriage to a Nambudiri woman with Vedic rites could be regarded as true marriage and that *sambandham* unions with Nayar women were a kind of concubinage. There seems to me no reason why we should not regard these latter unions as concubinage from the point of view of the Brahmans and (since they fulfilled the conditions of Nayar marriage) marriage from the point of view of the Nayars. This seems to me, in fact, the only possible interpretation, since the Brahmans are patrilineal and the child of a Brahman-Nayar union is not legitimized into the Brahman caste. The contrast from the Brahman point of view appears most sharply in the case of an eldest son who may marry one or more Nambudiri women with Vedic rites and may also have liaisons with one or more Nayar women. The Brahman wife's children are of course fully legitimized into the Brahman caste from birth. But the Nayar wife and her children traditionally had no rights of patrilineal descent or inheritance whatsoever, might not enter the kitchen of the Brahman house and might not touch its inhabitants.

Consistently with the difference in direction of *sambandham* unions, the *enangar* institution in these aristocratic Nayar lineages differed somewhat from that in the commoner sub-castes. In general, an aristocratic Nayar lineage had as *enangar* two or more lineages of a sub-caste higher than itself from which its women were want to draw husbands in the *sambandham* relationship. The linked lineage relationship was in these cases not reciprocal. A chiefly lineage might act as *enangar* for the lineages of one or two village headmen but had as its own *enangar* one or two chiefly or royal lineages of higher rank than itself. The Nambudiri Brahman lineages acted as *enangar* for the highest ranks of chiefs and royalty. In this case too the aristocratic Nayar lineage has of course no reciprocal ritual obligations towards the Brahman families with which it was linked. The functions of these aristocratic *enangar* were, as far as I can detect, the same as in the case of commoner Nayars. In particular, men of the higher ranking *enangar* lineages tied the *tali* at the pre-puberty marriage of aristocratic girls-appropriately, for it was from these and other such higher ranking lineages that the girls would later draw visiting husbands. Plural unions were customary in these aristocratic lineages as among commoner Nayars. Obviously, however, the choice of husbands became more and more restricted as one ascended the scale of ranked sub-castes, and at the top of the Nayar hierarchy it was restricted to Nambudiri Brahmans.

I turn now to my interpretation of Nayar marital institutions. To accomplish this it is necessary to classify the rights and obligations obtaining between 'spouses' and between 'fathers' and their 'children'. These fall into two categories : those of the *tali*-rite and those of the *sambandham* union. In relations between spouses of the *tali*-rite, the important rights are those of the woman. The ritual husband had, it is true, apparently at one time the right to deflower his bride. But the accounts of many writers indicate that this right was not eagerly sought, that in fact it was viewed with repugnance and performed with reluctance. The ritual husband also had the right that his ritual wife should mourn his death. But we may assume that this right had more significance for the wife than for the husband for it was not attended by offerings to the departed spirit. These could be performed only by matrilineal kin. The ritual bride's rights were complementary to her husband's, but for her they were of supreme importance. She had, first, the right to *have* a ritual husband of her own or a superior sub-caste before she attained maturity. Her life depended on this, for if she was not ritually married before puberty she was liable to excommunication and might possibly be put to death. She held this claim against her sub-caste as a whole exclusive of her lineage, or (in the case of aristocratic lineages) against a higher sub-caste. This group must, through the institution of the linked lineages, provide her with a ritual husband of correct rank and thus bring her to maturity in honour instead of in shame. It was the duty of her lineage kinsmen to see to it that some representative from their linked lineages fulfilled this right. The ritual wife's second right was that of observing pollution at the death of her ritual husband. I interpret this as a mark of proof that she had once been married in the correct manner and that this ritual relationship had retained significance for *her* throughout her ritual husband's life.

The *tali*-tier had no rights in his ritual wife's children except that they should observe pollution at his death. From the child's point of view, however, his mother's ritual husband must have been a figure of great symbolic significance. For a child whose mother had no ritual husband, could not acquire membership in his caste and lineage at all. The birth of a child before his mother's *tali*-rite was absolutely forbidden and, in the nature of the case, can scarcely ever have happened. If it did occur mother and child must certainly have been expelled and were most probably killed. The child's observance of pollution for his mother's ritual husband-like the use of the kinship term *appan* in Cochin—was a formal recognition that, for ritual purposes, he had been 'fathered' by a man of appropriate caste.

Turning to the *sambandham* union, it seems clear that the husband had no exclusive rights in his wife. He had only, in common with other men, sexual privileges which the wife might withdraw at any time. Again it is the wife's rights which are important. The wife had the right to gifts from her husband at festivals, gifts of little economic value but of high prestige value, for they established her as a woman well-favoured by men. But most significant was the woman's right to have her delivery expenses paid by one or more husbands of appropriate caste, that is, to have it openly acknowledged that her child had as biological father a man of required ritual rank. Her matrilineal kinsmen could if necessary press for the fulfilment of this right in a public assembly of the neighbourhood : in cases of doubtful paternity and man who had been currently visiting the woman could be forced by the assembly to pay her delivery expenses. But if no man of appropriate rank could be cited as potential father, women and child were expelled from their lineage and caste.

The *sambandhan* father had no rights in his wife's children. Here again, however, the child had one right in his possible biological fathers : that one or more of them should pay the expenses associated with his birth, and thus entitles him to enter the world as a member of his lineage and caste.

It is clear therefore that although the elementary family of one father, one mother and their children were not institutionalized as a legal, residential, or economic unit, and although individual men had no significant rights in their particular wives or children, the Nayars did institutionalize the concepts of marriage and of paternity, and gave ritual and legal recognition to both. It is here that I must contradict Dr. Leach's interpretation of the situation, for it is not true that 'the notion of fatherhood is lacking' nor is it true that 'a woman's children however they might be begotten, were simply recruits to the woman's matrilineage' (Leach 1955, p. 183). For unless his mother was ritually married by a man of appropriate caste and, unless his biological parternity was vouched for by one or more men[5] of appropriate caste, a child could never enter his caste or lineage at all. As I pointed out in both the papers quoted by Dr. Leach, the Nayars were aware of the physiological function of the male in procreation and attached significance to it, for they expected a child to look like his genitor. Like all the higher Hindu castes of India, they based their belief in the moral rightness of the caste system in part upon a racist ideology which involved the inheritance of physical, intellectual and moral qualities by a child from both of its natural parents, and which held that the higher castes were, by virtue of their heredity, superior to the lower castes. It was ostensibly for this reason that the Nayars forbade with horror sexual contracts between a Nayar woman and a man of lower caste, and that they expelled or put to death women guilty of such contacts. This racist ideology also provided a motive for hypergamous unions, for Nayars of aristocratic lineages boasted of the superior qualities they derived from royal and Brahmanical fatherhood.

Moreover, although individual men had no significant customary rights in their wives and children, marriage and paternity were probably significant factors in political integration. For hypergamous unions bound together the higher sub-castes of the political and religious hierarchies. Multiple sexual ties, as well as the *enangar* relationship, linked office-bearing lineages to each other and to their retainers in a complicated manner. And Nayar men phrased their loyalty to higher ranking military leaders, rulers and Brahmans in terms of a debt owed to benevolent paternal figures whose forebears had collectively fathered them and whose blood they were proud to share. The generalized concept of fatherhood thus commanded the Nayer soldier's allegiance to his wider caste unit, to the rulers of his village, chiefdom, and kingdom and to his religious authorities. It was associated with tender loyalty and with fortitude in war.

I cannot entirely blame Dr. Leach for underestimating the significance of Nayar paternity on the basis of his reading of my earlier papers. For in those papers I was concerned to emphasize the lack of rights of individual men in their spouses and children. It is true that in 1952 I wrote : 'Marriage...was the slenderest of ties, while as a social concept fatherhood scarcely existed' (Gough. 1952 : 73). I had not then realized the fundamental necessity to a Nayar of having both a ritual and a biological father of appropriate caste. Moreover, I myself confused the issue by referring to the *sambandham* partners as 'husbands' and 'wives' in my first paper (Gough, 1952) and as 'lovers' and 'mistresses' in my second (Gough, 1955a). For it was not until some time after I read Dr. Leach's paper that I decided to classify Nayar unions unequivocally as marriage and arrived at a definition of marriage which would include the Nayar case. In my own defence I must, however, note that in my paper of 1955, I mentioned that children must observe death pollution for their mother's ritual husband, and that in Cochin they used the kinship term *appan* for this ritual father. In both papers quoted by Dr. Leach, finally, I noted that sexual relations were forbidden between a Nayar woman and a man of lower caste or sub-caste, and that the current *sambandhan* husbands of a woman must pay her delivery expenses.

I regard Nayar unions as a form of marriage for two reasons. One is that although plural unions were customary, mating was not promiscuous. Sexual relations were forbidden between members of the same lineage on pain of death. It was also forbidden for two men of the same property-group wittingly to have relations with one woman, or for two women of the same property-group to have relations with one man. (This rule of course automatically excluded relations between a man and his biological daughter). Further, relations were absolutely prohibited between a Nayar woman and a man of lower sub-caste or caste. These prohibitions are directly connected with my second and more important reason for regarding these unions as marriage, namely that the concept of legally established paternity *was* of fundamental significance in establishing a child as a member of his lineage and caste.

Granted that Nayar unions constituted a form of marriage, we must I think classify them as a clear case of group-marriage. This was the interpretation to which I inclined in 1952 (Gough, 1952 : 73) and it is, I now think, the only interpretation which makes sense of the descriptive material I have presented. The *tali*-rite, as I see it, initiated for each individual Nayar girl a state of marriage to a collectivity of men of appropriate caste. First, the rite ceremonially endowed the girl with sexual and procreative functions. (The mock menstrual seclusion before the rite is relevant to this, as is the actual defloration.) Second, the woman's natal kinsmen surrendered the newly acquired rights in her sexuality, though not in her procreative functions, to a male representative from outside her lineage. This appears in that rules of etiquette associated with incast prohibitions came into force from this date. Third, rights in the woman's sexuality were received by her *enangan* as representative of the men of his sub-caste as a whole. This appears in that the individual *enangan*, as a special sexual partner, was dismissed at the end of the ceremonies and might approach the woman again only as one among a series of equal husbands. In the commoner sub-castes the *enangan* was of the same sub-caste as the woman, and through him as representative sexual rights in the woman were conferred on all men of her sub-caste as a collectivity. They were also in fact extended to any man of higher sub-caste who might favour her with his attentions. In aristocratic lineages the ritual husband was of a sub-caste higher than the woman's, and through him, as representative, sexual rights in the woman were conferred upon all men of higher sub-caste as a collectivity. Fourth, the *tali*-rite, by providing the woman with a ritual husband who (in my view) symbolized all the men of his sub-caste with whom the woman might later have relationships, also provided her children with a ritual father who symbolized the correctness of their paternity. The children acknowledged their debt to him by mourning at his death.

The later *sambandham* unions, by this interpretation, involved the claiming of sexual privileges by men all of whom were potential husbands by virtue of their membership in a sub-caste. The husbands had, however, no individually exclusive rights and could be dismissed at the woman's wish. Their duties as members of their caste were to provide the woman and her lineage with children and to acknowledge their potential biological paternity through birth-payments which legitimized the woman's child.

The Definition of Marriage

I have called the Nayar unions marriage because they involved the concept of legal paternity. It is clear however that such a form of group marriage will not fit the *Notes and Queries* definition of 'a union between *a* man and *a* woman such that children born to the woman are recognized legitimate offspring of both parents' (my italics). For legitimacy in the case of the Nayar child required both a ritual father and a 'legalized genitor' of appropriate rank, and indeed a child might have more than one 'legal genitor' if two or more men had jointly paid the expenses of his birth.

As a tentative move toward a new definition which will have cross-cultural validity and will fit the Nayar and several other unusual cases, I suggest the following :

> 'Marriage is a relationship established between a woman and one or more other persons, which provides that a child born to the woman under circumstances not prohibited by the rules of the relationship, is accorded full birth-status rights common to normal members of his society or social stratum'.

A few footnotes to this definition may help to vindicate its inevitably clumsy phraseology. 'One or more persons' (in place of 'a man') will bring into the definition both group-marriage of the Nayar type and also true fraternal polyandry'.[6] It also brings within the definition such unusual types as woman-marriage to-a-woman. 'Under circumstances not prohibited by the rules of the relationship' would bring into the definition various problematic cases. It is possible for example that there are patrilineal societies in which a husband may legally repudiate a child illicitly begotten upon his wife by another man, without divorcing the wife herself. In this case the previous establishment of the marriage would *not* ensure full birth-status rights to the child, for the rules of the marriage relationship would have been broken through the circumstances which led to his birth. 'Full birth-status rights common to all normal members...' is a compressed reference to all the social relationships, property rights, etc. which a child acquires at birth by virtue of his legitimacy, whether through the father or through the mother. For patrilineal societies the phrase 'full birth-status rights' will include the rights which a child acquires in his *pater* as a person and in his *pater's* group. It will include, that is to say, the legitimization of fatherhood, or mere precisely, of 'father-sonhood'. The phrase is, however, broader than any concept of specific rights in a particular father. It will therefore take care of a case like the Nayar in which all rights are acquired *through* the mother but in which a relationship must be established between the mother and one or more other persons in order for these matrilineal rights to be ratified. Such a process may be called the legitimization of motherhood, or more precisely of 'mother-sonhood'. Moreover, 'full birth-status rights' is, I think, not only broader but more precise than 'recognized legitimate offspring', to the vagueness of which Dr. Leach took exception. The inclusion of 'society or social stratum' makes allowances for class or caste systems in which birth-status rights vary between strata. The case of the Nayars, who are a matrilineal caste in a predominantly patrilineal society, is an obvious example of this.

It should also perhaps be pointed out that this definition does not state that full birth-status rights cannot be acquired by a child except through the marriage of its mother, but only that marriage provides for the acquisition of these rights. The definition does not therefore exclude societies like the Nuer in which a man may legitimize the child of an unmarried woman upon payment of a legitimization fee, without becoming married to the mother (Evans-Pritchard, 1951 : 21, 26).

Prince Peter has objected to the *Notes and Queries* definition and, by implication, to any definition which would make the legitimization of children through the mother's relationship to another party the distinctive characteristic of marriage (1956 : 46). His reason for objecting is that in some societies like the Toda, 'marriage and legitimacy of the children can be looked upon as two different and separate concepts, and it may be necessary to go through a ceremony of legitimization of the offspring (the Toda *pursutpimi* ceremony) in order to establish who is the legal father, because marriage rites are insufficient in themselves to do this.'

However, it seems from Rivers' account that precisely what distinguishes the Toda institution which Prince Peter translates as 'marriage' (*mokh-vatt*) from that which he translates as 'concubinage' (*mokhthoditi*) (1957 : 35), is that a 'husband' held the right to legitimize some or all of his 'wife's' children by the *pursutpimi* ceremony, whereas a lover in the *mokhthoditi* union, being of a different endogamous group from the woman, does not hold this right (Rivers, 1909 : p. 526). A husband acquires the right to perform the *pursutpimi* ceremony, it seems, by virtue of arranged marriage to an infant or through payment of cattle to a former husband or to a group of former husbands of the wife. The Toda marriage union at its inception does therefore provide that a child born to the woman (under circumstances not prohibited by the rules of the relationship) *must be* legitimized before his birth ; the *pursitpimi* ceremony confirms his legitimacy by attaching him to a particular father and giving him rights in the father's patrilineal group. In the Toda case again therefore the concept of legal paternity is *the* distinguishing characteristic of marriage, even though the individual husband, because of polyandry, may be permitted to legitimize only some and not all of the children born to his wife. The Toda case therefore fits my definition,[7] whether we regard the pursutpimi ceremony as the final one of a sequence of marriage rites, or as a Legitimizing act which, under circumstances not prohibited by the rules of the relationship, one or another of the woman's husbands is legally obliged to fulfil.

I do not argue that all societies must necessarily be found to have marriage by my definition. There may yet turn out to be whole societies—or more probably whole social strata—in which children acquire no birth-status rights except through their mother, by the simple fact of birth. It is possible for example that some slave populations do not have marriage in this sense of the term. What I do wish to suggest however is that for most if not all the societies for which we now have information, including the Nayar, marriage as I have defined it is a significant relationship, distinguished by the people themselves from all other kinds of relationships. My definition should therefore enable us to isolate marriage as a cross-cultural phenomenon, and from there to proceed to the more exciting task : that of investigating the differential circumstances under which marriage becomes invested with various other kinds of rights and obligations. Some of the most important of these Dr. Leach has already listed for us.

NOTES

1. The fieldwork on which this paper is based was carried out in three villages of Kerala between September 1947 and July 1949 with the aid of a William Wyse Studentship from Trinity College, Cambridge. Writing it has formed part of a project financed by the American Social Science Research Council.
2. In America Miss Alisa S. Lourie, Douglass College, Rutgers University has recently worked on this problem, and I have been stimulated by correspondence with her and by reading an unpublished paper of hers, *Concepts in family Sociology*. In this paper Miss Lourie formulates a definition of marriage which is narrower than mine, but when her work is published readers will see that I was helped toward my definition by her analysis. I have also profited much from discussions with my husband, David F. Aberle.
3. A. To establish the legal father of a woman's children.
   B. To establish the legal mother of a man's children.
   C. To give the husband a monopoly in the wife's sexuality.
   D. To give the wife a monopoly in the husband's sexuality.
   E. To give the husband partial or monopolistic rights to the wife's domestic and other labour services.
   F. To give the wife partial or monopolistic rights to the husband's labour services.
   G. To give the husband partial or total rights over property belonging or potentially accruing to the wife.
   H. To give the wife partial or total rights over property belonging or potentially accruing to the husband.
   I. To establish a joint fund of property—a partnership—for the benefit of the children of the marriage.
   J. To establish a socially significant 'relationship of affinity' between the husband and his wife's brothers. (Leach, 1955 : 183).
4. Radcliffe-Brown expressed this view most recently and fully in his Introduction to *African Systems of Kinship and Marriage* (1950 : 73 seq.).
5. I do not know whether the Nayars believe it possible for two or more men to contribute to the formation of embryo. I think it possible that they did, for I found this belief among villagers of the Tamil country. Among these castes it formed part of a belief that several acts of intercourse are necessary to 'feed' the embryo and assist it to grow.
6. I agree with Dr. Leach that the Iravas of Central Kerala had true fraternal polyandry. My own enquiries produced evidence supporting Aiyappan's view that the brothers shares equally both sexual rights in the women and also legal paternity of the children in the

same manner in which they were co-owners of the ancestral property. The eldest living brothers at any given time was simply the legal representative of this corporation.

7. I agree with Dr. Fischer that Prince Peter's definition of marriage is a tautology and so of no assistance (1956 : 92). All that Prince Peter's second note shows (1957 : 35) is that several peoples of his acquaintance have different terms for different kinds of relationships between men and women. But unless we approach these with some guiding concepts of our own in mind, we cannot decide which of them to translate as 'marriage' and which as 'concubinage'.

REFERENCES

Buchanan, Francis (Hemilton) 1897 *A Journey from Madras through Mysore Canara and Malabar*. 3 vols. London.

Evans-Pritchard, E.E., 1951 *Kinship and Marriage among the Nuer-* Oxford.

Fischer, H. Th. 1956 For a New Definition of Marriage. *Man*. 92.

Gough, E. Kathleen 1952 Changing Kinship Usages in the Setting of Political and Economic Change among the Nayars of Malabar *J.R. Anthrop. Inst* 82. pp. 71-87.

Gough, B. Kathleen 1955a The traditional Lineage and Kinship System of the Nayars. (Unpublished manuscript in the Hadden Library, Cambridge).

Gough E. Kathleen 1955b Female Initiation Rites on the Malabar Coast, *J.R. Anthrop.* Inst. 85, pp. 45-80.

Hamilton, Alexander 1727 A New Account of the East Indies, 2 vols. Edinburgh.

Leach, E.R 1955 Polyandry, Inheritance and the Definiticn of Marriage *Man*. 1955, 199.

Lourie, Alisa S. 1957 'Concerts in Family Sociology'. (Unpublished manuscript kindly made available to this author).

Murdcck, G.P. 1949 *Social Structure*, New York.

Notes and Queries in Anthropolgy 1951 6th ed. London.

H.R.H. Prince Peter of Greece and Denmark 1956 For a New Definition of Marriage. *Man*, ; 46 ; 1957 : 35.

Radclife-Brown, A.R. & Forde, D. (ed.) 1950 *African Systems of Kinship* and *Marriage*. Oxford.

Rivers, W.H.R. 1906 *The Todas*, London.

11

FRATERNAL POLYANDRY IN MALABAR*

A. AIYYAPPAN

The Malabar coast seems to be the only place in the civilised world where fraternal polyandry still actively practised. The practice is, however, rapidly disappearing and perhaps no vestige of it may remain a generation hence. As the communities that have the polyandrous marriage are becoming conscious of the peculiarity of the practice and as occasionally their neighbours ridicule them on that account, the process of decline of fraternal polyandry is accelerated. Now there is a lot of confusion as to whether Nayar polyandry was a recognized institution or whether it was merely a sporadic irregularity that was regularised by Brahman landlord at certain localities where their power and influence were great. Unless care is taken to record all available facts relating to fraternal polyandry before it disappears completely, a legacy of confusion will be left about it too.

Sheikh Zeenuddin Mukhdom, an Arab traveller (1579-1580) in Malabar, after referring to the polyandry of the Nayars, gives us the following facts concerning the polyandry of the lower castes :

---

*Reproduced by permission of the authority of Man-in India from *Man in India*, 15(283). 108-118, 1935.

"The lower castes such as the carpenters, ironsmiths and others have fallen into the imitation of their superiors, the Nayars, with this difference, however, that the joint concern in a female is among these last limited to the brothers and male relatives by blood, to the end no alienation may take place in the course of the succession and the right of inheritance."

In his notes to this passage, Duncan (Asiatic Researches, Vol. V, p-14) adds :

"Five low castes Teer, Agaree (carpenter), Musalie (brass-founder), Tattan (goldsmith), Kollan (blacksmith) who live promiscuously with one or more women ; and sometimes two, three or four or more brothers cohabit with one woman. The child or children who are the offspring of this connection inherit the property of this whole fraternity ; and whenever the female of the house is engaged with either of the brethren, his knife is said to be hung up at the door of the apartment as a signal of its being occupied. It is however justice to add that this custom is said to be local and practised in a few of the southern districts ; and even among the five castes there is no prohibition against any man's keeping for himself either one or as many women as he can maintain."

Barbosa, a European traveller from whom we get the best account of the Nayar polyandry, has the following remarks to make on the fraternal polyandry of the Ilavans : —'Sometimes among them two brothers have one wife and sleep with her and hold it nothing wonderful'.

That there is no exaggeration at all in the accounts of both the Sheikh and Barbosa will be clear to all who have studied the castes referred to by them.

Legendary references to fraternal polyandry are very few. There is of course the well-known story of Droupadi, the daughter of the king of Panchala, marrying the five Pandava brothers. It was the third brother Arjuna who actually won the bride in the shooting contest, but the eldest brother insisted on his right of sharing the wife, their mother agreed with him and it was settled that each of the five brothers was to have connubial rights for a period of one year in the order of seniority and, if any one interfered with the rights of another he was to go out and do penance and perform pilgrimages for a year. Opinion is divided as to whether the Pandava marriage reflects any real polyandrous state or trend of the society in the Epic days of India. The Brahamans are however positively against fraternal or any other form of polyandry; it is said 'One man can have many wives, but a woman cannot have co-husbands (Aitareya Brahmana). Only one instance is known of a polyandrous marriage in the Buddhist Jatakas (Birth stories)... Princess Kanha was allowed to have at a time five husbands selected by her in a *svayamvara* assembly. Tradition in Malabar is poor in references to polyandry. Relationship terms of all or almost all South Indian castes reveal a state of affairs which we expect and which exist in a society wherein the fathers' brothers have the same status as the father himself. Among many of the lower castes polyandrous or non-polyandrous, the father is called *achau,* and the father's younger *pappan* (*Pali* for father). All the wives of the father's brothers, and all the sisters of the mother are 'mothers' grouped according to age as 'big mother' or 'little mother' and all their children are regarded as brothers and sisters. Except among the matrilineal sections, levirate of some form is to be found among all the primitive people inhabiting the Ghats. Among the Nayadis, who are not polyandrous, instances are not wanting of one brother making over his wife to another and also of an elder or younger brother marrying the deceased brother's widow.[6] Going in search of traditions of levirate the oldest instance we have of it in Malabar is in a very popular folk-song of a Tiyya hero Aromat-chekon that is sung by villagers all through the Malayalam-speaking countries. The hero is mortally wounded and is brought home. Before he breathed his last, he asked his younger brother not to forsake his widow; later in the story we read of the son of the widow by the brother avenging the death of the Chekon (Knight). Now the Tiyyas are matrilineal, and polyandry is unknown among them, but their fellows in the more southernly part of the

Malabar district and the Cochin state, who are styled, as suits the fancy of the person, Ilavans, or Tandans or occasionally, Tiyyas (Tiyyans) but ought to be, strictly speaking, called Ilavans, still practise fraternal polyandry. Internal evidence collected will show that the matriliny of the Tiyyans is not the genuine of the Nayars, but an imitation of the latter, in certain aspects of it.

Between the type of polyandry that prevails among the Kandyans of Ceylon and that in Malabar there is a very close similarity. There, it is said, it was obligatory for every farmer to go and work for some time for the feudal lord, and that necessitated periodic absence from home and consequently leaving the wife in the charge of a brother. From known facts of the history of the Ilavans (and Tiyyas) it is fairly certain that they came to Malabar from Ceylon and were the first planters in the country specialising in coconut cultivation. When they came they would have brought with them also this institution of polyandry. The Ilavans are the lords of the artisan classes who are the most ardent adherents of polyandry nowadays. The artisans of Malabar are said to have once upon a time struck work and left in a body for Ceylone and were brought back with the assistance of the Ilavans who were commissioned by the king of Ceylong to look after them. Whatever the historical value of this legend, it shows that that the two groups of people that practise fraternal polyandry, viz., the artisans and the Ilavans are closely associated and perhaps they might have come into Malabar from the same locality. No artisan marriage can take place without the permission of the Ilavan chief or his agent accompanying the marriage procession.

Both the Ilavans and artisans are strictly patrilineal. Their social organisation is broadly as follows : There are, firstly, some subcastes which are divided into *illams* and *kiriyams*. There is no intermarriage between the subcastes. A man inherits his mother's *illam* and *kiriyam*. Two persons having the seme *kiriyam* are said to be *kiriyam* sister or *kiriyam* brother, i.e. *kiriyam* is exogamous. A few patrilineal families usually constitute a *taravad* ; the members of a *taravad* are all descended from one ancestor. A man or woman inherits his or her father's *taravad*. (The word *taravad* is usually rendered in English as 'house-name' and is a common feature of the social organisation of Malayalam and Telugu-speaking peoples.) So we find that the *taravad* exogamy is there to prevent the marriage of close relatives on the father's side and the *illam* exogamy to prevent similar marriages on the mother's side. Members of a *taravad*, when it has grown in numbers, are still held together by the fact that they have a common family god whom they all join together to worship, and also a common *sarpa-kavu* (a clump of trees where serpent images are kept for worship). When the *taravad* is too unwieldy for such meetings, there takes the "division of the serpent" and the accessories used for the performance of funeral rites. People though they belong to the same house or clan, will not henceforward observe death-pollution for those who have separated by division, as for all social purposes two new clans are brought into existence.

Marriage among the Ilavans and the artisans is patrilocal. Though they have the joint family system, their families do not grow to the extent they do in the case of the Nayars. Normally in an Ilavan family there will be found one or two elderly men, their common wife, married sons and their wife or wives, unmarried sons and daughters. Married daughters will be away with their husbands of whose house-holds they become full members. A father having a marriageable son seeks a bride who would be suitable for him, and the first person he consults is his wife's brother. The parents of the girl will be glad if the bridegroom has several brothers too, for in the event of the death of the eldest brother, she will be looked after by the younger brothers, other economic motives also come usually into play e.g., of the two brothers one may be working away from home and can come home only very occasionally ; so though the two brothers marry a common wife only one of them is with her actually, the other being only a visiting husband, on whom also devolves the fatherhood of all the children born.

Whether at a marriage all the brothers are made copartners ceremonially, or whether there is only an understanding that though only one is married, the others should have access to the wife, there is no clear indication. The common practice is for the eldest brother alone to go to the bride's house to fetch her on the day of the marriage ; then at the ceremonies by which the 'tie is created' by 'drinking milk' all the brothers are seated in a row on the right of the bride, and all of them are given the sweet drink that makes them co-husbands of the woman. In an area where fraternal polyandry has disappeared, I once saw at an Ilavan's marriage a small boy was placed by the side of a grown up elder brother of his who was the bridegroom at the milk-giving ceremony ; the people had no intention whatever of making the little boy a partner in the marriage. A forgotton usage had a momentary, though unnecessary, resurrection in the minds of the elderly members of the marriage party.

Another episode from a polyandrous family of blacksmiths throws some side-light on the regulations of fraternal polyandry. The common wife of five brothers became too weak to look after the comforts of all of them. The youngest of the brothers who was not much older than his own eldest son expressed a wish to have a new wife for himself. The wife advised him that the proper procedure was for the eldest brother to marry again a younger woman and for them all to share her.

The simple form of polyandry where several brothers have one wife in common is giving place to several new forms. The brothers may divide themselves into two or three batches for purposes of marriage ; or they go on for some time with one wife, then some of them leave the joint concern and have separate wives for themselves ; others remain in the partnership and also have additional wives. I was told of an interesting instance of a marriage of a member of a polyandrous group at which, in order to deprive him and his bride of any monopoly of each other, five of his brothers and three common wives of all of them sat in a row at the milk-giving ceremony, on either side of the marrying pair.

The complicacies which are pointed in the foregoing paragraphs are rather rare, and are the results of jealousies which, in most normal cases, are absent ; and it is a wonder how they maintain such harmony. In fact, I was told by a very intelligent member of a polyandrous group that the disintegration of joint families is prevented by the brothers having a common wife, as, through her influence, all fissiparous tendencies are avoided. There is a saying in Malayalam 'Four men will join and get along well together, but not four women'.

There seems to be very few rigid rules for the internal regulation of the married life as in Ilavan house-hold. The knife which is placed on the door-frame to prohibit other husbands from entering, is no more heard of. Some simple turns are arranged by the mother when the bride is still young. In the beginning, during the honeymoon, the brothers go to the bride's house one after the other and are feted alike, for periods ranging from a week to a fortnight. As very often nowadays the number of brothers in polyandrous marriage is two only, there is very little necessity for any elaborate regulation in their sexual life. Sometimes, among the artisans, even parallel brothers become co-husbands. Similarly own sisters and even parallel sisters become co-wives of brothers. The latter arrangement helps the maintenance of domestic peace, owing to the wives being already close relatives.

If one asks the child of a polyandrous family for his father he would reply, "I have three fathers. Whom do you want ?" Descriptions like 'big father', 'small father', 'short father', 'fair father', 'dark father', are not at all uncommon. I have found in some families fathers showing a particular partiality for children who resemble them closely. Coming to the question of inheritance, Thurston was obviously wrong in recording that property went down through the eldest wife. All the children born to the brothers have equal right, so that the superiority of the eldest brother or the oldest of the wives does not come in for consideration at all.

When asked to explain to me the advantages of the polyandrous marriage a well-to-do Ilavan told me,—

> "It keeps all the brothers together ; union and co-operation gives them strength, and therefore, their community ranks as the best agriculturists in their country. You can be sure that your children are your own. A woman will

have one or other of their husbands always by her side, so that her tendency to sin is obliterated."

My informant agreed with me in thinking that polyandry meant a great strain on the women.

Polyandry now survives particularly in the marginal areas among the less advanced members of the castes in whose midst it is now found. That it was once more wide-spread also is clear. Fraternal polyandry which is rarely practised, and that only by some minor and numerically small sects among the Nayars of Travancore and the Paliyans of the Travancore Hill, is due to the difficulty of getting wives. Some very poor members of the Nayar community of Travancore practise fraternal polyandry, because of the difficulty in maintaining a family. The Ilavans now have the normal sex ratio and as they are mainly as agricultural people, it would be advantageous for them to have more women married into a joint family. So neither the idea of economy nor paucity of women explains the Ilavan polyandry. The Ilavans are never known to have practised female infanticide. Unlike the Kandyans of Ceylon they had no feudal lord to serve for long terms.

NOTE

1. As the widow's children are not regarded as the posthumous children of her deceased husband (cf. the Toda custom) there is no classic "Niyoga" of the Hindus involved here.

12

POLYANDRY IN MALABAR*

K. RAMAN UNNI

The former district of Malabar and the Native States of Travancore and Cochin constitute the linguistic State of Kerala today. This paper discusses non-fraternal polyandry in the southern half of the district of Malabar. This type of polyandry among the matrilineal Nairs in several parts of this linguistic area has been dealt with by a good number of writers. Drs. K.M. Kapadia and M.S.A. Rao appear to be the most recent of the writers who have attempted a discussion of the subject in the light of available records.[1] Inspite of this our knowledge of polyandry in this region, particularly of the non-fraternal type, is considerably sketchy. Dr. Kapadia in the illuminating discussion refers to the absence of any allusion to polyandry in the vast Malayalam literature of the 18th century.[2] My search through a collection of proverbs has equally failed to single out any proverb referring to polyandry.[3] In spite of this, there is no reason today to question its very existence in the past. There is, on the other hand, obvious need to learn more about it from the elderly persons of rural Malabar. Little is known about the conditions which governed polyandrous mate selection among the Nairs and nothing worthy of note seems to have

*Reproduced by permission of the Indian Sociological Society from *Sociological Bulletin* VII (1 & 2) : 62-79, 123-133, 1958.

been recorded about the nature of customary relations between the spouses.

This paper discusses the data which I have gathered first hand from an area of comparatively little social change in Malabar. (The names of talukas and reference to boundaries are those as existed before the State of Kerala was formed). My enquiries were directed to collecting all available data from elderly informants and observing what influence of a polyandrous past, if any, could be seen in the institution of marriage today. Among my informants were one elderly woman whose mother was polyandrous and another whose mother's mother was polyandrous. Among the rest of my informants were a few who had a fair degree of clear memory of polyandrous practice seen and heard about during their young age. In reconstructing the picture of sub-caste distinctions and intra-sub-caste differentiation into groups I have depended on the information which could be collected from well-informed men and on observation of what exists today.[4] A part of the data was collected in April 1950 and the rest during April and May in the years 1955 and 1956.

My study was mainly restricted to two villages, Munnurkode and Karatukurssi which are three miles apart and are nine miles interior from the town and railway station of Ottapalam in Walluvanad *taluk*. These and the few other villages mentioned at length and within a radius of about six miles and are in the southern part of the same *taluk*. In a wide sense this study may be regarded as covering south Malabar, i.e., south of Calicut *taluk* or south of the Kora river.

The discussion which follows does not throughout bear reference to the two villages for the reason that any one village or a group of contiguous villages did not present the conditions and features relevant for present consideration. In spite of persistent efforts the yield of data from informants has not been adequate for discussing the various aspects of polyandry with reference to one or a few specific cases.

The existence of polyandry in the past among the Nairs and the continuance of its off-hand appearance in the twenties of this century are evident from the cases cited by my informants. These cases will be described in the relevant contexts in the following discussion. To understand the limitations within which polyandry worked in the past it is necessary to consider at the outset the factors which narrowed the field of choice of mates among the Nairs.

The Nairs in the two villages mentioned belong to several sub-castes which, on the basis of their social status and ritual rank can be roughly classed into three groups as high, middle and low.[5] In the high group are the sub-castes of Vellayma Sudra Nairs, Nair-Panikkars, and Kiriyatil Nambiars, the first being numerically large in the group.[6] With rare hypergamous alliances each of these sub-castes tended to be endogamous. The middle group is formed of the sub-castes of Ayikara, Ulladan, Vatekat and Pallichan each of which was generally endogamous. The low group is constituted of the endogamous sub-castes of Atikurssi, Veluthedan and Vilakathiravan. Each of these groups rendered services of ritual, occupational and ceremonial nature to the higher group or groups, the Sudra Nairs of the highest group rendering a few services to the family of the Nambutiri Brahmin of the village. The Nambutiri who ritually and religiously ranked the highest was also the only ultimate owner of the lands with his '*janmam* right' which was a form of overlordship. Till quite recently nearly all the lands in each of these villages was the *janmam* property of the family of a Nambutiri. All the Nair sub-castes were in general tenants and the Sudra Nairs formed a bulk of the tenant class who did not cultivate but rented out the land to other sub-castes of lower rank or the polluting labourers of the caste of the Cherumas. The position of these sub-castes in the pattern of land tenure will be pointed out later.

Nearly all the Sudra Nair *tharavads* (matrilineal joint families) in one or a few villages were a dependent group rendering services of ritual and ceremonial nature to their Nambutiri overlords. These services were to be rendered only a small number of Sudra Nairs on a few occasions in a year. The sense of dependancy, however, was firm and deep rooted, and Sudra *tharavads* owing allegiance of this kind, were known as the Adiyar of the Nambutiri families. The Adiyar *tharavads* professed to have a reflected prestige primarily arising from the sub-caste rank of their overlord Nambutiris. For this reason the Adiyar groups of different Nambutiris in different villages would often be of a differential level of reflected prestige. This sense of prestige tended to close each Adiyar group of Nambutiries of different sub-caste ranks as an endogamous one. In the village of Munnurkode, for instance, 10 Sudra Nair *tharavads* in the beginning of this century formed a major section of the Adiyar group of the Nambutiri family located in the same village, the rest of the same Adiyar group remaining in other villages where the Nambutiri had extensive rice fields. It is also not unlikely, as a few informants conveyed that each Adiyar group in some villages for generations remained endogamous except for accepting the patrilineal Nambutiris as visiting husbands.

Sometimes coinciding with this group and often as a part of it was the *enangar* group of *tharavads* which also had a tendency to be endogamous. Except for occasionally accepting Nambutiri husbands or more rarely husbands from title-holding and wealthy Nair *tharavads* (Sthani-*tharavads*), the *enangar* group in some villages remained endogamous for generations. The *tharavads* of an *enangar* group were bound by reciprocal obligations of ritual, ceremonial and social importance. If marriage mates were not available within the *enangar* groups, a *tharavad* could, with the consent of the Nambutiri overlord find out a *tharavad* outside the group and maintain *enengar* alliance with it. Thus for the *tharavad* which initiated such an allieance its *enengar* group became larger, a process which could continue. Sometimes in its distant estate of garden crops and rice fields a few members of a *tharavad* would go and settle down, and this truncated *tharavad* would find itself in need of creating *enengar tharavads* in the neighbourhood. In selecting an additional *tharavad* as an *enangar* the important criterion was the rank of the Nambutiri whom that *tharavad* served as an Adiyar family. An *enengar* group would not comprise *tharavads* which served Nambutiris of different ranks, a fact which became often explicit in such remarks of my informants as "we are Adiyars of Nambutiripad and they are Adiyars of the Nambutiri in their village. Some fifty years ago our women would not take water from their houses Nambutiripad definitely ranks higher."

In Walluvanad *taluk* in general and in the villages of focal interest in this study in particular, two other important sub-castes who ranked above Sudra Nairs were the Kiriyatil and the Charna Nairs who were chiefly concentrated in areas where lands belonged to the wealthy pre-British Nair chiefs who held hereditary titles. These Nair chiefs are today known by the generic term Sthani[7] but their social status vary according to the titles, powers, rights and privileges ascribed to them by a few powerful pre British rulers (Rajas). Nairs under them were also their tenants, chiefly non-cultivating, as the Sudra Nairs under the Nambutiris. The Kiriyatil in their relation to the Sthanis were known as their *adukalakar* (kitchenmen) for the Kiriyatil men were to serve as cooks at feasts in the *tharavads* of Sthani Nairs.[8] The women of Kiriyatil also had ritual and ceremonial services to be rendered to the Sthani women. The Charna (attached Nairs) were the armed retainers under the Sthanis. Corresponding to the Adiya-prestige scale among the Sudra Nairs under the Nambutiris the Kiriyatil Nairs also tended to form Sthani-wise number than the Nambutiri families and the relative rank of the former was often disputed either among them or their spokesmen. It was also not unusual to find some Sthani families on unfriendly terms for decades and the respective Nairs under their power formed or were coerced to form cleavage in the groups. Thus marriage between Kiriyatil Nairs who were under the overlordship of different Sthanis would take place to a very limited extent. Among the lower Nair sub-castes in general under Nambutiris and Sthanis, similar tendencies sought more feebly and much less effectively to restrict the field of selection of a marriage partner.

The divisions of sub-castes of Nairs are not so simple as pictured here However, in any group of a few villages traditionally one would not find more than two or three high sub-castes of Nairs except that the Charna Nairs had a wider distribution. To mention a few more sub-castes of Nairs there were the Eruma Sudra Nairs who were retainers of families of Nambutiris of low rank. Among the Kiriyatil Nairs were Kiriyam Nambiar, Kaka-kiriyam, Pattikiriyam and Munnutil-kiriyam. Similarly among the Charnas were a few of which Agathu-Charna-Nairs had a relatively wide scatter. In addition were the Menon which included the sub-castes of Paricha-Menon, Agathu-Charna-Menon, Purathu-Charna-Menon, Menon Panikkar, Patola-Menon, the relative rank of each often varying from *taluk* to *taluk*. The process of differentiation of Nairs into a wide variety of sub-castes is a field as yet unexplored. In Walluvanad *taluk* Kiriyatils ranked higher than Sudras and Charna Nairs were below Kiriyatils, while in Calicut *taluk* Purathu-Charnas ranked higher than Kiriyatils. In the generic term Sthani mentioned in this study there were some families of pre-British chieftains and their commanders. Each of these families developed into a sub-caste named after its original place name or *tharavad* name. Thus arose the sub-castes of Eradi, Vellodi, Thirumalpad, Nedungadi and Kartavu, each of which was numerically very small and was above the Sudras and the Kiriyatil Nairs. In this study all these sub-castes who branched off from the Nairs are regarded as the Nairs except when specifically named.

How the overlordship and ritual superiority of the Nambutiris and the power of the Sthani families restricted in a variety of ways the range of marriage within the Nair sub-caste is a fact which seems to have escaped the notice of all writers. It is possible that this feature of strictly rigid restrictions in the range of choice for mate among the Nairs existed when the Nairs rendered military service in pre-British days. Speculatively it can even be said that the restrictions of this kind were more rigid in those times. The Nair men for military service were drawn chiefly from the Charna Nairs under the Nair chiefs, and some sections of Menons under the bigger chiefs or Rajas. It is doubtful if the Sudra Nairs under the Nambutiries were ever recruited as soldiers.

In areas where neither the Nambutiris nor the Sthani Nairs owned lands, the *janmam* right of the land belonged to either wealthy temples or to pre-Britith rulers (Rajas). The temples were generally managed by the Nambutiris or the Sthani Nairs, and they were thus powerful over the Nair tenants of the temple lands as well. The high caste Nairs of the Menon group were originally those who served the powerful royal families and became differentiated into sub-castes on the basis of importance of the roles they discharged. They also tended to form prestige groups which sought husbands from a higher sub-caste, caste or group within the same sub-caste. Often the same sub-castes under two Rajas did not rank equally. The Menons under the Walluvanad Raja were regarded as lower than the Menons under the Zamorin Raja. In some places the Sudra Nairs and the Charna Menons often disputed their relative ranks. In places where there was no dispute about the relative rank of sub-castes or the order of prestige groups the higher would rarely take wives from the lower. And the highest always tended to accept husbands as increasingly as possible from the Sthanis, Rajas or Nambutiries. Owing to the working of the ideas of rank and prestige, in each high sub-caste of Nairs, there were a few families which accepted husbands in this manner and tended to make it an exclusive practice.

My data regarding the shades of difference between the sub-castes and the formation of prestige groups within each sub-caste under the Rajas are rather sketchy but it seems that marriage among them was regulated by principles analogous, if not similar, to those under the Nambutiris and the Sthanis. It is certain however, that the *enangar* group was a feature in all areas and each *tharavad* could, if found essential, expand its *enangar* group. However, everywhere the distinction was drawn between the new *enangar* and the old *enangar* ; the former was always held in higher esteem and relations therein were more informal. It is also certain that in the landed property of the Nairs the overlordship of the Nambutiries, the Sthanis or the Rajas, in some form or other existed all over South Malabar.

Roughly coinciding with the hierarchy of the groups of Nair sub-castes (the high, middle and low) were the classes based on the nature of land ownership and land tenure,—and these classes were a feature in general all over South Malabar. These were to state in a simplified form, the Janmis, (the owner overlords), the Kanakaran (an intermediary), and the Verum-Pattakaran (a second intermediary) who would often himself be the tiller. As noted already the Janmis were the Sthanis. In areas where the Nambutiris were the Janmis the Sudra Nairs were generally the holders of *kanam* tenure. The sub-castes roughly corresponding to the rank of the Sudra Nairs were the holders of *kanam* tenure under the other category of the Janmis. In some areas the Janmis including the Nambutiris had chiefly Verumpatakaran under them without the first intermediary. The actual cultivation was done by tied labourers chiefly of the highly polluting caste of the Cherumas. The Verumpatakar who held their tenure under the Kanakaran, usually belonged, in small numbers, to the poor class of the high group sub-caste of the Nairs, and in majority, to the middle and low groups of sub-castes of the Nairs. The Verumpattam tenants generally had small holdings, a fact which kept them without fair chances of becoming increasingly wealthier. This feature of land tenure classes which existted in the villages of focal interest in this study also existed in a major part or nearly the whole of South Malabar. In the economy of South Malabar therefore, till late in the last century the Nairs were in general non-producers, and this is true of many villages till quite recent decades. In this tenancy system of produce sharing the traditional practice was that one-third of the net produce was taken by the Verumpattakaran and two-thirds went to the *janmi*. In the case of *kanam* land two-thirds reached the *kanam* holder and he paid a nominal rent to the *janmi*, Till 1793 *janmam* was regarded as the highest form of ownership but tenants were not evicted. And at the same time there was no clear evidence to say that *janmam* was an absolute ownership. In 1793 the Britishers recognised *janmam* as absolute ownership and consequently the power and prestige of the Janmis were enhanced, and they began to exercise their legal right to evict tenants frequently in order to rent out land at a higher rent and become wealthier.[10] Among the Sudra Nairs there was a tradition that they should not hold *janmam* property except under *kanam* rights, or less desirably as the Verumpattakar. If through an unusual channel a Sudra Nair became the *janmam* owner of some land he would surrender the *janmam* right to the Nambutiri of the village and remain as a *kanam* tenant under him. Instances of this kind were cited to me by some well informed Nairs in illustration of the superiority of the Nambutiris and esteem accorded to them.[11] The existence of the three classes based on the pattern of ownership and tenure influenced and even shaped the limited hypergamous preferences of the Nairs. The high group of Nair sub-castes remained ambitious of getting husbands from the Janmi class. Among the Nair sub-caste of the three groups hypergamy was rare, but within the sub-caste of the high group who were chiefly *kanam* tenants (the first intermediaries) the Verumpattam tenants under them, even when they belonged to the same sub-caste, were regarded as low. The Kanakaran's master-like attitude and Pattakaran's sense of dependeny created a social distance between them. The Nair *tharavad* with *kanam* lands would not accept husband from a *tharavad* which had exclusively *verumpattam* lands held under *kanam* tenants. Usually *tharavads* with such *verumpattam* lands were also poor but under *enangar* obligations this attitude of the *kanam*-prestige *tharavads* would, if unavoidable, be made lenient. The Nairs were highly sensitive to the social distance created by this *kanakaran-pattakaran* distinction and wanted to maintain it without creating situations in which the two classes would have to treat one another as equal. As marriage would create certain mutual affinal obligations in discharge of which the two classes would have to be treated as socially equal, it is avoided. Spatially marriage between distant *tharavads* was rare. An important reason for this was that among the Nairs, with rare exceptions, the husband visited the wife, a custom which still prevails to an impressive extent in many parts of rural South Malabar.[12] A distance of less than two miles seems to have been popularly conceived as normal for a visiting husband to walk up. However, marriage between *tharavads* three to four miles apart was not infrequent. Further the question of expanding the *enangar* groups within the sub-caste and on the same prestige level and within a reasonable distance accounted for this feature, namely, that affinal *tharavads* would not be very far from each other. In the twenties of this century, in the village of Munnurkode, happened two cases which illustrate what akward situations and group conflicts the acceptance of a visiting husband from a lower prestige group even as an exceptional case creates. In one case at the *talikettu-kalyanam* (the pre-puberty symbolic marriage of a Nair girl) ceremony in a *tharavad* the girl's father was not permitted by her *enangars* to discharge the formality of offering a cloth to her ceremonially. The *enangars'* protest was strong because the father belonged to a *tharavad* of a lower prestige group. The *enangars* threatened to stage a walk out and mar the celebrations ; the father yielded and allowed an *enangar* to represent him in giving the cloth. In another case, on the occasion of a big feast there was a similar threat from the *enangar* and many invitees to keep a woman's husband of a lower prestige group off from sitting at the dinner in the same corridor with the *enangar* group of his wife.

Thus for each *tharavad,* marriage was generally restricted to a locality, to a sub-caste, to an *enangar* group, to a prestige group, and to a land-tenure class. The level of wealth of *tharavads* also influenced the selection of mates, but it is likely that within an *enangar* group wealth was not a very important factor of consideration until about the close of the last century.

The above discussion reveals that polyandry had to work within a set of limiting factors. But were there factors which favoured the existence of polyandry ? If hypergamy reduced the number of marriageable women for the Nairs to marry a condition favouring polyandry would exist. The castes above the Nairs were numerically very small and the very nature of their means of living in relation to other castes kept them widely scattered. Consequently in the majority of villages the strength of each caste above the Nairs was, as far back as my informants could remember, of negligible proportion in relation to the number of the Nairs. However, their probable strength in the past particularly the population of the Nambutiries deserves a detailed consideration. In the villages of which I have some knowledge the castes above Nairs were, till three decades ago, the Ambalawasis, the Nambutiris, the Tamil immigrant Brahmins (Pattar) and the Canarese immigrant Brahmin priests (Embranthiris). In considering hypergamy the Sthani Nairs could also be regarded as forming higher sub-caste. Of these castes the Pottars generally married among themselves and had rarely an additional Nair wife who would be visited. The Embranthiris would be visiting husbands of Sudra Nair women but the Embranthiri families were very few not amounting to an average of one small family in three or four villages. The Ambalawasis is a common term for a group of castes devoted to temple services. The matrilineal castes of this group were the Pisharodys, Poduval, and Warrior who would be visiting husbands of Nair women.[13] These castes did not intermarry ; each had marriage within itself, could take the Nair wives and accept the Nambutiri husbands. Except a division of the Poduvals all other could marry Sudra Nair women or other Nair women of the rank of Sudras. The Pisharodys could also marry from the sub-caste of Kiriyatil Nairs (higher than Sudras) at least in some parts of South Malabar. The patrilineal Ambalawasi castes of Nambissan and Chakiyar were each very small in number and had no marriage with Nair women at least in the villages of which I have some knowledge. The Ambalawasis on the whole, married the Nair women only of the high group. Owing to the location of the Ambalawasis near temples they were on an average, very small in number in each village and their marital advent into the Nair population must have been limited as a consequence of accepting the Nambutiri husbands for their women. This necessity was highly limited for the reason that the Nambutiris have a much wider field of women to choose from. The necessity for the Sthani Nairs to find wives from among the rest of the Nairs (the high group sub-castes of the Nair) was much less limited for the Sthanis could marry in the Sthani *tharavads*, accept the Nambutiri husbands and also marry the non-Sthani Nair women.

The case of the Nambutiri males making hypergamous inroads into the population of the Nair women deserves a more detailed consideration. The location of the Nambutiri in the pattern of agricultural economy of Malabar has been already pointed out[14] ; ritually and religiously also they ranked the highest. They were also regarded as dominant for their power to interfere and settled disputes brought to them by their tenants. The social and political power of the Nambutiris started from about the 10th century but their necessity for matrimonial alliance with Nair women perhaps started much later.[15] According to E. Kunjan Pillai, 14th century can be estimated as the period when the Nambutiris developed the custom that only the eldest brother in a family could marry the Nambutiri women and the younger brothers took to the Nair women.[16]

This custom which led many Nambutiri women to remain unmarried, the affiliation of the children bornof the Nambutiri-Nair union to the Nair *tharavad*, high sickness rate due to the custom of purdah and outcasting of unmarried women for charges of immorality are some of the important factor which reduced the numbers of the Nambutiris by half in every two hundred years. The custom that younger brothers of the Nambutiris had to marry outside their caste continued upto the thirties of this century. Polygyny among the Nambutiris was rare and confined to cases of barrenness and absence of male issues. Pillai proceeding with the estimate of figures with reasoning based on diverse sources arrived, although not conclusively, at the figure of one and a half lacs of the Nambutiris in Kerala in 18th century and over five lakhs in 14th century when the total population would not be more than 10 to 15 lakhs.[17] If this is near the truth the figures he provides to demonstrate the dominance of the Nambutiris in ancient and mediaeval Kerala are relevant to the consideration of the hypergamous marriage pressure of the Nambutiris on the Nairs. The proportion of the Nambutiris to the Nairs was therefore definitely high and the hypergamous advent of the Nambutiris into the Nair population must have created high incidence of polyandry among the Nairs. In the light of this possibility it can be said that the remoter the period the larger the Nambutiri population and the higher incidence of polyandry. Theoretically therefore, polyandry also tended to disappear in the recent past with the process of reduction of the Nambutiri population. It has also to be noted that the Mysorian invasion at the close of the 18th century and the death of many Nairs and Nambutiris in it as well as their forcible conversion to Islam must have tended to reduce the incidence of polyandry. European travellers and others have recorded polyandry in mediaeval Kerala but it seems that it is only with reference to South Malabar, Cochin and parts of North Travancore, and these were the places where the Nambutiris were largely distributed. The Malabar Marriage Commission of 1894 pointed out that polyandry though widespread at one time lingered in Ponnani and Walluvanad *taluks.* These were and still are *taluks* with comparatively very high number of the Nambutiri families. The census reports of Malabar do not facilitate a break-up of castewise figures into categor-is relevant here and useful for a more detailed and possibly fruitful discussion. With our present knowledge it is also not certain if the Nambutiris initiated polyandry, but under the conditions outlined here they seem to have played an important part in initiating it. It is also not unlikely that the much discussed *talikettukalyanam* among the Nairs was originally a marriage and under the pressure of the Nambutiris it was relegated to a form of symbolic marriage at a younger age to leave the Nair girls open for engagement with them.[18]

The military life of high caste Nairs and hypergamy among the Nairs also deserve consideration. My informants believe that polyandry was more among the Sudra Nairs than among the Charna Nairs. Extensive enquiries among the sub-castes which were armed retainers are likely to yield some useful data today. The Sudra Nairs were always under the Nambutiris and the cases of polyandry in my record are of the Sudra Nairs and a section of the Kiriyam Nairs. The military career of the Nairs must have reduced their male population since they always formed the militia. The sub-castes which chiefly devoted themselves to the profession of arms should therefore have had only a low incidence of polyandry. More investigation in other parts of Malabar today can throw more light on this possibility. But there again remains the problem of having sexual partners for the mobile soldiers and until archival research can tell us more about the degree of mobility of such soldiers and the nature of their residence and duration of battles it is not possible to proceed further with the analysis.

If Nairs practised polygyny there would have arisen a disbalance in the ratio of unmarried men to women, a condition favouring polyandry. But what has been mentioned by some writers as polygyny among the Nairs was either an exaggeration of rare cases in some parts of Malabar or a misleading name given to a form of concubinage. The question of polygyny and concubinage will be dealt with at a latter stage.

II

The cases of polyandry cited by my informants with as much details as could be provided by them are briefly enumerated below :

1. Village-Munnurkode. In a Sudra Nair *tharavad* a woman had four husbands. She died in about 1870 A.D.
2. In the same village in another Sudra Nair *tharavad* a woman had two husbands of whom one was a poor Nambutiri tutor in the Nambutiri overlord's family in the village. The second husband, a Sudra Nair belonged to the village Kallusi three miles away. He was the first husband and for a couple of years both the husbands visited her but after that she disliked the Nair husband and divorced him. This woman died about 23 years back.
3. In the same village in another Sudra Nair *tharavad* a woman had two husbands, the first from the village Panamanna, three miles away, and the second from a village about five miles away. The second husband started as a resident tutor of the children in that *tharavad* at frequent intervals in a year. He became a lover of the woman and was later recognised as her husband. This woman died about 55 years back. She had in addition a poor Nambutiri visiting her privately but without the knowledge of the headman of the *tharavad* or her two husbands. One of her husbands was poor and the Nambutiri who was less poor gave her frequent gifts.
4. In the same village in a *tharavad* of Ulladan caste of the Nairs a woman had two husbands, one from the same village and one from the neighbouring village. She died about 25 years back.

5. Village-Vengasseri. This is about six miles from Munnurkode. A woman of the Sudra Nair *tharavad* had two husbands until about twenty years back.
6. In the same village in a Sudra Nair *tharavad* a woman had two husbands. She died about 30 years back.
7. Village-Karakurssi, about 13 miles from Munnurkode. A woman of a Sudra Nair *tharavad* had two husbands. The second husband started as a lover and was later recognised as her husband. She had an additional Nambutiri visiting her without the knowledge of her two husbands. She died before the twenties of century.
8. In the village of Kizhoor, a mile from Munnurkode, in a *tharavad* of Charan Menon two women had two husbands each. One of these women died about 40 years back and the other about 30 years back.
9. In the village Karakurissi in a Sudra Nair *tharavad*, one woman had two husbands. The woman died about 50 years back.
10. Village-Kolapilli. In a Kiriyatil Nair *tharavad* one woman had two husbands. She died about 50 years back.

More *tharavads* in different villages where polyandry existed were pointed out by my informants but they could not name the women or state the number of husbands or the time when polyandry disappeared in those *tharavads*. The sub-caste of these *tharavads* were the Sudra-Nair, Kiriyatil Nair, Veluthedan and the Ulladan, the last two having two cases each. Some informants were vague in giving details but asserted that polyandry existed among the Nairs including Menons except in the Sthani *tharavads*. Among the matrilineal castes the Ambalawasis do not seem to have practised polyandry.

It is possible that polyandry had a higher incidence in wealthy *tharavads*. If *tharavads* on the basis of wealth are classed as high, middle and low (as judged almost concurrently by my informants), it is found that four out of ten *tharavads* listed above, belong to the high class and four to the middle class. Ten is too small a number to divide classwise to form any reasonable judgement. But a few of my informants with a wide acquaintance with *tharavads* in several villages, implicitly meant that the high and middle class *tharavads* had a higher number of polyandrous women. The *tharavad* (Case No. 8) was the wealthiest of the ten and was owning an elephant, a symbol of opulence and prestige. A member of this *tharavad* told me that polyandry was likely to be less common among the low group sub-castes of the Nairs as well as the *tharavads* of the low class.

Traditionally among sub-castes below the Sudra-Nairs, the lower the sub-caste of a *tharavad* the less wealthy it was. The high, middle and low groups of sub-castes therefore roughly coincided with the corresponding classification of the Nair *tharavad* based on wealth. An old man who originally belonged to the village of Peruvamb in Palghat *taluk*, told me, "I have heard that polyandry existed in Palghat *taluk* long ago but it was very limited and far between and in *tharavads* of affluence." All my informants emphasised that polyandry was never practised by more than one or two women in a *tharavad*. One cannot say if this was a regular feature of the Nair polyandry through centuries but it is possible that a small disparity in sex ratio led only to a limited incidence of polyandry in the past.

All polyandrous unions started with one husband ; the second husband used to be originally an occasional visitor to the wife's *traravad* and later became her lover. As a lover or even as a visitor, he could convey his desire to be the second husband of the women of his choice. The woman's consent was necessary, for she was to initiate the question of acceptance of the proposal. In the matter of acceptance the *tharavatilamma* (senior most woman of the *tharavad*) had an important voice. If she agreed she would take up the matter with the *karanavan* (the male head of the *tharavad*) who would usually give the sanction, but would sometimes do so in a rather half-hearted way : Is it necessary that she should have a second man ? If she is so particular about it, let it be. "Beyond this finalising there was no ceremony or elaboration in recognition of the acceptance of an additional husband. It was not common that sexual *liaison* preceded acceptance of a man as husband. A woman would not have adequate opportunity for illicit sexual intimacy with a man. In the Nair *tharavads* the freedom of women to move out unwatched as extremely limited, and their behaviour was disciplined by the senior male members. Indoors, the *tharavatilamma* played an effective role in maintaining discipline. The possibility of knowing a man, responding to his approaches and desiring him as an additional husband worked within these controls. Sometimes the senior women members would render connivance to a woman of their *tharavad* if she was approached with conjugal intentions by a man highly desirable for his wealth, *tharavad* prestige and reputation for individual qualities. Some of my informants pointed out the limited possibility that an additional husband could be as an extra-martial sexual partner who gained recognition as a husband. It is not fully unlikely that this possibility was greater at a very remote period in the history of polyandry among the Nairs.

It appears that the consent of the first husband was more of a *post facto* nature if he had not known of the progressive step by which the second one started gaining access. It is more proper to say that the first husband accepted the situation rather than giving a formal consent. The second husband might well be a friend of the first but irrespective of this possibility co-husbands have to be accommodating to each other.

On an understanding between them the husbands visited the wife in turn. Not set rules guided the husbands in spacing the turn of each but on important festival days such as *onam*, the first husband was preferred to the rest, to spend the night with the wife. If all the husbands happened to be present on such an important day the situation was tackled in this manner. The visiting husband would usually be in the portico at about the time of retiring after chatting in the company of the male members of the *tharavad*. The wife would convey through a very elderly woman or a child that the bed had been spread for the first husband in the room. The first married one would thus be received into the room while the others would be provided with beds either in the portico or in the common hall inside the house but on the same night the woman would not sleep with more than one husband. There could rarely be husbands whose *tharavads* were four to six miles away. Such husbands would visit much less frequently but they were expected to maintain same regularity.

The husbands were jointly to provide the wife with such items as cloth, oil, etc. which were not usually supplied to her from her *tharavad*. Each husband would undertake to supply one of these items but in addition each would give the wife gifts of ornaments, brass and bell metal vessels which were to be her personal properties.[20] Not uncommon but less preferred were gifts of cot and materials for making beds of considerable bulk. Handy curios from distant markets such as an ivory image of gold or a fancy article of some value made an occasional and much appreciated gift if a husband could afford and avail of it. In the annual cycle the three important festivals of Vishnu, Onam and Thiruvatira were occasions when the husband had to send fruits of the season in good quantity, chiefly bananas of different strains, and papadams (wafers of rice and blackgram) and cooking oil to the wife. These were not only meant for luxurious feasting on the occasion but were also symbols of the continuing marriage relationships. The non-supply of these goods on such occasions meant a serious rupture in conjugal relations and an imminent divorce, or it would be regarded as a confirmation of divorce if the husband was not visiting the wife for months. Supply of goods like oil on other occasions such as the wife's delivery, her birthday, the birthday of children was customary but was not basically necessary for the continuance of marriage relationship. A poor husband would be excused and sympathised with if he failed to comply with this customary dues.

Was the wife bound by obligations of annual visit to the husbands' *tharavads*? This custom today in monogamous unions seems to be a time-honoured one from a remote period. The details available regarding two of the cases cited, each with two husbands show that the wife went and enjoyed a brief stay for a few days in the *tharavad* of each husband once in a year. "Ammai parkuka" which means the stay of an elderly Nair wife in her husband's *tharavad* as Ammai (mother's brother's wife) of a large number of members there, is even taday a coveted one for it brings to the Nair wife a restful change as an honoured kin.

The question of assigning paternity of the children to one husband or the other was not regarded as one essentially to be solved. Efforts were made at it on the basis of the child's resemblance to one of the husbands but such efforts were not direct, formal or strictly deliberate. The elderly women played the role by taking the infant in arms, dandling and remarking "Oh, he is definitely taking after so and so; his colour, nose and face reveal that resemblance." Often this remark might be overheard by the husbands and in due course the growing child would get confirmed as the issue of one or the other of the husbands. There would be children whose resemblance to any of the husbands was questionable, and whose paternity could not therefore be established. But physiological fatherhood did not bind the polyandrous husband by rigid obligation to his children, a fact that could be inferred from the diverse nature of opinions of my informants on the matter. In monogamous unions the father had to discharge some obligations more definitely expected of him. At the occasion of the Talikettukalyanam of his daughter the father had to make a ceremonial supply of *pudava* and *karimbadam* (a long loin cloth and a coarse shawl) to her. He had also to supply a large number of items, except rice required to conduct the pompous feast held on the occasion of her puberty ceremony. If the father failed to supply these, the needs would be met by the daughter's *tharavad* ; but if the father was absent on the occasion, a member of an *enangar tharavad* was nominated to make the formal offerings of the cloth and shawl. In addition, for feasts on the occasion of birthday and marriage of the children the father had to supply a major part of the requirements except rice. Of the polyandrous unions recorded details are available for two, each having two husbands. In one case the fatherly obligations were discharged by the husbands jointly and in the other each husband separately did it for his children.

It is also to be inferred that sons were not bound by clear rules of obligation of participation in the funeral rites of their mother's husbands. In instances of established paternity the eldest son was to take part in the funeral rite and all children of the dead father were to observe death pollution. It is doubtful if in all cases of polyandry on record this practice was followed. In monogamous unions, all children had to observe death pollution and at least one son, preferably the eldest, was to participate in the father's funeral rites. If the father was a Nambutiri or a Pishorody or Warrior the Nair sons had no pollutions and were not to take part in such rites. If the father belonged to a higher prestige group among the high group of sub-castes of the Nairs his maternal kin would question the right of his sons to take part in the death rites. An instance in point which happened twenty five years back revealed that the sons facing objection in such a context were helpless to press any claim and had to resort to the alternative of conducting the rites in their own house. However in the twenties of this century there were cases of sons taking part in the death rites of their fathers who belonged to higher prestige-groups without facing any objections. In polyandry hypergamous husbands were very rare and yet informants could not provide a definite answer regarding the question of participation of sons in the death rites of their mother's husbands. Two of the informants believed that if the husbands of a woman belonged to *enangar tharavads* her sons had to take part in the death rites of her husbands and this was not necessarily father-wise. From these facts it also emerges that values of rank and prestige and the significance of *enangar* group were emphasised and preserved and the question of fatherhood as such as of secondary importance.

In the same manner, it is doubtful if in polyandry, all reciprocal obligations between the *tharavad* of each husband and that of the wife were carried out as in monogamy except when the two *tharavads* were formerly *enangars.* Between *tharavads* of spouses of the same sub-caste, there were reciprocal obligations carrying the force of a remote tradition. When a child was born in one *tharavad,* a representative from the other had to pay a visit and see the child and if the mother of one of the spouses dies, the *tharavad* of the other had to despatch goods for a day's feasting during the period of death pollution,

These and other obligations of a minor nature continue to be discharged in a major part of rural Malabar today.

Although data are lacking, it is possible to believe that polyandrous marriages were nearly as durable as monogamous ones. The main reason for this might be the fact that after her first marriage, the woman at a mature age took additional husbands at her own discretion and choice and in doing so her mature psycho-sexual disposition must have played an important role. This was true of the man as well, since initially he posed for her to choose if desired. In this context it has to be noted that the additional husbands were usually either widowers or men not young enough to contract first marriage with young girls. Divorces, however, occurred for reasons such as the husband's repeated inability or failure to supply the essential items such as cloth, his progressively decreasing frequency of visits or a marked disinterest in and indifference towards wife exemplified in various aspects of his behaviour. In the matter of divorce, the first married husband did not merit any special consideration for his seniority. A wife would however keep a tolerant attitude towards the least liked husband if his *tharavad* was one of higher social status and prestige. She would be advised by her kin to do so since an alliance with such a *tharavad,* even by the feeble link of polyandry was regarded as desirable. A husband could divorce his polyandrous wife but such cases, in the opinion of my informants, might be much less than those of the wife divorcing one of her husbands. One of the reasons for this might be the fact that a polyandrous woman's judgment about the qualities of her husband is comparative, and a husband who falls short of her expectations is increasingly disliked by her and in due course is discarded. In the case of a man, clandestine visits to a woman could be kept up but it was disgraceful to him to remain without a recognised sexual partner.

The procedure involved in dovorce was not a strictly formal or standardised one, as was the case with monogamous unions until recent years and even today it is rarely so. A husband who is to be divorced would be told by his wife not to visit her house any more. Inspite of this, if he visited her house, an elderly male member would remind him not to persist in it. In rare cases a rejected husband would not withdraw from the scene until the *karnavan* commanded him out. Often the wife's consistent dislike for a husband, exhibited in diverse ways, was sufficient for the husband to sever the union. A husband could divorce his wife by the more simple procedure of stopping his visits, and the wife had to regard it as a confirmed case of divorce if she did not receive from his customary supply of goods due at the next occasion or a few successive occasions. Divorce in all cases was not life-long and there were cases of reunion a few months or some years after divorce.

One rarely comes across a reference to polygyny among the Nairs. My enquiries reveal that while polyandry was just permitted, polygyny would be tolerated. In cases of polyandry recorded, no husband was known to have an additional wife. Yet the possibility that a husband of a polyandrous woman could have another wife was not completely ruled out. This possibility was highly limited by the fact that a man has to maintain his wife at the expense of his *tharavad* which would not provide him with supplies for two wives. The male members of a *tharavad,* barring some of the wealthy *tharavads* in which some allowances were given to grown males, generally had no other source of income. This allowance in kind or cash was meant for expense at their discretion and fancy. A man with such an income could afford to maintain a second wife but his *tharavad* would usually not accord her full recognition as a second wife. Excluding her from invitation to feasts, discouraging any initiative on her part to visit the husband's *tharavad* and denying her opportunities to pose herself at par with the first wife, were the methods by which the second wife would be effectively differentiated by the husband's *tharavad.* Rarely a second wife would tactfully manage to make the attitude of her husband's *tharavad* relaxed and she would succeed considerably if her husband co-operated or his first wife tolerated such effort. However co-wives of a man would hardly have any acquaintance between them, and under no circumstances they would ordinarily have co-residence even for a day in the husband's *tharavad.* The husband's conjugal bond with the second wife was no less durable than that with the first wife and to the best of the knowledge of my informants the second wife did not have other husbands. There may be a rare instance of a man having three wives but no specific case eould be cited by those who spoke about its probability. Cases of a Nambutiri having more than one Nair wife, although rare are known to elderly men in the villages. Equally well known are the cases of the Brahmins (Pattar) who in addition to a Brahmin wife had a Nair wife. The case of a Nair having more than one Nair wife was, however, extremely rare.

This account of polygyny leads to the necessity of distinguishing it from concubinage. A man's continued sexual intimacies with a woman which his *tharavad* or local sub-caste people would not rebel against and would ignore rather than give a semi-recognition may be termed as concubinage. The necessity to rebel against it would arise if the woman was distinctly of a lower caste or of a sub-caste far too below. A Sudra Nair, for instance, could have a concubinage belonging to the sub-caste of the Ulladan or the Vatekat Nairs, but not further below. In Malayalam the word that can in this context be equated with concubinage is *swakaryam* which literally means 'secret' or in a loose sense 'private'. One would say, he has two *sammanthan* (visiting marriage relationship) and in addition one *swakaryam*, or alternatively "he has two known *sammantham*, (two wives) and one unrecognized (concubine)". Concubines with two or three masters who know each other as sharing concubinal rights over the same woman were also not rate. Concubines of the men of the high group of the Nair sub-castes belong to the middle group of sub-castes or to very poor *tharavads* of the high group which had for their subsistance a confirmed dependancy on *tharavads* of the same group for generations. A concubine would not aspire to become a recognized wife for the very fact of her being concubine was due to the restrictions barring a publicly recognised union with her. She was to be visited with some amount of professed secrecy and she was not to be the only source of gratification of sex need of her master. An unmarried man in his thirties would not be credited with celibacy but would be accused of living a life of loose morals or condemned as being in the clutches of a concubine if he had any. A married man with a concubine would find it easier to maintain secrecy of his visits to his concubine. He could after his supper leave his *tharavad* in his routine way to visit his wife and instead of turning to his wife's *tharavad* he could spend the night with the concubine. Polyandry or monogamy did not therefore repel concubinage but favoured its existence as a tolerated form of extra-marital sex gratification. An important factor which perpetuated concubinage was that the major number of *tharavads* of the high group of sub-castes possessed lands as the first intermediaries (*kanam* rights) and the middle and low sub-castes were sub-tenants under them on simple lease (*verumpattam*). Tenancy on simple lease was the most insecure since the leaser could change the tenant every year if he liked. Each *tharavads* of the middle and low group of sub-castes, apart from its occupational services, depended on one or more of the *tharavads* of the high group of sub-castes to supplement its income by rendering occasional services of a miscellaneous nature. However, a marked degree of dependance on the part of a *tharavad* adversely affected the prospects of its becoming a concubinal *tharavad* of a member of the master *tharavad* on which it depended. It was repugnant if a man made a dependant servant woman the object of his sexual desire even if she belonged to the same sub-caste. A Malayalam proverb ridicules this possibility by saying that one should not make a pillow of a broom, which means that one should not make one's maid servant a target of his sexual desires.

The distinction drawn here between polygyny and concubinage was not easily agreed upon by some of my informants, but they were aware of the basis of such a distinction. It is likely that the distinction if recognised and maintained will be rewarding in any future intensive study of the past processes and present patterns of the institution of marriage among the Nairs.

Did the Nairs ever have fraternal polyandry ? It appears that it existed in some parts of South Travancore where Nair women permanently lived in the *tharavads* of their husbands (virilocal residence). An elderly Nair belonging to North Travancore told me that he had heard of the Nair brothers having common wife in parts of South Travancore where the traditional form of residence was virilocal. But he added, "One wonders if those Nairs could be regarded as the Nairs because the high Nair sub-castes there have much of Tamilian feature including the dialect of Malayalam they speak." My casual enquiries with a few Nairs of North Travancore had yielded me some information which make me bold to say that in South Travancore there was a limited distribution of non-fraternal polyandry among the Nairs and rare cases of it in rural corners continued in the thirties of this century. Cases of levirate among the Nairs of South Travancore were cited to me by the Nairs who belonged to North Travancore. Rare cases of levirate are said to have occurred even in North Travancore where there was no tradition of it.

K.M. Kapadia points out that K.M. Panikkar has recorded that the Nair polyandry was of the fraternal type. It is fully possible that when K.M. Panikkar wrote about polyandry his familiarity with South Travancore led him to say that the Nair polyandry was only fraternal. My informants conurrently rejected the idea of even a remote possibility of Nair polyandry being fraternal in *tharavads* with visiting custom. My enquiries also reveal that fraternal polyandry would never have existed among the Nairs of North Travancore, Cochin and Malabar. In the whole of this area, sororate and levirate were traditionally absent and a man's relationship with his wife's sister or brother's wife was one of avoidance. In some places in this area it is more correct to say that this relationship was not one of familiarity though not one of deliberate avoidance. Specific study of the Nair *tharavads* of South Travancore is bound to reveal structural variations in the light of which we can understand how fraternal polyandry could function with the virilocal practices in that area.

In the major part of North Travancore in Cochin State and South Malabar, visiting custom prevailed. It is fully probable that polyandry existed in this whole area with regional fluctuations in its incidence. It seems to have disappeared at a much early period in this whole area except in some parts of Walluvanad *Taluk* where it lingered into the early decade of this century.

Whether polyandry of a very remote past and the context in which it worked can be characterised strictly as shown in the foregoing discussions is questionable. The picture of polyandry presented here can be regarded as what existed at the close of the 18th century and during the 19th. The restrictions on choosing husbands seem to have developed from a remote past correlated with the process of social differentiation among the caste of the Namburities. It is doubtful if in the 16th century Nambutiri sub-castes had scattered so widely with groups in each sub-caste with varying degrees of rank and prestige based on ritual rights and privileges and ownership of extensive lands. Foreign travellers from the beginning of the 16th century have recorded polyandry but it is not reasonable to believe that all aspects of polyandry remained stable from 15th to 19th centuries.

The evolution of land tenure and forms of land ownership and the beginning of British rule must have effected the fortunes of many Nair families and consequently their rank in the prestige order within the local sub-caste group must also have been affected. This must have in turn led to revision of preferences in the choice of husband. Data for an analysis of this direction are scanty and require to be collected from various published sources or to be collected afresh.

The influence of the polyandrous tradition still seem to be lingering in some aspects of the marriage institution of the Nairs of these villages. My data show that roughly over 20% of the Nair women who are over 45 years of age, residing in the two villages mentioned, sought divorce from the first husband to accept a second one who had courted her to that effect or at least posed temptingly as the more desirable one. A good number of such cases is in well-to-do families belonging to the high class among the Sudra Nairs of the two villages. In a few of these cases the first husband submitted to the situation and vacated when he found that a second one was definitely in the making. Cases of divorce and remarriage among women of any age group, particularly among those who have visiting husbands, do occur even today although rarely. Women whose husbands are employed in distant towns and who are not under the constant control of a brother or a mother's brother or any male guardian are a category among whom exist cases of extra-marital sexual partners. In poor families such cases occur often with the tacit recognition of the woman's male guardian of the household. The important fact is that such women, wealthy or poor, do not suffer from any serious social stigma provided they have not violated the sub-caste regulations of marital choice of today. Very rare cases of women having two extra-marital partners now residing in the two villages came to my notice. The concubinage of the type described still lingers on. Instances of a restricted form of prostitution in the sense that the woman caters to the Nairs or members of a higher caste who are known to her, are well known to my informants, and is a feature which is not likely to have existed a few decades ago. Such 'prostitutes' are not socially ostracised or no particular social disability is imposed on them. Reviewing the cases of divorce and extra-marital unions it is possible to remark that in these villages among all classes of Nairs in general, there is no social expectation of a rigid marital fidelity on the part of a woman or a man.

My familiarity with these villages and my inference from a study of the several cases of sexual laxity permit me to offer a more acceptable interpretation of the situation today. It is not simply the tradition for polyandry that creates the present tolerant attitude towards a little laxity of morals. Partitions of *tharavads* into small households have created a large number of small matrilineal family units. As I have shown in a paper on Visiting Husbands in Malabar, many families today need a male member to be in charge of its affairs chiefly for the reason that the ever increasing number of males are employed in distant towns without enough means or convenience to keep their wives with them. This need of a male member is to a large extent being met by modifying and often increasing the traditional roles of affinal and lineal kin. However, there is a gap and there are women who need males who have a sincere concern for their affairs in the process of rural life and living. To a considerable extent the problem of rural life and living for most of the Nairs is to manage their lands in the present context when the former landlord-tenant and tenant-cultivator relations have become seriously ruptured. The need on the part of some women for males having a real interest in them is to be understood against this background. There are men who want to take advantage of the situation and make such needy women a limited target of their extra-marital or pre-marital ventures. This is likely to be the reason why some of the extra-marital ventures on the part of men and women result in rather lasting than mere temporary relationships. Every effort is now being made to obviate this need by increasing the role of affinal kin and by a shift from visiting custom to virilocal or uxorilocal residence. The modern role of affinal kin, chiefly of the visiting husband, and the shifts in marital residence have been illustrated in my paper on Visiting Husbands cited elsewhere. Such efforts have become quite successful in many villages and among the different classes of Nairs. However, in the opinion of several of my informants the past patterns of marriage which accommodated monogamy, polyandry, concubinage, divorce and re-marriage among the Nairs and the conditions obtaining today as outlined here are together responsible for the current feature of a limited laxity of sexual morals.

III

Considering polyandry as characterised in the foregoing discussions it will be rewarding to look into the various functions served by polyandry. The data are not adequate for a functional analysis on the principles developed by Robert Merton. However, an attempt is here made to point out the various functions to the extent the data permit of doing so.

Although the units to which the functions are relevant are here pointed out, these units are frequently overlapping or do not permit of a strict division, as far as the relevancy of the functions to unit is concerned. Polyandry served several manifest functions ('objective consequences for a specified unit') and latent functions ('unintended and unrecognised consequences'). Keeping in mind the possibility of confusion between motives of behaviour and function, a possibility which Merton repeatedly points out, it is found that an enumeration of these functions can help to understand analytically the significance of polyandry. Manifest Functions :

(1) From the point of view of the polyandrous woman and her *tharavad* polyandry enhanced the prestige of each, particularly when the husbands were men of some individual merit or reputation. To the woman it was also a recognition of her eligibility to have more than one husband in the sense that her beauty or sex appeal had also played a part in attracting more than one husband. Even in monogamy married woman at the zenith of a quarrel and exchange of hot words with another would say, "Do you know who is visiting me ?", implying thereby a threat that there are stronger hands to champion her cause. (In some cases it is possible that the individual merit of a man was a factor which motivated a *tharavad* to consent to his being accepted as an additional husband.)

(2) A widower could without great difficulty find a wife and thus save himself from the possible disgrace of remaining without a recognized sexual mate. This was a function to the widower as well as his *tharavad* in that polyandry tended to eliminate the necessity of one's finding a mate from undesirable groups such as that of the sub-tenant (*pattakaran*).

(3) To the *tharavad* as a whole the free and sincere services of more husbands who would be specialists in some occupations, would be available. There were 'open occupations' which could be followed by several castes and sub-castes including the high group sub-caste of the Nairs. In this category of occupations are Ayurvedic medicine, childrens' therapy, astrology, curative and preventive magic. Teaching the three Arts as well as Sanskrit, practising and teaching a form of physio-therapy, teaching a form of gymnastics chiefly for self-defence, mastering and giving instructions in Kathakali (folk drama), training oneself to be

well informed on local matters including property deals and money transactions or procedures. In several of these the Nairs often excel although not always necessarily motivated by professional interest for profit.

(4) To the sub-castes which received husbands from a higher sub-caste or caste, polyandry was an adjustment to the situation of excess of males over females available. It also created sub-caste solidarity to the extent it obviated the necessity of finding wives from lower sub-castes as a permitted practice. A sub-caste which permitted polyandry had therefore little reasons to be linked by hypergamy with a lower sub-caste. In the same manner polyandry strongly tended to create and maintain the solidarity of the prestige group. In a measure it also tended to keep the tie between *enangar tharavad* for if a woman's first husband from an *enangar tharavad* failed to discharge his conjugal obligations he would not have to be divorced since an additional husband of choice is permitted.

(5) To the extent polyandry was a consequence of accepting the Numbutiri husbands it also created a channel for the slow transfer of the private property of the Nambutiri's younger brothers into the possession of the Nair women. Apart from jewellery and other articles there were several cases of the Nair wives who received waste lands and paddy fields on *kanam* tenure from the Nambutiri husbands. Any Nambutiri husband would do so with the consent of his eldest brother and for the Nambutiri families which were usually very wealthy, giving for the sake of a younger brother would not amount to more than a negligible drain. The Sthani Nair husband could equally provide the Nair wife with property and other gifts. Scores of cases of the Nair women in several villages feasting on the purse of their Nambutiri husbands and also acquiring wealth including landed property were narrated by my informants.

Latent functions :

(1) A sterile but otherwise desirable husband would not have to be divorced by a woman to ensure the possibility of getting children. A *tharavad* with a polyandrous woman could thus have a more remote chance of becoming extinct or facing the necessity of adopting a child. In the early part of this century there were *tharavads* which adopted girls through fear of extinction.

(2) A woman's desire for extra-marital sex gratification would not have to be suppressed or would not lead to liaison with the staff of men of lower sub-castes serving in her *tharavad* in various capacities with whom she would have more opportunity of contact and freedom of speech. In this sense it kept up the prestige of the *tharavad* without the strain of the women going astray.

(3) To certain extent polyandry removed the necessity of having affinal relatives from places far and wide. It also contributed to the solidarity of the group under a Nambutiri or a Sthani overlord. Such a group had therefore little reason to have affinal relations under another overlord and to fear and respect him as occasions would demand. This function was perhaps more important in pre-British days when the small chieftains had often hostile relations among them. The visiting custom itself with the minimum of conjugal obligations in monogamous unions, has served this function to a less extent even when groups under two overlords had affinal ties.

The manifest functions mentioned here are those which my informants seem to have recognised. While dealing with data which relate to a remote period there are several difficulties in making a functional analysis, particularly when the data were not originally collected with this end in view, or when it is extremely difficult to get relevant data for a given period of a few decades. The functions indicated here show the possibility of a wider scope for further analysis in this direction. The functions pointed out here chiefly are from the standpoint of the high group of sub-castes of the Nairs. The paucity of data also do not permit a satisfactory consideration of the dysfunctional aspects of polyandry. If polyandry was in part a custom perpetuated through the necessity of accommodating the Nambutiri husbands among the Nairs it also led to an overvaluation of the same practice leading to the phenomenon of girls over-growing marriageable age awaiting solely for suitable Nambutiri husbands. But it is doubtful if this dysfunctional feature existed when polyandry had a fairly high incidence. It was also dysfunctional to the sub-castes that a more desirable woman could be acquired as a mate not by a healthy competition among eligible husbands but by a spirit of accommodation. At the same time, to the extent the spirit of accommodation supplemented other factors making for unity among the sub-castes it must have been functional in several situations. In general it can be stated that there was the possibility of dysfunction to the extent polyandry contributed to make the social structure too rigid or too remotely predisposed to develop structural changes as an adjustment to the external pressures with the passage of time. The functions as pointed out here can be regarded as applicable to the pattern of polyandry as existed in the latter half of the 18th century. Several of these functions must have existed at earlier periods as well.

The value which govern the patterns of polyandrous and monogamous unions in the past, in a measure, appear to be currently influencing marital choice and sex life of the Nairs in rural Malabar. A detailed study of the present institutions of marriage and family among the Nairs of South Malabar will reveal how the old values of group affiliations and rank and prestige strive to find expression in or shape the characteristics of these institutions today.

NOTES

1. K.M. Kapadia, *Marriage and Family in India*, Oxford University Press, Bombay (1955), pp. 76-84 ; M.S.A. Rao, *Social Change in Malabar*, Popular Book Dept., Bombay, (1957), pp. 90-92.
2. Ibid.
3. Twelve Hundred Malayalam Proverbs, Mangalore (3rd edition, 1904) ; Thousand and one Proverbs, R.V.R. Press, Trivandrum.
4. The names of sub-castes as presented here do not tally with what is recorded in the Malabar Gazetteer. This is presumably because in briefly dealing with the caste system in the whole of Malabar, the Gazetteer makes only a broad distinction between North and South Malabar.
5. This division into three groups is based on the concurrent opinion of my Sudra Nair informants. The sub-castes of Nairs in other villages who may roughly be regarded as belonging to these groups are also, at times, in this study referred to in terms of the respective group to which they belong.
6. The Nair Panikkar and the Kariyam Nambiar were originally the Nairs but were re-labelled by pre-British chiefs on the basis of offices assigned to them. They were not to render any service to the Nambutiris as was the case with the Sudra Nairs.
7. For convenience the term Sthani is here regarded as including the Samanthans (the pre-British chieftains) who are in Walluvanad *taluk* today the sub-castes of the Tirumulpad, Eradi and the Vellodi. The term Sthani in this study also refers to the pre-British Rajas except when the term Raja is specifically stated. Literally Sthani means a position holder and the term is in current use in a major part of S. Malabar to refer to high ranking Nair families who held titles from pre-British chieftains and big chiefs.
8. The Sudra Nairs in a mood of gossip or sportive ridicule would refer to the Kiriyattils as the 'Kolli Untikal' which means 'firewood feeders' (with reference to their role of cooking.)
9. A search through all published records can reveal much more sub-castes but it is doubtful if the origin of all the relative rank and prestige of any sub-caste all over Malabar could be known from such sources.
10. Dr. A. Aiyappan, in *Iravas and Culture Change*, Madras (1945), discusses with considerable clarity the effect of this British intervention on the peasantry of Malabar. Report of the Malabar Tenancy Committee (Madras, 1940) shows that tenants were evicted in very large numbers with the increasing realisation on the part of the Janmis that they could exercise their ownership rights as they liked.

11. This fact does not appear in any published accounts of the Malabar tenancy system. My informants are aware of several cases of surrender of Janmam rights to the Janmi in the past.

    E.M. Sankaran Nambudiripad in his dissenting minute to the report of the Malabar Tenancy Committee (Vol. I Madras, 1940, p. 73) has well summarised the feature of dominance of the Nambutiris as Janmis and has also referred to the role played by this dominance. In recent years there have been other studies which among other things also contribute to our knowledge of some aspect or other regarding the position of the Nambutiris and the Sthanis in Malabar society. P.K S. Raja in his Mediaeval Kerala (pp. 232-263) shows how the Nambutiris slowly increased their hold on the mediaeval Kerala politics.

    Dr. K.N.S. Namburitipad in his unpublished thesis, "A Survey of Occupational and Employment Structure in some Malabar Villages," (1949) has reviewed the position of Janmis in South Malabar in the 19th century. He also gives figures (p 63) of the very large proportion of acreage under cultivation by tenants.

12. K. Raman Unni, Visiting Husbands in Malabar, *Journal of M.S. University of Baroda*, Vol. No. 1, March 1956, pp. 37-56.

13. There is another matrilineal Ambalawasi caste, Nambissan, which was a very small one and scattered into a few places. The Poduvals were divided into Aka Poduval and Pura Poduval and the latter were further divided into Mala Poduval and Chenda Poduval, all named after the nature of their temple services. Another Ambalawasi caste, Marar, was of a low rank but they could not have Nair wives except in a few places in Malabar. The patrilineal castes of the Ilayad and Muthad (or Mussad) were also sometimes mentioned as the Ambalawasis but they were also small in number and scattered and it is doubtful if they could have Nair wives except in a few places.

14. There are also at the same time many folk sayings and stories about the innocent nature of the Nambutiris and their lack of shrewdness in dealings. It is often said that this is one of the reasons why they nearly always wanted the Nairs or the Pattars as managers of their affairs connected with property and income. In each village one could find a couple or more *tharavads* or the Nairs which swelled up its wealth at the expense of the Nambutiri family.

15. Ilamkulam Kunjan Pillai, *Some Problems of Kerala History* (in Malayalam) part III, National Book Stall Kottyam, (1956), p. 96.

16. Ibid.

17. Ibid, pp. 86-100.

18. Several interpretations have been placed on Kettukalyanam but it is still not possible to state anything conclusively about it.

Dr. Aiyappan's study 'The Meaning of the Tali rite', (*Bulletin of the Ramavarma Research Institute*, Trichur, July 1941) is a check against those interpretations which regard it as a marriage.

19. Regarding the military life of the Nairs and the various hypergamous possibilities of the past in various parts of Malabar more studies will be possible when researches into the problems of Kerala History yield more results.

20. Oil for smearing over the body and applying on the scalp before bathing is used in large quantities by women in Malabar. A husband who can afford to supply such items in large quantities would never economise on that since it affects his prestige to do so.

21. Robert Merton, *Social Theory and Social Structure*, Illinois. 2nd Edition, (1951), p. 63.

13

POLYANDRY IN KOTA SOCIETY*

DAVID G. MANDELBAUM

The Kotas of the Nilgiri Hills in South India are not polyandrous in the strict sense of the term. A woman may have but one husband and can acquire another only by divorce from or after the death of her previous spouse. What Kota polyandry amounts to is that a man's brothers have free sexual access to his wife, and when a man is ill or incapacitated or in any way unable to fulfill his husbandly duties, then his brothers take his place. The brothers are, in effect, secondary husbands.

The Kotas are the neighbors of the famed Todas on the Nilgiri plateau. Unlike the Todas, whose whole culture pivots around the care of buffalo, the Kotas have more diversified interests. They are agriculturalists, but also keep herds of cattle and buffalo. A large part of their livelihood is earned by handiwork; they are the aboriginal artisans of the Nilgiri area and provide the other tribes with iron tools, wooden utensils, and pottery. In addition, they are professional musicians who furnish the music that is required for the ceremonies of the other tribes.

---

*Reproduced by permission of the American Anthropological Association, from *American Anthropologist* 40(4) : 574-583, 1938.

There are seven Kota villages, each divided into three exogamous fathersibs. The same three sib names occur in every village, but each village sib counts as a distinct social entity. A man belonging to the aker *gens* may not marry a woman of the same gen in his own village, but is permitted to take a wife from the aker gens in any of the other villages. Marriage is a simple affair; the bridegroom bows to the feet of the bride's father, pays a token fee of four annas and a bride price ranging from ten to one hundred rupees. Residence is patrilocal. The normal household consists of several brothers and their wives and children living together under the paternal roof. When the growing families can no longer be accommodated in a single house because of the limitations of space, each of the married brothers establishes his family in a separate house.

A man may have more than one wife and so the Kota marital system includes true polygyny as well as fraternal polyandry. A woman lives only in the house of her legal husband and he is recognized as the father of the children she bears. The husband has precedence to his wife's attention and favours. But in the absence of the husband, any of his brothers have the right and the obligation to act in his stead. It is a right in the sense that a husband may not attempt to interfere and may not exhibit any signs of jealousy when he finds his brother with his wife. It becomes an obligation when the husband is away from the village overnight. No woman will sleep alone in a house lest the sorcerers from the nearby Kurumba tribe find her an easy prey. Therefore, the husband delegates one of his brothers to sleep with his wife while he is away. Similarly, when a man is unable to accompany his wife on a ceremonial visit to another village, one of his brothers is duty-bound to go along with her and to remain at her side constantly, as would the husband himself. Not infrequently also, a man may want to conduct a liaison on his own and may conveniently divert the care and the attention of his wife to his brother while he himself goes about his affairs.

Although any one of a man's brothers may be the biological father of his wife's child, only the husband is recognized as the sociological father. When a child patently resembles its progenitor rather than its sociological father, any levity on the subject is sternly discouraged. The mother's husband is thus the father of the child in every sense of the word, save the biological. In no way may a man question the right of his brothers to have intercourse with his wife.

This right applies not only to an individual's uterine brothers, but to his classificatory brothers as well. All the male parallel cousins of a man and all the male members of his gens who are of his own generation are classed as brothers. Since the sib groups are small, the number of classificatory brothers is restricted. Nonetheless there may be ten to twenty men standing in the fraternal relationship to an individual.

Underlying the practice of sharing wives among brothers is the operation of a principle whose presence may be discerned in other phases of the culture, the principle of the equivalence of brothers. Just as every members of a group of brothers has equal sexual rights to the wife of any one of them, once the husband's precedence has been allowed, so do brothers share equally in other things. In the economic sphere, a group of uterine brothers till the paternal fields together and mutually partake of the harvest. When brothers live together, they divide the various tasks. One brother acts as herdsman, some as blacksmiths, others work in the fields. The proceeds of their labor are pooled, and each one enjoys an equal part of the total income. When the paternal inheritance is to be divided, it is parcelled out equally among all the sons.

The kinship system further reflects the operation of the principle of fraternal equivalence. A man calls the children of his brother by the same terms as he uses for his own sons and daughters. This is true for the children of classificatory brothers as well as for the children of real brothers. The brothers of one's father are equated with the real father and are called "younger father" or "elder father" according to their age in relation to one's own father. The presence of this particular type of kinship system is not to be taken as either the cause or the effect of the fraternal principle. There are societies which possess this kind of system and which do not have the idea of fraternal equivalence, and conversely, there may be cultures in which the fraternal principle exists and which have an entirely different type of terminology. The concurrence in Kota culture only means that the terminological aspect of the social structure is in symmetrical accord with a dominant social motif.

The presence of this principle is also apparent in the Kota religion. There is a paramount triad of gods composed of "Elder Father God", his brother "Younger Father God," and "Mother God". The junior male god shares the wife of the other. It is not so much that "Younger Father God" is a co-husband, but that Kota deities, like Kota men, have fraternal rights to the wives of their brothers. In this culture as in many others, the attributes and behavior of the deities are direct projections and elaborations of patterns valid in the society.

Incidents in the folklore illus trate the cultural setting within which the formula of fraternal equivalence works. There is a tale of two brothers, the elder called Katpedkamaten, the younger Parkul. In the words of the story ;

> The elder brother became the headman of the village and always walked about with a leaf umbrella (a symbol of wealth and dignity). He had many servants. When the time for sowing came, the men spread manure over the fields. The elder brother told the younger to carry manure with the servants but the younger brother took his loads of manure and poured them into the bushes instead of over the fields. When the elder brother heard of this and berated Parkul, he replied, "I am your brother, not your servant. If you work, I will work; if you stand with a leaf umbrella, so should I." Katpedkamaten grew angry and beat his brother with a stick . . . . Then an old man rebuked him with the proverb, "Even if a man becomes a king, to his mother he is only a son and to his younger brother he is but elder brother." And the old man went on to tell Katpedkamaten. "Bring back

your young brother, for when an elder brother sits, then also must the younger brother sit."

To this episode the informant added his own comment that "Until today, brothers who live in the same house are equal in position. When each has his own house and his own land, then only may one have more than the other." There is absolute economic equality among a group of brothers who live together. When they no longer live in one household, they still are bound to render economic assistance to a brother who is in need. If a man suffers any misfortune, it is his brothers who come to his aid, who cultivate his land, do his craft work, care for his family. The essential economic solidarity of the fraternal group is maintained even though the brothers no longer pool the proceeds of their work.

The fraternal equation does not prevail with mathematical infallibility. In certain circumstances it may come into conflict with another cultural axiom and be cancelled out. One such situation arises in the case of the priests. There are one or two men in each village who perform the sacerdotal duties, occupy a priestly office, and are scrupulously segregated from contaminating contacts. Thus the Kota priest may not eat from vessels used by laymen; he must occupy a certain reserved portion of the house when he visits the home of a fellow villager; he may no more join in the ordinary social dances than a bishop may publicly demonstrate the tango. Since women are most potently charged with ceremonial pollution, and since the priest must be most carefully insulated against such pollution, the rules which regulate the contact of the priest with women are stringent. He may have only one wife and may not have intercourse with any other woman. The wife of the priest partakes of his sanctity and she, in turn, may not have intercourse with any man but her husband. It is in this respect that the principle of the equivalence of brothers gives way before the more demanding principle of the segregation of the priest and his wife from contaminating mundane influences. The brothers of a priest do not have access to his wife since that would impair her sacrosanct nature. The priest may not have anything to do with the wives of his brothers since they would trespass his consecrated presence. The priestly principle is dominant over the fraternal principle because its effective rating, to use Professor Linton's phrase, is higher. That is, the society is more concerned with preserving the purity of the priests than it is in consistently equilibrating the rights of brothers. The priesthood complex has greater potentialities, in this instance, for influencing societal behavior than has the fraternal complex.

Sometimes the application of the concept of fraternal equivalence overrides some other fundamental of the culture. A basic observance is that a woman may not be forced into an association repugnant to her. A girl may be married off to an elderly man for the sake of the bride price he pays, and many kinds of social pressure will be exerted on the girl to persuade her to abide by her parents' choice. But if she adamantly refuses to stay with one husband, she is usually able to get another. In the numerous legal cases concerning illicit sexual relationships, the crucial point at law is whether the woman willingly formed the alliance or whether she was forced into it. If it was voluntary, her partner's penalty is light; if involuntary, it is more severe. The volition of the woman is of primary importance. But when a woman dislikes the brother of her husband and refuses him, she is ultimately forced to tolerate the relationship. In this case the woman's will is disregarded because of the paramount idea that brothers must enjoy equal privileges.

The conflict of the same two principles but with opposite results occurs in the remarriage of widows. If the equivalence of brothers were the most powerful social coefficient in this instance also, a widow would be compelled to marry one of her deceased husband's brothers. As it is, the levirate is the preferred remarriage ; it is socially approved, but yet is not compulsory. Should a widow refuse to marry one of the brothers, she may not be coerced into the match. She must then surrender to the brothers all the property left by the deceased and must even give them the jewels given by her late husband. The fraternal principle demands that the material possessions be equally distributed among the brothers if there are no sons to inherit, but the brothers are defeated should they attempt in this case to over-rule the maxim that a woman's stubborn will must prevail.

The question then arises as to why a woman may reject the brother of her husband after her spouse is dead, but may not do so while he is alive. The answer is that the refusal while the husband is alive immediately disbalances the fraternal prerogatives, denying to one brother what the other possesses. But when the widow remarries to some one not in the fraternal group, then none of the brothers have access to her and the equivalence is maintained.

The Kotas themselves do not calculate this outcome with deliberate nicety. Indeed, they are hardly aware of the existence of the fraternal principle. That, however, does not militate against its reality and influence. Even the members of the highly verbalized societies of Western civilization do not consciously formulate the basic configurations of their cultures.

Nor does the fraternal principle have the same meanings for all the tribesmen. One informant rationalized the practice of fraternal polyandry on the grounds that it encourages friendship between a man's wife and his brothers, and when it becomes necessary for the brothers to aid the wife and the children, they are not reluctant to do so. The polyandrous custom, in this informant's understanding, created a sort of aboriginal insurance policy for one's family. Less articulate informants merely returned the stock answer, as their rationale for polyandry, "We follow this custom because our forefathers did."

Individual variations likewise occur in the application of the principle. A man who recently died left behind him little property and no close relatives to pay for the expenses of his funeral. It was clearly the duty of his parallel cousins, in their capacity as classificatory brothers, to provide for the cremation. They did not feel impelled to do so since the deceased had been a man of little consequence and, as they would not inherit from him, any expenditures for the funeral would be sheer loss. In the end the husband of the dead man's sister and his widow's brother provided for the necessary ceremonial display. For if the hody had been ignominiously disposed of, the disgrace would have redounded to them, his nearest of kin. The parallel cousins were men of some rank and any adverse criticism of their action would not harm them greatly. But in other instances in which parallel cousins were obligated to provide for the funeral of a classificatory brother, they unhesitatingly did so. Some men feel constrained to fulfill their social obligation, others may ignore it.

The principle of the equivalence of brothers extends to a group of sisters. Thus a man has sexual access to all the sisters of his wife. The sororate is preferred, but is not compulsory. If a newly married couple find that they are not compatible, the husband may exchange his wife for one of her sisters. But the equivalence of sisters is not as thorough going as is the fraternal principle because a set of female siblings may be married off into different villages and will not frequently meet ; therefore a sororal group does not constitute as right a social and economic entity as does a fraternal group.

A noteworthy topic of inquiry in a society which permits a number of men to share the same woman is whether any friction arises over the uniform allocation of privileges. Among the Kotas, as in other cultures where polyandry or joint uxorious rights are sanctioned, any manifestations of sexual jealousy within the fraternal group are drastically squelched. There is a tale of a man who asked his brother to keep away from his newly acquired second wife so that more of her time might be available to her husband. For this mild and seemingly reasonable request, the husband almost was outcaste, had to pay a heavy fine and send the woman to live with his brothers for a time. The slightest sign of sexual jealousy between brothers arouses the relatives and the sub members of the jealous man to bring all the persuasion and social force at their command to eradicate the symptoms of jealousy.

This is not to say that jealousy outside the fraternal line is unknown. A husband will not usually tolerate any sexual relationship between his wife and a man who is not one of his brothers. If he suspects such a relationship, the husband will threaten the paramour, or remove his wife from temptation or utilize any of the devices available to jealous husbands in other societies beside the Kota. Whatever the root causes of jealousy may be in Kota culture, they are certainly as deep lying and are perhaps similar to those operating in Western societies. Since Kota men are conditioned to exclusive sexual possession of their wives in respect to most males, it seems likely that they may have the desire for personal possession in respect to the fraternal males also. The feeling for individual privilege which is socially encouraged in the one circumstance may carry over into the other. Since the dictates of the culture so effectively repress any manifestations of such sentiments, it is difficult to find many direct evidences of intrafraternal jealousy. But there are certain indirect clues.

There is a proverb which says, "Do not climb a rope down the face of a cliff (as is sometimes done in gathering honey), except in the company of your male cross-cousin." The implication is that one's brothers are not to be trusted too far.

Another clue is the prevalence and frequency of quarrels among brothers. While the assertion of individual aggression is rigidly tabooed in the sexual sphere, there is no restraint of hostility in other matters in which a group of brothers share rights. Violent disputes among brothers occure about property division, about distribution of inheritance, about the allocation of work then a joint enterprise is being conducted. It is my impression that intrafraternal disputes are more numerous and more vehement than other kinds of quarrels. It may be that the hostilities generated by sexual jealousy within a set of brothers find their outlet in the economic relations of the fraternal group.

Polyandrous societies are not as rare as it was once thought they were. The Eskimo, Tibetan, and Wahuma cases have long been known. Recent reports indicate that a number of North American tribes practiced the custom, among them the Shoshoni, Paviotso, Northern Paiute, Pawnee, Wichita, Kitsai, Arikara, and Comanche. The Comanche in particular institutionalized the exchange of wives in a manner similar to the Kota system. The Lhota Nagas of Assam also extend the rights of a husband to his brother. In South India polyandry is of especially frequent occurrence. Six polyandrous tribes have been reported from Cochin; the Nayars of Travancore and the Irava of British Malabar have this form of marriage ; while the Todas are the classic example of a polyandrous people in the textbooks of Anthropology.

The historical aspects of Kota polyandry frame a significant problem. Before the English came up to the Nilgiri plateau, its inhabitants were relatively isolated from the main currents of South Indian life. Contacts with the people of the lowlands were few since the journey up the hills was hard and hazardous. Soon after the Europeans discovered that the climate of the plateau was a life-saving refuge from the fevers of the plains, roads and later a railroad were built in the wake of the English came Tamilians and other lowland Hindus. Within the last fifty years, the advent of these newcomers has effected significant changes in the tribal culture. New deities have been adopted, new legal procedures have appeared, new fashions in dress taken on, new methods of cultivation practised. It is striking that there has been no change in the practice of polyandry. Other of the tribal institutions, economic, religious, political, have been affected, yet polyandry flourishes with full vitality.

Such has not been the case in other polyandrous communities. Dr A. Aiyappan says of Irava polyandry, "Wherever modern European culture has penetrated and modified indigenous culture, polyandry is giving way to monandry...." Only among the rural and remote Irava does polyandry still exist. Aiyappan ascribes the absence of jealousy and discord among Irava co-husbands to several causes: the joint marriage ceremony, the desire to limit heirs, the supervising influence of parents, the force of public opinion.[4] Among the Kotas, however, there is no joint marriage system nor any desire to limit the number of heirs, nor any particularly potent supervision by parents. The one common factor that remains, is public opinion. But public opinion is an omnibus term which may encompass any number of differing social forces and phenomena.

To delineate the reasons why Kota polyandry has stood steadfast in the face of the influx of new customs, let us return to the cultural motif which was found to underlie the functioning of polyandry. The encroachment of foreign concepts has not yet invalidated the principle of the equivalence of brothers. Inheritance, marriage, family organization are still influenced by this factor. Since the principle continues to function in other phases of the culture, it is understandable that it should continue to work in the matter of polyandry. It continues to work because the fraternal principle is still economically justified. The economic set-up is usually the part of a culture most vulnerable to change and it is precisely here that the fraternal principle finds its primary validation. Although new crops are being cultivated, although the old inter-tribal commerce has broken down, although the material equipment of the household has been revised, the major economic pursuits of Kota men are still blacksmithing, music and agriculture. Each of these occupations demands the cooperative effort of a team of men. In blacksmithing, at least three must work together : one to operate the bellows, one to hold the iron, a third to wield the hammer. In music, the minimum number for a land is five players. In agriculture, it is becoming easier for a man to care for his fields alone but cooperative effort is more efficient. The groups that work together in the smithy, in the fields and in providing music, are generally groups of brothers. Since the Kota depends on the economic cooperation of his brothers for his livelihood, it is small wonder that the close knit ties of the fraternal group hold their grip and that the principle of the equality of brothers yet prevails. A proverb which aptly states the case says, "If the mother dies, there is no good food; if the father dies, there is no happiness; if a man has no brothers, he has no strength of arm."

The economic dependence on group effort is the condition that makes the supreme civil penalty, outcasting, so powerful a force toward social cohesion. One who persistently disregards the rules of the culture in regard to the fraternal principle or in any other important respect, is outcaste and denied communication with his fellow tribesmen. He consequently is unable to earn a living since he cannot single-handedly make tools or provide music or reap a full harvest. The one man in the tribe who has for some time defied the consequences of being put into the Kota Coventry, is the one man, a school teacher, whose livelihood does not depend on the traditional occupations. He is now strenuously campaigning for reforms in the tribal habits of wearing long hair, of eating carrion, of protracted menstrual and childbirth seclusion. A number of young men have come to support him. But in the matter of polyandry, the reformer seeks no change. There is neither incentive nor opportunity for altering this tribal custom.

Kota polyandry then, has remained unimpaired because the underlying functional principle and its economic validation have remained intact. Not that the economic factor is the only important element motivating the fraternal principle. Childhood conditioning, family organization, emotional attachments also play a significant part. But the economic props will probably be affected before the others and then polyandry will be threatened. When imported tools completely supplant the articles of Kota manufacture, when no income is to be derived from musical services, when improved agricultural techniques and availability of hired labour make the Kota more independent of his brothers, then it well may be that the equivalence of male siblings and the practice of polyandry will no longer be maintained.

The factors responsible for the continued preservation of polyandry in this tribe need not be the same those operating in other polyandrous societies. The Todas have a form of polyandry similar to that of the Kotas and Toda polyandry too, continues to flourish. But Toda economy and social organization are vastly different from that of the Kotas and the resistance of the Toda institutions may be due to reasons different from those posited for the Kota case. It is to be noted, however, that Toda economic life has changed even less than Kota within the last half century. A study of what has happened to polyandry among the Todas and studies of other polyandrous peoples would make the Kota instance more meaningful. A deeper insight into the nature of the cultural processes may best be secured through the comparison and integration of controlled bodies of evidence regarding culture change in various societies.

Through Kota society there run certain dominant themes which link seemingly disparate elements of the culture, motivate the cultural dynamics, establish the basic configurations of the society. Within the scope of these basic configurations, there is room for individual variation in some matters, no allowance at all for personal deviations in other matters. A dominant personality will utilize all the leverage permitted within the configuration to introduce changes. The principle of fraternal equivalence is still current because it is economically worth while. If its economic value should fall, then we may look for a corresponding decline in the practice of polyandry.

14

POLYANDRY IN THE KOTA SOCIETY : AN APPRAISAL*

I. VERGHESE[1]

Introduction

Though Mandelbaum contends that the Kota are not polyandrous in the strict sense of the term, yet he considers them as polyandrous on the grounds (1) a man's brothers have free sexual access to his wife and when a man is ill-capacitated or in anyway unable to fulfill his husbandry duties, then his brother takes his place. The brothers are, in effect, secondary husbands; (2) in no way a man may question the right of his brothers to have intercourse with his wife ; (3) this right applies not only to individual's uterine brothers, but to his classificatory brothers as well ; (4) even if a woman dislikes the brother of her husband and refuses him, she is ultimately forced to tolerate the relationship ; (5) the principle of equivalence of brothers extends to a group of sisters, whereby a man has free sexual access to all the sisters of his wife (1938 : 574, 577, 578).

He characterizes the Kota polyandry as an extension of

---

*Reproduced by permission of the Indian Anthropological Society from the *Journal of the Indian Anthropological Society*, 3 (1 & 2) : 141-152, 1968.

the principle of equivalence of brothers, especially in economic matters which, according to Berreman, is also valid for Garhwal Paharis, fraternal polyandrous people of Jaunsar Bawar and other Himalayan areas and probably Tibet (1962 : 70).

Based on Mandelbaum's writing, Fischer concludes that with these people (Kota) "polyandry is a form of polykoity and that it generally does not have the form of polyandry" (Prince Peter, 1963 : 112). In Fischer's opinion, their polyandry "must be considered more as a form of economic collaboration with attached rights of sexual intercourse for the partners than as a form of marriage." Cooper opines that more sharing of a wife is not polyandry unless a woman is actually married to more than one man (cf. Lowie, 1961 : 114). Murdock supports Cooper's insistence that the term "polyandry" be reserved exclusively for a form of marriage which is socially sanctioned and culturally patterned (1960 : 25). More sharing of wife in the absence of bond of marriage has been termed as "cicisbeism" by Piddington (1960 : 115) and Prince Peter (1963 : 21-22), and as "disparate polyandry" or "tolerated promiscuity" by Grottanelli (Prince Peter, 1965 : 92).

Quoting Shortt (1869) Westermarck states that although polygyny is sanctioned by custom, the Kota are in practice monogamous (1903 : 439). Thurston also states, "The Kotas as a rule have one wife and polyandry is unknown among them. But polygyny is sometimes practised." (1909 : IV : 22).

It is clear with these divergent views that there is some ambiguity as regards the understanding of polyandry and also whether any form of polyandry really exists in the Kota society. As it is not my intention to enter into a discussion on the theoretical issues of polyandry, in this paper I would confine my discussions to the traits of the Kota which have been characterized as polyandrous by Mandelbaum and to examine such traits in the light of my data. I shall also discuss some of the factors that are associated with polyandry and examine them in specific reference to the Kota society.

The Kota

Numbering 1113[2], the Kota are confined to seven villages

in the Nilgiri hills of Madras State. Speaking a dialect of their own, they are also fluent in the dialect (Badagu) of their neighboring Badaga and in Tamil, the language of the State (Madras). They are primarily agriculturists. Among other occupations on which they subsist, are blacksmithy and pottery which are traditional, and domestication of cattle.

In their religious observances, the Kota have adopted some rituals and practices of the Hindu religion. They are proud of the fact that they are the only people on these hills who have successfully resisted all the efforts of Indian and foreign missionaries to christianize people of other faiths. They are strictly a patriarchal people.

The Kota residents of Trichagadi[3] strongly react to the allegation that they practise polyandry. None of them admitted to have ever heard of any society, other than the Toda, giving sanction to a man to exercise his right of sexual pleasures with his brother's wife. Of a total of 175 marital unions concluded in the last four decades, 168 (96%) are monogamous and 7 (4%) polygynous. The wives in respect of any of the polygynous marriages are not real sisters.

Polyandrous Traits and the Kota View

(*i*) A matter relating to one's sexual indulgence with his brother's wife is neither taken to the *koot* (village panchayat) nor the latter entertains an issue of this kind, whereas extra-marital relationship of a woman with any other man is entertained by the *koot.* This suggests that sex relations of a woman with her husband's brothers are not punishable, though not publicly permitted (cf. Fuchs, 1963 : 131).

The Kota consider a man's relationship with his brother's wife as an act of adultery.[4] But all that her husband can do under such circumstances, is to either condone his wife by warning her not to be disloyal to him (husband) in future or to divorce her. The reason offered by the panchayat elders for not entertaining an issue of adultery is that such an occurence is the concern of only one family or that of the brothers involv-ed, and giving publicity to it only breeds bitterness among the families of brothers, together with lessening of their prestige and honour. The reason offered may not be convincing but it does suggest that sex relations of a woman with her husband's brothers (adultery) is socially disapproved though not strictly forbidden, as in the case of four societies in Murdock's (1960 : 265) sample.

The Kota marriages are mostly by courtship. A boy selects his mate and informs the same to his parents who, then, arrange for the marriage. Marriage by elopement is also prevalent among them. According to this practice, the one who takes a woman (married or unmarried) away to his own house either by physical force or by enticement for a night, can claim his wedded relationship with her. In either types, the parents themselves have only little to say than to abide by their son's choice, and the own brothers may or may not be consulted or even informed about the matter earlier. Fortyfive instances of elopement marriages were recorded, of which excepting thirteen (28.88%) where the men concerned had exercized force in leading the women to their (men's) houses, the rest (71.12%) were all preplanned. In respect of an elopement marriage of a married woman, if she is a party to the planned elopement, the aggrieved husband has no means of holding her. Her new husband, however, has to pay damages to him within a period of three months at double the rate of bride price which the aggrieved husband might have paid for marrying her. Failing to clear off the damages within time, may entail the meeting of the *koot*, which may impose conditions for immediate settlements of the payment or for the return of the woman to her first husband. What is important to note here is that out of forty-two instances of preplanned elopement marriages, in two cases men had enticed their real brothers' wives and claimed wedded relationships. Whereas in one instance the payment (damages) had been made promptly, the other was not made. The matter had been reported to the *koot* which had allowed seven more days' time for the payment. Thus, even a real brother is not spared from evading the payment of damages.

(*ii*) Whenever a man goes out of his village, involving his absence from home for a night or more, he usually asks one of his brothers to take care of his wife and children. If no adult male is at home, the assignee may even stay in his brother's house during nights until his brother returns. In his inability to accompany his wife to her natal home or elsewhere on a social or ceremonial visit, a man requests one of his brothers to accompany her.

Assigning one of his brothers (preferably an already married brother) to care for his wife and family during his absence, though is customary, does not entail any right on the assignee to demand sexual favours from her as a matter of right. If any such matter comes to the notice of her husband, he certainly warns his wife or else he may even divorce her. In 1958, a Kota, stationed elsewhere on a Government job, had divorced his wife when the latter had confessed at an advanced stage of her pregnancy that she was going to get a child through his brother who was looking after her during her husband's absence from the house for about a year. Following the divorce, his brother married her. I have recorded three more instances where sexual contacts with brothers' wives had resulted in divorces. Those appear contrary to Mandelbaum's statement that

> "in the absence of the husband from the village overnight, any of his brothers have the right and obligation to act in his stead" and that "in no way a man may question the right of his brothers to have intercourse with his wife" (1938 : 574).

A question arises, then, as to why at all a man is assigned for the purpose. The Kota have two answers to offer : (1) as a safeguard from the treacherous Kurumba sorcery (Verghese, 1966) which Mandelbaum himself admits (1938 : 577). According to a Kota belief, a woman or a group of women, if unaccompanied by an adult male, may easily become a prey to Kurumba sorcery. Therefore, a woman needs company of an adult male to save herself from such dangers; and (2) it is likely for a man and a woman to indulge in sex (if they could be potential mates), and opportunity prevailing, they do it and keep it a secret. Hence, not only that a Kota expects his brother to protect his wife from others when he is absent but also that his brother should abstain from having any sexual relation with her. That a brother is sent to accompany one's wife is also on account of their patrilineal system and kinship bonds.

(*iii*) Customarily, a widow may not remarry until the dry funeral ceremony[5] in respect of her deceased husband has taken place. It may take place in the same year or within a period of three years. This being the mourning period for the widow, she is not to go back to her parental house, and instead, she is required to continue her stay in the same house (of her deceased husband). Uptil the day of the ceremony, a brother of the deceased stays with her if she has no adult son. They may or may not indulge in sex but if the widow conceives in the meanwhile, the man is duty-bound to marry her immediately after the dry funeral ceremony has taken place.

A Kota widow, however, is at liberty to remarry a man of her own choice. As Mandelbaum admits,

> "If the equivalence of brothers were the most powerful social coefficient . . . a widow would be compelled to marry one of her deceased husband's brothers . . . but . . . should a widow refuse to marry one of the brothers, she may not be coerced into the match" (1938 : 575).

Trichagadi houses four widows in independent households and six others as dependants in other households. In spite of the Kota view that a woman is a valuable economic asset to a family, the number of widows, particularly those who run independent households, can be interpreted as a significant drift from polyandrous practices, in general, and if there was any among the Kota.

(*iv*) Though rarely practised, the Kota recognise a man marrying a woman on behalf of the bodily deformed brother.

This is done because, in the Kota view, an unmarried life is sinful and the fear that the deformed brother may not otherwise be able to secure a wife by himself. The one who marries so, keeps his real intentions hiding from the wife until she has conceived, for a woman is tabooed from seeking a divorce or remarrying during her pregnancy. Once she gives birth to a child, it is hoped, that out of her love for the child, she may get reconciled to the fact that she was meant to be the wife of the deformed person and not the one who actually married and cohabited with her. One such marriage had occurred in 1963 and it continues. When asked about his brother's (the one who had actually undergone the marriage ritual) right to sexual pleasures with his wife, he promptly reacted to it saying 'how is it possible, she is not his wife anymore and my wife cannot be his wife also'.

(*v*) Mandelbaum (1938 : 575) asserts that not only uterine brothers have a right to sexual intercourse with their brother's wives, but that the right extends to classifi catory brothers as well. This statement even theoretically is seen wanting in exceptions, even if the Kota are polyan drous to the extent Mandelbaum describes them to be. I shall give an example of a situation where sexual relation ship of a man with the wife of his classificatory brother would amount to incest. Each Kota village is divided into three exogamous clans. Let me name them as A, B and C. A girl of the A clan, for example, by marrying aboy of

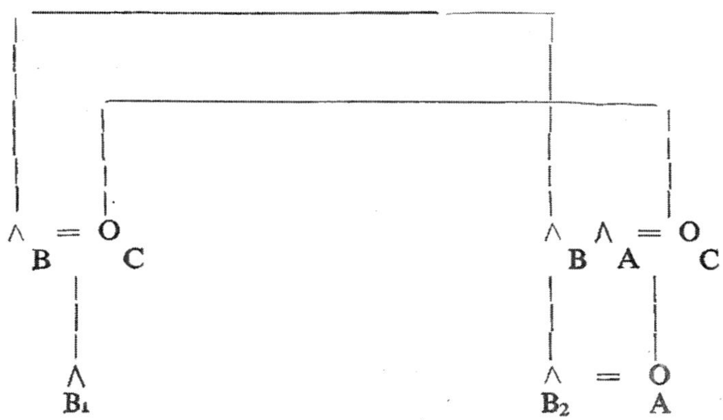

Here B_1 and B_2 are classificatory brothers, but A is the (classificatory) sister of the former and wife of the latter, and therefore B_1 's relationship with A would amount to incest.

the B clan, is tabooed from having relationship (sexual) with her mothers' sister's sons who may also be the members of the B clan and are classificatory brothers of her husband.

(*vi*) Towards the end of his paper Mandelbaum writes that the Kota polyandry is similar, in form, to that of the Toda.

Among the Toda, as Lowie (1920 : 44) states, when a man marries a woman, it is understood or the Toda society sanctions that she becomes the wife of all brothers (who normally live together) including those brothers who are born subsequently, and their rights over her are shared ; no dispute ever arises among the husbands and the very notion of such a possibility is flouted by the Toda mind; all brothers are reckoned the child's fathers and the legal parenthood is established by the bow and arrow ceremony (1960 : 264). Besides, as Murdock says that the Toda show indifference to adultery. Among the Kota it is not so. Mandelbaum (1938 : 574) has himself stated that a Kota woman may have only one husband and can acquire another only by divorce from or after the death of her previous spouse. Prince Peter (1963 : 89) rightly comments on this point of Mandelbaum that 'in the light of River's description of Toda polyandry this hardly appears to be the case and there seems therefore to be very little justification for making such a pronouncement "

The Kota Vis-a-Vis Factors Favournble to Polyandry

(*a*) The principle of the unity and solidarity of the sibling group offering an explanation for and an advantage of polyandrous (fraternal) practices is emphasized by Radcliffe Brown (1960 : 64) and Leach (1955 : 185).

> "A normal Kota household," writes Mandelbaum, "consists of several brothers and their wives and children living together under the paternal roof, and when the growing families can no longer be accommodated in a single house because of the limitations of space, each of the married brothers establishes his family in a separate house" (1938 : 574).

My investigations show that the divorce which took place during the period of my field work, on the ground that a man committed adultery with his brother's wife, broke the only fraternal joint family which existed in the village uptil then. Apart from this, it is the practice now-a-days that an older son establishes a separate household soon after his younger brother is married. Six out of the sixty-eight households of Trichagadi accommodated not more than two persons each, while their married brothers live separately. Three out of these six households contain only a widower each, who could very well be accommodated with his brothers. Limitation of space, therefore, is not the criterion among the Kota for the brothers to live separately.

Prince Peter states, "only an intesification of the unity and solidarity of the sibling group can bring about adelphic polyandry". (1955 : 180). In case of the Kota, jealousy and quarrels amongst brothers are not new to them. In explaining the origin of their clan system, it was extreme jealousy between two brothers and the desire of the younger to marry his elder brother's wife were brought to the limelight by my informants. Though legendary, as it appears to be, it relates the decision of one brother who, in order to possess all his brother's wealth and his wife, attempt to kill the brother.

In explaining the Kota polyandry as an extension of the principle of fraternal equivalence, Mandelbaum writes :

> "a group of uterine brothers cultivated lands jointly and shared the harvest; living together in joint families, they divided among themselves the various tasks such as herding cattle, blacksmithy and work in the fields; their entire proceeds were pooled and the total income was evenly distributed amongst themselves" (1938 : 582).

But, in the present context, the changes that have ushered in the Kota society are phenomenal, and in effect, fraternal equivalence or solidarity in economic sphere does not meet with any success. For example, the total absence of fraternal joint families has restricted a Kota's concern more towards his own nuclear family. As in the field of agriculture, blacksmithy endeavours are also seldom undertaken jointly by brothers. Their blacksmithy produce are no longer in great demand since cheaper imported tools have flooded the nearby markets of Ootacamund. Cooner and Kotagiri, which are frequented by the Kota themselves. The Kota musical services to the Badaga neighbours (in the past a set of Kota brothers constituted a team for the purpose) which had been for long, a substantial secondary income to them have now been lost due to a vast majority of the Badaga opposing to the Kota music, substituting it by the Kurumba music[6]. The large-scale settling of Harijans in the around of the Kota villages offering manual labour in the agricultural fields and in herding cattle for nominal wages in cash and kind, has made the Kota more independent of his brothers.

(*b*) Leach believes that polyandry is intimately associated with an institution of property rights and has hypothesized that "adelphic polyandry is consistently associated with systems in which women as well as men are the bearers of property rights." (1955 : 183). Dunlop opines that polyandry is sometimes due to a high bride price. (cf. Kapadia, 1959 : 71).

Dowry is not at all a part of the traditional Kota marriage transaction. Now-a-days, however, bride-price ranges from Rs. 10 to 250 but is not compulsory. The only compulsory payment is of *vakispanm* (a token fee of 25 paise coin) which the bridegroom offers to his father-in-law which binds the marriage. Moreover, elopement marriage of an unmarried girl involves absolutely no amount payable by either of the parties. As regards the property rights, all property-movable or otherwise—are exclusively in the hands of males. A woman surrenders whatever possessions (jewelry) she brings with her on her marriage, to her husband. Property transmission is done from father to sons, in the absence of the latter, to the former's brothers.

(*c*) Polyandry has often been attributed to economic hardship (Kapadia, 1959 : 71 ; Iyer, 1961 : 140), and it has been observed that polyandry is related to sex specialization in which woman makes only an insignificant contribution to subsistence (Heath, quoted by Berreman,

1962 : 64). Murdock (1960 : 36) also opines that where women make an insignificant contribution to the economic life, polyandry becomes a satisfactory adjustment.

The Kota women contribute as heavily as do men to subsistence, particularly in respect of pottery and handicrafts which are exclusively theirs, and in agriculture. In fact, a women is considered an economic asset to the household, and the chief reason attributed to the polygynous practices among them is to gain additional economic assets for the household. Therefore Cunningham's (Westermarck, 1903 : 504) contention that the difficulty of raising the sum for securing a wife (see point b) and the expense of maintaining women may perhaps account for polyandry, in part, has no relevance in the Kota society.

(*d*) Rockhill (Lowie, 1920 : 44), Walton (Berreman, 1963 : 346) and Rev. Rebsch (Westermarck, 1903 : 504) attribute the pressure on the land and a desire to maintain family lands intact or to transmit them undivided to fraternal polyandry.

The revenue data show that in Trichagadi, a total of 156 acres[7] of lands are owned in fifty-four names (men). Excepting two married brothers who possess six acres of land in common (undivided) the rest are all independently owned. In three of the instances, division of property has taken place amongst brothers even when their fathers were alive. Further, it is noted that between brothers, some own lands and some have sold away theirs. In two cases the land-owners had leased out their lands to other Kota, whereas their own brothers cultivated the lands taken by them on lease from the nearby Harijans.

> "If two brothers have separate wives, their children will have separate economic interests, and maintenance of the patrimonial inheritance in one piece is likely to prove impossible" (Leach, 1955 : 184).

So is exactly the case with the Kota.

Traditionally, the Kota are not an agricultural tribe, and

so the question of feeling any pressure on land (in the past atleast) does not arise. They often express concern over their static population for over five centuries. Increasing death rate among them, particularly those of infants and children, is attributed by them to the ill-will of the sorcerous Kurumba neighbours. According to the 1867 Census, the Kota population was 802, and it is to be wondered that one full century has added only 311 individuals to their populace. Further, lack of desire to limit the number of heirs by the Kota is emphasised by Mandelbaum himself (1938 : 581).

(*e*) According to Rivers (cf. Kapadia, 1959 : 77) polyandry implies certain privileges of leviration. On the death of one brother, the others have first right over the widow. This view is also shared by McLennan (cf. Westermarck, 1903 : 3) and Aiyappan (cf. Kapadia, 1959 : 77). According to the latter, with the prohibitions of sororate and levirate, it is difficult to consider adelphic polyandry even as a survival.

Levirate and sororate (both senior and junior), though not prohibited in the Kota society, are infrequently practised. They are, however, not the preferred marriages. In Trichagadi, I found a lone instance of levirate. A man left behind his wife and six children at his death. An elder brother of the deceased was then a widower with no children. He adopted three sons of his deceased brother. Five years later, in 1963 he married their mother. He was then aged fifty-eight. The woman tells me, 'he found my sons too good to him in his disabled age. It was a token of gratefulness that he married me in the invalid age of both of us'. Besides, only two cases of sororate (one senior and one junior) were remembered by my informants, to have taken place two decades ago. Fear of ill-treatment to children by non-related step-mother or a step-father was returned as the cause for all the cases of levirate and sororate.

(*f*) Murdock (1960 : 25) opines that despite the paucity of cases, there seems reason to assume that polyandry may sometimes be due to a scarcity of women resulting from the practice of female infanticide. John Mogey (Prince Peter, 1965 : 94), on the other hand, asserts that female infanticide joins the rejected explanation for the practice of polyandry.

However, considerable excess of males over females is favourable to polyandry (Iyer, 1961 : 140).

No available literature on the Kota gives any clue that they ever practised female infanticide. As far the Kota themselves, the practice is repugnant and one of their major arguments with which they claim superiority over their Toda neighbours is that the Toda were practising female infanticide. As regards the proportion between the sexes in the Kota population, it has been actually the women who mostly outnumbered men, as can be seen from the census figures, some of which are given below :

Year of Census	Males	Females	Total
1901	582	685	1267
1911	547	616	1163
1921	563	641	1204
1931	562	559	1121

Conclusion

The Kota society, as I have discussed in the foregoing passages does not greatly correspond with the writings of Mandelbaum. Instead, the practice (polyandry) is alluded to with disgust and contempt by the Kota. Notable amongst the features of their society which stand in the testimony to the absence of what Mandelbaum calls "the principle of fraternal equivalence" are (1) a man's sexual indulgence with his brother's wife being treated as an act of adultery ; (2) the oft-repeated practice of elopement marriages with brother's wives ; (3) mode of inheritance, and fragmentation of lands between brothers and the absence of joint families, and (4) non-preference of sororate and levirate marriages and their rare occurrences. The Kota society appears also to be inconducive to be a polyandrous on for reasons such as (1) significant contribution of women to the subsistence of the family and the realization of men of their economic importance ; (2) females outnumbering males in their relative strength ; (3) desire to multiply their population, and (4) presence of a good number of widows living in independent households.

To sum up, a few polyandrous traits are today scantily and vaguely seen in some of their practices, which are also fast fading out, as can be judged from the way the Kota repudiate them. On the one hand, their society is seen wanting in fraternal equivalence and solidarity, and on the other, its structure and function show no sign to be conducive to be polyandrous.

NOTES

1. I am very fortunate in getting the comments on this paper from Dr. Surajit Sinha for which I am indebted to him. I wish to express my gratitude to my colleagues of the South India Station of the Anthropological Survey of India, Mysore, for reading an earlier version of the paper and offering criticisms and suggestions.
2. The population figures were collected in one of my field trips to all the Kota villages from December, 1960 to February, 1961.
3. My data are confined mainly to Trichagadi, the biggest of the seven Kota villages. It has a population of 252. The data presented in this paper are, in part, the outcome of my field work between February and June 1965 for an ethnographic study of the Kota, sponsored by the Anthropological Survey of India.
4. "When sexual intercourse takes place outside of marriage between two persons of whom atleast one is married to another person, it is called adultery". (Murdock, 1960 : 261).
5. The Kota cremate the dead. In each village, a bone from each dead body is preserved to be burried collectively. The ceremony of burying the bones is called *var thav* (dry funeral), and is celebrated more like a festival.
6. The Kota eat buffalo flesh and therefore the Badaga consider them as unclean. Besides, as I have elsewhere (1966) discussed, the Badaga patronise the Kurumba in order to appease them, as they are themselves dreadful of the Kurumba sorcery.
7. 4,840 square yards make an acre.

REFERENCES

Berreman, D. Gerald. 1962 Pahari Polyandry : A Comparison, *Amer. Antrop.* vol. 64

——1963 *Hindus of the Himalayas*, Bombay.

Fuch, Stephon 1963 *The Origin of Man and His Culture*, Bombay.

Iyer, L.A. Krishna and Balaratanam, L.K. (Ed.) 1961 *Anthropology in India*, Bombay.

Kapadia, K.M. 1959 *Marriage and Family in India*, Bombay.

Leach, E.R. 1955 Polyandry, inheritance and definition of Marriage, *Man*, vol. 55

Lowie, H. Robert 1920 *Primitive Society*, London.

——1961 *Social Organisation*, London.

Majumdar, D.N. (Ed.) 1955 *Rural Profiles.*

——1962 *Himalayan Polyandry*, London.

Mandelbaum, G. David 1938 Polyandry in Kota Society, *Amer. Anthrop*, vol. 40.

Murdock, George Peter 1960 *Social Structure*, New York.

Piddington, Ralph 1960 *Introduction to Social Anthropology*, London.

Prince Peter (HRH) 1955 Polyandry and the kinship group, *Man*, vol. 55.

—1963 *A Study of Polyandry*, The Hague.

—1965 A Study of Polyandry—Book Review, *Cur. Anthrop.*, vol. 6.

Radcliff-Brown, A.R. and Daryll, Forde (Ed.) 1960 *African System of Kinship and Marriage*, London.

Saksena, R.N. 1955 *Social Economy of a Polyandrous People*, Agra.

Thurston, Edgar 1909 *Castes and Tribes of Southern India*, vol. IV (Kota), Madras

Varghese, I. 1966 The Kota : their dreaded life of Kurumba sorcery, *Bulletin of the West Bengal Cultural Research Institute*, No. 1 & 2.

Westermarch, Edward 1903 *The History of Human Marriage*, London.

Census of India, Reports 1901, 1911, 1921 & 1931.

PART FOUR

POLYANDRY IN THE EAST AND NORTH EAST INDIA

15

A NOTE ON POLYANDRY AMONG THE GALLONG : AN ANALYTICAL APPRAISAL

BIMAN KUMAR DAS GUPTA

In the eastern part of India, the Bhot of Sikkim (Prince Peter, 1962 ; Das Gupta, 1964), Gallong of Arunachal Pradesh (Srivastava, 1962 ; Lal and Das Gupta, 1979) and Lhota Naga of Nagaland (Mills, 1922) are said to be practising polyandry. The Gallong who inhabit the lower regions of the Siang district of Arunachal are known to be a polyandrous community who allow the brothers to have access to the wife/wives of other married brother(s). They are, however, surrounded by other tribal groups such as the Minyong, the Tai, the Bori, the Boker, and the Ramo who do not favour polyandrous union.

One characteristic concomitant of Gallong marriage is the heavy bride-price. One has to give 2, 3, or 4 mithuns and a number of *tadok* (costly bead necklace) to get a fairly beautiful bride. For more beautiful brides, the price may shoot up more. A beautiful girl is an asset to the family and may bring prosperity to her father. The young boys while meeting one another express their liking for one girl or the other. Then often jokingly a boy would tell, "I shall give two mithuns for her", while the other would retorts, "I shall give four". A Gallong belle is, therefore, more a commodity and in the system of exchange, she is received in exchange of mithuns and *tadok*. Once she is purchased by family. She is accessible to all uterine brothers because (1) she becomes a property of the family, and (2) many such brides cannot be purchased for all the brothers individually as that would mean unimaginable expenditure. Side by side, a Gallong marriage ritual continues for 2,3 years during which period a number of visits is paid and loads of exchanges of fish, utensils and liquor are made before the girl is brought in the family. There is also the allotment of gift for mediator, initiator, agnatic and affinal kins and so on (Lal and Das Gupta, 1979). And it is obvious that polyandry would persist in the background of such expensive set of rituals, high bride price and elaborate exchange of gift. Society, therefore, has deemed it necessary to allow brothers to have access to the wife of another brother.

Apart from the bride-price and enduring rituals, the other factor which helps polyandry to thrive is the shortage of marriageable girls. When a survey of a few Gallong villages was made, the percentage of females in relation to total population was seen to be around 52% which means that there should be no dearth of brides. In a community where the number of women is more, polyandry will naturally rouse demographic imbalance. But then how it is matched. It has been observed that the Gallong society allows polygyny also. The *mirem* (rich) folk who can afford to purchase more girls do so and thus polygyny acts as a safety valve and helps the marriageable girls, who would otherwise be left idle, to get exchanged and lead a conjugal life. In one particular village where only three cases of polyandry have existed, twelve polygynous marriages have been noted. Thus in the Gallong society the richer people are considered rich not only by the possession of more cash, more mithuns and more beads but also by being the husband of a number of girls. Girls, therefore, are marker of richness after marriage and an asset before marriage.

People themselves see polyandry as a norm, as a social prescription. But it is strictly restricted amongst the uterine brothers and no cousin is allowed access. That way a Gallong wife is chaste in the family of uterine brothers. Srivastava (1962), however, notes that even clan members (i.e.

members belonging to the husband's clan) are allowed. But this seems to be too romanticising the whole issue. The fact remains that a Gallong bride is for all the brothers of the husband to whom she is married. Marriage of a Gallong girl is always with one brother. At no stage of the rituals other brothers are involved. This is true to all other groups mentioned as polyandrous by Peter (1963). The elders argue that logistically polyandry is beneficial to them. They being basically *jhum* cultivators get allotment of plots of land in the hills, falling within their village area, from the village headman. If all the brothers socially and emotionally cling together centering one wife, fission of arable land would not take place. Otherwise coming up of more nuclear families would naturally mean depletion of forest areas. Moreover, often one of the brothers with the wife may remain in the temporary house constructed in the *jhum* field and guard the crop or complete any incomplete part of agricultural operation. Since any brother can have access to the wife, this arrangement would cause inconvenience or commotion to none. It seems, therefore, rational that taking cognizance of all these factors the elders prescribed the adelphic type of polyandrous union for the healthy perpetuation of the community in the specific ecological locale. But their neighbours the Miniyong deprecate the custom and tell that since a Gallong bride is purchased, she is used in any way the family likes her to be treated. It is noteworthy that side by side, in any Gallong village a number of nuclear families based on monogamous marriage are also seen because whenever a family hoards some wealth sufficient enough to procure another bride or when any brother accumulates some money through subsidiary earnings from jobs or petty trading, another bride is purchased. In this case, the brother separates out from the natal family to start a new household. When a brother separates out if he has no separate source of earning, he may get a share of parental plot or may approach the village headman for a separate *jhum* plot. But even then the brothers of his natal family would accept him visiting their wife or he would not mind other brother(s) in the natal family visiting his wife in this new household. Though Piddington (1950) would refer 'many of the fraternal polyandry as forms of cicisbeism', infact it is this symbolism and sentiment of possessing common partner that acts as cohesive factor in a Gallong family. They are to struggle hard to earn more and hoard enough to acquire the potentiality of possessing a separate wife and even then won't mind sharing the same with other uterine brothers. The only reason to possess wife independently is, therefore, to get the status of a father because otherwise one who is ritually married will always enjoy the honour of paternity. It is this aspiration that is tending them to monogamy. In any polyandrous community, however, polyandry, polygyny and monogamy exist side by side.

As we analyse the kinship terms of the Gallong, we get some explict indications of polyandry. This is corroborated by the equations of the following kinship terms.

1. mother = father's elder brother's wife
   = father's younger brother's wife
2. wife = elder brother's wife
   = younger brother's wife
3. father = father's elder brother
   = father's younger brother

The Minyong who are the neighbour of Gallong, do not follow these equations. The above procedure of clubbing together a category of kins and designating them by one term do exemplify that polyandry is still an accepted norm in their mind.

We have noted earlier that in one village only three cases exist where the uterine brothers are bound together by polyandrous ties. There have been many instances where the brothers on becoming economically better off have procured another bride and have established separate household. Whatever that might be, whether the brothers are independently married or not they have access to the wives of elder or younger brother. But the children born to the wife will always go to the elder brother or the brother to whom the wife is married. Thus the observation made by Berreman (1962) in respect of a non-polyandrous tribal group in north-western Himalayas that the brothers 'share the wife's sexuality and not the reproductivity' holds true in Gallong and probably the same may be said in respect of all other polyandrous communities of the world. Among the Gallong, polyandry as the only prescriptive system of marriage is not to be found. Chandra (1983) reminds us that even in the north-western Himalayan polyandrous societies of the Kinner and Sirumese, polyandrous unions go by 28% and 8% respectively while monogamous and polygynous marriages exist side by side. Thus considering all these factors, it seems probable that bride-price, specific economic system and economic condition have combined together in the persistence of polyandry in the symbolic system of the Gallong. But due to the absence of any obligatory principles shift to monogamy or polygyny is possible. In present days, polyandry is not often adhered to as better education, job opportunities, shift of residence pattern often make the younger generation to avoid polyandry. Yet there has not been any out burst or effort to do away with it.

To sum up the content of the Gallong polyandry, we must assert that qualitatively the Gallong are polyandrous because polyandry is in their symbolic order. Though there is no pressure of norm to pursue polyandry, yet the respect for norm has helped them to retain it in their symbolic system. Even in their polyandrous system they have got a very high sense of chastity to be preserved within the family of uterine brothers. To the Gallong, a girl is a commodity and a bride is an asset and often a marker of affluence. The people, of course, suggest that the polyandry is suited to their geographical set up and to their economy. The present day tendency to go for polygyny or monogamy is probably to acquire the prestige of fatherhood which under polyandrous situation becomes the monopoly of one brother, usually the eldest.

ACKNOWLEDGEMENT

I am thankful to Dr. Ranajit Kumar Saha for his useful suggestion while this paper was under preparation.

REFERENCES

Berreman, G.D. 1962 'Pahari Polyandry; A Comparison *American Anthropologist*, vol. 64 : 1.

Chandra Ramesh 1983 'Marriage forms in north-western India in the perspective of evolution'. Paper presented in the seminar on 'Marriage practices in India' held under the auspices of Anthropological Survey of India at Nagpur in February, 1983.

Das Gupta, Biman Kumar 1964 'A Report on the Reconnoitre Survey in Sikkim'. Report submitted to Anthropological Survey of India (unpublished).

Lal, P.N. and Das Gnpta Biman Kumar 1979 *Lower Siang People* Memoir no 50 Published by Anthropological Survey of India, Calcutta.

Mills, J.P. 1922 *The Lhota Naga,* London.

Peter, Prince of Grece 1963 *The Study of Polyandry* Mouton and Company, The Hague

Piddington, Ralph 1950 An Introduction to Social Anthropology, vol-I.

Srivastava, L.R.N. 1962 *The Gallong,* Published by NEFA Secretariat, Shillong.

Vergheese, I 1968 Polyandry in Kota Society: An Appraisal *Journal Indian Anth, Society* vol 3, nos. 1 & 2 (combined) Calcutta.

16

THE SO-CALLED POLYANDRY AMONG THE GALLONGS*

NIRANJAN SARKAR

All societies have faced the problem of evolving some mode of control on the sexual impulse of the individual members. Because the uncontrolled sex drive, next probably to hunger and thirst, has the potentiality of wrecking the cooperative nature of the inter-personal relationship of its members upon which thrives the social life. The reckless competitions over sexual favours and the resultant strain may destroy the numerous inter-personal bonds which go in the making of the human association. But no society can carry such regulation too far. Because a society has to grant sufficient means of sexual gratification for reproduction and thus to prevent population decline. So all societies have solved this problem by some combination of incest, exogamy, endogamy, prohibited and preferential types of mating.

It is intended to examine here the nature of the mechanism of social regulation of sex among the Gallongs of Arunachal Pradesh.

---

*Reproduced by permission of the authority of Man in India from *Man in India* 53(2) : 128-134, 1973.

The institution of marriage plays a major role in the regulation of the sex impulse among the Gallongs. The parents arrange the marriage of their sons and daughters. The boy's father has to pay bride-wealth of several *mithuns* (*Bos fronialis*), cows and brass bowls to the bride's father. So only the very few rich parents can arrange the marriage of all the sons without much difficulty. But it is otherwise among most of the families. The marriage of the first or at best the second son can be arranged in time. But it becomes delayed for others till the bride-wealth is arranged. This is done in two ways. In one, the bride-wealth, received in the marriage of daughter, is used by the parents to arrange the marriage of another son. In the other, the parents have to arrange the bride-wealth by purchase.

It is observed that in many families there are adult sons whose marriages have yet to be arranged due to lack of resources. And here is a social situation where the lack of any outlet for sexual gratification at an explosive age may pose a problem to their social life. The Gallongs have tackled this problem by permitting the unmarried younger brothers sexual access to the elder brother's wife. This same permissive sexual access has been extended in the reverse direction also. It means when any of his younger brothers marries, the elder brother also has the permissive sexual access to the younger brother's wife. This extension is probably granted to ensure that the latent jealousy that the elder brother entertains against his younger brothers for having sexual access to his wife does not come to the surface and thereby makes this arrangement vulnerable. If we consider some aspects of their social life, it become clear why they opted for this mechanism.

Formerly the Gallongs used to generally live in single-clan villages. Their land tenure and the myths show that their migration was based on clan-basis. The village used to be known after the clan founding it, and the proprietorship of the whole area of the village would vest on the members of that clan only. The girls and boys of the village belonged to the same clan. So the incest rule and clan exogamy would not permit any sexual relation between them. It is believed that such a relation would bring supernatural punishment not only on the offenders but on the whole village and the clan.

Even if there are a few families belonging to other clans in the village, as is found to be the case in many villages now-a-days, this social problem remains unsolved. It is true that premarital sexual relation between the boys and girls of different clans does not infringe the laws of incest and clan exogamy. But such a relationship brings another difficulty in its train. If such a relationship is discovered, the aggrieved parents of the girl brings the case before the *kebang* i.e., the council of elders. The *kebang* imposes in such a case, the customary fine of a *mithun* which the seducer has to pay to the aggrieved party. A family can ill-afford such a luxury on the part of the sons as then the livestock gets depleted and the chance of arranging marriage for the still unmarried sons gets further delayed. Sexual relation with the married women of these families is held adulterous and it also invites the same penalty as in the previous case.

Slavery was in practice among them before the establishment of formal administration in their area. Sexual relation between the members of the master's families and the slaves was regarded as a heinous crime. If such a relationship was discovered, the guilty slave was killed and the member of the master's family was ostracised. If a free man had sexual relationship with a slave woman of another master, the free man would be compelled to pay heavy fine to the aggrieved master and then he would be expelled from the village.

So the only group of women, with whom they could think of having sexual relation, was the wives of the members of the same clan. The wives of clan-brothers are from other clans and have come to this villages after marriage. Neither the incest rule nor the clan-exogamy would be a bar in permitting sexual relationship with them. Srivastava writes in the chapter on types of marriages :

> 'Polyandry is the most prevalent form of marriage...most important factor leading to the prevalence of polyandry is, perhaps, the economic pressure on the family. The prohibitive amount of bride-wealth does not permit each

individual to have a wife for himself. Generally, the eldest brother is married to a girl and the amount of bride-wealth is given jointly by the family. As the economic condition of an average family is not always sound, the family may not allow the remaining brothers to bring wives, but they are allowed sex rights over the woman brought by the eldest brother. The woman is duty-bound to allow all the brothers access to her. As an extension of the custom, even the members of the clan of the husband have been granted sex right over the woman by the society, but the wishes of the woman are often honoured. If she is averse to a particular person, he, in that case, cannot insist on intercourse' (Srivastava, 1962 : 74).

So the only safe course available to a Gallong family, was to permit the unmarried sons sexual access to the wife of the son already married. Such an arrangement, being within the family, would be easier to regulate. It would also ensure the solidarity of the sibling group.

Such a relationship between a woman and more than one man may be either polyandry or cicisbeism. If these associating men are brothers, it is called either adelphic polyandry or fraternal cicisbeism. Polyandry is 'the marriage of one woman to more than one man' (Prince Peter, 1969). But if there is no marriage, a group of men living with one woman, having sexual relations with her and even procreating children, cannot, strictly speaking, be considered polyandrous. For this reasons, I shall reserve the term *cicisbeism* (from the 18th century Italian *cicisbel*, a *cavaliere servante* or attendant lovery for such an arrangement between the sexes, wherein one or more of the male partners is not relaled to the woman in marriage, each of the men involved in this way to be known as *cicisbeo*, and not as a husband, (ibid : 21-22). According to the Notes and Queries of Anthropology, cicisbeism is a more or less permanent union of a woman with one or more men without giving them the full status of consort (1951 : 118). So while polyandry is a particular form of the marital institution, cicisbeism is not. So it becomes essential to understand what type of institution marriage is.

The Notes and Queries definition of marriage is : "Marriage is a union between a man and a woman such that children born to the woman are the recognized legitimate offspring of both partners". (1951 : 110)

Murdock writes of marriage as "a complex of customs centering upon the relationship between a sexually associating pair of adults within the family" (1949 : 1). In the spectrum of such a relationship he mentions four functions fundamental to human social life—the sexual, the economic, the reproductive and the educational, without provision for the first and third, society would become extinct, for the second, life itself would cease ; for the fourth, culture would come to an end...(ibid : 10).

Leach is of the view that,

'The institutions commonly classed as marriage are concerned with the allocation of a number of distinguishable classes of rights. In particular a marriage may serve :

A. To establish the legal father of a woman's children.
B. To establish the legal mother of a man's children.
C. To give the husband a monopoly in the wife's sexuality.
D. To give the wife a monopoly in the husband's sexuality.
E. To give the husband partial or monopolistic rights to the wife's domestic and other labour services.
F. To give the wife partial or monopolistic rights to the husband's labour services.
G. To give the husband partial or total rights over property belonging or potentially accruing to the wife.
H. To give the wife partial or total rights over property belonging or potentially accruing to the husband.
I. To establish a joint fund of property—a partnership—for the benefit of the children of the marriage.
J. To establish a socially significant 'relationship of affinity' between the husband and his wife's brothers (Leach, 1961 : 107-108).

According to Prince Peter's definition,

> "marriage is the union between man and woman in the form recognized by their society entitling them individually to the specific kinship status of husband and wife, jointly to that of spouses with reciprocal rights and obligations, and to the procreation of legitimate children within the union" (1963 : 23).

If needs to be stressed here that though economic pressure of bride-wealth among the Gallongs may not allow all the brothers to get married, but each family tries to get all the sons married. In fact the rich families get all the sons married.

Among the Gallongs, the sexual intercourse between the wife and husband is obligatory but that between a woman and her husband's brother is only permissive. She is expected by the society to allow sexual access to her husband's brothers. But she may at times express her unwillingness to have a sexual union with a husband's brother, which choice she cannot exercise when her husband is involved.

Even Srivastava states,

> "...Though the polyandrous custom of society does not maintain much difference between a father and his brothers, yet we find here separate kinship terms used for them... . The term for father is used for him only, no matter that he is in fact a sociological father. The brothers of father are termed differently, and even distinction is made between the elder and younger... (1962 : 62-63).

The relationship of affinity between the wife's paternal family and her husband is close, while the relationship between the wife's paternal family and her husband's brother is just the extension of the previous relationship.

> "Sociological parenthood is more important than the biological one and, as a matter of fact, the latter has no specific value. As all the brothers live together and have access to all the wives, nobody knows by whom the child has

been begotten. The brother, who performed the ceremonies of marriage, is recognized as the child's father" (ibid : 62).

In another place, he states, "Apart from having sex relations with the women, the other brothers or the clan members have no right over the children born to her' (ibid : 75).

The responsibility of nursing, tending and rearing the child to physical and social maturity squarely rests on the woman and that brother who has under gone through the process of the wedding ceremonies with her. And the descent of the child is always traced from this brother.

When all the brothers are under the parental roof, the economic interest and for that matter the economic activities of one brother and his wife may not be very different from those of the whole household. But when a brother and his wife establish a separate household, the whole gamut of their economic cooperation, based upon a division of labour by sex, comes into effect and their family is sustained by their joint economic endeavours. The children inherit the property—inherited as well as acquired—of the mother and the father and not that of the father's brothers.

So it is seen that all the mates of a woman, even if they are brothers, are by no means on a par ; and the one, who actually marries her and goes through the wedding ceremonies, can legitimately be regarded as the husband. Monogamy with fraternal cicisbeism i.e., socially sanctioned cohabitation by the wife with the husband's brothers is the correct description of the observed social facts.

REFERENCES

Leach. E.R. 1961 *Rethinking Anthropology*, London.
Murdock, G.P. 1949 *Social Structure*, New York
Prince Peter, H.R.H. 1963 *A Study of Polyandry*, The Hague.
Srivastava, L.R.N. 1962 *The Gallongs*, Shillong

17

POLYANDRY AMONG THE LEPCHAS OF SIKKIM : A DEAD OR DYING INSTITUTION

SAMIT GHOSAL

The institution of polyandry as a marital form, vis-a-vis, the *Notes and Queries*' definition of marriage (p. 110), initiated a great deal of scholastic arguments both on the definition of marriage itself as well as on the defining elements of polyandry. Since we assume polyandry as a form of marriage and the *Notes and Queries*' definition on marriage has been found inadequate and subjected to severe criticism, it is of prime importance to find out a workable definition of marriage before proceeding to the scientific exploration of the institution of polyandry as a marriage form.

Among the vast number of definitions available in Anthropological literature, the definition of marriage offered by Gough appears to be very much provocative, which states,

> "Marriage is a relationship established between *a woman* (italics mine) and one or more other persons, which provides that a child born to the woman under circumstances not prohibited by the rules of the relationship, is accorded full birth-status rights common to normal members of his society or social stratum" (1959 : 32).

Here she most cunningly accommodates the matrilineal Nayar type polyandry as well as the true fraternal type, even it also brings within the definition such unusual types like 'woman to woman marriage' among the Nuar (Evans-pritchard, 1951 : 108). The only lacuna in the definition is its consideration of 'a woman', since it can not explain the 'polygynandrous' union in Jaunsar Bawar, which is some sort of a combination of polygyny and polyandry, where the existence of more than one woman is evident (Majumdar, 1960 : 72).

To me, formulating the definition of polyandry based on a single criterion is like balancing a pyramid on its point. Polyandry is reported to have distributed throughout the world and each and every one is different from the others in its uniqueness. It is worthy to have a definition of polyandry in empirical terms, in configurational or multifactorial fashion. This must allow for the possibility that in any one case not every element in the configuration will be present, and that every element present will not necessarily be there to the same degree. The proposed definition should be substantial rather than formal. The key concept of the polyandrous union is the socially sanctioned legalised sexual relation of a woman with a group of persons who are considered to be her husbands and to have legitimised the children born out of such relationship. The husbands should have joint responsibility for the well being of their wife and children. The union, at least at any one stage, must be accompanied by some form of ritualistic or religious ceremony which expresses the sanction of the group upon the union.

The misconception arises in Anthropology from the notion of husbandhood as an attribute of an individual. If we begin to think in the way that individuals are representing an institution, to my feelings, much of the above mentioned problem can be solved. In the polyandrous society fatherhood or husbandship is a social relationship rather than a biological one. Each individual husband is same in 'representant' level but different in 'representation' level so far wife's social relation is concerned.

With the lead provided by the above theoretical exercise

we would examine the nature of polyandry among the Lepchas of Sikkim. The Lepchas, a mongolian tribe of Sikkim, are believed to be the original inhabitant of Sikkim and neighbouring areas of West Bengal, Nepal and Bhutan. In Sikkim they are mainly concentrated in the Lepcha reserve of Zongu in North Sikkim. They are patrilocal, patrilineal people having exogamous clans.

The polyandry among the Lepchas of Sikkim is of adelphic or fraternal type, where the co-husbands are brothers. A woman is supposed to have but only one legal socially recognised husband and can acquire another only by divorce from or after the death of her previous husband. What the Lepcha polyandry amounts to is that the husband's fraternal brothers have free sexual access to elder brother's wife, even if they did not participate in the wedding. The brothers may be called as "secondary husbands" (Mandelbaum, 1938 : 574).

Although any one of a man's brothers may be the biological father of his wife's child, only the husband is recognised as the sociological father. A woman lives only in the house of her legal husband and he is recognised as the father of the children she bears. The younger brothers jointly share the sexual rights of the elder brother's wife. This type of plural mating was called "polykoity" by Fischer (1952). In adelphic polyandry "the woman does not contract different successive marriage. There are no reasons for this, since the social position of her children is guaranteed completely by the fact that she is married" (cf. Fischer, 1952 : 114, as quoted in Leach, 1955). Among the Lepchas a man may have more than one wife and so the Lepcha nuptial system includes true polyandry as well as polygyny, which is called 'polygynandry' by Majumdar (1962). But polygynandrous union or family is very rare among the Lepchas due to their poor economic condition and only wealthy and affluent families can afford an additional wife. The character of the Lepcha polyandry in Sikkim can be stated in Leach's words as, "it is clear that two separate rights are distinguished. Firstly, there is the right in the wife's sexuality which marriage serves to vast partly, but not completely, in their person of the first husband.

The sexual rights of the other husbands are exercised, not by virtue of the marriage, but through the individual consent of the first husband and the joint wife. On the other hand, the ritual of patrilocal marriage—the essence of which is that a man conducts his bride from her father's house to his own—serves to establish a relation of affinity between the wife's family as a whole and the husband's family as a whole. The wife's family has no interest in what sexual arrangements pertain unless it is proposed to extend the rights of sexual access beyond the limits of the husband's sibling group (1955 : 185).

Gorer writes on the Lepcha polyandry,

> "it is permissible for a man who feels himself unable to cope with his field work, either on account of physical weakness or because he has other work which takes him a great deal from the neighbourhood, to invite an unmarried younger brother to live with him and to share his fields and wife. The co-husband is co-opted without any sort of ceremony, but thereafter he is no longer free in the choice of a wife of his own; if he desires one he must make the request for a wife of the same *ptse* as the shared wife, exactly as if he was taking a second wife in the normal course of events. The co-husbands sleep with their common wife on alternate nights, but all the children are presumed to be begotton by the first husband, and he alone has to observe the pre-natal precautions" (1938 : 171).

To become a *lama* is considered a most desirable achievement for a Lepcha. The monastic training required to be a *lama* has several stages including compulsory staying in the *gompa*. A *lama* may enter married life but his increasing involvement in catering the needs of the people as a religious specialist and commitments towards the *gompa* force his prolonged absence from family life and home. If he does not have a brother to look after his field and his family, he will face grave economic crisis. Polyandry is one of the means best suited to cope-up such a situation. In actual practice the husband who always stays in the house, carried on the matrimonial life. Nakane's observation on two actual cases of polyandry reveals that polyandrous brothers do not share the wife in the same way in terms of the relationship between husband and wife. In the first case three polyandrous brothers shared a common wife, where one was a monk studying in Tibet, another was a trader mostly absent from home and the eldest brother actually lived with the mutual wife. In the second case, where two brothers shared a wife, the elder brother was a devout *lama*, his younger brother was a peasant and actually lived with their wife (1966 : 242).

I personally came across a case where two brothers were sharing one common wife. She was married to the elder brother. The younger brother was not in a position to afford another bride-price and the wife was being shared with the elder brother as against his service in cultivation.

As regarding the persistence of polyandry as well as its genesis, the general notion among the Lepchas of Sikkim that it was an effective custom to keep the property undivided. Similar views were expressed by Aiyappan (1935), Barreman (1962) and Leach (1955). Westermarck writes, "A widely cited economic advantage of fraternal polyandry is that it keeps family property, especially lands, intact in a patrilineal, patrilocal group" (1922 : 185f). Moreover, a wife of two brothers in possession of a joint property can expect a higher standard of living than the wife of a man with only one share of his paternal property, she will enjoy the advantages of a comparatively young husband. Though it is not uncommon that a young brother who had joined in a polyandrous union later establishes a separate household and takes another wife. Usually this is done amicably by the mutual agreement among the brothers. In most of the cases the cause of dissolution of polyandrous unions were due to disagreement in economic matter but never on jealousy over the sexuality of the wife. For the Lepches of Sikkim sexual activity is devoid of any emotion or aesthetic consideration, and as same as food and drink, and like food and drink it does not matter from whom you receive it, so long you receive it.

Gorer (1938 : 160) traced some sort of analogous relationship existing between polyandry and the customs of levirate and sororate. It is customary among the Lepchas that a man can inherit the wives of his elder brother and all the younger sisters of his wife but not the vice-versa. A man can also have permissible sexual relations with the above mentioned relatives. But in no circumstances can the formal wife of a younger brother be shared by his elder brother. Gorer states,

> "with the wives of their real elder brothers the Lepchas have in theory a right to use force; if they will not copulate willingly, the younger brothers are considered to have contributed to the marriage price of the bride and therefore to have, as it were, a legal right. In point of fact, such a use of force never arises, the Lepcha women know that their husband's younger brothers have the right to access" (ibid).

The Lepcha kinship terms for collaterals are also collaborating the above hypothesis. The terms for father's brother 'elder' and 'younger'—are employed no doubt to distinguish father from them only by prefixation. The etymological meanings of these terms suggest that father's brothers are also fathers who are, however, distinguished from one another on the basis of age difference. In mutual behaviour both father's elder and younger brothers are to be treated on a par with father.

Inevitably the polyandry in Sikkim, as it is in everywhere throughout the Cis and Trance Himalayas, had long seen its prime days. Due to the acculturation of alien ideas and values from the plains the institution of polyandry has become inept now-a-days. It has also lost much of its institutional settings and condition of genesis in which in was operative. Some of its objectives were replaced by the forces of modernity. One of the reasons for the persistence of polyandry was that they had to put an effort to check the population growth and thus avoiding rapid increase of the potential claimants to the household property, fragmentation of joint labour and above all, pressure on land. Now various job opportunities made possible the pressure on land reduced at a minimal level and solved the problem of economic stringency to some extent. The role of polyandry as a controlling mechanism for population growth has partly replaced by the prolonged period of lactation. The growing urge for individual property has ushered out the principle of equivalence of brothers. Berreman (1962 : 68) opined that there is a gross correlation between polyandry and a shortage of women, and monandry and a surplus of women. There might have been a shortage of women when the Lepchas were in hunting gathering stage long ago. Because hunting economy always discourages the growth of female folk. Presently as an agricultural population there is hardly any imbalance in the sex ratio of the Lepchas of Sikkim. There is 956 females per 1000 males in Zongu, North Sikkim. Again to become a *lama* is not that much prestigious as it was earlier because religion itself has lost much of its significance as a controlling mechanism. Another methodological problem is to identify the polyandrous family. As a rule monogamy has prevailed at first, the second husband is incorporated at a later period quite informally without any ritual, on the basis of mutual understanding because the system is looked down upon by the neighbouring Nepalis who are monogamous people, and the co-husbands find it too much embarrassing to publicly acknowledge the polyandrous relationship. One has to depend completely on guessing by studying the behaviour of the woman with her husband's brothers outside the house, mostly at fields or in market and on the secondary sources of information from the neighbours.

Again it is not uncommon among the Lepchas that an adult unmarried younger brother, living under the same roof, will share the sexuality of his elder brother's wife without sharing any responsibility towards her. But a polyandrous system means more than a sexual liaison, there should be a definite system and understanding between the co-husbands regarding economic cooperation and joint responsibility as member of a single corporate unit. Though the system of polyandry is breaking and the Lepchas have more or less become monogamous, it is permissible for a younger brother to sleep with his elder brother's wife during his absence until he gets married. This sort of an affair can be called cicisbeism and hardly a marriage. Cicisbeism, which grants legitimate sexual access of two or more men to the same woman coterminously is not polyandry, because it does not confer on cicisbeo the possibility of being recognized as the pater of any of the children the woman bears.

REFERENCES

Aiyappan, A. 1935 Fraternal Polyandry in Malabar. *Man-in-India.* 14 : 108-18.

Berreman, G.D. 1962 Pahari Polyandry : A Comparison. *American Anthropologist.* 64 (1) : 60-74.

Evans-Pritchard, E.E. 1951 *Kinship and Marriage among the Nuar.* London : Oxford.

Gorer, Geoffrey 1938 *Himalayan Village.* London : Thomas Nelson.

Gough, E. Kathleen 1959 The Nayars and the definition of Marriage. *The Journal of the Royal Anth. Inst.* 89(1) : 22-34.

Leach, E.R. 1955 'Polyandry Inheritance and the definition of Marriage'. *Man.* 55 (199) : 182-85.

Majumdar, D.N. 1960 *Himalayan Polyandry.* London : Asia Publishing House.

Mandelbaum, D.G. 1938 'Polyandry in Kota Society'. *American Anthropologist.* 40(4) : 574-83.

Nakane, Chie 1966 'A plural Society in Sikkim'. In C. Von Furer-Heimendorf (ed.). *Caste and kin in Nepal, India and Ceylon.* Bombay. Asia Publishing House.

Routledge and Kegan Paul 1951 *Notes and Queries on Anthropology.* London (6th edition).

Westermark, Edward 1922 *The History of Human Marriage.* vol. III. New York : Allerton Book Company.

PART FIVE

POLYANDRY IN INDIA : SPECIAL ISSUES

18

POLYANDRY IN ANCIENT INDIAN SOCIETY

PALASH CHANDRA COOMAR
MANIS KUMAR RAHA

The polyandry in modern India was studied by some eminent scholars like, W.H.R. Rivers (1906), S.C. Das (1893), A. Aiyappan (1932, 1935), K.P. Chattopadhyay (1957), K. Gough (1959), Furer-Haimendrof (1964, 1966), G.D. Berreman (1962, 1975), D.G. Mandelbaum (1938), Prince Peter (1955, 1963), K.M. Panikkar (1918) and D.N. Majumdar (1955, 1963) and many others. Many of them carried out their studies among specific polyandrous societies of a particular area and thereby studied polyandry of that society. But researchers such as S.D. Singh (1978), K.M. Kapadia (1984), Iravati Karve (1965), John Muir (1877), D.P. Vora (1959) and a few others threw light on this particular type of institution as practised in ancient India. The ancient literary evidences clearly indicate the prevalence of polyandry in both *Vedic* and post-*Vedic* periods. The present paper in brief concerns with the past history of polyandry as prevalent in ancient India.

There is controversy among the scholars about the existence of polyandry in ancient India, particularly during the *Vedic* period. The later *Vedic* texts also give references about the opposition to the practice of polyandry. The *Aitareya Brahmana* (800 B.C.) declares that a man may have several wives, "but one wife has not many husbands at the same time" (cf.

Singh, 1978 : 69). Some asserted that the same was non-existent in that period. MacDonnel and Keith's view was that polyandry was never a *Vedic* institution, as according to them, no Vedic literature had given clear indication of the presence of this institution (1912 : 115-116). Almost same is the view of Meyer (1930 : 115). Upadhyay also concedes to the idea that polyandry could be a pre-*Rg Vedic* custom but became defunct during the *Rg Vedic* period (1974 : 124). Kane also could not locate a single *Vedic* passage which clearly referred to the practice of polyandry (1974 : 554). Altekar believes that this custom was "practically unknown to Hindu society" of the olden days (1973 : 112). While Horner opines that "the custom did not obtain at the time of the rise of Buddhism" (1930 : 40), Jayal thinks that polyandry of Draupadi is an isolated "single case" (1966 : 95-96).

But inspite of the denial of the existence of polyandry in ancient India by the above scholars, it can forcefully be said that during the *Rg Vedic* era, polyandry was known similar to the gods and men. Many ancient literatures like the *Vedas*, the *Sutras*, the *Smritis*, the *Mahabharata*, the *Ramayana*, the *Kamasutra*, the Buddhist as well as Jaina texts etc., all have given evidences of the incidences of polyandry in ancient India. Polyandry in one form or the other was no doubt in practice from Tibet in the north to Sri Lanka in the south in ancient times. And it is still in existence in Tibet, many Himalayan regions, some parts of south India and also in Sri Lanka. Polyandry among different ethnic groups living there presents different patterns and has different origins and developments.

The *Rg Veda* has highlighted the existence of polyandry in that period by giving examples of the twin Asvins the *Rg Vedic* gods, who won Surya, the daughter of sun-god who accepted her as her husbands and shared a common bed. It is significant that the text finds no fault with the conduct of persons practising polyandry. There is not a single word of expostulation or condemnation possibly because this kind of behaviour was expected and accepted in that society. This custom was not viewed with disapproval.

The *Rg Veda* also refers to the case of Maruts and their wife Rodasi,

> "who with her hair dishevelled and in mind fixed on her lords, woos them to unite with her, like Surya, mounting the chariot of the twin Asvins. And the bright Maruts cling to their young wife, who be longs to them all" (Singh, 1978 : 48-49).

In fact the *Rg Veda* refers more than once to Rodasi as the common wife of the Maruts. Besides the divinities like the twin Asvins and Surya and the Maruts and Rodasi, the Visva-devas were also involved in the institution of polyandry. Hence at least in some cases gods too could innocently be described as polyandrous, like some human groups. Besides the existence of polyandry among the divine races the practice of polyandry as custom was in existence in the early Aryan society.

Infact the ancient *rishis* found nothing unusual and improper in the idea of two persons sharing a common wife and 'tracing their ancestry to such a union' (Singh, 1978: 51).

> "The plural "husbands'' actually occur at a number of places in the *Vedas* and the *Sutras*, and the assertion that the expression is "simply generic" does not carry conviction." (*ibid*)

The system of *niyoga* or levirate was often considered as the substitute for polyandry. Some scholars think that it may be treated as an attenuated relic of polyandry (MeLennan, 1970 : 81-83, 90, 97 ; Briffault, 1927 : I : 681-682).

> "The appointed kinsman performs *niyoga* for restricted purpose of begetting a son. When a man's funeral rites are performed, the *didhisu* (wooer) the brother-in-law claims the widow as full wife for love, property and progeny". (ibid : 53-54)

No formal marriage ceremony was required for this kind of relationship ; it was taken for granted from the society. Sometime the brother-in-law became secondary husband during the lifetime of the departed brother. Polyandry was also thought to be practised by some migratory people or people preoccupied with war.

The *Atharva Veda* which has also given illustrations in regard to polyandry, supports the *Rg Vedic* belief that for every girl, Soma is her first husband, Gandharva the second, Agni the third, and the fourth one is the human being whom she actually marries. This mystical legend clearly indicates the practice of polyandry in that period. Some other passages also mention some more proofs of polyandry. One of such proofs has been given in one of the verses of the *Atharva Veda* when king Soma returned a Brahman his wife. The verses of the *Atharva Veda* clearly indicate that a woman at a time may have as many as ten husbands. "They must be contemporaries, so that it becomes essential for the brahmana to stress his suppressive primacy". (Singh, 1978 : 64)

The *Atharva Veda* is an important document which provides us enough evidences to prove the existence of polyandry among both the non-Aryans and the Aryans and was also among the Brahmans and the *rishi*. From the analysis of different passages inference may be drawn that during that period polyandry was unquestionably in existence.

The *Taittiriya Samhita* also refers like other *samhitas*, to "noble husbands" and four offspring in relation to single wife.

Thus all these evidences available in the ancient India clearly establish that polyandry is neither *non-Vedic* nor entirely non-Aryan. It may be thought that both before and after their arrival in India, the Aryans were "in the closest possible contact with populations among whom polyandry was an established social usage" (Briffault, 1927 : 1 : 698). Singh in his book *Polyandry in Ancient India* states that

> "But to nail polyandry down to the names of the non-Aryan, Tibetan or Dravidian tribes or castes to the exclusion of the Aryans would amount to falsification of history. They were also likewise polyandrous. This is also not correct to say that they did not know monogamy or polygyny. The trend was undeniably in the direction of monogamy as many passages testify ; and the *Atharva*

> *Veda* even compares a pair of human spouses to be inseperable *cakravakas*,..." (1978 : 69-70).

The Mahabharata and the Ramayana have given more evidences on polyandry in ancient India. The illustration in the *Mahabharata* and the *Ramayana* are more vivid and colourful. There we find the evidences of 'promiscuity and unregulation; of polyandry and polygyny; of group marriage and monogamy of celibacy and license ; and of *niyoga* at times almost indistinguishable from polyandry or cicisbeism' (Singh, 1978 : 76). In the period of the *Mahabharata* that both the Brahman and the Kshatriya caste people practised polyandry, remains unquestionable. The Brahman priests' approval for Draupadi's polyandry, though some Kshatriyas were against it, is also equally significant. Some Indologists are of opinion that the Pandavas belonged to a non-Aryan tribe because polyandry was found to be practised by some non-Aryan tribes till today. (Kapadia, 1984 : 55). To avoid conflict and discension among the brothers the five Pandavas accepted Draupadi as their common wife, Rishi Narada also advised them to accept Draupadi as their wife, after citing the example of Sunda and Upasunda, the demon brothers of yore who had fought for a woman.

The Pandavas belonged to such a group or tribe among whom intimacy between a woman and her brother-in-law was not considered unusual. This cultural trait was not unknown to *Vedic* Aryan. This closeness between a woman and her brother-in-law could not be indifferent from polyandry and hence could be viewed as a particular pattern of sexual behaviour. The same was in vogue among the Pandavas. Though the *Vedic* Aryan were involved in such intimacy, they had strong faith towards one husband for a wife system. Vasistha cited other type of marriage rule allowing the younger brother to handover his wife to the unmarried elder brother who, in turn, accepted the younger brother's wife as his own wife. The younger brother then with the permission of the elder brother, married her again. Even if the offer is considered as symbolic, a system that brothers used to share single wife may be thought as prevalent at that time. So when the elder brother first accepted the younger brother's wife, he was also considered to be her husband. The reference of polyandrous marriage of Varksi and Jatila Gautami is available in the early Indian texts. The *Mahabharata* gives evidence of polyandry through the story of Princess Madhavi, daughter of the King Yayati about whom Sarkar (1928) in his book *Some Aspects of the Earliest Social History in India (Pre-Buddhist Ages)* feels that

> "She was jointly the queen to four contemporary and neighbouring kings (viz., Haryasva of Ayodhya, Divorce of Varanasi, Usinara of the North-West, and Visvamitra of Kanyakubja . . . " (1928 : 155).

The *Adi Parva* of *Mahabharata* mentions that Brhaspati, younger brother of Ucathya, had a free and rightful access to Mamata, the wife of Ucathya. Brhaspati could indeed force himself upon her despite her physical condition or strong protest. Singh considers it a classic example of fraternal polyandry 'in which the legitimacy of the progeny is properly assured by Mamata's nuptial knot with the elder brother' (1978 : 58). Mamata never felt it as *adharma* as she was quite used to such a relationship. Her objection was for her physical condition, and not for any moral aversion. So this illustration indicates that this type of plural marriage was known during the time of Mahabharata. It is also significant that human society at that age never viewed it with disapproval and found no fault of the conduct of Brhaspati.

The Kauravas of *Mahabharata* were found to be accustomed to the custom of *niyoga*, a type not much different from polyandry. The family history of Pandavas discloses that Satyavati approached Bhisma, her step son, with a request to cohabit with the widow of his younger brother to beget a child which Bhisma rejected. He suggested his step mother to take help of the Brahmans to beget a child. When both Bhisma and Vyasa, the elder brothers of Vichitravirya were approached by Satyavati, their mother, to have progeny from their younger brother's widows namely Ambika, and Ambalika, Bhisma did not find any thing unusual about this offer. We also get evidence from the story of Dirghatamas that he was permitted to be the second husband of King Balin's wife which is very similar to polyandry. Therefore from these illustrations we can say that the elder brother might also have sex relation with the younger brother's wife. Pandu elsewhere spoke to the king Kalmasapada Saudasa who gave permission to his wife Madavanti to beget a child with the help of a stranger and Asmaka is the result of the union between queen Madavanti and Vasistha. Identically both Kunti and Madri adopted this system. Kunti had three sons and Madri obtained two sons through *niyoga* system but their husband Pandu would like to have more. Singh in this connection observes,

> "Kunti's case smacks as much of *niyoga* as of polyandry or cicisbeism, in as much as the *niyogas* are not confined to one person ; while Pandu still lives with his wives without renouncing his conjugal rights over them" (1978 : 131).

This type of conjugal relation was accepted only for the continuity of the line of descent. Possibly for this reason only a widow, who was either barren, in the post-childbearing age or very aged was deferred to resort to the system of *niyoga*. Indeed *niyoga* was popular and quite acceptable custom in the ancient India. It was a common usage of the past that a brother or any kinsmen or other person the wife of a childless man enables to conceive a child. Briffault regarded this *niyoga* as an "attenuated relic of polyandry" (1927 : 670). Singh also feels that, "*niyoga* thus becomes something similar to polyandry or remarriage in actual practice" (1978 : 132).

Illustration of polyandry is also available from *Ramayana*. Rama did not find the marriage of Sugriva with his deceased elder brother Bali's widow, Tara as unusual. Rather, he supported Sugriva. Both Bali and Sugriva shared Tara and Ruma as their common wives. The evidence helps us in thinking that the *vanaras* used to practise both fraternal as well as other types of polyandry. This view is also confirmed by Bali's willingness to easily accept Ravana's offer to share everything including their wives. This offer of Ravana, could no doubt be taken as which clearly points out the free and easy an indicator of polyandry practised by the Raksasas. Bibhisma likewise married Mandodari, the wife of his elder brother, Ravana. Briffault (1927 : 682-683) is of opinion that the marriages referred to in the *Ramayana* between Rama and Sita, Laksmana and Urmila and the two cousin brothers of Rama with the two cousins sisters of Sita is a kind of polyandrous group marriage, though this view is not widely accepted. Viradha suspected Rama and Laksmana to have shared Sita as their common wife when he saw them together in the forest. Sarkar also suspects that Sita was the common wife of Rama and Laksmana (1928 : 151). The conversation between Sita and Laksmana when latter was hesitant to leave the former in the forest, and go to the help of his elder brother Rama at her bidding is quite significant in this regard. Sita accused Laksmana that he liked to see Rama dead so that he might get Sita as his wife. It thus appears that Sita was familiar with both polyandry and brother-in-law marriage i.e. levirate. Rama also had knowledge about the practice of an elder brother's wife living with younger brothers. In the *Jataka* we see that Panchapapa, the wife of King Baka of Kasi, was also the wife of Pavarika and thus illustrates an example of non-fraternal polyandry. The *Jataka* tells us that a woman "may have husbands eight. . . yet on a ninth she sets her will" (cf. Singh, 1978 : 147). Kautilya's opinion in this context is that "no kind of marriage should be prohibited provided that it pleases all those who are concerned with it" (ibid : 148).

From some *Puranas* we have another type of polyandry. Matsya Puranas tells us the story of *Ahuki* who was given marriage to the princes of Avanti. As this type of marriage was not respectable in the past the practice was unexplained.

From *Kamasutra* we get evidences that polyandry of this type was persisted in certain parts of India. Vatsyayana refers to this custom popular in some countries like the Bahtika, Strirajya and the province of Gramanari. Chakladar thinks that this type of rather unusual custom no doubt refers to a system of polyandry carried to a refined excess (1929 : 49-50). Chandragupta-II also married his elder brother's wife without any criticism from the society.

We have thus given only a few examples on polyandry and similar custom from different ancient Indian literatures and scriptures. There are many more such examples in those literatures and scripture.

From the above discussion it is apparent that though the early Indian texts have mentioned some cases of polyandry, this institution was naturally grown in the Indian society of that era and there is no reason to believe that the same was unknown or uncommon in ancient India or this was looked down or disowned. Polyandry was in existence in ancient India and the same has been perpetuated in some present day societies inhabiting in different parts of India.

REFERENCES

Aiyappan, A. 1932 Nayar Polyandry. *Man*. vol. 32, No. 99.

—1935 Fraternal Polyandry in Malabar. *Man in India*. vol. 15, No. 2.

Altekar, A.S. 1973 *The Position of Women in Hindu Civilization*. 2nd Edn. Delhi.

Briffanlt, R. 1927 *The Mothers*. 3 vols. Goorge Allen and Unwin Ltd. London.

Chakladar, H.C. 1929 *Social Life in Ancient India : Studies in Vatsyayana's Kamasutra*. Greater India Society Publication. No. 3, Calcutta.

Chatopadhyay, K.P. 1957 On Polyandry. *Journal of the Asiatic Society of Bengal, Science*. vol. 22, No. 2.

Das, S.C. 1893 The Marriage customs of Tibet. *Journal of the Asiatic Society of Bengal*, vol. 62, pt. II, Calcutta.

Furer-Haimendrof; C. Von 1964 *The Sherpas of Nepal: Buddhist Highlanders*. John Murrey. London.

—1966 *Caste and kin in Nepal, India and Ceylon*. Asia Publishing House, Bombay.

Gough, E.K. 1959 The Nayars and the Definition of Marriage. *Journal of the Royal Anthropological Institute*. vol. 89, pt-I.

Horner, I.B. 1930 *Women under Primitive Buddhism*. London.

Jayal, S. 1966 *The Status of Women in the Epics*, Delhi.

Kane, P.V. 1974 *History of Dharmasastra*, vol. II. pt-I. 2nd. Edn. Poona.

Kapadia, K.M. 1984 *Marriage and Family in India*. Oxford University Press, Calcutta.

Karve, I. 1965 *Kinship Organization in India*. 2nd Edn. Bombay.

MacDonell, A.A. and Keith, A.B. 1912 *Vedic Index of Names and Subjects* 2 vols. London.

Majumdar, D.N. 1955 Family and Marriage in a polyandrous village. *The Eastern Anthropologist* vol. 8, No. 3.

—1963 *Himalayan Polyandry*. Asia Publishing House, Bombay.

Mandelbaum, D.G. 1938 Polyandry in Kota Society. *American Anthropologist*. vol. 40.

McLennan, J.F. 1970 *Primitive Marriage : An Inquiry into the origin of the Form of capture in marriage ceremonies* (originally published in Edinburgh, 1865) ed. W.H.R. Rivers. P. Chicago.

Moyer, J.J. 1930 *Sexual Life in Ancient India*. 2 vols. London.

Muir, D. 1877 On the question whether Polyandry ever existed in Northern Hindustan. *Indian Antiquary*. vol. 6.

Panikkar, K.M. 1918 Some Aspects of Nayar Life. *Journal of the Royal Anthropological Institute*.

Prince, Peter 1955 Polyandry and the kinship group. *Man* vol. 55.

—1963 *A Study of Polyandry*. The Hague.

Rivers. W.H.R. 1906 *The Todas*. Macmillan. London.

Sarkar, S.C. 1928 *Some Aspects of the Earliest Social History of India (Pre-Buddhist Ages*). London.

Singh, S.D. 1978 *Polyandry in Ancient India*. Vikas Publishing House Pvt. Ltd. Lucknow.

Upadhayaya, B.S. 1974 *Women in the Rg Veda*. 3rd Edn. Delhi.

Vora, D.P. 1959 *Evolution of Morals in the Epics*. Bombay.

19

A NOTE ON DIFFERENTIAL SEX-RATIOS* AND POLYANDROUS PEOPLE IN INDIA

KANTI PAKRASI

The great disparity between the two sexes in the population of India has been a matter of considerable demographic interest in successive census-return since 1872. In 1901 there were only 963 females per 1000 males. This phenomenon of male-excess persists even in the latest 1961 census-return for India (male : 22, 62, 93, 620; female : 21, 29, 41, 462). The fact that women were continuously outnumbered by men in India has duly been admitted in different periods by government officials, demographers, actuarial experts and others interested persons in the field. In the *Census Report of India* (1951) it has thus particularly been emphasized that : 'a deficiency of female arises in all parts of India as a biological phenomenon' (p. 60).

Uneven distribution of sex-ratio throughout India still upholds the existence of the above 'biological phenomenon' in distinct zones and as a consequence,

> 'There are recognizable geographical bands where there are more than 1000 females per 1000 males. If districts

*Reproduced by permission of the authority of Man-in India from *Man in India* 44 (2) : 161-174, 1964.

> and states are arranged according to the sex-ratio, a curious pattern except for eastern Madhya Pradesh and Bihar largely on account of their tribal population, seems to emerge on either side of latitude 20°. It will be seen that the sex-ratio is appreciably lower in the north of latitude 20° than south of it' (Census 1961, p. xvii).

As a matter of fact, in the north of this demarcating latitude low sex-ratios are discernible, particularly in Punjab and Uttar Pradesh.

> 'In Punjab, Ambala (812), Simla (731), Ferozepur (848), Bhatinda (837), Sangrur (840), and Patiala (830) form a compact block of low ratio. The other compact area occurs in Uttar Pradesh with Saharanpur (825), Dehra Dun (766), Muzaffarnagar (841), Meerut (843), Naini Tal (719), Rampur (871), Pilibhit (842), Bareilly (834), Budaun (837), Mathura (838), Agra (840), Shahjahanpur (826), Farrukhabad (839), Etawah (847), Kanpur (811), Lucknow (839), and Sitapur (859)' (Census 1961 : p. xviii).

In close proximity of this geographical tract of female deficiency, we find the location of one of the famous polyandrous groups of India. The polyandrous Khasas of Jaunsar Bawar, a pargana of the Dehra Dun district (Uttar Pradesh) conform immediately with the general demographic pattern of the said compact belt of low ratio in North India in having conspicuously high proportion of males among themselves. It has been shown that among the Khasas, great disparity between the two sexes has been in existence consistently from as early as 1901 when males per 100 females were 126.9. Maximum excess of males (131. 2) among the Khasas was observed in 1921.

In this context it would be profitable to refer to what was commented on the disparity of sex-proportions among the Khasas by noted anthropologists like Dr. D.N. Majumdar and Dr. R.N. Saksena who had intimate experience about the polyandrous folk of Jaunsar-Bawar. Dr. Majumdar (1960) wrote.

> 'It is said that female infanticide was prevalent in the area some 25 years ago. Now-a-days, though infanticide is no longer practised in this area, yet no significant changes in the sex-ratio have taken place in recent decades' (1960 : 18).

Under the circumstances, it becomes really difficult to lay stress on any causal relations that might exist between the customs of female infanticide resulting in high male excess and polyandry. It appears more plausible that the Khasas, irrespective of their marriage custom, exhibit the same 'biological phenomenon' of female deficiency as the inhabitants of Dehra Dun district as a whole, and other geographical tracts of low sex-ratio in Uttar Pradesh and Punjab.

It is to be noted that polyandry as a form of marriage has, on the other hand, never been reported to exist among those people like the Bedees, the hypergamous Rajput, the Khatris, the Chouhans, the Sikhs of Uttar Pradesh, Rajputana and Punjab, among whom historical evidences of female infanticide are available. (*Census*, 1911 and Das, 1956 and 1957). Even if it is admitted that the cruel custom of female infanticide was notably instrumental in bringing about consistent high male excess and consequently polyandrous marriage among the Khasas of Jaunsar-Bawar, then it is expected that among those people of Punjab, U.P. and Rajputana, who practised almost ritually the custom of female infanticide, polyandry should have eventually crept in as a social element in their respective cultures. But authentic evidences are absolutely lacking to justify such expectation.

Again, this question about the assumed relationship between dearth of females due to infanticide and polyandry among the Khasas has aptly been discussed by Dr. Saksena (1955). He wrote with regard to the distribution of population in Jaunsar Bawar.

> 'It will be observed that the population of this region is almost static and the net increase in the population is

showing a downward trend, as would be evident from the following analysis :

Mean decennial growth rate (1881-1901)+13.3
" " " " (1901-1921)+ 8.8
" " " " (1921-1941)+ 3.6
" " " " (1941-1951)+ 1.4

Another interesting feature of the population is the disparity in sexratio which is said to have exerted its influence on the form of marriage and helped polyandry. But this sex-disparity is not peculiar to Jaunsar-Bawar alone. In the whole of the district of Dehra Dun, excluding Jaunsar-Bawar where sex-disparity already exists, the same disturbed sex-ratio is noticeable. According to the Census report of 1951, there were 1,77,423 males and 1,26,135 females. But certainly polyandry cannot be said to exist in other parts of Dehra Dun district' (p. 17).

In order to gain an insight into the problem of chronic low female proportion together with its peculiar spatial dispersion in India, attention is invited to what has been written in this regard in the 1951 *Census Report of India.* This information, it is hoped, would especially help in appraising the merit of the issue under reference. In India (1951) the sex-ratio (number of females per 1000 males) was 947. The lowest value was 883 in north-western India and the highest 993 in southern India. The sex-ratio was found to be less than 1000 in every division of northern India and north-western India without any exception.

TABLE 1

Sex-ratio at birth during 1941-50

State	Average	Highest during decade	Lowest during decade
Madras	948	959	937
Madhya Pradesh	939	946	921
Bombay	935	937	931
Uttar Pradesh	857	874	843

With regard to female deficiency in India it has been shown in *Census Report* (1951) that in Madras during 1941-50 for every 1000 male children born there were only 948 female children, and the following results have further been supplied to us.

It is written,

> These figures are very instructive and three points should be noted about them : *First*—In every case, there is a definite excess of male births over female births; *Second*—The excess is very much more pronounced in Uttar Pradesh (North India) than in the other three States (which may be taken to be broadly representative of South India, Central India and West India) ; and *Third*—The lowest and highest values recorded over a period of ten years do not differ very much ; and this fact shows that the occurrence of an excess at birth is not an accident...
> 'We must accept the existence of a male excess at birth as a fact. A deficiency of female arises in all parts of India as a biological phenomenon. It is believed that this happens in almost all parts of the world' (pp. 59-60).

In the backdrop of such geo-demographic situation it is in South India that the second notable group of polyandry practising people is met with. Of these people the Todas, the most discussed tribe of Nilgiri Hills, maintain a conspicuous position like the Khasas of North India in showing high male proportion in their population since 1872. But for such masculine nature of the Toda population the eminent anthropologist Dr. Rivers (1906) had the occasion to comment on the tribe. On the strength of population data furnished by the genealogical records of 359 Toda families, Dr. Rivers built up a hypothesis for explaining the constant feature of female deficiency on account of infanticide and continuing practice of polyandry among this tribe. In this regard he tabled a concrete point in suggesting that

'It is possible that at their first arrival in the Nilgiri

> Hills, the Todas has few sources of food, and has a severe struggle for existence; that they therefore adopted the practice of female infanticide, and that polyandry followed as a consequence' (1906 : 521).

Further, he wrote, 'All accounts of the Toda agree in attributing to them the practice of female infanticide, though at the present time, the Todas are very chary of acknowledging the existence of the practice' (1906 : 478).

Taking a clue perhaps from the discussion made by Dr. Rivers, the *Census Report of India* (1911) reiterated, 'the crime (female infanticide) was also common amongst the Todas of the Nilgiris who, being polyandrous, had no great need of woman and, being poor, did not wish to rear superfluous offspring' (p. 216). Again, Dr. Rivers asserted that,

> 'there is no doubt whatever as to the close association of the polyandry of the Todas with female infanticide. It has certainly, however, diminished in frequency, and the consequent increase in the proportion of women is leading to some modification in the associated polyandry' (1906 ; 518).

If it were true that the proportion of women among the Todas began to increase due to decreasing practice of infanticide by the beginning of the present century, then it is obvious that some time later, say 25 to 30 years, the female sex-ratio must show an appreciable improvement amongst them But, the available facts point to an interesting state of development. In 1902 there were 132.2 males per 100 females among the Todas according to Dr. Rivers' own estimate. Peculiarly enough this demographic feature of male excess continued to exist even in 1931 when the sex-ratio happened to be the same as shown by Dr. Rivers.

Incidentally, it is important to note that since 1872 the male proportion among the Todas never dropped down to the lowest limit of 127.4 per 100 females which was, on the other hand, noticed long before in 1901. It is thus evident that irrespective of the prevalence of female infanticide or its declining influence, male excess continued to dominate as a biological phenomenon in the Toda population. Under the circumstances, the question remains : Would it be reasonable to assume any direct causal relation, as asserted by Dr. Rivers, between (i) practice of female infanticide, (ii) increasing proportion of males, and (iii) marriage of one woman with more than one man at a time in the group concerned ?

Further, that polyandry as a form of marriage should necessarily be governed always in a population by the detrimental impact of female infanticide seems to be unjustified. This would amply be evident from the fact that besides the Todas who are suspected of infanticide there are in Travancore and Cochin (Kerala) of S. India *sixteen* other castes and tribal groups who have been reported to practise polyandry but never female infanticide, (Iyer, 1939 : 41 ; Mandelbaum, 1938). These people are (1) Izhuvans, (2) Kammalans, (3) Kaniyans, (4) Karvazhi Pulayas, (5) Kotas (Nilgiri Hills tribe), (6) Malayarayans, (7) Mannans, (8) Muthuvans, (9) Nayars, (10) Paliyas, (11) Panans, (12) Parayas, (13) Pulayas, (14) Ullatans, (15) Uralis, and (16) Velans.

On the other hand, it is moreover significant to note that some of these polyandrous people register a male sex-ratio below 100 while some more than the limit of equality. The groups which show for a considerable period consistently high female ratio (more than 100) are the Izhuvans, Kammalans, Karavazhi Pulayas, Ullatans and the Velans. Contrary to the above, the Kaniyans, Kotas (a tribe), Malayarayans, Mannans, Paliyans, Parayas and the S. Pulayas have an excess of male in their respective populations. In this context the Mannans, Pulliyans and Pulayas deserve special mention since they have been maintaining a constant high male proportion from the past (vide Table-3).

In order to appreciate the significance of the varying sex-proportions among the castes and tribal peoples mentioned above, it is imperative to make a close study of the wider demographic situation that has conditioned the population make-up of Travancore as a whole. It has been shown in *Census Report of Travancore* (1931) :

> 'During the past decade the female births in Travancore averaged 944 per 1000 male births, and the sex-ratio in 1931 was 987. In India the proportion of female to male births during the decade 1911-20 was 933 and the sex-ratio in 1921 was 945' (p. 134).

Further it is found in the report that the sex-proportion at birth varied considerably from year to year within 1920-21 and 1929-30 and ratio of female to male births was higher in the earlier part than in the latter part of the decade in question (maximum 972 in 1923-24 and minimum 948 in 1929-30).

> "The causes of these variations are not known and owning to the absence of separate vital statistics for different races, castes, and religions, it is not possible to ascertain whether the variations are shared by all the communities or are confined to any particular community or communities'.
>
> 'The sex-ratio of children under one year may probably give a better indication of the degree of masculinity at birth than the imperfect vital statistics. In the population of Travancore in 1931 there were 991 female children to 1000 male children under one year.... It is noteworthy, however, that this ratio is very nearly equal to the sex-ratio of the aggregate population, the former being 991 and the latter 987' (p. 135).

Incidentally, it is interesting to note that the males have been continuously in excess in Travancore-Cochin during the time gap covering 1901 and 1931, but since 1941 the proportion of females has begun to increase very slightly over that of the males. In 1951 there were 1008 females per 1000 males in Travancore-Cochin (*Census Report of Travancore-Cochin*, 1951, p. 67).

Viewing the problem of differential sex-ratios from a slightly different standpoint it can be stated that an excess of male proportion in a population does not necessarily lead to polyandry. It would be evident from the fact that there exist some caste people like the Kanikkars, Malapantarams, Mala Vetans (Vetans and Vettuvans) in Travancore-Cochin (Kerala) who show continuously high male ratio among themselves from long past, but they practise neither polyandry nor female infanticide. Table 4 will speak for itself in explaining the issue raised here.

In this regard it would, then be sociologically interesting to examine how the polyandrous form of marriage has been operating as an established custom among the caste-group consisting of the Mannans, Malayarans, Palliyans, and others, but *not* among the caste-group including the Kanikkars, Malapantarams, Mala Vetans, and others, though it is a fact that under more of less similar ecological conditions each one of these castes has been strikingly maintaining continuous male excess in their population over different decennial counts since 1901.

Meanwhile let us have a look on the other side of the issue. Discussing various points related to the sex-ratio pattern of Travancore Cochin, the Census Report (1931) for this State has stated that while Trichur and Quilon districts have an excess of females, Trivandrum has males and females almost in equal strength. But Kottayam district stands conspicuously apart from the rest in maintaining all along a male excess in the population since 1901. Sex-ratios in Kottayam, district vary from 951 females per 1000 males in 1901 to 977 females in 1951, the minimum 939 being found in 1921.

It should be noticed at once that it is in this Kottayam district that irrespective of marriage-practices, caste people like the Malapulayas, Malayarayans, Mala Vetans, Muthuvans, Ullatans, Uralis, and others show more males than females, as has already been pointed out above, in their respective population. They are living particularly in the following *taluks* of Kottayam district, which strangely enough started with a deficit of females even as late as 1901.

With respect to this sort of disturbed sex-ratio continuing for more than half a century, one may be tempted to conclude that it is the general demographic peculiarity of female deficiency of Kottayam district (and for that matter of Travancore-Cochin as a whole), that has perhaps been reflected in the sex-

TABLE 2

Sex-ratios for the *Taluks* in Kottayam district

	Census year					
	1901	1911	1921	1931	1941	1951
1. Changanachery	959	963	917	944	954	942
2. Kottayam	948	953	956	969	994	1012
3. Minachil	954	958	946	967	961	988
4. Devikulam	695	799	856	799	823	852
5. Thodupuzha	979	931	924	937	961	968

composition of the population of each one of the castes and tribal people concerned. Under the circumstances, is it not more reasonable to propose that the custom of marriage of one woman with more than one man at a time has functioned independently of the observed fluctuation in sex-ratios among the people concerned ?

With reference to what has been discussed so far it is amply clear that the biological phenomenon of male excess (or female deficiency) remains as a longstanding demographic characteristic of India's population as a whole. This feature is particularly conspicuous in northern and north-western India. But why should such an affair persist in India ?

> 'It is less easy to find a satisfactory explanation of the causes which, in the greater part of India, have produced a deficiency of females. It does not seem to be due to any appreciable extent, to their concealment at the Census, nor can any correlation be traced between the proportions of the sexes and climate, season of gestation, food, consanguineous marriages, and the like' (*Imperial Gazetter of India*, 1907 : I : 480).

As against the above situation, it is a noteworthy social fact that the polyandrous people of India are concentrated in two distinct geographical tracts only—one in the north-west sub-Himalayan region of Uttar Pradesh and the other in the south-western marginal areas of Travancore-Cochin (Kerala).

In spite of the fact that compact blocks of low ratio of females are immediately recognizable in regions like Punjab and Uttar Pradesh, polyandry as a custom has never taken its root in any group, except among the Khasas, residing in the said geographical belt. Is it not interesting to probe how in the land of male-dominated population *only* the Khasas have retained the practice of marriage of one woman with more than one man at a time ? Pursuant to this, it can again be posed : Should the biological feature of continual male excess be an essential pre-requisite to keep polyandry going in the community concerned ?

With special reference to the disturbed sex-ratios of the

TABLE 3

Census Report-wise distribution of population and sex-ratios among different polyandrous communities of India

Castes and Tribes practising polyandry in India	Census Report for the year	Population		(Sex-ratio males per 100 females)	Reference
		Male	Female		
1	2	3	4	5	6
		A. South India			
1. Izhuvans (Illavans, Tiyyans, Chouans, Thandans)	1901	91524	92980	98.4	L A.K. Iyer
	1931	132875	143774	92.4	
2. Kammalans (artisan classes)	1881	342438	349862	97.9	L.A.K. Iyer & Census Report
	1931	22085	23461	94.1	
3. Kaniyans (Panikans)	1931	1950	1891	103.1	L.A.K. Iyer
4. Karavazhi Pulayas (Mala Pulayans)	1901	14	12	116.7	,, ,,
	1911	17	28	60.7	
	1931	125	129	96.9	

(*Contd.*)

5. Kotas (a tribe of Nilgiri Hills)	1911	547	616	88.8	Census Report
	1931	562	559	100.5	
6. Malayarayans	1911	1294	1318	98.2	
	1921	1486	1372	108.3	L.A.K. Iyer
	1931	1606	1576	101.9	,, ,,
7. Mannans	1901	615	557	110.4	,, ,,
	1911	647	592	109.3	
	1921	587	511	114.9	
	1931	665	611	108.8	
8. Muthuvans	1901	409	399	102.5	,, ,,
	1911	195	184	106.0	
	1921	122	135	90.4	
	1931	649	652	99.5	
9. Nayars (of Travancore)	1931	431154	437257	98.6	Census Report
10. Palliyans	1921	165	134	123.1	L.A.K. Iyer
	1931	266	217	122.6	
11. Panans	1901	1403	1378	101.8	,, ,,
	1931	1771	1832	96.7	
12. Parayas	1931	72158	70206	102.8	,, ,,
13. Southern Pulayas	1931	36782	36610	100.5	,, ,,

(Contd.)

1	2	3	4	5	6
14. Pulayas (including the Southerners)	1911	93235	91979	101.4	,, ,,
	1921	99420	96764	102.7	
	1931	183815	181355	101.4	
15. Todas (A tribe of the Nilgiri Hills)	1901	451	354	127.4	W. H. R. Rivers and Census Report
	1911	426	322	132.3	
	1931	340	257	132.3	
16. Ullatans	1911	2197	1918	114.5	L.A.K. Iyer
	1921	1604	1803	89.0	
	1931	2242	2879	77.9	
17. Uralis	1901	106	114	93.0	,, ,,
	1911	169	197	85.8	
	1921	129	101	127.7	
	1931	454	462	98.3	
18. Velans	1901	4009	4230	94.8	,, ,,
	1931	5205	5690	91.5	
		B. North India			
19. Khasas (of Jaunsar-Bawar)	1901	28349	22752	124.6 (a)	D.N. Majumdar R.N. Saksena
	1911	30518	24294	125.6 (b)	
	1921	31567	24056	131.2	
	1931	31922	24857	128.4	
	1941	32345	25305	127.8	
	1951	32704	25765	126.9	

TABLE 4

Census Report-wise distribution of sex-ratios among some selected polyandrous and non-polyandrous castes of Travancore-Cochin

Polyandrous castes	Ref. Census year	Sex-ratio (males per 100 females)	Non-Polyandrous castes	Ref-Census year	Sex-ratio (males per 100 females)
1	2	3	4	5	6
1. Mannans	1901	110.4	1. Kanikkars	1901	105.4
	1911	109.3		1911	116.0
	1921	114.9		1921	109.5
	1931	108.8		1931	112.5
2. Malayarayans	1921	108.3	2. Malapantarams	1901	155.0
	1931	101.9		1911	131.1
				1921	147.8
				1931	142.9
3. Paliyans	1921	123.1	3. Mala Vetans	1911	114.0
	1931	122.6		1921	99.7
				1931	101.7

caste people of Travancore-Cochin, it is all the more imperative to realize that while the event of continuing high male proportion or otherwise in any group should be examined within the appropriate demographic context, customary practices like polyandry or other forms of marriage are to be appraised in their proper societal framework. To put the idea more concretely, it is suggested that instead of ascribing simply a generalized relation between polyandry and high male concentration (due to female infanticide or other biological factors) in a caste or tribal group concerned, it would be better to study thoroughly the nature and functions of the *social structure* that has sanctioned or otherwise marriage of several men with one woman at a time, and at the same time caused demographic imbalances affecting increased male or female proportion over a long stretch of time within the group concerned.

ACKNOWLEDGEMENT

I am thankful to Prof. R. Mukherjee, Head of the Sociological Research Unit, Indian Statistical Institute, Calcutta, for the active guidance he offered me in the preparation of the paper in his unit.

REFERENCES

1. Imperial Census of India 1881 *Madras Presidency*, vol. 4 (Tables).
2. Imperial Gazetteer of India 1907 vol. I, (Descriptive).
3. Census of India 1911 *India*, vol. 1, Part I, (Report), Ch. vi, para 275-278, pp. 214-18.
4. Census of India 1911 *Madras*, vol. xii, part II, (Tables).
5. Census of India 1931 *India*, vol. I, part I, (Report), p. 205.
6. Census of India 1931 *Travancore*, vol xxviii. parts I and II (Report and Table).
7. Census of India 1931 *Cochin*, vol. xxi, parts I and II (Report and Table).
8. Census of India 1951 *India*, vol. I, part I-A, (Report), ch. 2, p. 54-62.
9. Census of India 1961 *Final Population Total*, Paper I, 1962.
10. Dass, M.N. 1956 'Female Infanticide among the Bedees and Chauhans, Motives and Modes', *Man in India*, vol. 36, no. 4, pp. 261-66.

11. ——1957 'Movement to supress the custom of female Infanticide in Punjab and Kashmir', *Man in India*, vol. 37, no. 4. pp. 280-93.
12. Iyer Krishna L.A. 1909 *The Cochin Tribes and Castes*. Higginbotham and Co., Mount Road, Madras.
13. ——1937-1941 *The Travancore Tribes and Castes*. vol. I, II, III, Government Press, Trivandrum, South India.
14. Iyer, Krishna, L.A. and N.K. Pillai 1931 'The Primitive Tribes of Travancore' in *Census of India* (1931), vol. I, Part III (Ethnographical).
15. Majumdar, D.N. 1960 *Himalayan Polyandry*, Asia Publishing House, Bombay.
16. Mandelbaum, D.G. 1938 'Polyandry in Kota Society' in *American Anthropologist*, vol. 40, p. 574.
17. Rivers, W.H.R. 1906 *The Todas*, MacMillan & Co., Ltd. London.
18. Saksena, R.N. 1955 *Social Economy of a Polyandrous People*, Institute of Social Science, Agra University, India.

20

BOW AND ARROW CEREMONY OF THE TODA—AN INTERPRETATION*

B.B. GOSWAMI

Introduction

The Toda are the well known pastoral tribe of Nilgiri district, Madras. Their present population is nearly a thousand. The Toda *munds* (village) are generally off the main roads surrounded by a green meadow on which domestic buffaloes graze. It is usually composed of huts, dairy, temple and cattle pen. The Toda are divided into two endogamous groups named Tartharol and Teivaliol. They are patriarchal people following the custom of fraternal type of polyandry.[1]

Under this custom as biological fatherhood remains unknown, it is socially established by a performance known as 'bow and arrow' (*pursutpimi*) ceremony. This ceremony is an exemplification of conventionality for solving the biological problem of the Toda society.[2] Very recently, I had the opportunity of witnessing the observances of this ceremony which have been described in the pages that follow. It may be mentioned here that many writers have written on the Toda (Harknes, 1832 ; Breeks, 1873 ; Marshall, 1873 ; Rivers, 1906 ; Thurston,

*Reproduced by permission of the Director, Anthropological Survey of India from *Bulletin of the Anthropological Survey of India*, XIV (1 & 2): 35-39, 1965.

1909 ; etc.) but none of them has given observational description of the ceremony[3] or a correct interpretation.

Background

The woman of Melgarsh clan who received bow and arrow from the man of Nodrs clan was educated up to Class XI in an educational institution situated in the town of Ootacamund, the headquarters of Nilgiri district, Madras. Both of them belonged to Tartharol group. (For convenience, henceforth I shall designate the woman as X and the man as Y). Y, though not much educated, was economically well off, for his father had a number of buffaloes. He with two other members of his clan (whose duty was to look after the buffaloes) was living with X in the same house. When X became pregnant, Y arranged the bow and arrow ceremony (*pursutpimi*), held on the 24th October, 1965, which was the first new moon day of her seventh month of pregnancy. Another function (as a part of *pursutpimi*) was held on the previous evening, i.e., on the afternoon of the 23rd October, 1965, called *Oorvasth*. Both the ceremonies were held in the *mund* of Y situated at about 20 km. west of Ootacamund.

Observed Events

First day : When I reached the place on the afternoon of the 23rd October, 1965, I observed two groups, one consisting of men and boys (25) and the other of women and children (15) distinctly separated from each other. The ladies, with their curled hair, dressed in spotless clean *putkuli* (cf. Marshall, 1873 : 50) and displaying their traditional gold and silver ornaments, were seated ; men in their impressive masculine appearance stayed apart from them.[4] The gathering was smelling of rancid butter with which the Toda, men and women both, anoint their bodies.

I noticed X, at a distance of three yards away from the female group and under a *Kiaz* (*Litsaea wightiana* Benth ad HK. cf, Rivers, 1906 : 738) tree, cooking rice in an earthen vessel (supplied by the Kota tribe) placed over a few stones. Her bare body was covered by a *putkuli*. She appeared impressive, shy and modest. When she faced any problem, she requested the advice of the elderly ladies (comprising mostly of the members of X's group). She made attempts to light the damp firewood by a match stick but when she failed, a young woman of her clan brought some clarified butter from the nearby hut and placed the same at a distance. She picked up the butter and poured it on the faggots to light the fire.

Then the above mentioned woman gave her a fountain pen, and with the same she made two dot marks on the top of each of her two thumbs (which symbolised the attainment of her puberty). When this was going on, one Toda man brought two pieces of wood (conical pegs) of about 11 inches in length. He tapped the pointed ends of those inside the ground. Both were then wrapped with pieces of rag, of which one was tied with a red thread. The peg with red thread symbolised male deity and the other female deity.

In the meantime, two of the male clan members of Y with the assistance of X's father constructed a crude symbolic Toda temple with *Kiaz* branches and leaves, and placed six bamboo reeds out of which four contained clean stream water. Then some other male persons brought a female calf and over the left side of the middle portion of the calf clean spring water was poured from one reed to the other. The water thus sanctified was then poured into a leaf-cup, which X held in her hand. She drank the water after raising the cup to her forehead. She repeated the same thrice using a fresh leaf. After this, she bowed before the temple ; the men threw away the reeds in the nearby gorge.

X then returned to her cooking pot and with a piece of wood examined whether rice was cooked or not. Finding everything to her satisfaction (actually it was not cooked properly), she took out some rice on two leaves and placed one of the same before the male (the peg was at her right side) and the other before the female peg saying '*pirn podia, piri podia*'. She then also tasted the food which she took out for her on a separate leaf from the earthen pot. This ceremony symbolised the attainment and completion of puberty and maturity.

After that she marked two dots by slight bums on the carpo-metacarpal joint of each thumb and on each wrist by seven rolled up lighted rags. While doing so she received the help of a male member of her clan. It appears that the ceremony is a declaration of attainment of seventh month of pregnancy (each rolled rag symbolising a month) and a crude form of communion with the supernatural.

Thinking so the rites have been completed she expressed her desire to join the group of women. But the ladies present asked her to remain at a distance. One of the ladies of the clan of X went forward to pour buffallo milk, which she was carrying in a bottle, in a leaf-cup held by X. X was asked to drink that milk. This was performed thrice and after that only she could join the group.

All the people then went inside the house where they sang songs over light refreshments. It continued up to 7.30 p.m. after which the guests dispersed.

Second day : On the 24th October, 1965, the bow and arrow ceremony was held. Even though it was raining from the early morning, the house of Y was full of Toda men and women in their traditional dresses. Some of the Toda came from far off *munds*. It was reported that a group of the Toda paid Rs. 56 to the taxi owner for to and fro journey from their village. There were 86 (Male=53, Female=33) Todas and 34 Badaga men present during the ceremony. There were also present a few Tamilian and Malyali men and women with whom the members of the *mund* had business connections.

By about 11.45 a.m., a few male members of the moiety of the couple made a triangular niche in the *Kiaz* tree near which Y performed *Oorvasth* ceremony on the previous day. Inside the niche a lamp was placed.

After this Y and X together, in the group of other men and women, started for the spot. After reaching near the tree Y remained behind, whereas X lighted the lamp with a match stick and to protect it from the dripping rain water, an open umbrella was tied by a few persons in oblique angle with the tree. Mother of X placed a brass plate containing honey comb, butter and some grains at the foot of the tree. X was then asked to bow before the lamp. This ceremony is called *parsh-kumkudi*. This was followed by the ceremony of salutation called *kolmelworted* which has been described below.

The Toda men and women were seated separately in two different rows. The couple, accompanied by the mother of X and a male clan member of Y, first went before the group of Toda men and saluted each of them. First Y then X crouched before each of the Toda male guests to be saluted (see Rivers, 1906 : 320), the latter in turn placed the right then the left foot on the head of him or her. Most of the guests present gave rupee one each to X and Y as presentations. The money was collected by the mother of X.

After completing the Toda men's row, the couple greeted the group of the Badaga men. They were standing. The couple went before each of the Badaga present and bowed before them, the latter blessed Y and X by touching their forehead. Many of them also presented cash money. The couple did not go to the other people. Thereupon Y and X went before the group of women who were sitting in a row to whom only X saluted in the traditional manner. They also presented cash money to each of them.[5]

X then went again before the niche and stood there gazing at the burning lamp. And Y accompanied by a few members of his clan went to the nearby forest to bring bow and arrow. For doing so he took the consent of the father of X. He returned after fifteen minutes with a crude toy like bow and arrow.[6] He went before waiting X and asked her permission to present bow and arrow to her. To which she enquired that whose bow and arrow it was. Y gave out a standardised answer delivered by the members of his clan in such occasions (see Breeks, 1873 : 19-20). The same question and answers were repeated thrice. Thereafter only she took the bow and arrow from the hands of Y, raised those to her forehead and then placed the same at the foot of the tree.[7] After doing so, she touched the ground with her forehead before the tree. Portions of honey comb were given to the couple for tasting.

The party then returned to the hut and a few men to express their joy and merriment, started singing and dancing. It was started by five persons holding each other's hand (some were holding umbrellas on their heads as it was drizzling) and keeping steps, moved round clockwise. Number of dancers swelled as the people joined the group while the dance was on.

In all two dances were held. Praises were showered by the dancers on the clans of X and Y through their songs composed then and there.

While the ceremony was going on, the mears were made ready by a few Toda men. After the dances, guests dispersed to take their lunch. As usual men and women sat in separate groups. In the group of men, the Badaga, the Toda and others sat separately but there was no such distinction in the group of women. The food, consisting of rice, bean curry and *ghee*, was first served to the Badaga and then to the others, for the Badaga hold an honourific position to the other tribes of the Nilgiri district. The food was served on banana leaves by a body of active and young Toda men. When the guests finished their lunch, the couple collected the leaf-plates jointly ; X folded and picked up the leaf-plates and deposited those in a basket held by Y. When the basket was filled, Y emptied it at a nearby bush. The significance of this custom is probably to show the couple as subservient to the persons assembled for witnessing the ceremony.

After this X and Y jointly presented Rs. 11 to a Toda of another group (Teivaliol) who had come to witness the ceremony. Money was presented ceremoniously as a gesture of honour to the group for supplying priests to the Toda temples. Thereafter, guests dispersed to their respective villages bidding best wishes to each other.

Discussion

The detail report of Rivers (1906, 315-323) shows that in the past the ceremonies were distributed over longer time and space. What I observed is the condensed form of the whole thing.

The rites of passage observed are transitional, dynamistic, direct and contagious (Gennep, 1960 : 42). All details regarding territorial passage have been omitted to the extent possible. At certain places the account given by me differs from what Rivers (*ibid*) wrote. For instance, X did not bring 'two pieces of wood' as reported by Rivers (*ibid* : 316) ; though she did not stay in *puzhars* (*ibid*) during the ceremony held on the first day, she was considered as impure and was incorporated into the company of women through the same ceremony described by Rivers (*ibid* : 317) ; during the wrist joint burning ceremony, she was assisted by a male person.

In connection with bow and arrow ceremony the significant changes noted by me from the reportings of others are the following :

1. Rivers (1906 : 319) stated that the ceremony is performed in the village of the pregnant woman. In the case observed by me, it was performed in the village of her husband.
2. Though the author, Rivers and Thurston have noted that the lamp was placed in a triangular niche in a *Kiaz* tree, Marshall stated, "...at the foot of some (emphasis mine) tree she places a lamp" (1873 : 214) and Breeks wrote "...a jungle tree in the stem of which a convenient hole can be found to place a small earthenware lamp" (1873 : 19).
3. Husband did not cut the triangular niche as stated by Rivers (*ibid*).
4. The couple did not go to collect materials to prepare bow and arrow. Only the husband went. It may also be noted that he went to bring the materials after performing the salutation ceremony. Rivers stated the opposite (*ibid* : 320).
5. X after receiving the bow and arrow returned to the village with the guests present while the lamp was burning ; whereas 'according to Rivers and others (*ibid* : 321 ; Breeks, 1873 : 19 ; Marshall, 1873 : 215 ; Thurston, 1909 : 143) she should have stayed there till the following day. Moreover, all the other details given by Rivers (*ibid*) were not at all performed.

One can also delineate many other important features of the Toda society from the afore-described ceremonies. Priest has no function and religious rites play no role in the rites of the pregnancy ceremonies. Fire is considered to be the emblem of supernatural power (*Swami*). During certain rites women are considered impure. The Toda temple and cattle play significant role in the rites of passage.

The Toda's regard to the Badaga was exemplified by serving of food first to them and then to the others.

During the dancing ceremony, all the Todas irrespective of their own clans praised the clan of X and Y. That showed the unity of the group. A payment of Rs. 11 to Teivaliol group, by X and Y jointly, was an expression of gratitude to the other group for performing certain religious functions. It appears that the value of presentation made to the couple by the guests assembled has been more or less standardised.

Meaning of the Ceremony

As has been said the agglomeration of the ceremonies can be interpreted as transitional rites, of which the presentation of bow and arrow is a warrant for attaining social fatherhood. It will be of some interest here to analyse the latent meaning and symbolic significance of the ceremony.

Rejecting the opinion of many that the 'bow and arrow ceremony' is a *tali* ceremony, Rivers suggested :

> "Since the ceremonies are only performed at the first pregnancy or when it is desired to change the fatherhood of a child, it seems clear that they closely resemble marriage ceremonies which have been postponed till shortly before the birth of the first child or what is more probable, pregnancy ceremonies resembling those customary in India, which have acquired social significance and have come to resemble marriage ceremonies." (1906 : 322-323).

I believe this interpretation is rather confused and disorganised for he had failed to understand the intellectual condition of the Toda and symbolic manifestation of his emotions and thinking.

To me (following psycho-analytical analysis), the bow and arrow ceremony symbolises the passing of the 'life force' of a clan into the uterus of the woman of another clan. The life force is symbolised by the arrow[8] which shoots into the uterus of the pregnant woman. It is significant to note that the arrow is made of grass blade. Though the word 'arrow' is used by the Toda in many different ways and contexts (for details see Rivers, 1906 : 586) but everywhere it has the quality of piercing. The bow symbolises the Toda universe. (They have special attachment for the arched-form for instance the front of the house, rainbow, etc.). The materials used for making bow and arrow are jungle shrubs. These are the products of nature, the attributes as well as qualities of which are life, tenderness and growth. These are given on a new moon day because, it is believed, that growth of the moon will have sympathetic effect on the development of the child in mother's womb.[9] For the Toda, seventh month is auspicious for firstly it is an odd month ; and secondly, only on the seventh month, the woman is competent enough to take the life force. She nurtures the life force for an odd number of months (approximately three months) inside her own body and then gives birth to a child.

Under the fraternal polyandry of the Toda, extension of the life force of the clan is important. The individual is only a tool to perform it and hence the person responsible for pregnancy has no importance. The woman before accepting bow and arrow from a man asks about the symbol of his clan thrice (to ascertain the authenticity of the statement) for the future child will be known after his clan. And this interaction between the clans was hailed by all the members present during the dances.

The Toda believe that life should give life, and so for those *pursutpimi* was not performed during the life time; it is positively performed during the funeral (Rivers, 1906 : 366) ceremony. Also it may be noted that if a child is born due to the sexual intimacy between a man and a woman of different Toda groups, the performance of the ceremony is not at all required, for the life force of the clan of one group is of no importance to the other.

NOTES

1. When a Toda boy decides to live with a girl, he approaches her guardian and negotiates for the amount of endowment to be reciprocally exchanged. If negotiation succeeds, the guardian of the

damsel passes her to the house of the man, after performing a few simple and formal ceremonies. The girl thenceforth lives in the house of the man. If the man has brothers or near relatives living in the house, they also can have sex relations with the woman (Thurston, 1909 : 142).

2. It has been noted that in due course of time, the ceremony may not be performed at all for under the instructions of medical authorities. (to check the spread of venereal diseases) and due to the impact of 'modernism' (!) the Toda men and women are reported to have developed a liking for monogamous conjugal life.
3. The observations of the ceremony have been filmed and music tape recorded by Shri S.K. Chattopadhyay on behalf of Anthropological Survey of India, Government of India.
4. Some of the Toda men unlike their traditional coiffure were clean shaven. On enquiry I was informed that a party of the Toda recently went to Nanjangud temple in the neighbouring district of Mysore, where they offered their hair and beard to the deity—a custom common in many south Indian temples.
5. I was reported that money collected during the ceremony totalled Rs. 260.
6. The bow and arrow were made of a twig of shrub (*Sophra glauca*) and 'a blade of grass called *nark*' (*Andropogon schoenanthus*) (Thurston, 1909 : 143).
7. Immediately a group of young boys who were watching the proceedings, whistled and shouted to express their merriment.
8. "Freud has pointed, spears, swords, staves, etc., are all penis symbols" (Skeels, 1965 58).
9. I am thankful to Dr. D.K. Sen who had suggested on the important phase of human transitional features and its relation with therhythmic movement of the celestial cosmos.

ACKNOWLEDGEMENT

I am thankful to Dr. D.K. Sen, Director, Anthropological Survey of India, for providing me the opportunity of undertaking a study of the ceremony. My grateful thanks also go to Miss Piljain for providing certain valuable suggestions in the field.

REFERENCES

Breeks, J.W. 1873. *An account of the primitive tribes and monuments of the Nilgiris.* London.

Gennep, A.V. 1960. *The Rites of Passage* (translated from French originally published in 1908). London.

Harkness, H. 1832. *Neilgherry Hills*, London.

Marshall, W.E. 1873. A Phrenologist among the Todas. London.

Rivers, W.H.R. 1906. *The Todas*. London.

Skeels, Dell, R. 1965. *Guingamor and Gurrehes : Psychological symbolism in a medieval romance in The Anthropologist looks at Myth*, (ed) John Greenway, Austin.

21

WOMAN'S ROLE IN A POLYANDROUS CIS-HIMALAYAN SOCIETY : AN OVERVIEW[1]

G. S. Bhatt
S. D. Jain

The Approach

The role concept is employed by the very people anthropologists and sociologists seek to study. Every society classifies its population in accordance with the jobs, offices or functions which individuals assume and the entitlements or responsibilities which fall to them (Nadel, 1957 : 20). How does the polyandrous social system of Jaunsar Bawar classifies its female population with regard to woman's obligations and rights is the main theme of this paper.

The phrase 'woman's status' in the notion of woman's rights is not objective empirically as rights are to be inferred and not observed. On the other hand, one's rights in society flow from the obligations of others oriented to one's social position and rights and obligations contained therein. Wife's rights flow from husband's obligations towards her position and vice versa.

Rights and obligations are interdependent though obligations tend to be more objective than rights. Both rights (status) and obligations (roles) constitute the contents of social position, and its contents are normatively defined

(Johnson, 1968 : 15). Hence, in main, description of a role solicits description of such normatively defined behaviour as is obligatory for the actor in the relevant social position. In the performance of a role, actor's awareness of his/her obligations and rights as seen by society is of crucial methodological importance. Positional norms tend to be reinforced structurally-functionally.

Every society tends to pattern its roles in the network of social relationships crucial to the functioning of each role. Therefore, besides the normative patterning of a role, two other aspects of role are of crucial importance in the functioning of role. They are one, social position and its total complex of inter-relations with other social positions and, two, the occupant of a social position in contingent reference to the occupants of other social positions with whom the occupant of the social position, under reference, interacts. Of equal importance are the norms of ascription and achievement as woven round sex, age and stratification.

Fraternal polyandry, as practised in Jaunsar Bawar, is the sole referent to this paper. Jaunsar Bawar, the two *parganas* (revenue divisions), constitute the Chakarata tahsil almost the hilly northern half of the district of Dehra Dun. As a distinct geographical-ethnic entity of the district, the area of Jaunsar Bawar forms part of a wider cultural complex of fraternal polyandry. This complex ranges over the adjacent block of Jaunpur (distt. Tehri) and Nowgaon and Purola (distt. Uttar Kashi). Thus, ranging over the river systems of the Jamuna and the Tons in Uttar Pradesh, the complex spreads over the adjoining polyandrous tracts of Himachal Pradesh from Sirmaur to Kulu-Kashmir from where the people of Jaunsar Bawar trace their God's (Mahasu's) migration.

Of all these polyandrous tracts only the area of Jaunsar Bawar was under the direct administration of the British. Others were administered by different princedoms. The areas underlying the blocks Purola (Rawain), Nowgaon and Jaunpur were administered by the princedom of Tehri. After independence, whereas the areas of Rawain-Jaunpur merged in the state of Uttar Pradesh under the normal rules of administration, the ethnic status of Jaunsar Bawar has been subject to change and fluctuations. From a partially excluded area in 1935, the inhabitants of this area attained the status of a tribe (1967) the Jaunsari tribe, inspite of having caste-stratification. Now moves are afoot to deschedule them (Bhoria, 1975 : XX/2).

As a consequence of this protective discrimination, polyandry in Jaunsar Bawar acquired political-vested interest (Bhatt, 1978). Whereas in Rawain-Jaunpur, as a preliminary survey done by the authors, reveals that polyandry is viewed shameful and its practice is denied at first contact, in Jaunsar Bawar it is accepted as a say of life, as a means to the claims of tribal status by the elite. Because of the opening it received under the British, polyandry in Jaunsar Bawar has been studied in depth as well as in detail. The present paper fills in a gap and that is of presenting a description of polyandry from the perspective of woman's social position in polyandry.

Ecological and Structural Antecedents of Polyandry

In this hilly terrain of towering mountains, deep gorges and wide-open valleys of the Himalayas, the socio-economic life of the people has tended to configurate in small nucleated villages. It mainly depends on labour intensive, terraced cultivation mostly undertaken for eking out subsistence. Local agriculture suffers from paucity of land. It is supplemented by the rearing of sheep and domestication of animal, by forest produce and occupations subsidiary to agriculture, and to the interests of the land-owning agriculturists.

Growing denudation of forests and their denial to the people, opening of roads, growing impact of motor transport, monetary market economy, trade and commerce, cash crops, education, party-politics and growing administrative integration of the region, are tending to change economic-social antecedents of polyandry. This precipitates structural-functional constraints which impinge upon the traditional roles of male and female.

In the multi-caste structure of villages of the region, are found a few stereotyped castes. They have well-defined relative statuses and fall into three stratified groups (Majumdar, 1963 : 64). First is the high caste group consisting of zamindars, Brahmins and Rajputs, owner-cultivators who carry a lion's share in land and in the social-economic structure of power. The second, i.e., the intermediate group consists of the Nath (agriculturist-cum-diviner-cum-astrologer-cum-priest to the Brahmin and the Rajput in the sacred bath at Hardwar), the Baddoi (carpenter-cum-mason), the Bajgi (drummer and beguiler on sacred-secular occasions, custodian of the lore of the cult of Mahasu, accompanist to dancing Bajgi girls, tailor and barbar). Tailoring is caste-free since many Rajputs and Brahmins too have taken to it.

The lower group consists of the Kolta and sparely found castes like the Dom, the Chamar and the Mochi. Functioning as the skinner, the currier and the tanner, the Dom occupies the lowest rank. The Dom and the Kolta are ex-untouchables. The Kolta is landless agricultural labourer, described as serf in earlier studies. Attempts have been made to free him from the traditional structure of bonded labour. The tradition does not allow the Kolta to enter the temple and the houses of high-caste men. This notwithstanding, in agricultural operations, a Kolta and his master, particularly his wife, may be found working side by side. In the get-together for singing and dancing, girls from different castes do not observe any social distance. Incidentally, the Kolta and woman form the backbone of regional agriculture.

The dominant norm of polyandry (48.3%) goes with monogamy (34.3%) and polygyny (17.4%). One husband having two wives is the usual pattern of polygyny. In polyandry, the dominating pattern consists of two husbands sharing two wives in common. It is followed by the patterns of two husbands sharing one wife, three husbands two wives, three husbands one wife and four husbands two wives. Other varying combinations of one to six husbands and wives to occur but they are not significant numerically.

The Brahmin and the Rajput share almost equal and the highest incidence (54.6% and 53.4% respectively) of polyandry, followed by the Kolta (43.7%), the Baddoi (37.5%) and the Bajgi (26.3%). In the practice of polygyny, the Kolta and the Baddoi share an equal and the highest incidence (37.5%) followed by the Brahmin (20.0%), the Bajgi (15.6%) and the Rajput (4.4%). The Bajgi has the highest incidence (57.9%) of monogamy, followed by the Rajput (42.2%), the Brahmin (25.4%), the Baddoi (25.0%) and the Kolta (18.8%).

The overall disparity of sexes (82 female for 100 males) and its stratificational variations are significant indicators of polyandry. The Bajgi has the highest ratio of females (105) for every hundred males, followed in order of descent, by the Brahmin (88 F.), the Rajput (79 F.), the Baddoi (74 F.) and the Kolta (60 F.). The highest disparity of sexes at the lowest level (the Kolta) points to a possibly low span of life and a higher rate of mortality of the Kolta women as they have to sustain hardwork with a highly insufficient standard of living. The highest ratio of females among the Bajgis goes with the highest incidence of monogamy. At Hanol, the Bajgis show a greater socio-economic diversification and independence from the traditional social economy. Because of her economic role, ranging from that of the housewife to that of dancing girls of easy virtues, the Bajgi woman is a greater asset.

On the regional stratificational ladder, polyandry gets a higher incidence where dependence of the traditional social economy is greater. At these levels (the Brahmin, the Rajput and the Kolta), the disparity of sexes is also comparatively higher. The generation-depth and size of family are positively corelated with the status of caste, with larger size and greater generation depth going with higher status. The need of keeping land intact and of maintaining a dependent source of labour supply and of economizing the resources of household living at the higher level and lack of economic avenues as a check against the break up of polyandrous family at the lowest level, seem to be the possible functional explanations of this phenomenon. A singly head of family often tends to resort to polygyny to have more helping hands in agricultural work.

Since a set of brothers usually born of a mother shares one or more wives in common, here fraternality is matrilineally defined. As per customary-legal norm of *sautiya bant* (division as per no. of co-wives), in the case of division in family, property is divided into as many shares as there be co-wives, with each share going to the offsprings (males) of one co-wife. Woman's rights as entailed in her social position, in Dr. Majumdar's view, indicate the presence of matriarchal base.

Thus, matriliny and matriarchy are juxtaposed with the otherwise patriarchal, patrilocal and patrilineal social system.

The Worldview About Woman

Being the hub of household and agricultural activities, woman is viewed as an asset. Yet, in the belief-system of the people, woman is suspect of poisoning males, avarice of material comforts and sensuous pleasure. In a folksong a husband says to her wife, "I shall not allow you to visit *mait* (father's house). Seeing the youngmen of your village you will dissolve amorously in the way asofoetida does in water". Besides wife, an unavoidable necessity, woman is, outside wedlock, an object of romance as well. In the people's worldview woman has many facets.

Thus runs a stanza of a folksong ; "Because of giving birth, she is the mother ; because of giving sensuous pleasure, she is the wife ; because of being worshipped she is the goddess ; and she is the *Kalika* (a goddess) when she destroys". The goddesses (Kalika, Durga and Deolarhi, the mother of God Mahasu) the people believe in, are benevolent to man. In the magical beliefs and the world of spiritual beings female has malevolent faces as well. Woman can be a witch. As *herh*, a female spiritual being, she is out to outwit and seduce males by taking the appearances of a beautiful belle. Always dressed in white, the *pari* (fairy) can please man with sensuous pleasure but at his own cost. When disturbed and annoyed she gets malevolent. Woman is a reality as well as a mystery, goodness and evil at the same time and a labourer, a child-producing machine as well as an object of romance.

Woman in Jaunsar Bawar is placed into two prescribed social positions, viz., *dhyanti* and *ryanti*. The synonym *dhyanti* denotes daughter of family and village. Both these terms are terms of reference. Derived out of *dhyanti*, the term *dhyanti* is a term of address for woman in her father's village. As a term of reference, *ryanti* denotes wifehood and woman's social position in her husband's house. In ordinary reference a woman is either a *dhyanti* or a *ryanti*.

In the social position of *dhyanti* woman is daughter, grand-daughter, great grand-daughter, sister, father's sister and *jost* (beloved). In the position of *ryanti*, woman is wife, co-wife, elder or junior, mother, grand-mother, daughter-in-law and mother-in-law. Viewed differently, the social positions of *dhyanti* and *ryanti* imply contrasting but inter-dependent and structurally set roles of females and rights and obligations implied therein. *Dhyanti* and *ryanti* can be conceptualized as role-sets in which status linked with the sequence of age, plays the crucial role of a structural determinant.

The Social Position of Dhyanti

Notwithstanding a definite preference for male progeny, birth of a daughter is viewed neither inauspicious nor a burden in the way it does where the custom of dowry is the most prevalent and dominant norm of marriage. Being a helping hand in household works from kitchen to fields and forests, daughter is not unwelcome member of family. In food and clothing she is accorded treatment equal to sons. Daughter's socialization takes place in the close association of her real mother and in the company of mothers some of which may be of her age.

Passing the age of infancy, daughter is obliged to look after younger siblings and work as baby-sister. Children of both sexes are playing together but girls mostly play by imitating the activities which the woman is obliged to undertake. As a daughter grows, she usually starts helping her mother and family in kitchen work, in fetching drinking water, fire-wood and grass for cattle, in tending and grazing cattle and by collecting seasonal herbs and by participating in and learning agricultural operations which grownup woman is required to undertake. Daughter is not particularly trained in knitting, needle-work, spinning and weaving as these are male's prerogatives. To look after guests in the family is daughter's obligations[2].

A woman is preferred as a wife for her proficiency in household and agricultural works. Woman's right to education is not denied ; at the moment, it is just not preferred. Formal education for girls, in the people's view, does not prepare them for the duties they are expected to perform in future life. It rather complicates the arrangement of matrimony. Our survey reveals (Bhatt and Jain, 1974) that out of thirteen unmarried Brahmin girls, between the ages of five to fifteen years, only one studied upto class one and none was going to school. Among twenty-two Rajput girls (4-22 years in age), one unsuccessfully studied upto class ten, one upto six, one upto five and six were studying in classes 1-4. This is because the village studied is situated on the side of motor road to Chakarata and is more under the impact of economic diversification generated by modern economic forces of change. The Bajgi women of Hanol, in the age group of 25-30 years and residing in their *mait* (father's houses) showed a better record of primary education than the then female generation in the shcool-going age. This is attributed to the fact that about twenty-five years back (in fiftees) school was housed in the heart of the village and the then teacher took inspiring interest in his work. In education, as expected, the Kolta woman lags most.

After the age of childhood, there is a gradual segregation of sexes because males and females have to be trained for different departments of socio-economic life. As a girl enters adolscence, she gradually draws into a circle of female friends of her choice, some of whom may be of her age, some younger and some seniors. Here she is gradually initiated into the art of group-singing and dancing which are quite common while at work in the fields and on the occasions of festive fairs and in the evening get togethers with the yougmen of the village. After the day's work and evening meals before sun-set, young boys and *dhyantis*, both married and unmarried, gather in the village quadrangle (*anganrh*) to sing and dance, to smoke and exchange wits and frivolities. Use of cigarettes and drinks are not tabooed to woman. In these gathering *dhyanti* gradually learns about the mysteries of male-female relationship, and she gradually enters the role of a romantic beloved for which there is ample expression in the local folklore and even in practice, against which now there is definite resentment.

To marry the *dhyanti* of is her eldest father's or brother's responsibility. In her first marriage arranged normally between the ages of five to fifteen years, she does not have any choice.

But as divorcee she has but a limited choice. The extent of choice in matrimony depends on woman's age and personality. By custom bride-price is token (rupee one) and dowry is confined mainly to five utensils. To celebrate marriage bride is taken in procession by her party to bridegroom's house. Only in the well-to-do high caste families, bridegroom's procession is taken to bride's house where marriage is solemnized through the classical Hindu rituals. On reaching groom's, bride is taken to her real mother-in-law sitting near the hearth in the kitchen. She touches the feet of her mother-in-law who after giving her a present of some ornament or money, accepts her as her daughter-in-law. Other mothers-in-law repeat the ritual in order of seniority. After that she is made to sit with the bridegroom, generally the eldest brother, or the brother in whose name the bride may be brought, and after both are fed with rice cooked in milk (*khir*), marriage is considered complete.

Marriage neither dissolves nor does it lessen or render distant the relationship between a *dhyanti* and her family of orientation. In the role of father's sister and/or grand-father's sister, *dhyanti* may play a decisive role in arranging marriage of her brother's sons and daughters. To expect gifts of clothes, eatables, grain, ornaments and money from her parents, brothers and brother's sons is a privilege of the married *dhyanti*. To be invited to her parental house on festive occasions is again a privilege of a married but young and issueless *dhyanti*. Rather, it is her right in the exercise of which she may visit her parental house uninvited. Of course, as *dhyanti* grows in age and gets burdened with the responsibilities of wifehood and motherhood, she gradually becomes unmindful of latter privilege.

In an annual cycle, visits to parental house are many as festivals of merry-making follow almost every busy agricultural season. Visits to parental house are the periods of rest and relaxation after hard agricultural work. During such visits to parental house, besides helping her mother or sister-in-law in the routine work of the family, '*dhyanti* is more entitled to enjoy a gay and unrestricted life.... She moves about in the village and takes part in all rejoicings, dancing and singing on the festivals' (Majumdar, 1963 : 318). All these are customarily denied to a woman in the role of *ryanti*. And, what is more, she is allowed to, and generally does, indulge in affairs with village youth and young guests from other villages. Presence of *dhyantis* adds colour, frivolity, mirth and romantic aura to festive fairs. All this relaxation is not possible if the husbands are also present there. By custom, generally, husbands are not present on such occasions.

In such fairs, *dhyanti* may negotiate a remarriage after breaking the existing one if she were dissatisfied with it. The deserted, the deserter and the divorcee, both real and prospective, try their luck in such festive fairs in the midst of singing and dancing and merry-making that usually goes late upto night. This normative permissiveness to *dhyanti*, the *dhyanti* affair, 'the double standard of morality for woman' in the words of Dr. Majumdar, is not unrestrained and a sheer laxity. Here woman is highly selective and choosy, quite conscious of drawing distinction between respectable woman and prostitute. However, this practice is now resented and is being checked, particularly the possibilities of sexual lapses with outsiders. But, if such a friendship does occur, it is *josti*, something sacred and other worldly. That is why lovers and beloved ones are normatively obliged to get each other's name tattooed on the innerfold of their left arms. In a folksong, a beloved asks her paramour : "The younghood is not return ; get my name written on your left arm".

Dhyanti does not have right to inherit. She does have the privilege of receiving help and maintenance from her family of orientation in the exigencies of desertion by husband, divorce, loss of support in in-law's house in old age, destitution and incompatibility with husband or in-laws. When a woman has to fall back upon the support of her family of orientation for a longer period, a field may be tilled in her name and she may be helped from the returns of its produce. In case of division in family, she is obliged to go along with her uterine kins. On the death of her husband, after the mourning period is over, her brother is normatively obliged to present her a nose-ring of gold and of silver in case of the Kolta woman.

Tradition enjoins her to touch the feet of parents, brothers and parents-in-law.

The Social Position of Ryanti

Marriage is the gateway to *ryantihood.* Proposal comes from the side of male and it has to be from outside parental village of *dhyanti.* In our survey, 41% of married women were brought as virgin (*ghar-dhyanti*) and 59% as divorcees. Remarriage of divorcee, widow and even of known lax is not a stigma. Nor is it a problem provided woman to be remarried were of good physique and proficient in agricultural work. Divorcees, young widows and spinsters hardly pose any problem to the social system.

Widowhood does not have a high incidence. Only very old and infirm women may remain widow. On the death of the eldest husband, all the wives take off their nose-ring and enter the state of temporary widowhood till the mourning is not over. Then, those accepting presents of clothes and ornaments from the remaining husbands, re-enter the old marital status and those refusing it, return to their parental house and remarry in due course of time. If younger husband dies, wife is not obliged to take off her nose-ring.

Ryanti's field of daily routine ranges from household work to agricultural operations. Early in the morning she fetches drinking water from the water source. Males share with her in milking of cows and buffaloes and churning of milk. She usually fetches wood for hearth, grass for cattle and leaves for manure. Cleaning cattleshed and collection of cowdung is her job, and if there be a need she helps by tending and grazing cattle. She undertakes cleaning of house, scrubbing of wooden floors, washing of clothes (generally light) and husking of grain. All agricultural operations, excepting ploughing, levelling and combing, are undertaken by her. Transplantation of paddy, sowing and seeding are her specializations.

In the traditionally patterned division of labour among *ryantis*, co-wives, based on age and status, the above female activities are generally allotted to the young *ryantis.* The seniormost *ryanti* (mother-in-law or co-wife) becomes the head and generally undertakes cooking. Their seniority notwithstanding, the very old and infirm recedes into the background. The senior *ryanti* and also one in the period of rest and recuperation after childbirth, refrain from out door work and stay at home looking after the children of co-*ryantis* and daughters-in-law. Before evening meals are served, *ryantis* are obliged to wash the legs of their husbands with hot water and message them with oil. They also wash and message each other's legs. In taking meals, *ryantis* follow males. In sickness and childbirth, a woman is looked after by her co-*ryantis* and female in-law(s).

This inter-personal obligatory cooperation and division of labour is crossed with conflict and co-*ryantis*' rights and obligations against each other. In the event of a husband's death, a co-*ryanti* had a right to chose a husband from the remaining ones whom she would prefer to live with. If there be division in family, a barren *ryanti* can demand a share in the children of co-*ryantis*. Tension and conflict between co-*ryantis* may arise because of the preference for a particular husband, barrenness of a *ryanti* and fecundity of others and shirking of work and preferential treatment to a *ryanti* by a particular husband or husbands. Tensions and conflicts among co-wives do not result in as much division in family as in dissolution of marriage.

A *ryanti* woman is not obliged to observe *purdah*. As a festive occasion draws near, a young *ryanti* may compel her husband to send her to her parental house as a part of her previlege. It is a matter of prestige with her that she must be brought back from her parents' house by someone from her husband's side. She is endowed with an exclusive right over the dowry she brings and gifts (including money) she receives from relatives, in-laws, husbands and keeping of poultry. If in need of money, husband can borrow it from his wife and has to return it with interest if dissolution of marriage follows.

Woman does not have right to possession over the ornaments given to her by her husband's side. Ordinarily, woman expects her husbands to provide her with food, clothing, shelter, ornaments, medicine, affectionate and loving treatment and even with smoke and drinks; and an ordinary woman doubts in her belief if a single husband can fulfil all these expectations of woman. Tradition allows the Brahmin female to eat fish but not the Brahmin male. Woman has right to dissolve marriage on the grounds of rough treatment from the in-laws, overwork in husband's house, incompatibility with co-wives, taking of another wife by husband, agedness of husband, insufficiency of food, clothing and ornaments received from husband's house, compulsion to cohabit with a husband she was not brought for or she did not like and death of the husband she was meant for and any other cause a woman may develop. If a young Brahmin girl feels that her husband is not smart, she may ask her parents to dissolve marriage.

Woman's right to dissolve marriage goes with her liability to pay compensation to her husband. Compensation includes expenses incurred by husband's side to celebrate marriage to feast bride's party. Since woman does not arrange her marriage, she is made liable for which parents are responsible. She is often made to dissolve marriage and remarry because of her parents', particularly father's or brother's wish. Rising amount of compensation because of rising costs, tends to affect woman's status negatively of which the new generation is quite conscious. Here woman of today, in group discussion on the problem, pleads for the retention of her right to dissolve marriage without her liability to pay compensation to the husband she divorces.

As *ryanti* a woman is expected to be loyal to the polyandrous system of family. Many a woman have felt constrained to dissolve marriage because of their preferential weakness for a husband at the cost of loyalty to the system. In fact, in the polyandrous set-up of family, sexual adjustment between husbands and wife or wives is crucial to the functioning of family. As wife, woman is obliged to fulfil husbands' demand for sex to beget children, preferably male progeny. Barrenness results in marital maladjustment leading to dissolution of marriage or it results in taking another wife. Normatively sanctioned privileged prerogative over wife or wives in sex, results in demands of sex from other husbands as and when occasion permits—in night and day and inside and outside the house. Under the circumstances, woman is obliged to bear the strain of multiplicity cohabitation.

Woman's resentment against this practice of sexual sharing of wife is also increasing. As she may be heard pleading that she is a human being and not a cow. Now, in many marriages, this question of sexual sharing of wife is decided at the time and part of settling matrimony, and in many cases, contrary to the arrangement already decided upon, if forced to be shared, woman may prefer to dissolve marriage. Practice of the traditional norms of polyandry, reinforced because of the grant of tribal status to the people, coupled with growing resentment against them, has tended to precipitate variant forms of family on the polyandrous and mutually constraining obligations for woman.

Depending on the resources of family, the tendency of taking as many wives as there be the number of brothers with one wife in the name of each, coupled with the growing use of kinship terminology of monogamous structure of family in the joint household, is definitely discernible now. In such situations sexual sharing of wives, a sort of group marriage in disguise, may be found if it is commonly agreed upon by the brothers concerned. Behind the growing facade of monogamy, the dominant traditional norm of polyandry permissiveness seems to continue as an underground cultural strain.

Woman's name is not called in her in-law's house. She is located and known after the village she comes from, and this becomes the basis of locating a *ryanti's* children. Mother does not discriminate between sons and daughters though, as already indicated, a mother is more close to her daughter(s), so much so, a mother knows all about her daughter, even about her amorous affairs if any. On festive occasions mother often insists on inviting daughter for a visit. Mother's role and her social position are to be accorded respect and veneration. This expectation is extended to the social position of mother-in-law in relation to that of daughter-in-law. To receive bride first of all is mother-in-law's normative prerogative which signifies the structural significance of her social position.

Drawn from varied backgrounds and age-groups and

with varied rights and privileges, mothers-in-law and daughters-in-law develop the pattern of constrained cooperation of relationships in which the role of the mother-in-law tends to be dominant. Preference for cross-cousin in marriage and or for a bride from the parental village of mother-in-law seems to be a structural device to smoothen their relationship. However, cases are not wanting in which has been found constraint to dissolve marriage because of strained relations with mother-in-law. This constraint in the structure of family tends to come up where a family moves towards modernization along with the traditional base of social economy.

The Ritual Social Position

Birth of a girl is not associated with any ritual inauspiciousness. The purificatory ritual of *chhatthi* is observed in the birth of a male as well as female. In the case of female child, the ceremony of ritual shaving or the first crop of hair is not observed. In the pre-puberty age, an unmarried girl, carries a purifying ritual status. The Bajgis of Hanol, to celebrate the ritual of *chhatthi*, invite an unmarried girl to sprinkle milk over the mother and the child to signify their ritual purification.

Menstruation is associated with woman's ritual impurity. When in menses, woman refrains from cooking food, from fetching water and from entering agricultural fields having bulbous plants. Appearance of first menses is not associated with any ritual. The ritual of menstruational pollution is not observed in the smaller families of low caste men having single wife. In childbirth woman is confined for ten days to be purified by a ritual bath.

Here woman is not a ritual partner of male. Observation of ritual fast and ritual worship and propitiation are male's prerogatives. Woman, like the Kolta, is not allowed to enter the temple and if she does so, she has to sacrifice a goat, actually or tokenly, to appease the god and to ward off the defilement caused by her. She is not permitted to touch the temple-priest at Hanol. The priest is required to purify himself by a ritual bath and to forego even the only one meal allowed to him, if a woman sits on the wooden plank over which he may be sitting.

To attain fecundity, woman undertakes pilgrimage to the Mahasu temple at Hanol. With a goat to sacrifice she enters the temple. There she receives from the priest, the grains of rice already offered to the deity. Afterwards in the compound of the temple, the goat is sacrificed and she shares the meat with the officials and servants of the temple. On being back to her house, she cooks the rice in milk and eats the preparation (*khir*) to attain fecundity. This is the ritual of *beej lena.*

Widowhood is not inauspicious. Use of coloured clothes is not tabooed to her. In the event of woman's death, the corpse of the widow and the married is dressed in a set of new clothes not used before. Every woman keeps a set of new unused clothes in her bag (now box) in which even husband is not permitted to look into. The corpse of a *ryanti* is given the make up (*singar*) of a married woman. It is not done in the case of widow.

Both the widow and the married are cremated. The bier of both is covered by red cloth. The corpse of an unmarried girl is not dressed in a set of new and unused clothes and her bier is covered by white, in place of red cloth. In the performance of *shradha*, woman's ritual status is equal to that of man.

NOTES

1. This paper is based on the data collected in the summer of 1974 in the villages of Koruwa, Chilharh, Chatra and Hanol to prepare a report on the 'Changing Status of Woman among the Polyandrous People of Jaunsar-Bawar'. This study was Commissioned by the National Committee on Woman's Status through ICSSR, New Delhi.
2. Certain caste-wise variations in *dhyanti's* obligations towards her family of orientation are discernible. Among the Brahmins and the Rajputs tending and grazing of cattle is not an economic occupation whereas among the Koltas it is so. Among the Koltas, young and old *dhyantis* and even *ryantis* generally take to it to eke out a living. Among them, a *dhyanti* may also help her father or brother by working as a wage earner. Here and there, among the low and the poor, *dhyantis* have been found

obliged to supplement income by trading in their virtue (Gupta, 1975 : XX).

REFERENCES

Bhatt, G.S. 1956 Jaunsari Lokgeeton Mein Romance (in Hindi) *Prachya Manav Vaigyanik*, vol. 3.

——1977 Economic Role of Woman and its Status Consequences in a Polyandrous Society (unpublished).

——1978 From Caste Structure to Tribe : The case of Jaunsar Bawar, *The Eastern Anthropologist* 3: 1.

——1980 Constraints of being Polyandrous—Tribal : The Case of Jaunsar Bawar in *Family Marriage and Social Change on the Indian Fringe*, S.M. Dubey, P.K. Bordoloi and B.N. Borthakur (eds.) Cosmo Publications, New Delhi.

Bhatt G.S. & S.D. Jain 1974 Changing Status of Women in a Polyandrous Society (Jaunsar Bawar) ICSSR, New Delhi (unpublished).

Bhoria, K.S. 1975 The Case of Jaunsaris as a Scheduled Tribe, *Journal of the Lal Bahadur Shastri National Academy of Adm.* XX : 2.

Chandra, H. 1975 Trafficking in Women and Prostitution in Jaunsar Bawar *The Journal of the Lal Bahadur Shastri National Academy of Adm.* XX : 2.

Gupta R.N. 1975 From Green Hills of Purola to the Brothels of Delhi and Meerat, *The Journal of the Lal Bahadur Shastri National Academy of Adm.* XX : 2.

Jain, S.D. 1980 Women's Status in Marriage and Family in a Polyandrous Society in *Family Marriage and Social Change on the Indian Fringe* S.M. Dubey, P.K. Bordoloi and B.N. Barthakur (eds) Cosmo Publications, New Delhi.

Johnson, Harry M. 1968 *Sociology—A Systematic Introduction*, Routledge & Kegan Paul, London.

Majumdar, D.N. 1963 *Himalayan Polyandry*, Asia Publishing House, Bombay.

Nadel, S.F. 1957 *The Theory of Social Structure*, Cohen & West London.

22

STATUS OF WOMEN IN POLYANDROUS SOCIETY*

S.B. Nandi

Bachofen (1861) advanced the hypothesis that in the history of marital institutions, the initial state of promiscuity was followed by matrilineal descent and maternal rule. Disapproving Bachofen's and Morgan's (1877) conjecture of universal primal state of promiscuity another pioneer evolutionist, McLennan (1876) explained that matrilineal descent originated due to uncertainty of parenthood resulting from polyandry. He thus associated matrilineal descent and maternal authority with a variable, none the less universal, era of polyandrous union. Despite differences on the genesis of the matrilineal social system most scholars agree that matrilineal institutions consistently favour a high status for women although, even among such distinguishably matrilineal societies as the Khasis and Garos of Assam or the Nayars of Kerala, it is the maternal uncle who wields considerable influence and authority in his sister's household. Women of such polyandrous societies as the Nayar of Kerala having the traditional matrilineal system of descent and inheritance enjoy a high or at least an egalitarian social status (Panikkar, 1918 : 266). But the questions arise : What about

*Reproduced by permission of the authority of Man in India from *Man in India*, 57(2) : 137-151, 1977.

the position of women in a polyandrous society with partilineal social system ? Do women enjoy a favourable or an egalitarian status in such communities ? Is there any correlation between social status and scope of sexual choice for women in a society that permits multiple mating for them or is founded on polyandrous union ? Herein is an attempt to discuss these firstly in the light of recent field experience on the polyandrous Bhotia of North Sikkim adjoining Tibet and then with aid of cross-cultural data. Unlike the well-defined legal status, however, social status is a relatively abstract concept. While legal status precisely define the statutory position and grant specific legal powers to enforce legal rights and obligations to an individual or legally constituted body, social status, in Linton sense is "any position in the social system". It is simply a collection of rights and duties and "a role represents the dynamic aspect of status". (Linton, 1936 : 113). The assessment of rights, duties and privileges of women, the roles accorded to them in different economic, social and ritual spheres, therefore, appear relevant for evaluation of their status in a society.

The northern most part of Sikkim comprised of Lachen and Lachung Blocks is almost exclusively the home of the Bhotia (Druk pas) who came from Paro[1] and who practise fraternal polyandry. The community inhabiting at Lachen introduces themselves as the Lachenpa. They have a mixed pastoral-agricultural economy. For exigencies of climate, pastoralism in the cis-Himalayas is associated with transhumance. With seasonal changes in climate and conditions in pasturage, the transhumant Lachen pas move up and down at a streteh of 38 miles of mountainous territory between the Thanggu (12.850ft.) at the north and the Lachen valley (8,950 ft.) towards south. Beside rearing *yak*, common domestic cattle, *zho* (hybrid of *yak* and common cattle), sheep, goat, mule and pony, they raise potato, radish and turnip in the limited cultivable patches of hill slopes around the Thanggu. With the coming of winter in October, the community, keeping pace with the seasonal southward advance of snow-line moves down to the Lachen valley halting on their way temporarily at places like Kalep, Yathang, Tolam, Yunga and Chungsema for utilisation of the growth in pasturages there. The Lachen valley and Thanggu are the winter and summer headquarters of the community respectively. Every family maintains at the least a couple of cottages one at the Lachen valley and another at the Thanggu region. The restricted cultivable land at places like Menshit-hang, Denga and Latong, south of Lachen is utilised for producing maize, wheat, millet and apple. The animals born and adapted to living in higher altitudes nearer to the perpetual snow-line, cannot endure the summer at the Lachen valley. As the winter retreats, the community also moves up in May with flocks. None is supposed to return to Lachen with flock even a day earlier than the date announced by the elected Headman, *Pipon* in the community council, *jom sa* for return of the entire community lest he draws advantage of the fresh growth in the valley pasturage for his animals. And anyone, who infringes on this norm is heavily penalised. In this way, the transhumance is regulated by the members of the community in this harsh mountain environs for survival.

Prior to the closure of the Indo-Tibet border in 1960 the Lachen pas also supplemented their economy by trade with the Tibetans. Men travelled with their surplus produces of potato, radish, turnip and apple as well as essential commodities like sugar, tobacco, bamboos, wooden and iron implements, kerosene, chemical paints in caravans across the mountain passes and in exchange or by the sale-proceeds acquired wool, *yak* meat and fat, butter, mineral salt, wheat, barley and so on for consumption and sale. The rugs and carpets made of Tibetan wool generally by the women folk were also sold in the markets of South Sikkim and Darjeeling. After the closure of the border, however, the trade activities diminished. Scarcity of wool adversely affected this home-industry and domestic economy. Surplus farm produces as well as livestock and their products are now sent to the markets of South Sikkim. Within such ecological and economic settings the robust, resolute and industrious Drukpa women have significant economic functions. Nevertheless, they do not seem to enjoy an egalitarian status with men.

A housewife is unchallenged mistress in purely domestic sphere. Notwithstanding the same, in patrilocal residence she has to abide by some major instructions of her co-husbands. The latter, however, do not interfere with her day-to-day management of household. Married women remain constantly at work at the service of her spouses and caring of children. She leaves bed never failing, at dawn approximately an hour earlier than the male members, feeds the milch-cattle in the house and serves breakfast to all the members of the family. Thereafter, she takes the animals to the nearby pasture to be brought back again before sunset. Besides cooking and serving meals, cleaning used utensils and clothes of all the members of the family, bringing water, collecting heavy leads of firewood from the forest, she assists in cultivating land whatever time at her disposal permits. She participates in all agricultural operations except ploughing ; prepares the soil by means of hoe and do threshing, grinding and storing. A woman in advanced stage of pregnancy, however, refrains from carrying heavy loads and using hoe for cultivation. There is cooperative interdependence between sexes. Men build and repair terrace walls, huts, village paths and the Public House, *mang khim* where the village elders assemble ; women excavate and bring heavy stones and sand. Most households have indigenous handlooms, *ogongs*, made by craftsmen of the community ; women weave colourful yarns for their traditional apparels like *kho* and *pangden*. Men procure wool ; women dye, spin into yarn and make garments for all. They weave beautiful rugs and carpets ; men sell them in distant marts. Women occasionally earn daily-wages knitting woollen garments, rugs and carpets employed by neighbours. Such female casual workers get five or six rupees, two meals and indigenous millet beer, *chang* for working eight hours in a day. Normally, she retires to bed after attending to all domestic chores when the male members are already asleep. A Lachen Pa male is also hard-working but he is not as constantly at work as a female. A man finds leisure for drinking and gossiping with neighbours sitting in the warmth of the kitchen-fire. The charge of family-finance is held by the male head, usually the eldest brother who is considered as the custodian of property. In matters like marriage of a daughter, acquisition or disposal of property and the like the eldest husband discusses with his wife and male siblings but the final decision rests with him.

Inspite of substantial contributions in the austere economic life, women's right is not recognised in the matter of transmission of landed property. This social disability makes them dependent upon men. They do not succeed as heir to the paternal immovable property. However, some sort of bilateralism is followed in regard to transmission of movable property. Jewelleries, not endowed to daughter-in-law by a woman during her life-time, are inherited by her unmarried daughter, if any. Otherwise, these are divided equally among the married daughters and the daughter-in-law. Again, obviously on social security consideration, an unmarried daughter is usually allowed a reasonable share of the livestock owned by her deceased father, and the male siblings are liable to incur expenses essential for her marriage. Even the eldest male spouse cannot dispose of his wife's personal belongings like jewelleries, ornaments and other valuables without her consent.

A male child is more welcome in the family. When a child is born kins and affines express pleasures, bless the new-born with a scarf, *khada* and cash amount varying between three to ten rupees. The affines also present butter, rice, flattened rice, fruits, meats, tea and millet-beer to show affections. In the case of first child-birth and subsequent male births more substantial gifts are presented, and if the first issue is a male, the gifts and enjoyments are in great plenty.

Descent is patrilineal and children belong to the father's clan. Children use the term father, *apa*, for addressing the eldest male spouse of their mother ; and her other co-spouses are addressed as uncle, *aku*, though anyone of them may be the biological father. The maternal uncles are addressed by the term *ashang*. Thrice in a year members of the patrilineage assemble to make offerings, *lache*, to the departed ancestors. A woman looses her natal clan membership after marriage and becomes affiliated to the clan organisation of her co-husbands. A brief flash of women's prestige is seen in customary marriage negotiations. But even in this, masculine dominance is superimposed. Maternal uncles of boys and girls have significant roles in such negotiations. Consent of a girl is generally taken by her eldest maternal uncle before negotiations begin. Customarily, it is the maternal uncle of a prospective bridegroom who has to make the first approach to his counterpart of the bride making a gift of a considerable quantity of millet-beer. Negotiations get underway, only if the liquor is accepted by the bride's uncle. Moreover, a heavy amount has to be paid for the bride varying between five hundred to one thousand rupees. In fact, however, the eldest maternal uncle of the bride obtains clear approval from the girls' father before he undertakes negotiation with his counterpart on the other side.

Parents think seriously of their daughter's marriage after she is fifteen. But they have to wait for the initiative that must come from a prospective groom's side. It is considered undignifying and socially degrading for a girl's family to make the first approach. Besides, it may also generate suspicion in the boy's family about the girl's character that she may bear some inherent defect or social stigma. The conjugal relations between the wife and the co-husbands are founded on mutual understanding and reciprocity. She addresses her co-spouses by the term, *chi*. A married woman wears *pangden*-rectangular multi-coloured piece of cloth hanging from abdomen. She, however, uses foot-wears just as a man does in the extreme cold environment.

Although uterine brothers share a common wife hardly at any point of time they live together at the residence. Customarily, the second son embraces Lamaism. He is taught religion and ethics in the monastery. Ploughing, smoking, slaughtering of animal and consumption of fresh meat preparation, which retains soul matter for sometime is forbidden to him. If possible, the parents construct a hut for him in a plot alloted in the monastery area. Except the above constraints there is no bar in his residing home. But he has to go to the monastery to attend to his duties during all rituals. One or two other brothers are often away from home either encamping near the pasturage tending the main body of the livestock or near the cultivable fields miles away from the settlement for farming or trading in the marts of South Sikkim and Darjeeling.

It is true that within such polyandrous social structure while men have extremely restricted choice, married women enjoy wider scope for legitimate sexual gratification. But she is not absolutely free in making her own selection among the multiple mates. Because, it is prerogative for the eldest male spouse to have the wife with him as bed partner at night if he is at the residence. Generally, the other co-spouses have access to her when the eldest spouse is away from home. Occasionally, however, the wife gives vent to her feeling of resentment for any action of her eldest husband by going to sleep with another of her cospouses. Sometime, at midnight she may withdraw from the eldest spouse or the latter may also ask his wife to go away from him thus sending her to sleep with any other of his brothers in a different room and seriatim unions occur. So, there is a tacit understanding among the male siblings in the matter of cohabitation with the common wife. Sexual jealousy is not given a place scrupulously in the mind. Family solidarity is maintained in the interest of keeping property united and ensuring economic security. Thus, in sex life, a woman appears to be in a relatively privileged position. She gets variety in enjoying sex and her sex instinct or appetite is not blunted by association with a sole mate throughout her life. Nevertheless, it is difficult to agree that such sex-privilege enhances her social status comprehensively.

A married woman has to maintain fidelity and loyalty to her husbands in the strict sense of the term. Unfaithfulness on the part of wife leads to dissolution of marital bond. And in such an event the payment made for bride is demanded back. There is no social constraint for remarriage of a divorcee but if she does it, her new consorts have to pay compensation to her former spouses for the expenses incurred during their marriage. If, however, the separation is due to ill-treatment meeted to her by her spouses or parents-in-law, maintenance is demanded from the ex-spouses usually in the form of a share of the livestock owned by them.

Because of automatic Lavirate once married, a woman normally enjoys considerable social security. If the eldest husband dies she remains the wife of other surviving brothers and no ceremony is required. Consequently young widow is rare in the community. There are instances of children living with the divorcee. If a younger brother leaves a polyandrous family and marries again, the father of his new consort has to pay compensation in the form of a head and a thigh of *yak*, some millet-beer and cash-money, amounting to five hundred rupees to his former spouse in the polyandrous unit particularly if the withdrawing man was blessed by presentation of scarfs during marriage rite by kinsmen and thereby formally bound by ties of wedlock. In a polyandrous family, a person is ignorant about his or her actual biological father. A child learns to regard mother's eldest spouse as father (*apa*), while her other co-spouses are introduced as uncle (*aku*). A withdrawing husband cannot claim any offspring of the conjugal group as his own even if he is personally certain of his male parentage for a specific progeny. On the demise of wife, the widower siblings, if they like to remarry, have to abide by the custom of sororate. Failure to do so makes them liable to pay compensation to the unmarried sister-in-law. Again, refusal on her part to marry deceased sister's husband makes them eligible to claim compensation. Conformity to norms of behaviour and traditional pattern of bio-social relationship between men and women are partly ensured by these means.

The fair sex among the Druk pas have little voice in community decision-making. The community council is constituted of males only. It is during the absence of adult male members that a female represents her family unit at the general meetings of the community that meets more than once in a year, to avoid penalisation. Male head of an unit is liable to pay fine of five rupees to council for being absent in a meeting. A household without any adult male, however, is represented by its female-head and is required to be paid half that amount as punishment for absence. Thus, women have secondary importance in public affairs and community decision-making.

Women have insignificant role in the religious life of the community. Separate monastery exists for the nuns. Women may make offerings at the general monastery on festive occasions, but are prohibited from making prayers regularly or participating in the rituals there. It is presumed that presence of women in the sanctity of monastery is not conducive for meditation by the *lamas.* Men refrain from attending to the rituals in the nun's monastery. After marriage of a daughter or a son, a mother is expected to pray regularly in the nun's monastery on eighth, fifteenth and thirtieth day of every Tibetan month.

Women's subordinate position is further evident in their exclusion from participation in the community New Years's Day festival, *Loshong* in which males, usually heads of families, get together in a grand day-long feasting at the Public House. Every housewife sends specially prepared food-stuff, tea and millet-beer which the elders take pleasure in sharing among themselves as an expression of community solidarity. After lunch when five girls and an equal number of boys dance together, the women may come and enjoy the show.

The Lachen pa are conscious that women have a subordinate status in their society. This is evident from the differences made between men and women in raising the height of funeral pyres. In the case of a female corpse eight and in case of male seven successive tiers of fire-wood are laid for consuming the body into flames. Among the Drukpa Bhotias of north-east Darjeeling it is raised nine tiers high in the case of the female corpse and a layer less in the case of a male one. This discrimination is explained in the way that women are one degree below men in the society. So the funeral pyre is raised higher to make amend the low status of the fair sex in the community when she goes to the other world.

It may appear from the above discussions that there is some kind of a dichotomy in the status of women among the Lachen pa community. Indeed, while women enjoy considerable authority in the domestic sphere and some privileges in sex-life in this polyandrous society men dominate in all other facets of life. There is exploitation of their labours. It is not only that descent and inheritance are traced along the male line but male children are more welcome. Above all, women are neither economically independent nor have they any significant role in community decision-making. Women have to abide by the decisions of the male elders in the community council. Their ritual status is low. And also in the emic view of the community it is recognised that women have a lower position in society during the life-time which need be compensated after death. Hence, it will not be correct to say that women enjoy an egalitarian, far less, a superior status in this polyandrous community.

Cross-Cultural Data

Although adequate data status of women in patrilineal polyandrous societies of other areas of the world are not available and no objective criterion for evaluation of women's social status has yet been determined, some relevant facts and comments pertaining to such societies may be examined here. Rivers (1966 : 566) reported that among the patrilineal Todas of the Nilgiri Hills although women have such freedom, they are unimportant in ritual life. The exclusion of women from the dairy cult, the culture-focus of the Todas reflects the attitude of the community towards the sex. Women undoubtedly have a subordinate position in the Toda society. In patrilineal Kota society (which of course, Mandelbaum considers not polyandrous in the strict sense), the principle of fraternal equivalence is given so much importance for maintenance of economic solidarity among a group of brothers that even if a woman dislikes the brother of her husband she is ultimately forced to tolerate and her will is disregarded (Mandelbaum, 1938 : 577 : 78). This does not indicate favourable position of women in the Kota society. Among the patrilineal Khasas of Dehra Dun women are denied of all rights to own property (Saksena, 1953 : 97). The rule of village exogamy is strictly adhered to and although a woman, as *dhyanti* in her parental village enjoys inordinate latitude (Mazumdar, 1955 : 86), her freedom of movement is restricted when she resides in her husband's village as *ranti.* Disloyalty and infidelity are taken seriously. Such misdemeanours may lead to dissolution of marriage in which case she has to leave all her ornaments and jewelleries behind. In popular saying, a girl after her marriage is compared to the 'carcase of an animal' so that parents can have no interest in her marriage (Aiyappan, 1940 : 32). Among the polyandrous Thandans (Tiyas), Kammalans and allied artisan castes in Kerala who practise patrilineal descent and inheritance, and have patrilocal residence, women have a position inferior to men. Children remain with father even after dissolution of marriage (Prince Peter, 1963 : 531-534). Thus in all these patrilineal polyandrous societies women do not enjoy status-superiority, even egalitarian status with men.

But double standards exist in regard to the status of women within polyandrous societies which have matri-patrilineal structural dichotomy. In such societies women have superior status when they have right over property and when post-marital residence is uxori or matrilocal. Prince Peter (ibid : 315) reports that in the most common *bag-ma* type of patrilocal polyandrous union among the Lahulia going together with patrilineal descent and inheritance the wife has an inferior position, whereas, in *mag-pa* polyandrous union with concomitant matrilineal inheritance and matrilocal residence, a Lahuli women enjoys superior status position. She can take as many husbands as she desires. Younger brothers of a *mag-pa* bridegroom do not have access normally to the elder brother's wife. Children of the heiress take her name. She takes husbands unto herself to beget children to succeed as heir to the property she received from her progenitors A *mag-pa* husband can be turned out by his wife without any obligation to compensate him. Similar double standards also exist in regard to position of women in Ladaki dichotomous society (Prince Peter, ibid: 346).

In Kandyan Sri Lanka women have superior position when the marriage is matrilocal *binna* form in which the husbands go to live with the family of a young woman than in patrilocal *diga* union. In the former kind, the co-husbands do not have right on the property of their consort which is reverted to her parents if she dies childless. In case of divorce, children stay with the mother (Prince Peter, ibid : 131).

Until 1890, when polyandry was popular among the Nayars of Kerala and men had not themselves assumed rights and legal and moral responsibilities of their children, a woman had hardly any obligation to her husband other than granting of sexual privileges. An individual had no legal right in a particular wife (Schneider and Gough, 1961 : 360). Panikkar (ibid : 366), categorically comments,

> "... as far as Nayers are concerned, their women enjoy equality with men. They can hold property in their own right and enter the professions they chose. ... On the whole I am inclined to say that women is Malabar among the Nayar at least enjoy, greater liberty, with regard to individual conduct, family relationship and social life. This no doubt is due to the influence of matrilineal customs." (1918 : 266).

In the changed context, a Nayar woman as reported by Gough (ibid : 363) ranks lower than men. She has to show respect to her husband and in the presence of her kin remains standing before him.

Opler (1943 : 44) examined the available data on the Nair, Toda, Kota, Tibetan, Wahuma, Pawnee, Shoshoni and the Marquesan and found that women enjoy egalitarian status in these polyandrous societies. He dealt with the problem of status and role of women in these communities and despite inadequacy of evidences, could demonstrate the favourable position of women in the Tibetan, Shoshoni and Marquesan societies. Hence further discussion on each of these communities here appears to be redundant.

But about the Tibetan polyandry Linton writes,

> "In Tibet all arable land has long since passed into family holdings. Many of these holdings have become so small that they barely suffice to support a conjugal group and could not do so if they were further subdivided. It has become customary for one son in the family to go into religious life, thus relinquishing his claim on the family land. The other sons marry a single wife, work the family holding for the support of this woman and her children, and pass the holding on to the children intact. Inspite of female infanticide the position of woman is high. The wife usually takes charge of the finances of the family and may dominate her spouses ..." (ibid : 183).

From Prince Peter's report (ibid : 418-542) it is also evident that in *mag-pa* matrilocal union among the Tibetans in which an heiress takes husbands unto herself, the male spouses are treated as servants of the wife. Wife is the mistress of the household. It is apparent therefore, that inspite of the practise of female infanticide women have high status among the polyandrous Tibetan lower classes as they have some degree of economic independence. Women in the polyandrous Shoshoni tribe of America who gather pinon nuts for subsistence also have considerable economic independence which attributes to their favourable position. In non-fraternal Marquesan polyandrous union a number of unrelated men join the household of a woman. She has power of directing her male co-spouses as she retains control over the domestic economy.

Conclusion

It appears, therefore, that women enjoy favourable social position in societies that not only accord them scope of multiple sexual choices but economic independence and control over family finance as well. Economic freedom for women in preliterate societies is associated with the rule of matrilinal inheritance and matri or uxorilocal norm of residence. Wider scope of sexual choice, even if it is of non-marital form does not exclusively attribute status-superiority to the fair sex. Sex along cannot be a test of status. This is evident from the fact that women among the patrilineal, patrilocal Druk pa Bhotias, Khasas, Todas, Kotas, Thandans and Kammalans do not hold enviable social position. Moreover, we find that those polyandrous Lahuli and Kandyan women who, respectively, enter into *bag-ma* and *diga* forms of union enjoining pursuance of patrilineal principle of inheritance and patrilocal norm of residence do not enjoy such favourable position as those who go through *mag-pa* and *binna* forms of connubial relationships that automatically enforce matrilineal inheritance and matrilocal residence. The polyandrous Tibetan, Shoshoni and Marquesan women are also reported to have egalitarian social status as they have economic independence or control over domestic economy. Although Burgess (1943 : 44) in his review also expressed doubt about the evidence presented by Opler, he agrees about the egalitarian status of women in these three communities. So one may agree with Opler's contention that the social regulation and sanction of multiple mating for women must further be associated with the social and economic conditions as promote an atleast egalitarian position of women, in societies where their favourable status is extended into the realm of sexual conduct and when society permits the occasions when multiple choices are made by them.

However, notwithstanding the favourable influence of the principles of matrilineal inheritance, succession and descent on the status of woman, masculine dominance practically prevail in the community affairs everywhere. Linton (1936 : 137) pointed out that men actually carry out the business of ruling in all societies. Indeed, physical deficiency has always been a formidable impediment for women in achieving equality with men in all spheres of life. Linton (ibid : 226) comments, "Even in the so-called matriarchal societies, majority of the leaders are always men. Women may be included, but if so they are persons of outstanding ability." And although the Marquesan women have unusual degree of sexual freedom and voice in social affairs (Linton, 1936 : 137, 226) they are no exception for this universal situation. Majority of leaders are men who decide on the will of the community. Similar situations also prevail in the Lahuli, Ladakhi, Kandyan and Tibetan polyandrous societies. Therefore, over-all social status-superiority of women in any contemporary society, remains a questionable proposition.

NOTE

1. (-Excerpts from a History of Sikkim, Joseph F. Roch, *Anthropos*, 1953, 48 : 935). The Lachen Pas also confirmed that their ancestors came from Bhutan in search of cultivable land and grazing field.

REFERENCES

Aiyappan, A. 1940 Some Aspects of the Khasas of the Cis-Himalayan Region. 6 : 1-44, *Jour. Asiatic Soc. Bengal*, 6 : 1-44.

Bachofen, J.J. 1861 *Das Mutierrecht*. Stuttgart.

Burgess, E.W. 1943-44 Review on M.K. Opler's paper : Women's Social Status and the Forms of Marriage. *Amer. Jour. Social.*, 49 : 147-48.

Linton, R. 1936 *A Study of Man.* London : MacMillan & Co.

Mandelbaum, D.G. 1938 Polyandry in Kota Society. *Amer. Anthrop.*, 40 : 574-583.

Majumdar, D.N. 1955 Marriage in a Polyandrous Society. *Eastern Anthrop.*, 8 : 85-110

Mc. Lennan, J.M. 1876 *Studies in Ancient History*, London : MacMillan & Co.

Morgan, L.H. 1877 *Ancient Society* (Indian Edition), Calcutta : Bharati Library.

Opler, M.K. 1943-44 Women's Social Status and the Forms of Marriage. *Amer. Jour. of Social.*, 49 : 125-146.

Panikkar, K.M. 1918 Some Aspects of Nayar Life. *Jour. Royal Anthrop. Inst. Great Britain*, 48 : 254-293.

H.R.H. Peter, Prince of Greece and Denmark 1963 *A Study of Polyandry.* The Hague : Mouton and Co. Paris.

Rivers, W.H.R. 1906 *The Todas*, London ; MacMillan & Co.

Saksena, R.N. 1953 Marriage and Divorce in Jaunsar-Bawar. *Vanyajati* 1 : 94-98.

Schneider, D.M. and Gough, K 1961 *Matrilineal Kinship.* Berkeley University of California Press.

INDEX